THE END IS NIGH

the END IS NIGH

BRITISH POLITICS, POWER, AND THE ROAD TO THE SECOND WORLD WAR

ROBERT CROWCROFT

OXFORD
UNIVERSITY PRESS

OXFORD
UNIVERSITY PRESS

Great Clarendon Street, Oxford, OX2 6DP,
United Kingdom

Oxford University Press is a department of the University of Oxford.
It furthers the University's objective of excellence in research, scholarship,
and education by publishing worldwide. Oxford is a registered trade mark of
Oxford University Press in the UK and in certain other countries

Published in the United States of America by Oxford University Press
198 Madison Avenue, New York, NY 10016, United States of America

British Library Cataloguing in Publication Data
Data available

Library of Congress Control Number: 2019938262

ISBN 978–0–19–882369–8

Printed and bound in Great Britain by
Clays Ltd, Elcograf S.p.A.

In memory of my Grandad, Melvin Arrandale

PREFACE

'The last sands of the hour glass were now slowly trailing out, and the strange tangle of fate was coming to its unravelling'.[1]

War and Myth

The weather in London on the morning of Sunday 3 September 1939 looked promising. There had been a few rain clouds in the sky first thing, but by 10.00 those had lifted. It was a perfect late summer's day. Yet though the weather may have been glorious, the national mood was anything but. Across the country, millions of nervous men and women were huddling around their radio sets and waiting for news. Fewer people than usual attended the Sunday church service, not wanting to be away from the radio. And when news finally came, it was not good.

Shortly after 11.15, the Prime Minister, Neville Chamberlain, spoke to his fellow citizens over the BBC. He brought grim tidings. As he read a prepared short statement Chamberlain sounded exhausted and dispirited. After years of arduous work, the most important policy of his government had finally disintegrated before his eyes. Deprived at last of any room for manoeuvre, the Prime Minister was forced to inform the public that, mere moments earlier, Britain had declared war on Nazi Germany. The conflict that would become the Second World War had begun. It was the crucial stage in an unfolding diplomatic and political crisis that culminated in Chamberlain's own removal from 10 Downing Street just eight months later.

The Second World War remains the closest thing that our civilization has witnessed to an apocalyptic event. Even eight decades on from the outbreak of war, its influence is, quite simply, astonishing. There is nothing quite like it. The planetary struggle between the Allies and the Axis powers constitutes a defining epoch of human history, its importance etched into innumerable aspects of our political, economic, social, and cultural lives. It shaped the political orders under which we live and, in many ways, determined the kinds of lives we are free to lead. It acts as a cultural breakwater: there is a *before* the war, and there is an *after* the war. The two are largely different worlds.

Modern Western culture finds in the Second World War something that answers our deepest civilizational needs. This is particularly true of the British. Generations after the guns fell silent it still occupies a central place in the public memory, conjuring up a ready reserve of slogans and imagery. The leadership of Winston Churchill and his colleagues in the wartime coalition government, and the feats of the armed forces—most famously the Spitfire pilots who won the Battle of Britain—enjoy a privileged place at the forefront of the national pantheon. They are symbols which fulfil the enduring human urge to memorialize the famous deeds of great men, or what the ancient Greeks called *klea andrōn*. Meanwhile the resilience of the British people under the pressure of bombing and the privations of war is similarly seared into memory. Facing down Nazi Germany and her allies, the Second World War was a 'good' war, fought for a virtuous cause. This conflict, an existential cultural event if ever there was one, provides us with a unique repository of national stories.

One of the most important of those stories is that of *how* and *why* the war occurred. Charting the road to war was of crucial importance for the people of the British Isles, because the Second World War destroyed Britain's world power, devastated her economically, and transformed her politically in directions that were of dubious merit. Nothing was ever the same again. So, to answer the questions of how and why, a series of robust national myths were constructed. These served partly to explain, but they had a second and more important purpose: they made the British feel better about what was, in reality, an utter catastrophe. They were a cultural anaesthetic.

Those myths were authored during the 1940s—by Churchill, the Labour party, the media, intellectuals, and the public themselves—and quickly became part of the mental map of all Britons. They remain entrenched to this day. At their core was an appealingly simple morality tale: that the Second World War came about because Britain had failed to stand up to the aggressive foreign policies of Adolf Hitler. The Conservative Prime Minister, Neville Chamberlain, lacked the moral integrity and strategic insight to craft a robust policy in response. Unwilling to recognize reality about the character of Hitler, time and again he made concessions to Nazi Germany, concessions which only made war more certain. By the time Chamberlain came to terms with the failure of appeasement, it was too late to stop Hitler without launching the most destructive war in human history. And those who understood the game the Fuhrer was playing—most obviously the maverick Conservative, Churchill—were exiled into the political wilderness by Chamberlain lest they upset his plans. This origin myth is connected to other important national stories; like all good dramas, there is more than one act to the play. The disaster wrought by

Chamberlain was followed by the salvation offered by Churchill, the Conservative rebels, and the Labour party in the form of the coalition government that replaced Chamberlain in May 1940. This new regime was underpinned by the resilience and stubbornness of the British public themselves. Together, the coalition government and millions of ordinary men and women united to lead the country through years of arduous struggle until eventual victory in 1945. And then the public ensured that a better, more egalitarian society was created upon the end of the war by electing Clement Attlee's Labour government with a mandate to establish a new welfare state and take large swathes of the economy under state control.

These three acts—one before, one during, and one after the conflict—make up the story of Britain and the Second World War. Even decades later, this remains the Authorized Version of national history. It is instantly familiar to British people, but will also be recognizable to international readers, for it is an indispensable component of the self-image that Britain has projected to the wider world. The outlines of the Authorized Version remain nestled at the very core of Britain's understanding of itself and its place in modern history. Even in the twenty-first century, Churchill still tops popular polls to identify the greatest Briton of all time; and his statue, ever watchful, stands silent sentinel in Parliament Square.

'The Continuation of Politics by Other Means'

Whether engaging contemporary polemicists or academic historians, Britain's road to war has long provoked vigorous debate.[2] The tone was set in the summer of 1940 with the publication of the iconic *Guilty Men*, written over a weekend by three left-wing journalists.[3] A vitriolic attack on those who had conducted British diplomacy in the 1930s, *Guilty Men* answered an urgent public desire to find people to blame for the policies which led to the fall of France, the evacuation from Dunkirk, and bombs falling on towns and cities across Britain. The book framed the popular mood and cast a long shadow over Chamberlain's strategy of appeasement. It was only reinforced by the publication, in 1948, of Churchill's own *The Gathering Storm*, the first book in his six-volume memoir *The Second World War*.[4] Churchill's pen was a flowing, elegant weapon: it depicted the man himself as a prophet who foresaw the coming danger, and charged his predecessors with a fatal combination of naivety, arrogance, and weakness that wrought disaster. This was a story of heroes and villains. Popular perceptions of the period were set in stone forevermore.

When historians began working on the period decades later, scholars such as A. J. P. Taylor, Martin Gilbert, David Dilks, and John Charmley risked committing cultural heresy by offering a more sympathetic assessment of British strategy.[5]

They suggested that British leaders of the 1930s enjoyed little in the way of political, financial, military, diplomatic, or social freedom that might have facilitated a more robust foreign policy. Moreover, they argued that it was clearly worth exploring whether a cataclysmic war might be avoided; the alternative—to embark upon a course of action that would certainly result in millions of deaths—was hardly ethical. By interpreting appeasement as logical, even inevitable, this 'revisionist' tendency among historians was always hugely controversial, and it never made much impression on a cultural memory shaped by *Guilty Men* and Churchill. A new wave of historians—most prominently R. A. C. Parker—reacted, countering that the revisionists were mesmerized by the self-justifications of failed policymakers, and that different, better choices were in fact available.[6] This approach gained widespread traction. The indictment of appeasement was back in the ascendant. The debates around the making and breaking of British strategy show no sign of abating.[7]

The End Is Nigh is a fresh account of British politics during the 1930s. It is a cynical story of political strife and conflict in Britain against the backdrop of international and imperial crisis. As such it paints a picture somewhat at odds with popular memory. From time immemorial, politics at the highest level has always been about power and ambition, manoeuvre and counter-manoeuvre. It is a competitive, and at times brutal, endeavour. It is one in which individuals scheme to satisfy their ambitions, intrigue to acquire authority, and plot to deny it to others. To that end they will utter whatever phrases and sentiments seem most useful at a given moment. They will construct alliances, cultivate relationships, and nourish enmities that may persist for a lifetime (or, perhaps, for just a few weeks). They will think constantly of their own self-interest, but at the same time they will rationalize that what is good for them happily accords with a wider good: of the party, the government, the country. This is politics. It is, surely, the real oldest profession.

In the 1930s Britain was confronted by a series of acute threats to her global power. This book argues that there quickly developed a dialectical relationship between the 'high-political' struggle for power and influence at Westminster—the everyday currency of British politics—and the question of what to do about these threats. Issues of international strategy, defence, and the Empire were omnipresent themes in political competition. To be sure, these were major problems with which leaders and parties were compelled to grapple; but at the same time, politicians *chose* to use these issues for political purposes, whether to stake a claim to power or to undermine rivals. They were converted into political weapons. Secrecy, intrigue, and plotting were prevalent. From Whitehall offices to Westminster clubs, political actors moved through a sea of chatter about who was up to what, and why. Rivalry and enmity spilled over into policymaking. Criticizing what others did offered a chance to enhance one's own distinctiveness and reputation. Moreover, major strategic decisions were influenced by anxiety about domestic considerations, with ministers keen to strengthen their position at home. The consequences of this for British policy overseas were significant. Foreign policy shaped high politics and, in turn, high politics shaped foreign policy.

When we apply this way of thinking about political behaviour to the mythologized 1930s, an unfamiliar picture emerges. Iconic figures such as Churchill no longer appear in quite the same light. We are compelled to rethink why things really happened, what drove events, and whether the explanations offered by participants were merely a gloss intended for public consumption. This is certainly a highly sceptical way of looking at politics, but it is perhaps of a piece with the equally sceptical age of the early twenty-first century. Trust in politicians is at an all-time low; we tend to see them as specialists in scheming, intrigue, and, occasionally, conspiracy. We imagine them as individuals who do not believe what they say, and in fact will say almost anything if it advances their interests. It is now almost a cliché to mistrust the pronouncements of politicians. This cynicism has gone so far that it is even an entrenched part of popular culture. When it comes to major questions of public policy, people would be justified in hoping their leaders might set aside considerations of political advantage in favour of a disinterested and objective appraisal. Yet that would, in reality, usually be wishful thinking.

Intrigue was a thriving trade in the 1930s. In Westminster and Whitehall, politicians did a booming business in plotting. To be sure, far more was at stake than the career success of those who competed to rule; the peace of the world and the future of the British Empire were at risk. Yet however grave these matters, the struggle that dominated British politics was not conducted in these terms. It was conducted in terms of personal relations, rivalries, and enmities at the hub of power. Relationships between the most influential individuals assumed central importance. These men jockeyed for position, parried the thrusts of their adversaries, and sought any opportunity for advantage. Strategic issues were understood not only in terms of the problems they presented, but also the personal political capital they might yield. Meanwhile high-political posturing at home plunged Britain ever deeper into the maelstrom of central European politics, with disastrous results. The survival of British global power and the world-system of her Empire—accumulated over centuries of struggle—were in danger. There is more. This high-risk linkage between domestic political ascendancy and British power abroad threatened to disrupt, and perhaps destroy, a democratic order which kept Britain remarkably stable during the turbulent years since the First World War. Whereas most European states had been pitched into deep crisis, Britain weathered the storm. The consequences of the enmeshing of British power with the search for advantage in Westminster and Whitehall finally became clear in 1940. As a result, the end was nigh for both British power in the world and, equally, a way of conducting democracy at home. One Britain—a highly successful one—passed away and slipped into shadow; another—arguably, a less successful one—was born.

It is not that the behaviour of prominent politicians was always and exclusively Machiavellian, with the good of the country brazenly sacrificed on the altar of naked self-interest. One must refrain from reducing Britain's journey into the Second World War to being nothing more than an unfortunate by-product of intriguing for political power—what Sir Thomas More bemoaned in 1513 when he wrote of the Wars of the Roses that 'the getting of the garland, keeping it, losing and winning it again, it hath cost more English blood than hath twice the winning of France'.[8] To suggest that would be misleading. It is, rather, that the politicians' perspectives on the policy problems they encountered, and the ways in which they framed and discussed them, were inevitably seen in light of the customary 'rules' of the political realm in which they existed. Within those parameters it was a conventional practice that crises were routinely manipulated for individual gain. Plotting, and speculating about plotting, was the norm. Adversity in foreign policy thus created enormous high-political opportunities; and international crisis became an instrument for the elimination of one's enemies.

Thus, while government was confronted with large, and dangerous, questions of national policy—and this naturally generated debate about how best to respond—the ever-present nature of these issues meant that British foreign and imperial policy *was* British politics during the thirties; there was no escape from it. Moreover, in the glare of domestic politics, a measured appraisal of British interests became impossible. With policy options limited by the proliferation of emotive rhetoric about 'honour' and 'justice', there was no scope for the genuinely imaginative, and counterintuitive, strategic thinking that might, perhaps, have led Britain out of the morass.

In his classic 1832 text *On War*, the great Prussian strategist Carl von Clausewitz famously observed that 'war is merely the continuation of politics by other means'.[9] It remains perhaps his most enduring maxim. What Clausewitz meant was that, when states can no longer achieve their aims or resolve their disputes through diplomacy, they may choose war as a device to seek satisfaction. This happens where the political issues are so acute that it is worth running the risks of military conflict. For Clausewitz, war is politics elevated to the next level. But I hope that a deliberate reworking of Clausewitz's aphorism is forgivable here: as we will see,

Britain's declaration of war in the autumn of 1939 marked the continuation of a long high-political struggle at Westminster by 'other means'. Earlier in the decade, India had been a continuation of politics by other means. So were crises over Abyssinia, rearmament, diplomacy with Hitler, international relations in central and eastern Europe, and the policy of territorial guarantees. A decision to actually go to war represented the further extension of politics—as did, in May 1940, the decapitation of the old regime and the erecting of another in its place. The continuities between peace and war were striking; the underlying dynamic was the same.

One is reminded here of the brilliant nineteenth-century Swiss historian Jacob Burckhardt: for him, history was nothing less than 'poetry on the grandest scale'. There is certainly something poetic in the story of Britain's approach to the Second World War. Ambition, folly, vice, lust for power, malice, and tragedy—all the hallmarks of epic literature—are to be found in abundance. This is a big topic that requires a macro-scale analysis, as well as a certain morbid curiosity. In attempting it, we are compelled to undertake a journey through what another celebrated historian, Hugh Trevor-Roper, called 'the haunted chambers of the human mind'.[10] That is because this is a profoundly *human* story; the book revolves around a cast worthy of Dickens or Trollope. Evoking personality is as crucial here as scrutinizing the alchemy of policy and, at times, these individuals make for a comic spectacle. The lives of the men were bound up in the intricacies of public affairs and policy, with its attendant cunning, rhetoric, dissembling, and ambiguity. They were part of it; but it was part of them. It was their life's blood. These men identified their interests with the *polis*, and its interests with their own. They circled around power like wasps around a jam jar.

Many of the most enduring historical stories provide searing accounts of societies at the intersection between flawed leaders, politics, and a devastating war. From Tacitus's account of the murderous Year of the Four Emperors to Plutarch's *Roman Lives*, these stories have resonated for millennia. The story of Britain and the Second World War is one of these; an important part of what the eighteenth-century philosopher Edmund Burke alluded to when he wrote of unrolling the 'Great Map of Mankind'.[11] Above all, *The End Is Nigh* is a demonstration of the grave consequences that follow when leaders fail. It is also a stark warning of the risks that emerge when the competition to rule a democratic *polis* overwhelms the system itself. These are, moreover, eternal conundrums. This may not be an attractive story, but it is certainly an exciting one.

ACKNOWLEDGEMENTS

I have been thinking about the history of British politics in this period for a long time. Primarily that is because democratic politics itself is such an ambiguous, and slippery, creature that a satisfactory understanding remains elusive. Yet I also find the political strife of the 1930s and 1940s so compelling that it is difficult to stay away.

In writing this book, I have accumulated many debts. It goes without saying that many historians have worked on this period, and the result is an astonishingly diverse and impressive body of scholarship upon which I have drawn with profit. Luciana O'Flaherty of Oxford University Press commissioned the project and offered helpful comments on the text. Her colleague Kizzy Taylor-Richelieu assisted with images. Sally Evans-Darby was a diligent copyeditor.

I am grateful to my colleagues and co-conspirators at the University of Edinburgh for kindnesses and good humour over the years. I must make particular mention of Paul Addison, Thomas Ahnert, Ewen Cameron, Martin Chick, Jeremy Crang, Trevor Griffiths, Fabian Hilfrich, Alvin Jackson, David Kaufman, Harshan Kumarasingham, Calum Maciver, Stephen McDowall, Zubin Mistry, Gordon Pentland, Julius Ruiz, Wendy Ugolini, and Ben Weinstein. I have benefited immensely from working alongside such a fine group of people. The administrative staff in the School of History, Classics, and Archaeology are exemplary professionals and make life far more straightforward than would otherwise be the case. Teaching remains a rich pleasure, and my students have provided much provocation and mirth.

Simon Green has always been a source of sage advice and invaluable support. Geoffrey Fry sent amusing emails aplenty, and much encouragement. Lee Bruce is a longstanding fellow traveller. The debt to my old secondary school History teacher, Paul Allen, grows by the year. A special thanks must go to John Bew for being so generous with his time; his work is an example to all scholars. My greatest intellectual debt remains that owed to my former supervisors, Owen Hartley and Richard Whiting. Life was never more fun than when I was working with them at the University of Leeds.

My Mum and Nan offered many welcome distractions throughout the process of writing. Walks with Henry always blew away the cobwebs. The book is dedicated to the memory of my wonderful Grandad, Melvin Arrandale, who passed away in June 2017, shortly after it was commissioned. Despite being very ill, he was thrilled when I was able to tell him that Oxford University Press had agreed to publish it. My Grandad was the finest man I have ever known, and I owe him more than I can express.

ROBERT CROWCROFT
November 2018

CONTENTS

LIST OF FIGURES

1

THE CONSERVATIVE ASCENDANCY

An Unexpected Equilibrium

We should start at the beginning. The interwar decades in Britain belonged to the Conservative party. Statistics alone do not convey the full extent of this remarkable ascendancy, but, even so, they are striking: for the almost twenty-one years of peace between the armistice of 11 November 1918 and the declaration of war on 3 September 1939, the Conservative party was out of power for just *three* years. At only one of the seven general elections during this period did the Conservatives fail to emerge as the largest party in the House of Commons. In 1918, the Conservatives stood as a coalition with the Liberal party faction led by the Prime Minister, David Lloyd George. This coalition secured 47.6 per cent of the vote and 478 parliamentary seats; 32.6 per cent of the electors and 335 of those seats belonged to the Conservatives. Four years later, in 1922, the Conservatives fought alone, winning 38.2 per cent of the vote and 345 Members of Parliament. Their nearest rivals, the Labour party, had just 142 MPs. Even a year later, when the Labour party briefly came to power in a minority government after the 1923 election, the Conservatives were still the largest party: with 258 MPs to Labour's 191, and almost 8 per cent more of the votes cast. In the general election that followed in October 1924, the Conservatives achieved one of the greatest triumphs in their history, emerging with 419 seats and 48.3 per cent of the vote. The Labour party, in contrast, could only muster 151 seats and 33 per cent of the electorate.

The 1929 election which led to the formation of the second Labour government was the sole contest of the interwar period which gave Labour more Commons seats than the Conservatives, but, even then, just barely—288 to 260. And the Conservatives still attracted 300,000 more votes than Labour. Following a period of instability amidst the World Depression which culminated in the threatened financial collapse of the British state, the Conservative party returned to power in 1931. This time it was in a coalition not only with Liberal factions but *Labour* leaders as well—including the Prime Minister James Ramsay MacDonald—exiled from their own party over their willingness to oversee contentious economies in public expenditure. At the October 1931 election, this self-styled 'National Government' garnered a huge 14.5 million votes, 67 per cent of those cast, and 554 MPs; 473 were Conservatives. The Conservative party alone won the backing of 55.2 per cent of the electors, and almost 12 million votes—against the 6.6 million who voted Labour. The Labour party was reduced to just 52 MPs. Four years later, and despite prolonged economic pain, the Conservatives still secured 432 seats to Labour's 154. The final general election held before the outbreak of the Second World War was yet another in a series of striking electoral successes.

For a total of eighteen years, then, the Conservative party governed Britain, either alone or as the dominant force in a coalition.[1] But what made this ascendancy still more remarkable was the fact that—according to conventional wisdom—*it was not supposed to happen*. After all, this was an era marked by the advent of mass democracy in Britain. Each of these seven elections included the participation of every male over the age of twenty-one in the country, with the result that the pre-war electorate of just over 7 million people suddenly grew to more than 21 million from 1918—a three-fold increase. Women also participated in general elections for the first time. Those over the age of thirty were granted the vote in 1918, and, from 1928, all women over twenty-one could participate. The latter measure increased the size of the electorate from 21 million to almost 30 million. This amounted to nothing less than a systemic and dramatic change in the character of the whole political process. New agendas and expectations were opened up, while fresh demands needed to be met—and these were initially thought unlikely to prove conducive to the success of the Conservative party.

Why was that? It had been a long-standing anxiety of Conservatives that universal suffrage would produce a mass electorate hostile to their party. Some had a positively apocalyptic view of the matter. By empowering not only the whole of the envious working classes but swathes of irrational women, mass democracy would overwhelm the Conservative party like a tsunami. 'Mobs', wrote the giant of Victorian conservatism, the Third Marquess of Salisbury, 'would not elect first-rate men'.[2] The events of the Russian Revolution during 1917, when the Bolsheviks came to power, offered a sombre lesson of what could follow from a sudden transfer of authority. Existing social arrangements might be destroyed by the sheer impatience of an excited electorate. The demand for urgency would unbalance the very political and legal institutions that had made democracy possible in the first place. Voters would be seduced by silver-tongued 'political adventurers' into believing that an ideal society lay just around the corner—if only they would lend their support at the ballot box.[3]

What was a deep-seated fear for Conservatives was a profound hope for their opponents. To those on the left, universal enfranchisement would finally provide the masses—in other words, the working classes—with the means to bend Parliament to their will and reshape the nation in order to redress the grievous socio-economic injustices they suffered. Being numerically preponderant, the working classes would naturally cleave towards 'their' party, the Labour party, and overrun the defenders of the old, pre-war order. The forces of 'modernity' and 'progress'—always defined in terms that conformed to left-wing totems—would reign supreme.

There were good reasons to expect radical socio-economic transformation of the kind feared by Conservatives to come to pass after the First World War. The Labour party had been formed in 1900 as the political expression of the trade union movement, and made gradual advances even on the restricted pre-war franchise. When the franchise was extended in 1918 the Labour party began to replace the fatally divided Liberals as the major anti-Conservative force in British politics. In 1918, Labour gained sixty-three seats; in 1922 they held 142 and this rose thereafter, to an interwar high of 288 in 1929. Universal adult suffrage was not the only explanation of Labour's remarkable success. It boasted a formidable group of leaders who were the architects of its credibility. Men such as Arthur Henderson, James Ramsay MacDonald, and Philip Snowden were determined to offer pragmatic solutions to the nation's challenges through Parliament, rather than imitate the Bolsheviks or socialists from the continent. They built the party, and its respectability, from scratch. Moreover the trade unionists were preponderant, not socialist intellectuals; and this meant that Labour's brand of socialism was mostly moderate, expressed in ethical terms, and concerned with the material well-being of the masses. It was all very British. Funded and underpinned by a union movement to which millions belonged, the Labour party posed a profound long-term challenge to the political system in an age of democracy.[4]

In the years prior to 1914, Britain had witnessed a surge in industrial disputes between trade unions and employers. Millions of working days were lost every year to strikes (40.8m in 1912 alone). British industry at times resembled a battleground. For some, this signified a welcome process of self-assertion by the weakest sections of society, with workers demanding a fair share of the economic pie. For others, it was potentially a challenge to the supremacy of Parliament and the rule of law. Trade union militancy lessened during the First World War but exploded again once the guns fell silent. The 1920s were a period of protracted economic and industrial crisis. Thirty-five million working days were lost due to strikes in 1919, 26 million a year later, and 85 million in 1921. In 1926—the climax of the struggle between state and trade unions in the form of the General Strike—an astonishing

162 million working days were lost to union action. Almost half of workers were now unionized. Every economic decision or trade fluctuation threatened to prove a flashpoint. The core reason for so much industrial unrest was the weakness of the British, and European, economy following the disruption of total war. Debts, the dislocation of trade, and the question of how to defend Britain's privileged global economic position bedevilled policymakers. And from 1929, Britain was afflicted by the Great Depression that followed the Wall Street Crash. For some, the fall of capitalism itself seemed to be at hand. This was an economy, and country, in profound disarray.

Meanwhile, new policy issues were already on the agenda. The pre-war Liberal governments had introduced a series of landmark measures of reform, including old-age pensions, sickness insurance, unemployment insurance, and wealth taxes. This was widely expected to be the thin end of the wedge, with future governments going further—additional welfare legislation, greater taxation, and a more expansive role for the state in everyday life. These changes signified the growing faith in the beneficence of government that would so dominate politics throughout the twentieth century. But the measures also strengthened the links between party politics and the material conditions in which the public lived: there were votes to be had in competing to dispense public services. The idea that the state could—and should— correct socio-economic problems through legislation remained contentious, on grounds of spiralling future costs and practicality. Yet political competition was unmistakeably moving in a new direction.

On the surface, then, this would not appear to be a situation pointing towards the political dominance of the *Conservative* party. The working classes were numerically preponderant in democratic, post-war Britain; the issues of the day were frequently industrial; and, in the aftermath of the war, the Labour party displaced the Liberals as the primary non-Conservative force. And yet, as election statistics lay bare, Conservative ascendancy was the outcome. Moreover, Britain itself was stabilized during these years of Conservative rule, and the kind of revolutionary situation that had occurred in many European countries never developed. How was this achieved?

Its principal architects were two of the most successful, yet subsequently reviled, politicians of the twentieth century: Stanley Baldwin and Neville Chamberlain.

'To Save Democracy, to Preserve It, and to Inspire It'

Interwar Britain was confronted by a profound challenge of democratic leadership.[5] The man who gave an answer to this problem—and in doing so shaped how all leaders thereafter would engage with the *demos*—was Baldwin. Born in Bewdley,

4

Worcestershire in 1867, his father, Alfred, owned a prosperous ironworks. Rudyard Kipling was a cousin. As a boy Stanley occupied himself exploring the rural area surrounding the works, explorations which inculcated a lifelong love of the English countryside. Educated at Harrow and then in History at Trinity College, Cambridge, Baldwin spent a quarter of a century working for the family business, which employed 4,000 workers and was listed on the London Stock Exchange. He was a humane employer with a strong paternalistic ethos. Baldwin did not enter politics until 1908, when he succeeded his father as Conservative MP for Bewdley. He remained an obscure backbencher for another eight years before being offered the role of Parliamentary Private Secretary to the Conservative leader Andrew Bonar Law in December 1916. After impressing Bonar Law, six months later he was appointed Financial Secretary to the Treasury. He held this post for four years, finally entering the Cabinet as President of the Board of Trade in April 1921.

In these roles Baldwin had proven a competent minister, but he was hardly a prominent figure in public life. Yet he unexpectedly emerged as Conservative party leader and Prime Minister in May 1923. His sudden rise began in October 1922 when the little-known President of the Board of Trade joined with the retired party leader Bonar Law to lead a revolt by Conservative MPs. This rebellion aimed to break the coalition led by Liberal Prime Minister David Lloyd George. There was mounting anxiety amongst backbenchers and junior ministers that Lloyd George and senior Conservative figures, including Austen Chamberlain, the incumbent leader, hoped to permanently subsume the Conservative party into a larger 'Centre party' under Lloyd George's control. This notion prompted Baldwin to affirm that 'there [is] no more important duty at present than to preserve the Tory party'.[6] He played a key role in spearheading a rebellion at one of the most famous political gatherings of the century. At the Carlton Club in Westminster—an exclusive members-only venue frequented by Conservative MPs—Baldwin helped to lead a *putsch* that destroyed the government, with Lloyd George being energetically denounced and the bulk of Conservative MPs demanding that the party reassert its independence. Baldwin himself launched a famous condemnation of Lloyd George as a 'dynamic force'. 'A dynamic force is a very terrible thing', he said. 'It may crush you . . . It is owing to that dynamic force that the Liberal party . . . has been smashed to pieces; and it is my firm conviction that, in time, the same thing will happen to our party'.[7]

The Carlton Club revolt brought down not only Lloyd George but also his Liberal protégé Winston Churchill and the senior Conservatives most associated with the coalition—including Austen Chamberlain who, like his father Joseph, believed in cooperation between like-minded Conservatives and Liberals. Other discredited Conservatives included Arthur Balfour, previously Prime Minister and an important party grandee. The coup was a formidable bout of 'giant-killing', creating a leadership vacuum in the Conservative party and leaving a legacy of mistrust, feuds, and strained relations.[8] With most senior figures tainted by the mark of collaboration, Baldwin was suddenly catapulted to the front rank of politics.

It is difficult not to interpret the Carlton Club revolt as being motivated by ambition on the part of the rebels. Austen Chamberlain and Lloyd George conceptualized the coalition as a device to dominate the political centre through an alliance of voter groups, neutralize the Labour party, and marshal resistance to socialism. Baldwin adopted an essentially identical approach. The core strategy may thus have been less contentious than the competition for power and places; or, to put it another way, the coup was about who exercised authority and who did not.[9]

Bonar Law emerged from retirement to replace Chamberlain as Conservative leader and Lloyd George as Prime Minister. Baldwin became Chancellor of the Exchequer in the new Conservative administration. Yet when terminal illness forced Bonar Law back into retirement in May 1923 after just seven months (he died in October), the once-obscure Baldwin suddenly ascended to both the party leadership and the premiership. Few, including Baldwin himself, would have predicted this development just a year before.

Baldwin remained Conservative leader for fourteen years, retiring in 1937. Though ambitious colleagues sought to supplant him, none of them were able to do so. Of twentieth-century leaders, only Clement Attlee, Winston Churchill, and Margaret Thatcher directed their parties for longer. Baldwin was also a member of that exclusive club of individuals to have been thrice Prime Minister. An initial eight-month stint as premier ended in January 1924, but he returned to Downing Street with the Conservatives' great election victory in November of that year. He resided there for half a decade. After the formation of the Conservative-dominated National Government under the titular Prime Minister and Labour exile Ramsay MacDonald in late 1931, Baldwin spent four years as Lord President of the Council. In this role he was, in practice, the real head of the government. And he returned to Downing Street for two more years, between 1935 and 1937, before retiring and handing over to Neville Chamberlain. But *how* did he attain such electoral success, and political longevity, in an unstable society?

Baldwin was one of the most skilful and successful politicians of the last century.[10] Cunning and highly creative, he rose to the challenge posed by high unemployment, prolonged economic crisis, and universal suffrage. In doing so, Baldwin did much to establish the parameters of democratic leadership itself. When he became Prime Minister in 1923, he led a country which had witnessed violent strikes and armoured cars deployed onto the streets of Glasgow. Lloyd George feared the establishment of 'an inevitable Soviet Republic' along the lines of what had emerged from the Russian Revolution.[11] If with hindsight we can say that these fears were probably exaggerated, at the time that was far from obvious. The economic chaos was certainly real. A policy of preferring inflation to unemployment had worked for a time, but increases in interest rates in 1920 led to a slump and rising unemployment, particularly in export trades. By 1921, unemployment stood at almost 2 million, and would remain above 1 million throughout the interwar era.

Moreover, unemployment was increasingly identified as a problem which the state had a direct responsibility to combat, as opposed to a fact of economic life—as was generally the case prior to 1914. The explanation for this transition is obvious. In an age of universal suffrage, politicians needed to offer 'answers' to the citizens' problems if they hoped to secure their votes. That meant party politics would be about how best to address these problems. As higher numbers of people went on the dole, the cost to the Treasury of paying unemployment insurance rose inexorably. Payments became more generous in order to prevent pauperization and maintain the fragile social peace. Between 1920 and 1924 the real value of unemployment benefit for a single man rose by 70 per cent, while for a married man with two children, the increase was 155 per cent. These costs threatened to derail the Budget. Austerity measures adopted as a result were deeply contentious.

Baldwin thus clambered to the top of what Disraeli called 'the greasy pole' of British politics at a challenging moment. In his own words, 'times are new and strange and extraordinarily difficult'.[12] He was confronted by an acute and insoluble problem, for the advent of universal suffrage marked the beginnings of a tendency that bedevilled leaders from Baldwin to Theresa May: unrelenting pressure on government to spend ever-increasing sums of money to meet public expectations. The state would need to continually grow in order to do this, taking on fresh responsibilities as it went. An electoral arms race had begun. The implications for party politics were transformational, swinging the advantage in favour of collectivism. What Baldwin termed 'the growing materialism of the age' was a major anxiety for him, for when combined with 'the mass mind' it could, he feared, lead to 'slavery'.[13] And yet Baldwin proved not only resilient, but remarkably successful.

His effectiveness was based on a wide-ranging strategy to smooth over social polarization by appealing to supposedly ubiquitous 'national', as opposed to class-based, values. As he put it, the goal was to 'prevent the class war from becoming a reality' in Britain.[14] Baldwin worried about political 'quacks' who would seduce the public by offering simplistic answers to complex questions and an easy route to Utopia. He sought an approach that would bind the country together, in contrast to the bitter divisions seen across Europe. This strategy had at least as much to do with presentation as actual policy. Baldwin was a prolific public speaker, making frequent addresses up and down the country, whether at party rallies, in Parliament, or at schools, friendly societies, churches, and civic events. In delivering them he drew upon a wide range of influences—religious, economic, literary, and historical—that would have cultural resonance with an audience in the first half of the twentieth century. Expressing himself in the language of fairness, decency, and moderation, Baldwin's political ethos enjoyed considerable appeal in a divided country. Outwardly presenting himself as a typical Englishman (with his background, Baldwin was certainly *not* typical), he worked to neutralize conflict and soften the sharp edges of economic instability. Baldwin understood, better than his peers, that Britain had been changed permanently by the experience of the First World War and the expansion of democracy: 'this post-war world', he told the House of Commons, 'is full of pre-war minds'.[15]

Importantly, Baldwin was the first Prime Minister to address the public en masse through radio broadcasts and newsreels in the cinema. Recognizing that 'public opinion today has a far greater weight in the moulding of governments than it ever had before', Baldwin set about communicating with, and shaping, that opinion.[16] In interwar Britain, mass newspapers were now complemented by the innovative media of radio broadcasts and cinema newsreels. These reached huge audiences. Whereas many of his contemporaries found the new outlets to be challenging, Baldwin mastered and dominated them. They were tools through which he could speak to a public anxious about the state of the country. He made regular addresses over the radio, and spoke into the camera for short films to be shown in cinemas. He was particularly good on the radio, where his understated style came across like an informal chat.

The historian Philip Williamson has demonstrated that Baldwin's public addresses represented *moral* appeals to moderation, and were devoid of much in the way of policy content or intellectual argument.[17] As Williamson writes, Baldwin 'enunciated not so much a party programme' as 'a public doctrine'.[18] To use a more contemporary phrase, the Conservative leader concentrated on crafting mood music. He presented a soothing image, typically being photographed or filmed with a pipe in hand. This 'pipe-smoking simplicity' reinforced the impression of Baldwin as being a straightforward fellow.[19] One admiring contemporary labelled him the 'Minister of Public Opinion'.[20]

During the approach to the 1926 General Strike which grew out of a prolonged dispute over wages in the mining industry, Baldwin went out of his way to be seen working for a fair solution. This ensured that when the strike materialized, and

1.5m workers across key sectors of the economy temporarily paralysed the country, the Prime Minister had already cultivated the image of being an honest broker. He could thus paint the unions as intransigent, and depict the Conservative government as upholding constitutionalism. Baldwin denounced the strike as 'a challenge to Parliament and the road to anarchy and ruin'.[21] 'Constitutional government is being attacked', he said.[22] Baldwin spoke of an attempt to institute a 'reign of force' by 'despotic power' and demanded the 'surrender' of the TUC.[23] When the General Strike was called off after just a few days, it was presented as a very public victory for Baldwin's approach to politics in an era of polarization. What Baldwin sought, above all, was cohesion and an 'atmosphere' in which society would hold together, constitutionalism would be defended, and socio-economic problems would be dealt with in a civil manner.[24] 'Moral values' were his focus, for 'good habits' were of more consequence than 'good laws'.[25] And this was not just a pose: Baldwin gave so much of his own money away to charity that he got into financial difficulties on several occasions.

What made this approach unique was that it developed linkages between a constitutional conception of politics and a quiet patriotism. Baldwin's economic outlook was that the negative consequences of capitalist competition needed to be carefully managed if social evil was to be avoided. He railed against 'parasit-ical' employers for their unwillingness to treat workers fairly and continually pushed management to be cooperative with unions.[26] But he also made a positive case for capitalism, arguing that whereas socialists decried it as 'the blackest curse that had ever fallen on mankind', in fact it had benefited 'millions of people' and raised the funds for even the unemployed to be kept in an 'unprecedented standard of living'.[27] As he wrote in 1935 during his final stint as Prime Minister, 'you see my job is to try and educate a new democracy in a new world and to try and make them realise their responsibilities in their possession of power, and to keep the eternal verities before them'.[28] By present-ing 'national' crises to the public, he was able to advocate 'national' solutions. In reality, of course, these were the solutions favoured by Baldwin and the Conser-vative party, and thus his rhetoric was far from non-political. But in the world of mass democracy, interpretations of public opinion, and efforts to organize it, had become the hinge of political action.

His rhetoric and style made a home for millions of Liberal voters in the Conser-vative party. The accretion of Liberal support was a crucial element in the Baldwi-nian hegemony. Newly enfranchised women were another important element of Baldwin's success. His government was responsible for granting full voting equality in 1928. By 1929, female voters outnumbered males. The Conservatives sought to tailor their message to these electors.[29] It was felt that women—as wives, mothers, and housekeepers—would be receptive to the party's message of 'responsibility' and economic prudence. Conservative propaganda aimed at women stressed, frequently in alarmist terms, the irresponsibility of socialism, and sought to offer a reassuring alternative. Women made up a large chunk of the army of Conservative activists—the party boasted 887,000 female members by 1927. This paid electoral dividends.

This electoral strategy also involved contesting the designation of Labour as the legitimate and default representative of the working class. The Conservatives worked to depict their 'socialist' opponents as sectional and divisive. The masses may have been working class, but they were also taxpayers and property-owners. They were savers and consumers. There was a long-standing tradition of working-class conservatism in Britain dating back to the Victorian era, and some of those voters assumed to 'belong' to Labour could be made receptive to a carefully crafted Conservative appeal that played on fears of confiscatory taxation and government profligacy. By rhetorically defining the Labour party as an exclusively trade union party, the Conservatives were able to erect barriers to its expansion beyond that base. Moreover, the Conservative party was quick to discern the transformational potential of the Great War as a political resource, frequently employing ex-servicemen as candidates. This imbued the Conservative party with a public—even *moral*—credibility that Labour could not hope to replicate. Labour had fourteen ex-servicemen in Parliament in 1924; the Conservatives boasted 200.[30]

The party also became ever more professional in putting across its message. It came to think of voters as—essentially—consumers, with the job of political leadership being to identify and meet (as well as shape) their preferences. One election agent declared, 'let no agent think that he has nothing to do with "sales". His business is to sell Conservatism to the public'.[31] This was aided by an estimated three-fold expansion in party membership during the 1920s, from approximately 560,000 members to 1.57m.[32] The professionalism of the Conservative electoral machine—for instance, in its detailed study of the messages that were likely to resonate with people in particular areas of a given town or city—was far in advance of rivals. In 1925, the Conservatives distributed 5.3 million pamphlets; by 1929, this had grown to 110 million. Posters were also employed on a vast scale.[33] Under Baldwin, the Conservative party was simply far more professional and imaginative than its opponents. The effort to define the new politics on Conservative terms was a sophisticated one.

Baldwin thus built a formidable alliance of voter groups with a vision of Britain as a 'property-owning democracy'.[34] Yet he was also magnanimous towards the Labour party. Baldwin understood that the Labour leaders were 'earnest and sincere men'—sensible Britons rather than Bolshevik fanatics.[35] He instructed Conservative MPs to be on cordial, even friendly, terms with their Labour peers, especially those of working-class background who were unfamiliar with parliamentary protocol; Westminster was not to be a bastion of privilege in which newcomers were humiliated.[36] Most Labour leaders were personally fond of Baldwin as a result. His strategy was to embed the Labour party within the political status quo, detaching it from any revolutionary aspirations, and then to defeat it in electoral conflict.

'Politically We Are on Velvet'

The year 1931 represented a crucial juncture in cementing the Conservative ascendancy.[37] The financial crisis of that summer precipitated the collapse of the second Labour government. With international trade in the grip of the World Depression, industries struggling, and unemployment nearing 3 million, the Labour government was split over cuts to public spending deemed necessary to stave off the possible financial collapse of the British state. A doomsday-scenario seemed to loom; in just one week in July, the Bank of England lost a quarter of its gold reserves as funds were withdrawn. The Cabinet fell into disarray over the economies deemed necessary to restore confidence in the national finances. The most contentious was a 10 per cent reduction in unemployment benefit. With the Cabinet fatally divided in August and the ministry collapsing, Baldwin—after standing back long enough for Labour's credibility to evaporate and its senior figures to descend into internecine hostility—finally, and very publicly, rode to the rescue. He agreed to forge a 'National Government' consisting of the Conservative party, elements of the Labour leadership disavowed by their party for their willingness to reduce welfare payments (including the leader and Prime Minister, MacDonald), and the Liberal party factions.[38] MacDonald would remain Prime Minister in name but Baldwin, holding the post of Lord President, would be the real leader of the government. The Conservatives overwhelmingly dominated the resulting coalition that endured until 1940. Indeed, its very name—'National'—embodied Baldwin's political outlook. As he himself put it, 'politically we are on velvet'.[39] The split within Labour's ranks was formalized the following month when MacDonald and the other Labour figures who had formed the National Government—at first hoping that it would be an emergency measure to restore financial confidence, after which they would return to their party—were formally expelled from Labour. MacDonald and his colleagues (most importantly the Chancellor of the Exchequer, Snowden, and Secretary of State for the Dominions, J. H. Thomas) were now prisoners of the Conservatives and held on to their offices largely through the indulgence of Baldwin.

At the October 1931 general election, the Labour party was portrayed as having not only almost bankrupted the country but as running away from responsibility and being unwilling to make painful choices. The Conservative party, on the other hand, appeared to have stepped in to save Britain from ruin. Baldwin's address to the public, filmed for newsreels and shown in cinemas ahead of the election, is worth viewing on the internet, for it shows his rhetorical style in full flow. Sitting behind his desk and projecting a calm, measured air, Baldwin said to his audience that:

> Every voter must remember that the future destinies of the country, and of the Empire, rest upon his or her decision. The country is face to face with a grave crisis. And the simple issue is this: whether the electors at . . . a time of national emergency are going to entrust the government of the country to the party which brought us to the verge of ruin and then ran away, because they had not the courage to face up to the crisis . . . On the one side are Mr Henderson's socialists, who by their extravagance wrecked the financial stability of the country and . . . deserted their posts . . . and left it to those who were prepared to put country before party to rescue the nation . . . I have no doubt as to the answer which the country will give . . . The only way to avert disaster and to set our country on its feet again is to return a National Government consisting of men of all parties resolutely determined to put the national interests first.[40]

Informed as it was by financial emergency, the result was a massive electoral triumph for Baldwin's strategy. It also left Labour in ruins for the better part of a decade. Stripped of credibility and having excommunicated several of its founding fathers, the Labour party descended into bloodletting and flirtation with extreme ideas. The 1930s were as close to a period of political hegemony as multi-party systems tend to permit.

The National Government implemented contentious cuts to public spending and navigated the dangerous shoals of global financial crisis. It also benefited from a recovery that gathered pace from 1932. Contrary to popular mythology, the so-called 'Devil's decade' was actually a good time for most of the country. Interest rates were held at a low level while the cost of living fell. This led to plenty of 'cheap money' sloshing around the economy and created relatively stable conditions for investment. Neville Chamberlain, as Chancellor of the Exchequer, was able to balance the Budget. A house-building boom and the growth of industries established to provide new consumer goods, like irons, radios, cars, and refrigerators, stimulated the economy. Average real wages were markedly higher than in the 1920s, and from 1934 the cuts in benefits made at the height of the financial crisis were restored. In the face of serious economic challenges, and operating in the new context of universal suffrage, by the early 1930s Baldwinian conservatism appeared to have established not merely an electoral, but also a striking socio-economic, equilibrium.

'Great Expectations'

Baldwin's mind focused on matters of presentation and persuasion.[41] He was generally happy to delegate actual policy to others. Yet he was determined not to permit Labour or the Liberals to propagate a 'fairy tale' that they were the principal authors of social reform, arguing that in the nineteenth century the pre-eminent reformers had been Conservatives like Disraeli and Salisbury.[42] To this end, Baldwin wanted social reform to mollify the democracy. The Conservatives needed, he said, to match the drive of Labour; 'sitting still' would be disastrous.[43] Baldwin was not stringent about achieving balanced Budgets (turning a blind eye to Churchill's acrobatics as Chancellor in the late 1920s) and remained more concerned about those things that would serve his larger goals. His outstanding colleague in delivering an expansion in social provision was Neville Chamberlain.[44]

The son of the great late-Victorian politician Joseph Chamberlain, and younger brother of former Conservative leader Austen—whom Baldwin had played a central role in overthrowing—Neville only entered politics in middle-age and was never fancied to soar to the heights reached by his father and sibling. He would ultimately eclipse them both. Tall and thin, Neville invariably wore starched collars and a dark suit and looked somewhat aloof. He was readily identifiable by the umbrella he was often photographed carrying (a custom that eventually earned him the public nickname 'the old umbrella'). A formidable administrator and technocrat with an austere air, Chamberlain possessed a striking capacity for hard work. He also shared his father's commitment to energetic social reform. Like Baldwin, Chamberlain's background was among the upper middle classes, not the landed elite; they came from the world of business rather than the gentry. He enjoyed, in Baldwin's judgement, a 'ruthless logic', 'precise reasoning and a severely practical mind'; he 'starts with the most complete knowledge of his subject that any minister could possess' and was 'devastating' to his opponents in Parliament.[45] He did, however, lack Baldwin's magnanimity, often giving the impression that Labour MPs were not merely wrong but 'dirt'.[46]

For five years between 1924 and 1929, Chamberlain served as Minister of Health. The ministry had a surprisingly broad remit, being responsible not merely for health but also pensions, housing, welfare, sanitation, roads, town planning, and local government. Chamberlain held a powerful grip on its agenda: within weeks of entering office, he devised a scheme for twenty-five measures of reform, from improvements to pensions to the rights of those who lived in rented accommodation.[47] Almost all of these measures were implemented over the coming years. One of his most significant policies was to construct an integrated scheme to cover unemployment, sickness, retirement, and support for widows and children; it was a contributory scheme, which people would pay into and receive the benefits as a matter of right, rather than being partly subsidized out of general taxation as a form of state charity.[48] Part of Chamberlain's motivation was rooted in recognition of the electoral appeal of such a programme, and he insisted that the scheme be an important part of the 1924 election manifesto.[49] Chamberlain did more than most to give policy substance to Baldwin's desire for reform.

After 1931, the National Government's priority was taking a grip on the economy; and Chamberlain was again the minister best equipped to deliver the policies required. In November, he replaced Snowden as Chancellor of the Exchequer, a position he retained until becoming Prime Minister in May 1937. From 11 Downing Street, Chamberlain implemented the policy of cheap money that worked to combat depression and stimulate recovery. He judged that a balanced Budget was crucial if low interest rates were to be maintained without stimulating inflation. Chamberlain's policy helped to restore international confidence in the British state's finances. Britain's experience of the Depression was less severe than that of most nations. In Chamberlain's own words, Britain 'had stood the test' of the World Depression with the 'greatest measure of success', compared to many other nations where it appeared that 'things are going to get worse'.[50] Rising real wages generated significant improvements in living standards for most of the electorate and stimulated a period of sustained growth and recovery, sufficient to even pay for a major rearmament programme after 1937. In his 1934 Budget speech, Chamberlain famously told the House of Commons that 'we have now finished the story of *Bleak House* and are sitting down this afternoon to enjoy the first chapter of *Great Expectations*'.[51] It was a nakedly political claim, but it was one that the Chancellor could get away with.

'Power Without Responsibility'

Baldwin's success was all the more remarkable for being achieved while presiding over a Conservative party that was deeply divided.[52] Baldwin himself had helped to create these divisions in 1922 by overthrowing the incumbent leadership. And his strategy of conciliation with opponents earned him the contempt of some within the party, particularly its more reactionary elements. The party's right-wing often saw their leader as a crypto-socialist due to his willingness to engage in progressive reform. Most significantly, Baldwin was subjected to frequent attacks from the media plutocrats Lord Beaverbrook and Lord Rothermere, owners of the *Daily Express* and *Daily Mail* respectively. They were the two best-selling newspapers in

Britain, with a combined daily circulation of 3.5m. The press lords were a major thorn in his side for years and ultimately sought to remove him from the leadership.

This campaign of harassment by Beaverbrook and Rothermere amounted to a vendetta. Baldwin's loathing for these men was total: to call them 'swine . . . was to libel a very decent, clean animal' as he put it, for they had become 'a peril to democracy'.[53] They depicted him as soft on socialism and likely to ruin both the economy and the Empire. The press lords, and much of the party, wanted 'Empire free trade', which meant creating an imperial economic bloc and abandoning free trade. By early 1931, the possibility of Baldwin being forced out over the issue was a serious one. The press lords—fast becoming 'megalomaniacal' in their ambitions—actually ran candidates against Conservatives at by-elections under their own 'United Empire' party. Baldwin eventually chose to denounce them publicly at a Conservative rally: 'what the proprietorship of these papers is aiming at is power', Baldwin warned his audience, and 'power without responsibility, the prerogative of the harlot throughout the ages'.[54] The entire political situation was transformed to his benefit a few months later with the financial crisis that led to the formation of the National Government. This left Baldwin's enemies out in the cold, a discontented minority who could increasingly be ignored.

One of the greatest tests of Baldwin's public leadership was not even a political issue. It came during his third and final stint as Prime Minister. In 1936 the desire of the new King, Edward VIII, to marry an American woman named Wallis Simpson—then in the midst of her second divorce—sparked a constitutional crisis that threatened to bring down the House of Windsor. It was an extraordinary episode. Simpson was regarded as a 'tart', and thought to be involved in simultaneous sexual relationships with other men including a married mechanic, the Duke of Leinster, and potentially even Joachim von Ribbentrop, Hitler's ambassador to Britain. She was believed to be motivated by money and 'entirely unscrupulous'.[55] Baldwin tactfully stressed to the Palace the public damage that a scandal might do to the monarchy if they were married. Traditional 'English' values were central to Baldwin's political armoury, and the Crown was hugely symbolic in national life.

The King refused to end the relationship, leaving Baldwin reluctantly, but firmly, to push him towards abdication. When he made clear that his solution had the support of the Labour leaders and Dominion Prime Ministers, the King relented and abdicated in December 1936, after just 327 days on the throne. And in Parliament, Baldwin delivered a speech on the issue that was one of the best of his career. The Prime Minister managed what was a huge shock to the national psyche with great skill in the twilight of his public life. One historian judged his handling of the abdication crisis, Baldwin's last major challenge just months prior to retirement in

May 1937, to be 'the closing and triumphant moment of his career'.[56] Baldwin himself recognized that 'now is the time to go'.[57] He resigned following the coronation of George VI, to be succeeded by Chamberlain.

Democracy and the Conservatives

In the years following the First World War, Baldwin's fear was that democratic politics would really amount to materialist politics, with politicians bribing the electors in return for votes. To counter this, he developed a new style of politics. The Conservative party responded not with materialism—for Labour would always enjoy more doctrinal and rhetorical freedom than the Conservatives to offer advantages through state action—but moderation. This stressed constitutionalism as well as democracy, patience as well as reform. Baldwin thus crafted a multi-dimensional coalition that dominated the centre ground. Presentation was at least as important to this as policy yet, as the historian Paul Addison observed, 'the social services of Britain, taken all in all, were the most advanced in the world' in 1939.[58] Alternatives to Baldwin's conception of democracy were gradually neutralized and by the mid-thirties, those who opposed his style of politics, not only outside the Conservative party but also within it, had been discredited and driven to the margins of public life.

The widespread lack of confidence in Baldwin within the Conservative party is difficult to understand—unless we bear in mind that success generates envy. His collection of political scalps included virtually all of the outstanding public personalities of the era. Few leaders have been as successful. Baldwin's partnership with Chamberlain, meanwhile, was a fruitful one. As Chancellor, Chamberlain gradually became the driving force of the National Government. The Liberal Herbert Samuel wrote in 1935 that the ministry was 'run by Neville Chamberlain. What he says goes'.[59] Baldwin himself described the Chancellor as 'the strong man' of the regime.[60] The axis between the two men represented more than mere party tactics. It represented a style of politics and an outlook on the horizons of government in an era of democracy.

But despite their success, the ascendancy of the Conservative party was perhaps less secure than it appeared. This would be exposed once Baldwin left the stage in 1937. For one thing, Chamberlain lacked Baldwin's conciliatory nature. 'More and more do I feel an utter contempt for their lamentable *stupidity*', he wrote of the Labour party. 'The fact is that intellectually, with a few exceptions, they *are* dirt'.[61] He was equally hostile towards dissent emanating from within Conservative ranks. That Chamberlain was condescending and visibly enjoyed taunting opponents would one day prove his undoing. Baldwin himself grasped the fragility of his creation and was often at pains to stress this. Chamberlain, in contrast, was less focused on lowering the temperature of politics.

There was a larger, more fundamental, problem as well. The Conservative party had performed a delicate balancing act, reinventing itself for the era of mass democracy. However, a series of major crises throughout the period repeatedly threatened to upset this. Up until the mid-1930s, when faced with these challenges the party had usually made the right calculations. But if the Conservatives should *miscalculate* during one of these crises, and their credibility sustain serious damage as a result, the edifice built by Baldwin and Chamberlain would be at risk. Just one badly handled episode may suffice to reverse fifteen years of success. And, crucially, such a development would offer an opportunity for those politicians who had been discredited by the Baldwinian hegemony—the Labour party on one side and critical elements of the Conservative party on the other—to escape their isolation and seek revenge. This is what happened in the second half of the 1930s, as storm clouds began to gather far away, in central and eastern Europe. The resulting eruption would change Britain forever.

For the moment, however, Baldwin could reflect on a unique achievement. With good reason did the Conservative Sir Henry 'Chips' Channon record in his diary that history would judge Baldwin to be 'half Machiavelli, half Milton'.[62] After Baldwin's death, Churchill himself acknowledged his old adversary to be 'the most formidable politician I have ever known'.[63]

EMPIRE AND INTRIGUE

Enter Mr Churchill

Winston Spencer Churchill is one of the most famous figures in human history. His physical features alone are unmistakable, while his wartime speeches remain a familiar component of British—indeed, Western—cultural memory. And it was perhaps Churchill, more than any of his contemporaries, whose decisions and ambitions influenced the shape of Britain's future. It is therefore worth introducing him in some detail. Though he could demonstrate poor judgement, the unusual variety of his life experiences and centrality to some of the key moments of twentieth-century history remains astonishing. Churchill's gift for both the spoken and written word placed him at the forefront of the public consciousness for half a century. His sheer brio was unique. He could deliver thunderous speeches in Parliament; inspire millions of people via a radio broadcast; and pen best-selling books. He was a man obsessed with his place in history—and to carve out such a place meant making history itself.

Churchill was born in 1874 at Blenheim Palace, Oxfordshire, the family seat of the dukes of Marlborough. His father was Lord Randolph Churchill, a senior Conservative politician in the late nineteenth century who served as Secretary of State for India and Chancellor of the Exchequer. Randolph liked to play the part of political insurgent and was deeply mistrusted by the Conservative hierarchy as a result. He had been the *enfant terrible* of the party in the 1880s, a dynamic force but lacking in sound judgement. It was undoubtedly from Randolph that Winston inherited many of his defining traits: impetuosity, hyperactivity, unembarrassed ambition, flexibility about principle, and a lifelong need for admiration. He was always regarded as a chip off the old block. His mother, Jennie, was a beautiful American socialite. On his father's side he was a descendant of John Churchill, the first Duke of Marlborough, who as Queen Anne's commander-in-chief during the War of the Spanish Succession was the greatest general of the early eighteenth century. Leading a European coalition, John Churchill thwarted the ambitions of the expansionist French monarch Louis XIV, the 'Sun King'. Winston was always acutely conscious of the legacy of his famous ancestor, and saw himself as the descendant of a world-historical family.

Educated at Harrow from 1888, Churchill proved capable in history and English but performed poorly in academic tests; he spent his time getting into scrapes and flouting the rules. He went to Sandhurst military academy in 1893 and treasured his time there. Like many young children, Winston was fascinated with military conflict. By the age of eight he had acquired an impressive collection of toy soldiers, and enjoyed manoeuvring them around imaginary battlefields. What *was* unusual was that he never grew out of the fascination. Even at the age of sixty-nine, Churchill was eager to personally cross the Channel with British forces on D-Day in 1944, only finally being talked out of the bizarre idea after a personal intervention by the king.

The premature death of his father at the age of just forty-five in January 1895 was a watershed in Churchill's life. Convinced that he too would die young, Winston resolved to leave his mark on the world. This was the source of the boundless energy that drove him for decades (and Churchill in fact lived to the age of ninety). It is also worth pointing out that Churchill endured a lifelong struggle with depression, and his bouts with what he called the 'black dog' could last for months at a time; it may be that he *needed* constant activity in order to fend it off.

After leaving Sandhurst he obtained a commission as a cavalry officer in the Queen's Own Hussars, and also began to dally in journalism. It was while on a trip to Cuba, observing the ruling Spanish put down a revolt, that Churchill developed his lifelong love for Havana cigars. By late 1896 Churchill was stationed in India and fought against Afghan tribesmen on the north-west frontier. He found the experience riveting. Two years later he was with the 21st Lancers during the reconquest of the Sudan; he took part in a famous cavalry charge at the Battle of Omdurman where he killed at least three men and engaged in hand-to-hand combat. During these conflicts Churchill secured a parallel contract as a war correspondent, reporting for the *Daily Telegraph* from India and the *Morning Post* from the Sudan. Churchill's dispatches, with their evocative descriptions of landscapes, peoples, and combat, proved such a success that he turned his experiences into two best-selling popular books, *The Story of the Malakand Field Force* and *The River War*. Churchill was evolving into a gifted writer and prose stylist. During his time in India he voraciously consumed classics of history and philosophy, being much impressed by Edward Gibbon's *The History of the Decline and Fall of the Roman Empire*, Thomas Babington Macauley's *History of England*, and Adam Smith's *The Wealth of Nations*. From these books he acquired his purple prose, evocative language, and certainty about the importance of 'Great Men'. Churchill's reading of history provided much of his worldview as well. From Macauley he imbibed a romantic and Whiggish notion of progress, and a conviction that everything would be all right in the end; but from Gibbon he absorbed an acute anxiety about the tragedy of civilizational collapse. For the rest of his life, Churchill's mood on public issues would oscillate between these two poles.

In early 1899 Winston resigned from the Army and took up a lucrative job as war correspondent for the *Morning Post*. He was sent to report on the South African War, Britain's conflict with the Boer states. He packed fourteen bottles of whiskey and forty of wine for the adventure. A journalist who met Churchill en route to the warzone recalled that 'I had not before encountered this sort of ambition, unabashed, frankly egotistical, communicating its excitement' but also 'extorting sympathy'.[1] On the front line, Churchill and other Britons were captured after a Boer ambush on a train on which they were travelling. Interred in a prison camp, Churchill famously carried out a daring escape and then crossed large swathes of enemy terrain to reach the safety of Durban. Whatever else can be said of Churchill, he did not lack individual courage. The account of his exploits, published in his *Morning Post* dispatches and then a book, *London to Ladysmith via Pretoria*, made Churchill a hero of the war and a household name. He briefly returned to the Army as a lieutenant and again took part in combat as the British fought their way through the Orange Free State, combining the role with his job as a war correspondent. Predictably, yet another book followed.

With these imperial escapades behind him, Churchill resolved to follow in the footsteps of his father and enter politics. Elected as the Conservative MP for Oldham at the 1900 election, Churchill quickly provoked trouble. Channelling the spirit of Randolph, he organized a group of young Conservative MPs to harass their leaders. He also attached himself to the cause of free trade, the central issue in British politics at this time. The debate between imperial protection and free trade would rumble on within the Conservative party for three decades, and being a free-trader was perhaps the only principle Churchill consistently adhered to. When no post was offered to him in the Conservative government of Arthur Balfour after 1902, Churchill increased the volume of his attacks on the leadership. Importantly, he also cultivated relations with senior Liberals. With the Conservative party dividing over trade and headed for an election defeat, in May 1904 Churchill crossed the floor of the House of Commons to sit on the Liberal benches. This highly unusual act earned Churchill the lasting enmity of the Conservative party as a rank opportunist and a traitor. Winston himself seems to have been serenely untroubled by the accusation, and by December 1905 he was under-secretary at the Colonial Office in the new Liberal government.

In 1908 Churchill was brought into the Cabinet as President of the Board of Trade, at thirty-three the youngest Cabinet minister for almost half a century. He was forging a close relationship with David Lloyd George, the rising star of the Liberal party. Churchill was the protégé and the 'Welsh Wizard' the mentor, a personal dynamic that endured until the latter's death in 1945. Both were quick to discern the electoral potential of social reform such as pensions and aid for the poor, and over the coming years guided the policies of the 'New Liberalism' with energy and verve. Churchill implemented statutory minimum wages in some industries; established state-run labour exchanges to help the unemployed find jobs; and introduced compulsory unemployment insurance. He was also enthusiastic in selling the measures from the platforms at mass meetings. Meanwhile he advocated major cuts in defence spending in order to finance his welfare measures. In a matter of just four years, Churchill had reinvented himself as a radical and progressive Liberal. It was not the last time he would change his hat.

Churchill was by this point married to Clementine (or Clemmie) with whom he had five children (one, a daughter, died before her third birthday). Theirs was a devoted marriage, though his wife was often left exhausted by Winston's energy and need for admiration. In 1910 his more reactionary instincts began to rear their head when he was appointed Home Secretary. In this role Churchill famously sent troops into the Rhondda Valley in Wales to deal with rioting miners. With the country wracked by large-scale union unrest, his practice of using troops to restore order made Churchill a long-time bogeyman of the Labour movement. By late 1911, Prime Minister Herbert Asquith was worried about the situation in Europe and put Churchill in charge of the Royal Navy as First Lord of the Admiralty. The boy who loved toy soldiers, and the young man who was always keen to get into combat, now had the chance to command military forces on a strategic scale. Predictably, he was no longer an advocate of cutting the defence budget; quite the opposite. Arguing that Britain must maintain a large lead over Germany in the size of its surface fleet, Churchill was to coerce the Cabinet into accepting his demands for more of the powerful dreadnought-class ships. He also set about modernizing the Royal Navy: shaking up personnel, revising command structures, and pushing for the development of faster ships with larger guns. He was a dynamic, innovative figure. And when civil war seemed possible in Ireland over the government's plans for Home Rule, Churchill responded to threats of revolt from Belfast Protestants by boasting that 'his fleet would have the town in ruins within twenty-four hours'.[2]

During the diplomatic crisis of the summer of 1914 that culminated in the First World War, within a divided Cabinet Churchill was a staunch advocate of military intervention in Europe. When the conflict began, he was predictably excited.

'Everything tends towards catastrophe, & collapse', he wrote to his wife. 'I am interested, geared-up and happy'.[3] Winston took a much closer hand in the conduct of operations than was customary for a First Lord, and during a brief visit to Antwerp in October actually found himself in charge of marshalling the city's defences against the German onslaught. His quite sincere offer to resign from the government if granted a senior command in the field generated roars of laughter around the Cabinet table. But his luck ran out shortly thereafter. Churchill was a strong supporter of using the navy to mount a diversionary attack on the Ottoman Empire, Germany's ally, through the Dardanelles. When the operation was launched in February 1915 it proved a disaster. Whether the concept was flawed or the execution was botched remains contentious. But by the time British and imperial forces were withdrawn in January 1916, 47,000 troops had been killed. The reservations that many people had about Churchill's character now crystallized into a conviction that he was simply too reckless. With the fortunes of the Asquith government at a low ebb and public confidence shaken, the Prime Minister invited the Conservatives to join a cross-party coalition; Bonar Law's price included the removal of Churchill from the Admiralty. The disaster at the Dardanelles thus offered his former colleagues in the Conservative party the opportunity to settle an old score. Not for the last time, Churchill's career seemed to lie in ruins.

In November 1915 he quit the government and returned to the Army as a Lieutenant-Colonel, in charge of a battalion on the Franco-Belgian border. But his section of the front was quiet, and by May a bored Churchill resigned his commission and sailed for Westminster. When Lloyd George replaced Asquith as Prime Minister several months later, he was able to persuade the Conservatives to permit his friend back into office as Minister of Munitions. Yet 100 Conservative MPs still signed a motion opposing Churchill's appointment, an unambiguous indication of the enduring antipathy towards him. In the post-war coalition, Winston was Secretary for War and Air and then Colonial Secretary. In those posts Churchill was typically energetic, whether improving the flow of munitions, pushing for military intervention during the Russian Civil War to try and throw out the Bolsheviks, or supporting the notorious Black and Tan paramilitary force in Ireland.

During the first years of peace, Lloyd George and Churchill hoped for a 'fusion' between their wing of the fractured Liberal party and the Conservatives. But this came to nothing, and, fearing that the Conservatives would soon jettison the Welsh Wizard, the two hit upon a different option. At the moment that a confrontation between a Turkish force and a British garrison at Chanak on the Dardanelles in September 1922 created a war scare, Churchill and Lloyd George floated the idea of fighting a general election on a platform of resistance to Turkish aggression.[4]

To be sure, British honour was at stake and Churchill was never shy about conflict; but the potential political effects in consolidating public opinion behind Lloyd George by playing the patriotism card were also very obvious. It was too brazen for the Conservatives, and when Baldwin instigated the Carlton Club revolt in October, the largest party in the coalition withdrew its support and the Prime Minister had no choice but to resign. Churchill lost his parliamentary seat at the election that followed.

After this latest setback Winston turned his attention to writing a mammoth—and lucrative—five-volume history of the First World War. *The World Crisis* was published between 1923 and 1931. Composed in Churchill's vivid and swashbuckling prose, it remains one of the great contemporary accounts. He also bought Chartwell Manor in Kent, set in eighty acres of private grounds. For the rest of his life this would be Churchill's beloved home, a place for respite and intrigue. Politically, he set about using speeches and newspaper articles to pitch himself as a right-wing Liberal, of an anti-socialist and constitutionalist bent. In other words—and not coincidentally—*precisely* the sort of person who Baldwin wanted within the Conservative party in order to broaden its appeal to former Liberal voters. 'Anyone can rat', as Churchill himself put it, 'but it takes a certain ingenuity to re-rat'—a quip which rather sums up his snakes-and-ladders approach to politics.[5]

In 1924 Churchill was adopted as Conservative candidate for Epping, which he won with a majority of 10,000 and would hold until retirement in 1964. To cement his party's new appeal, Baldwin offered Churchill the position of Chancellor of the Exchequer. Given the views of most Conservatives about their new colleague, it was a surprising appointment. Churchill later recalled that when Baldwin asked if he would take on the job, his first thought was, 'Will the bloody duck swim?' As Chancellor, Churchill took the disastrous decision to return sterling to the Gold Standard (which left the pound considerably over-valued and uncompetitive), cut defence spending, and struggled to achieve economic growth. However, he did make reductions in taxation and worked with Chamberlain in financing the latter's scheme to expand pensions. His overall record is complex given that the international economy was so unstable. During the General Strike Churchill acted as editor of *The British Gazette*, a newspaper set up by the government after the press was crippled by industrial action. Its circulation reached more than 2 million. Baldwin gave him the job because 'it will keep him busy, stop him doing worse things', but confessed to being 'terrified of what Winston is going to be like'.[6] Predictably, Churchill treated the dispute as a war, with 'the strikers as an enemy to be destroyed', and took to the role with gusto.[7] A daily diet of condemnation and demands for unconditional surrender were hurled at the unions. Determined to monopolize all publicity about the strike, within days Churchill launched a raid on the offices of *The Times* to commandeer its paper supplies for his own use. He even warned his old friend Beaverbrook that should he try to publish *The Daily Express* Churchill would requisition the printing presses to stop him![8] So electrified was Churchill by the General Strike that during one Cabinet meeting he almost came to blows with his closest friend Lord Birkenhead while arguing over what to do.[9]

By the time the government fell from power in 1929, Winston Churchill remained deeply distrusted by Conservative MPs. There was much admiration for his energy and abilities; one observer commented that 'He is the sort of man whom, if I wanted a mountain to be moved, I should send for at once'.[10] But there was also widespread concern about his lack of judgement, and enduring resentment at his youthful 'betrayal' of the party. As Neville Chamberlain put it, to other MPs Churchill resembled 'first class entertainment', like 'at a theatre'. 'The best show in London they say, and there is the weak point . . . they think of it as a show, and they are not prepared at present to trust his character and still less his judgement'.[11] Lacking a base in the party, and a committed free-trader as the tide of protectionism rose once again, Winston's future prospects were uncertain. He was also fifty-five years old. He needed *something*, an issue, which would connect him to the Conservative party and provide an outlet for his still-immense ambition. It was in this context, with the future of India within the British Empire emerging as a problem to be tackled, that Churchill reinvented himself once again.

The Irwin Declaration

It is one of the contentions of this book that the struggle over appeasement at Westminster in the *second* half of the 1930s can only be properly appreciated in light of the very personal battle lines drawn up over India in the *first* half of that decade. The Indian sub-continent represented a critical component of Britain's global power. Britain had been in India since the seventeenth century, and controlled the region from the eighteenth century. It offered a huge resource base and market that helped to underpin the riches of the Empire. British rule extended over not only modern-day India, but also what is now Pakistan in the west, Nepal in the northeast, and Bangladesh and Burma in the east. This was a vast land empire that stretched for 2,000 miles east to west, and the same north to south, with borders touching upon Persia, Afghanistan, Tibet, China, and Siam. That huge area—less a country, in truth, than a place—was home to a dazzling array of cultures, languages, and ethnic tensions. Successful rule over this vast area depended on clever policies and acquiescence from native elites. By the end of the 1920s, India's population stood at around 350 million. Order over this mass of humanity was maintained by a force of just 60,000 soldiers from the British Army. These were reinforced by an additional army of 174,000 Indians. Meanwhile the country was governed by its civil service, under a Viceroy appointed by London. The Viceroy possessed wide-ranging powers, but only around 500 of the civil servants were British, with many thousands more being Indian.[12] The Raj directly ruled over three-quarters of the population. The rest were governed by almost 100 'princely states'. These were usually small enclaves dating back to the days when the British signed treaties with local rulers whereby the latter retained their internal sovereignty but the British took control of their external affairs. This was an empire built on cunning, low-cost policies. A journey across the Indian Empire would cover as many miles as travelling from Madrid to Moscow; India was bewildering and complex. But controlling it enabled the British to dominate the Arabian Sea and the Indian Ocean, and to project naval power deep into the Pacific. It is not difficult to see why India was considered 'the jewel in the crown' of the Empire.

The question of how this vast land was to be kept within the Empire became a taxing one during the interwar era. The reason was that British control over India was increasingly confronted with a growing nationalist movement. Considering that rule by coercion was unpalatable to opinion at home, liberal constitutional reform seemed to offer the best device to retain India for the Empire. This might satisfy local demands for greater self-government whilst preserving Britain's imperial interests. Yet the matter generated immense rancour at Westminster, and became the subject of a bitter struggle within the Conservative party; some exploited this conflict as a means to enhance their own prospects. Nobody was more animated by India than Churchill, who threw himself into battle with his leaders and the mainstream of the British polity. The Conservative civil war over India, which saw Churchill seek to establish himself as the head of a powerful revolt by activists and MPs, poisoned Winston's relations with party leaders. It recalibrated relations within the party and left a deeply toxic legacy.

During the First World War, 1.5 million Indians had volunteered to fight for the British Empire. But in lending large sums of money to Britain to help meet the costs of the conflict, the country began to exert greater financial independence. The British Viceroy won the right to determine India's trade policy and promptly imposed tariffs which damaged Britain's exports to the sub-continent. Furthermore, in 1917, the Secretary of State for India, Edwin Montagu, announced that Britain would introduce reforms to give Indians greater political freedom, the purpose being 'the increasing association of Indians in every branch of government, and the gradual development of self-governing institutions with a view to the progressive realisation of responsible government in India as an integral part of the British Empire'. This was not a proposal for Indian independence, but a route towards a relationship analogous to Britain's connection with the Dominions of Australia, Canada, New Zealand, and South Africa. In other words, one day India would be largely self-governing, but on terms which left her a core part of British global power.

This was the strategy pursued throughout the interwar era. But the growth of Indian nationalism (a simplistic term for what were a series of culturally diverse movements), expressed in outbreaks of civil unrest, provoked anxiety. Many in Westminster feared that the policy of enhanced self-government was one of weakness that would embolden the separatists and ultimately deprive the imperial crown of its Indian jewel. Yet something had to be done about those who wanted independence. In 1919, British forces stationed in Amritsar in the Punjab had opened fire on a crowd of protestors during a curfew. Hundreds were killed, generating a major scandal on both sides of the world. The government was acutely aware that in a democratic age at home, rule by the sword was not an option. And the question of what to do about this began to generate serious ruptures within the Conservative party following the October 1929 'Irwin Declaration'.[13]

Edward Wood, Lord Irwin until 1934 and thereafter Viscount Halifax, was one of the most influential British politicians of the era.[14] As Irwin, he was Viceroy of India for five years between 1926 and 1931. As Halifax, he was Neville Chamberlain's Foreign Secretary from early 1938. The youngest of four sickly boys born to an aristocratic Yorkshire family, Irwin had no left hand and his arm was withered, but he was, nonetheless, a keen huntsman and served as an infantry officer during the Great War. A devoutly religious Anglo-Catholic, he was educated at Eton and Oxford, eventually becoming a Fellow at All Souls College. A Conservative MP from 1910, and then a member of the House of Lords from 1925, Irwin cultivated a detached, patrician air. He was tall, austere, and self-assured. An encounter with him left people with the impression of a straightforward, sympathetic man who would try to do the right thing. His combination of ruthless intellect and sincerity was a powerful one. But Irwin's penchant for moralizing could annoy many. He was also not above intriguing to get his own way. R. A. Butler found him slightly mystifying, a 'strange and imposing figure—half unworldly saint, half cunning politician'.[15]

In response to the growing instability, on 31 October 1929 the Viceroy laid out formal plans for India to achieve Dominion status within the Empire. This quickly became known as the Irwin Declaration. In making it, Irwin was playing a strong hand. He enjoyed an excellent relationship with Baldwin, was well connected in Conservative circles, and worked in harmony with the Labour government then in office in London. The fact that he was considered able to manage Indian politicians was another source of confidence. Meanwhile Indians found him eager to resolve problems. As such he enjoyed the latitude to devise a major blueprint for imperial reform.

What Irwin wanted to achieve was a policy of divide-and-rule. Through proposals for constitutional reform, Indian nationalists would be broken up into extremists and moderates. The former would be isolated, whilst the latter would be invited to play a role in India's governance. This would put Britain's long-term position on a firmer footing and secure core imperial interests—resources, trade, and military manpower—while satisfying indigenous demands. As Neville Chamberlain recorded of a conversation with Irwin, 'in spite of the immense difficulties . . . he is not without hope that a plan may be found which will satisfy the more reasonable Indian and at the same time secure the vital services for the ruling power'.[16]

Such was the objective. Achieving it was a challenge. Just two years earlier, an investigation into Indian reform had run into severe difficulties. Led by the Liberal Sir John Simon, this body had an all-British membership, including future Labour Prime Minister Clement Attlee, and excluded Indians. This caused suspicions that its investigation would be a whitewash. The arrival of the commission in India on 3 February 1928 was greeted by strikes and widespread protests. Nationalists refused to cooperate with the Simon Commission, and chose instead to draft their own constitution for a self-governing India with Dominion status. They threatened that unless this principle was conceded by the end of 1929, full independence would be sought through massive civil disobedience.

It was in this context that, in October 1929, the Irwin Declaration was made. It was a tactical decision. The Simon Commission had not yet finished its report, and so the Viceroy concluded that Britain had to say *something*. Moreover, in Irwin's mind 'there was nothing new' in the Declaration, for British policy was moving towards Dominion status anyway.[17] Making a formal proposal would, he told one MP, hopefully 'prevent serious trouble' and offer a means to flush out the moderates and force them to sit down and talk. It would provide a useful facade that 'will leave the essential mechanism of power still in our hands'.[18] Irwin proposed a roundtable conference in London, where British leaders and Indian politicians might work out the details. The Labour Cabinet supported this. As for the leader of the Conservative party, Baldwin's position was that 'if Edward backs it, it must be all right'.[19]

A Party Divided

But it was not 'all right'; far from it. Ominously, when news of Irwin's plan was conveyed to Conservative MPs at a party meeting, there was an audible 'gasp' of shock.[20] 'As far as I could see', Chamberlain wrote, 'no one in the party approved of what he had done'.[21] Backbenchers were in uproar. There was a widespread conviction that Irwin was capitulating to Indians out to wreck the Empire. Faced with revolt, Baldwin had to beat a retreat and withdraw his own support. He was 'depressed' and privately bemoaned 'the hopelessness of trying to liberalise the Tory party'.[22]

India became bound up with high politics at Westminster because the Declaration worsened the problems that Baldwin was already facing at this time over imperial protection and from those who hoped to engineer a change of leader. In 1929, Conservative spirits were low, having expected victory in the election. The ejection from office thus left Baldwin vulnerable. As the man who had presided over an unsuccessful election campaign running on the platform 'Safety First', he made for an easy target. Even a loyalist like the chairman of the Conservative party J. C. C. Bridgeman worried that Baldwin 'cultivates the attitude of being on a transcendental plane above the sordid turmoil of political life'.[23] It seemed unlikely that he would survive for long.

Churchill was one of those who sought to exploit the situation. He had already held several of the major offices of state—the Home Office, the Admiralty, and the Exchequer. And he was also one of the two or three best speakers in Parliament. This made him dangerous. Soon after the fall of the Conservative ministry in 1929, Winston began seeking to spearhead the party's attacks on Labour in the Commons, constantly sending tactical advice to Baldwin and advocating that the Conservatives confront Labour on 'all great imperial and national issues'.[24] As was the intention, this behaviour did not go unnoticed by his colleagues. Churchill's vigour made for an obvious contrast to Baldwin's understated style. In July 1929, Churchill launched an attack on the Labour government's decision to remove the British High Commissioner in Egypt, the Conservative Lord Lloyd, and appoint a replacement.[25] He seized the opportunity to fire a broadside at the government, but Chamberlain suspected that Churchill was *really* using the issue to try and establish himself as the most hawkish member of the Opposition front bench in the eyes of Conservative MPs: 'he has been trying to take the lead away from SB and thought he saw his way to make a real splash . . . and leave the House the hero of the day'.[26] This was an old trick for Churchill: in 1921, Lloyd George had written that Winston had a tendency to make dramatic declarations 'whenever there was a chance of a real limelight effect!'[27] Tellingly, around this time Churchill also began to qualify his lifelong support for free trade. To most Conservatives free trade was anathema and should be replaced by a tariff policy based on imperial protection. This created a gulf separating Churchill from the MPs and rank-and-file whose support he would need. Mainstream Conservative opinion was every bit as animated by the conversion of the Empire into a trading fortress ringed with walls and a moat in the form of tariffs as it was by India. Churchill's decision to modify his advocacy of free trade thus helped to lessen tensions between him and the backbenchers. He was 'depressed' by the shift.[28] But when push came to shove, Churchill had disregarded his beliefs and undertaken an important political leap that would improve his relations with fellow Conservatives at precisely the moment when Baldwin's hold over the party seemed to be fragmenting. The timing can hardly have been a coincidence.

If Winston wanted to seize the Conservative leadership, India was the safest bet he could place. In the aftermath of the Irwin Declaration, on 16 November 1929 Churchill thus penned the first of many articles in the *Daily Mail* in which he employed violent language to oppose Dominion status under the heading 'The Peril in India'.[29] He gave the impression of being 'demented with fury'.[30] During a Commons debate following the Declaration, Churchill enthusiastically 'punctuated every sentence' of other speeches critical of the policy with emphatic 'hear hears'.[31] And in early 1930 a Conservative faction, labelled the 'Diehards', began to coalesce in Parliament around the Indian issue. Churchill was its most recognizable figure. A new organization, the Indian Empire Society, was formed in March 1930, consisting of Conservative MPs and peers, former military officers, and civil servants who had served in India. This garnered considerable publicity and united politicians with activists. Employing apocalyptic language, its stated aim was to resist a 'dereliction of duty' on the sub-continent.[32] Churchill had chosen profitable ground on which to distance himself from Baldwin. In declaring war over the shift towards greater Indian self-government, Churchill began a circuitous journey that would one day lead him not only to 10 Downing Street, but a quite unique cultural immortality.

On the far side of the world, meanwhile, the Irwin Declaration also failed to anaesthetize critics. Partly that was because of the crisis in London. To try and save Baldwin's credibility and preserve the appearance of bipartisanship, the Labour Cabinet publicly stated that the Declaration involved no shift in policy. In some respects, of course, this was true: British governments had quietly been in favour of an outcome involving Dominion status for years. But *saying* that nothing had changed was hardly likely to elicit enthusiasm from nationalists. Civil disobedience promptly spread, stirred up by extremists like the Congress party leaders Mahatma Gandhi and Jawaharlal Nehru. Congress refused to participate in the proposed roundtable conference as it was not tasked with implementing immediate Dominion status. And Gandhi himself was imprisoned by Irwin in May 1930 for civil disobedience. Like many middle-class idealists (born to a merchant family, he had been educated in law in at the Inner Temple in London), Gandhi was happy to play the martyr. He was arrested, but inspired millions to follow suit with minor acts of disobedience. In this environment, Irwin had to agree to a crackdown. Over the course of 1930, the British imprisoned at least 20,000 Indians for disorder.

Sir John Simon, still completing the work of his commission, thought that Irwin had been 'very foolish' in making his Declaration, which was 'bunkum'.[33] He concluded that if Gandhi was any indication, the Indians were not ready for Dominion status. In June 1930 the Simon Report was finally published. It proposed Indian self-government in the provinces, but no radical overhaul of the central government. It also made no mention of Dominion status.[34] Conservative critics of the Irwin Declaration—almost the entire party—immediately rallied to Simon's recommendations. Lord Reading, Irwin's predecessor as Viceroy, warned that permitting self-government at the centre would only expose the cultural and religious divisions that existed in India, leading to 'bloodshed' on a huge scale.[35] Even Baldwin thought that Irwin was naively failing to recognize how shameless the nationalists would prove in demanding more.

The Viceroy, however, was a stubborn man. So he dug his heels in. He bizarrely blamed the civil disobedience on the illiberal attitude of the Conservative party.[36] He pointed to the willingness of moderate leaders to attend the conference as evidence for his view that majority opinion would be in favour of Dominion status. And he felt scorn towards the Simon Commission for showing a 'very grave lack of imagination'. The failure to signal agreement to Dominion status could, he insisted, 'provoke an explosion'.[37] Irwin thus sought to discredit Simon by demanding that the Cabinet reiterate the Declaration, express no support for the Simon Report, and announce that the conference due to take place in London between November 1930 and January 1931 would be a wide-ranging summit.[38] He threatened to resign if this did not happen. The Viceroy's gambit worked, and in July the Labour government gave way.

The political crisis grew when the Labour Cabinet invited the Conservatives and Liberals to participate in the conference. Baldwin agreed in hopes of salvaging a bipartisan solution that would keep a reformed India within the Empire. Irwin had by now devised a firm strategy to meet the objections of his critics. Control over finance, the civil service, defence, and foreign policy would remain in British hands.[39] The Viceroy also proposed the creation of a new federal system that would see the princely states employed to weaken the nationalists: the privileges of the former might disappear in an India that was entirely self-governed from the centre, and so they could probably be relied upon to favour a federal approach that safeguarded their power over their own enclaves.

The principal Conservative representative at the conference was Sir Samuel Hoare. He agreed that a federal system was the only way forward. But Hoare also used India as an issue on which to build a career. A hard-working and intensely ambitious man, Hoare was also vain and insecure. He had a penchant for accumulating honours and wearing their symbols on his clothes. He was resolved to secure a career-defining triumph through Indian reform.[40] Hoare's approach was to face all possible ways and advocate a policy that would curtail Conservative dissent while leaving him a free hand should he be appointed Secretary of State for India when the Conservative party returned to office. He conformed to the general mood of the conference in his willingness to support federal reform, but also made all the right Conservative noises about safeguards. 'The realities and verities of British control' must be guaranteed, he said.[41] Hoare was acutely conscious of party opinion, and very careful not to offend it.[42]

The conference ended on 19 January 1931 with agreement that the Indian polity would be reformed to give full provincial autonomy and more limited self-government at a central level. The precise details would be thrashed out a second conference, scheduled for the autumn. This sharply improved the climate in India: civil disobedience was called off and Irwin released the Congress leaders from prison. Within weeks Irwin entered into negotiations with Gandhi, and the Viceroy outmanoeuvred the Middle Temple martyr in what became known as the Irwin–Gandhi Pact of 5 March. In return for an amnesty for those who had engaged in civil disobedience and recognition of Gandhi's participation in future constitutional negotiations, Irwin secured Gandhi's acceptance of core British safeguards in a federal India. This was an important step. Moreover, with the Congress party endorsing the Pact quickly afterwards, they were now effectively locked in to a political framework devised by the British.

It was Irwin's last act as Viceroy. After five punishing years, his term came to an end in March 1931. The conference and the Irwin–Gandhi Pact had achieved short-term pacification. A long-term solution seemed plausible too. In Britain, however, the bitterness within the Conservative party was now obvious to all. Many felt that in even negotiating with Gandhi as an equal, Irwin was committing a blunder which underlined the declining willingness of Britain to exercise imperial power. Indeed, the real Gandhi was not the saint-like figure created by cinema and Indian propaganda; he was a shrewd operator. The novelist and left-wing intellectual George Orwell later wondered 'to what extent was Gandhi moved by vanity . . . by consciousness of himself as a humble, naked old man, sitting on a praying mat and shaking empires by sheer spiritual power'.[43] Lord Lloyd openly declared that in negotiating with Gandhi, Irwin was 'drinking tea with treason and actually negotiating with sedition'.[44] He feared that Britain was in the process of 'withdraw-ing' its 'legions'.[45] In the last resort the British Empire rested on two things: power and the will to exercise it. If the latter dissipated, the Empire would not stand.

Battle lines were thus being drawn up. And Baldwin's endorsement of federalism created opportunities for those who wanted to effect a change of policy—not to mention a change of leader. Churchill had already warned Baldwin that 'I care about [India] more than anything else in public life'.[46] In December 1930, with the conference underway, he delivered a speech in London clearly intended to chill the blood of his audience. 'The withdrawal or suspension of British control' in India would, he warned, mean 'either a Hindu despotism...or a renewal of those ferocious internal wars which tortured the Indian masses for thousands of years before the British flag was hoisted in Calcutta'.[47] He went on to attack the small and westernized Hindu elite who, by stirring up an artificial Indian nationalism, were threatening to unleash forces that they did not comprehend and could not control.

The divisions between Churchill and his colleagues were now apparent. He thus began searching for an excuse to resign from the Conservative Business Committee (analogous to an inner Shadow Cabinet) in order to attack Baldwin directly. In late January 1931, Churchill found his chance. He contrived a public row in the Commons with Baldwin, delivering a prepared speech that was clearly intended to be a set-piece assault on the leadership. Winston tore open the party's wounds once more, savaging the Irwin Declaration in 'a recital of the catalogue of errors and disasters which have brought us to our present position'. He argued that while Irwin was 'well-meaning and high-minded', he had made a fatal mistake in dangling 'the orb of power' before the 'gleaming eyes of excitable millions'. Churchill expressed his backing for the Simon Report before denouncing the conference and Hoare's participation in it. Drawing up a constitution in partnership with the nationalists would, he said, be to impose something which could not 'in any way represent the masses of India. The masses will be delivered to the mercies of a well-organised, narrowly elected, political and religious oligarchy and caucus'. Federal reform and the empowerment of Congress would constitute a betrayal of the '300 million people' for whom Britain had responsibility.[48]

With this outburst—and as Churchill almost certainly intended—Baldwin's patience finally snapped. The leader rose to his feet and declared that if the Conser-vative party returned to office in the near future it would implement the resolutions of the conference.[49] With this statement, Churchill finally had the justification he had been seeking. The following day he resigned from the Business Committee.[50] Tellingly, he forwarded his resignation correspondence with Baldwin to the press and allowed it to be published—a clear sign that he had choreographed events so as to make a splash.[51] Chamberlain wrote of Churchill's attack that 'I cannot help suspecting that it was deliberately prepared as a preliminary to his break with S.B. . . . If so, it was skilfully conceived and carried out with admirable verve and dash. It set everyone talking about him and raised his prestige to a higher level than ever'.[52]

Churchill thus tried on the hat of the political insurgent, falling back on his formidable powers of oratory. As the historian John Charmley noted, he boasted an array of strategic assets for this campaign: the support of Rothermere and his newspapers, about fifty Diehard Conservative MPs, and the views of party activists expressed through forums like the Indian Empire Society—all in addition to his own silver tongue and razor-sharp pen.[53] Rothermere's *Daily Mail*, delighted at the prospect of being able to assail Baldwin on India as well as tariffs, pushed Churchill's claim to the party leadership, declaring that 'he is the most discussed man in politics today'.[54]

An effort was now underway to use the question of India in order to raise a revolt in the Conservative party and break Baldwin's leadership. Margot Asquith, widow of the former Liberal Prime Minister Herbert Asquith, said of Churchill's 'fundamental disloyalty' that 'He is the falsest of political gods to worship'.[55] Davidson wrote to Irwin that 'Winston's game' was 'very obvious, as it always is. He is not the son of Randolph for nothing'.[56] Chamberlain perceived a 'serious danger' that Churchill would seize the leadership if 'something is not done quickly'.[57] Churchill was reported to be canvassing for the support of the *Daily Telegraph* and *Sunday Times*.[58] Of course, Chamberlain might also have been hoping to use the prospect of a Churchill insurgency to compel Baldwin to stand down and make way for himself. He was certainly of the view that 'I don't think Baldwin can survive' and 'Winston has left the Sinking Ship'.[59]

The political crisis at home thus outpaced the constitutional question in India. To put it another way, the struggle at Westminster was becoming increasingly detached from the actual substance of policy on the Indian sub-continent. The evocative language, and emotive symbols, associated with the Empire made for ideal political blunt-force objects.

At a meeting of the National Union of the Conservative party on 24 February 1931, Churchill was greeted with 'unequalled acclamation'. The Union passed a motion calling for 'firm rule' in India.[60] On 9 March, at a session of the party's India Committee (which was made up of 'mostly Diehards'),[61] Churchill moved a resolution against Conservative participation in the second constitutional conference scheduled for later in the year. He also advocated that this position should be publicly announced. Churchill was warned that publication of the decision would be 'a slap in the face for S.B.', but he 'pretended that [this] was a mere detail'—which rather suggests that a slap was precisely what he aimed to deliver.[62] The resolution

33

won the support of a majority, dealing a humiliating blow to Baldwin's authority.[63] One senior Conservative concluded that 'Winston . . . has stampeded the Conservative party'.[64]

If Baldwin fell, Churchill could now stake a strong claim to being his successor as the embodiment of party feeling on the Empire. His gambit looked to be paying off. Panic mounted as a result. It was compounded by the simultaneous culmination of the press lords' challenge to Baldwin over tariffs at the Westminster St George's by-election. And yet Baldwin reacted to this two-front assault with skill. On 12 March he delivered 'the speech of his life' by challenging those who might want a new leader to say so openly or get out of the way of 'those who have [a] superhuman task, on the successful accomplishment . . . of which depend the well-being, prosperity and duration of the whole British Empire'.[65] Being 'absolutely frank', Baldwin pledged that reform would only progress if British interests were safeguarded. It was a robust performance that temporarily silenced his foes. Then, as we saw in Chapter 1, Baldwin reframed the by-election as a referendum on the power of the tabloid press. Five days later he delivered his 'power without responsibility' speech in which he assailed the press barons directly. Two days after that, Duff Cooper won the election for the Conservatives by a margin of 5,710 votes. Against the odds, Baldwin was saved. He had passed the test of plutocratic power.

One Conservative observed that 'with his usual luck', Baldwin had 'scrambled out of it'.[66] Another remarked on Baldwin's aptitude for survival that 'God Almighty was so busy looking after Baldwin that He had no time to look after the rest of the World'.[67] If He had been involved, He had certainly been busy. The Conservative victory at St George's did not mean that Baldwin's colleagues agreed with him on India. Most did not. But it did mean the charge that his leadership was an electoral handicap for the party seemed false. Baldwin's opponents, chief among them Churchill, were unexpectedly deprived of a convenient justification for his removal. Moreover, Churchill and the press lords had looked too obviously gleeful about being subversive. Just twenty-four hours before the poll, for instance, the Indian Empire Society held a major rally at the Royal Albert Hall. Churchill was one of the speakers, the *Daily Mail* producing a headline on the 'Baldwin–Churchill India Duel'.[68] The timing was illuminating.

Into the Wilderness

As if the official Conservative victory at the by-election was not bad enough for Churchill, within months he found himself dangerously isolated and in financial difficulty. The crisis of August 1931 broke the Labour Cabinet, leading to the formation of the National Government and, following the October 1931 election, a House of Commons overwhelmingly dominated by the Conservatives. Faced with ejection from the party leadership at the turn of the year, by its close Baldwin was more powerful than ever. He led a broad-based regime that brought the Conservatives into alliance with Labour and Liberal factions. Thus, Baldwin felt no inclination to accommodate Churchill in the ministry.

An integral part of enduring myths about the 1930s is that Churchill was exiled into the wilderness by cowards and knaves unwilling to confront threats in Europe. However, the truth is that it was Churchill's failed bid to overthrow Baldwin which landed him there. He was an expert in the art of making enemies. Meanwhile the global economic downturn also cost Winston tens of thousands of pounds in lost investments. Facing financial hardship, Churchill was compelled to devote more time to journalism and even speaking tours to America in order to pay his bills and support an extravagant lifestyle. But what really ate away at him was his lack of political options. In this environment Churchill clung to the Indian question as a drowning man might cling to a life raft. He was convinced that 'the March of Events' would ensure India re-emerged as the key issue in national politics.[69] And so it proved.

Unsurprisingly, Hoare was Baldwin's choice as Secretary of State for India. He found himself with the punishing responsibility of managing a political crisis that dragged on until the passage of the Government of India Act in 1935. History has remembered Hoare in the same vein as it has Baldwin and Chamberlain: a pompous and cowardly twit complicit in the appeasement of Hitler. In reality, like his colleagues, Hoare had to work within the limits of British power and grapple with the question of how that power was to be preserved. Others, like Churchill, could avoid those difficult exercises altogether and confine themselves to defiant, emotionally satisfying rhetoric. Hoare's programme for a federal India was published in a White Paper in March 1933. The scheme offered a framework for maintaining British power, in that London would retain authority over the appointments of the Viceroy and the provincial governors. The Viceroy would exercise authority over 'reserved' areas of policy, while health and agriculture were devolved to Indian provincial government. An elected legislature, with two chambers, was structured by Hoare to make it almost impossible for Congress to obtain a majority. The federal government could not be dismissed by the Indians and the Indian Army—the 'ultimate power' on the sub-continent—would remain under British command.[70] If not for the hammer blow of the Second World War, this structure may have succeeded in achieving its aims. The Beaverbrook press began to mischievously float Hoare as 'a prospective Prime Minister'.[71]

But Churchill discerned a renewed opportunity in this. Seeking to incite MPs and peers, in early 1933 he organized a new Diehard venture in Parliament, the India Defence Committee.[72] He and Rothermere also formed an extra-parliamentary offshoot, the India Defence League, to act as a focal point for activist discontent. When it was launched with a headquarters in Westminster, the League found the backing of fifty-seven Conservative MPs, while former high-ranking officials in India and senior military figures numbered among its members. And local Conservative associations across the country began to pressure their MPs to adopt a firmer stance. Although most Diehards remained suspicious of Churchill for his past behaviour, he was still the outstanding figure in the faction. The Liberal leader Sir Herbert Samuel believed that if Churchill had not been there 'to give leadership and energy and to form a centre for this movement I believe that very little would have been heard of it from the beginning'.[73] It constituted, one historian observed, 'the nearest thing which the Conservative party had to a genuine grass-roots revolt' for a century, and Winston was its driving force.[74] Hoare complained that Churchill was 'completely unscrupulous', and had 'seriously disturbed a large number of Conservative MPs'.[75] He went on that 'it must . . . be constantly kept in mind that Winston is out chiefly to smash the National Government and that he will stick at nothing to achieve this end. India gives him a good fighting ground . . . no one at present can assess the strength of his forces, and I am sure that it would be a mistake to underrate them'.[76] A worried Hoare concluded that 'Winston . . . believes that India is a good battering ram'.[77]

From early 1933, then, Churchill undertook a series of increasingly violent manoeuvres to restore himself to the political position he had enjoyed during the preceding quarter of a century. If seizing the Conservative leadership was no longer feasible, at least he could force his way back into the inner circle. A rank-and-file insurgency led by Randolph Churchill had been a threat to the stability of the party in the 1880s; fifty years later, Winston tried out the same tactic. He established himself as a popular figurehead for Conservative anger over Indian reform, delivering chilling orations at mass rallies, harassing the government in Parliament, and launching scathing attacks through the press. He remained both recalcitrant and durable. It is important to stress that Churchill campaigned on India at least as strongly as he later did on Hitler. He hoped that a 'deep-throated growl' from activists would force MPs to withdraw support for Baldwin and Hoare;[78] the resultant crisis would then presumably compel Baldwin to make amends with Churchill.

The Government of India Bill elicited little enthusiasm on the government benches, and the great majority of MPs only supported it because their leaders pressured them to do so. Hardly any Conservatives were actual enthusiasts. There followed a steady stream of bitter revolts and close votes. One division in the Commons on 22 February 1933, called after a Diehard motion to back the Simon Report, saw no fewer than 245 Conservative MPs abstain rather than support the government. Then, at the Conservative Central Council six days later, a resolution moved by Churchill criticizing the principle of Indian self-government was only narrowly defeated; the margin of 189 votes to 165 was humiliating for the government. This was revolt on a dangerous scale, and Churchill ensured that the closeness of the result was circulated to the press.[79] He demanded the BBC let him broadcast to the nation and boasted that 'we represent three-quarters of the Tory party in the constituencies'.[80] For Hoare, the problem was that 'our case is a complicated case of detail, whilst the attack is an attack of headlines and platform slogans'.[81] He was terrified by the influence of 'Winston's partisans' and in agreement that 'three-quarters' of the activists were against him, fearing the break-up of the Conservatives.[82] 'Winston . . . has launched a very formidable assault', resulting in a 'battle royal' for control of the party.[83]

But, as so often in his career, Churchill misjudged when it mattered. Ahead of one Commons speech he was heard boasting of his intention to 'smash' the government.[84] And he refused to serve on a parliamentary Select Committee established to scrutinize the legislation, preferring to deliver violent speeches than immerse himself in the details of Indian government.[85] As one historian observed, this decision amounted to a virtual declaration of war on the leadership.[86] One backbencher accused Churchill of blatant opportunism motivated by the frustration of his own ambitions.[87] Geoffrey Dawson, the editor of The Times, thought that Churchill and his supporters were 'traitors' to the party.[88] At a meeting of the Central Council of the National Union of Conservative Associations in 1933, Churchill was heckled.[89] Baldwin publicly attacked the Diehards for seeking to 'destroy national unity' and 'split the Conservative party'.[90] In response Churchill threw down the gauntlet: he made a venomous statement to the press in which he charged Baldwin directly with 'pervert[ing] the power and abus[ing] the trust' placed in him'.[91] This too did him few favours.

Winston's appearance before the Select Committee in October 1933 to submit evidence was another failure; his grandstanding could not disguise his poor grasp of detail.[92] Moreover, whatever their reservations most Conservatives were flatly unwilling to destroy the government over constitutional questions relevant to a country on the far side of the globe. Attempts by the Diehards to secure wider backing, whether through the Central Council or the annual Conservative party conference, were repeatedly defeated by a margin of 2:1 or 3:1. Thus, whilst

Churchill could command the support of many, it was not enough to decisively break the control of Baldwin and Hoare. And though plenty of backbenchers were willing to work with Churchill on India, they still did not actually trust him—something which had always compromised his ambitions.

In early 1934 Churchill even attempted to 'impeach' Hoare after receiving confidential documents which suggested that the Secretary of State had manipulated evidence about trade with India presented to the Select Committee by the Manchester Chamber of Commerce.[93] Churchill's accusations stunned the government and created a scandal that threatened to kill Hoare's federal legislation and halt Indian reform.[94] A speech in the House of Commons during which Churchill unveiled the charges made abundantly clear the lengths to which he was willing to go; he had been in possession of the documents for a fortnight and during that time had seen Hoare socially, giving no hint of what he had discovered.[95] Though historians now know that Winston was correct about Hoare's behaviour, at the time he lacked the evidence to definitively prove the charge and his attack seemed motivated by spite.[96] Hoare feared, rightly, that Churchill 'intends to turn the whole business into ... an impeachment'.[97] Davidson remarked bitterly, 'perhaps that is why Winston has no friends'.[98] The Viceroy thought Churchill 'unscrupulous' with a 'designed' attack that 'savours of the middle ages'.[99] Hoare whinged privately that a 'bomb' had been 'thrown at my head': 'I might have been a traitor being arraigned by the Star Chamber in the sixteenth century'.[100] Given that he had been caught red-handed, Hoare's complaints read as rather pathetic self-pity.

Baldwin and MacDonald led a formal investigation into Churchill's accusations, but this proved to be a charade.[101] The charges could simply not be allowed to stick; bringing down Hoare and killing his Government of India Bill would make Churchill an indispensable force, someone the ministry could not afford to exclude. The investigation therefore ruled that Hoare had only 'advised' that evidence submitted to the Select Committee be altered, rather than actually tampering with it himself. It was a blatant cover-up, sanctioned at the highest levels of British government. But rather than allowing the Cabinet to writhe in embarrassment, Churchill still managed to bring disrepute on himself by accusing Baldwin of suppressing evidence.[102] Though historians with access to the full range of documentation can see this was true, at the time it turned what should have been an acute humiliation for the government into a referendum on Churchill's character and motives. In the Commons, Leo Amery—a man who was a more sincere imperialist than Churchill ever was—accused him of having the mindset that 'if I can trip up Sam [Hoare], the government's bust'.[103] MPs roared with laughter at Amery's assessment; they knew it to be true.

In pursuing Hoare and then accusing Baldwin of corruption, Churchill had taken an irrevocable step. Even other Diehards began to refuse to be associated with him. He complained that only a small number of them supported him on other policy issues,[104] which rather underlines that Churchill viewed the Indian question as a vehicle for this own career. A frustrated Churchill called in the press for constitutional reform not in India but at *home*: a 'timid Caesarism' had settled upon British politics, he wrote, threatening 'the end' of the 'parliamentary system'. He proposed that all householders should possess not one vote but two, in order to recreate a system that produced 'statesmen'.[105] The real target of Churchill's sally about 'statesmen' was obvious. He was effectively saying that because existing political arrangements elected politicians whom Churchill thought unsound and kept him out of power, the democratic system itself should be altered. As his campaign faltered, Winston was sounding increasingly desperate.

By late 1934 he was advocating to Rothermere that they expand the India Defence League in case 'we . . . decide to carry the war into the constituencies' and 'fight every by-election which affords the opportunity'.[106] This was an astonishing notion. Smarting from his humiliation, Churchill was flirting with the outright treason of running candidates against his party. Then his own son, Randolph—as 'handsome as a Greek god and twice as arrogant'[107]—decided to involve himself with the India Defence League against Conservative candidates at by-elections, even unsuccessfully standing himself at Liverpool in early 1935. Though Churchill was privately unhappy (in his impulsiveness, Randolph was a true Churchill), he publicly supported his son.[108] To most Conservatives it thus appeared as if the long-suspected Churchill conspiracy had finally come out into the open. That seemed to be confirmed during the by-election campaign when Churchill delivered a nationwide BBC radio broadcast in which he denounced the Government of India Bill as a 'monstrous monument of shams' that had been 'built by pigmies'.[109] His own constituency party in Epping passed a motion censuring him.

In the end, it was all for naught. Over the first half of 1935, Churchill's insurgency began to peter out. With his attempt to indict Hoare defeated, the Government of India Bill gathered unstoppable momentum as it slowly wound its way through Parliament. It still provoked resistance—on 26 February 1935, the largest Conservative backbench revolt of the century occurred when eighty-nine rebels supported a motion from Churchill that savaged the Bill—but not enough to actually block reform.[110] In August, Hoare's programme finally passed into law; within days, Baldwin began his third and final stint as Prime Minister. There was still no room in the government for the intriguer of Chartwell. That was it. Churchill had been defeated.

Fate and Fortune

There has often been a suspiciously teleological view that, by the interwar era, the British imperial system was doomed to disintegration and gradual dismantlement. The Empire was apparently too colossal in extent, and British strength (and will-power) too scarce, to retain such a privileged position of global power; policy-makers thus pursued a course of slow, but deliberate, retreat. Yet this is to read events backwards. As the eminent imperial historian John Darwin demonstrated, the basis for believing in an inevitable decline is, in fact, far from clear.[111] For one thing, in their own minds policymakers were committed to maintaining, and consolidating, Britain's international position. Britain was the *only* global power, and remained the pre-eminent actor on the world stage. Governments pursued an activist foreign policy intended to advance British interests and maintain the liberal world-system which she dominated. That system was underpinned by Britain's role as the globe's leading naval and financial power. The might of the Royal Navy was sufficient to defeat any realistic challenge, and its network of naval bases facilitated the projection of British power almost anywhere within reach of the sea. Britain's formidable commercial strength furnished it with a depth, and variety, of resources which most other great powers had little prospect of emulating. Moreover, during the interwar period relations with the Dominions were updated and strengthened through the granting of greater constitutional autonomy via the 1931 Statute of Westminster. The uninterrupted, easy flow of capital from London money markets throughout the British world-system created powerful incentives in favour of continuing the imperial network. Meanwhile formal (and expensive) British control over geographically crucial states such as Egypt was replaced with political and commercial 'influence' and 'partnership': this retained all of the advantages of empire and lessened the ability of local rabble-rousers to stir up trouble. The Empire had *never* been a one-size-fits-all enterprise; it had always been knitted together through quite different kinds of political structures, utilizing diverse economic, diplomatic, and military instruments to achieve Britain's larger strategic objectives.

This fusion yielded a highly flexible system; indeed, it was perhaps this that accounted for its resilience. The secret of British power was the (by the standards of most empires) liberal, relaxed nature of its apparatus and the deep appeal of the global system of which it was the hub. The First World War had certainly inflicted monumental harm to the nation's wealth and strength. Yet far from being finished by the 1920s or 1930s, Britain and its Empire remained a leviathan on the inter-national stage. It was, in fact, the Second World War that inflicted irreversible damage and sealed the fate of Britain's global position.

Between 1929 and 1935, Churchill audaciously exploited the issue of India in order to try and provoke a realignment of power within the Conservative party. In doing so he made himself a popular figurehead, a dangerous force, and a wrecking ball. But his campaign failed. Discredited and distrusted, by 1935 he seemed a spent force. Suspicion of Churchill's motives had been entrenched by his conduct. To do justice to Winston, it is important to stress that he saw the world differently to Baldwin—or, for that matter, to most anyone. Part of the explanation for Churchill's lifelong recklessness was his thirst for conflict. Whether chasing combat on the Indian frontier as a young man or lobbing oratorical artillery across the Commons, Churchill loved a fight. He was so in his element at moments of danger that he frequently sought them out; politically, he even engineered them. Robert Cecil once said of Churchill that 'war is the only thing that really interests him in politics'.[112] Senior Conservatives expressed concern over his 'inevitable intoxication with the idea of using force'.[113]

But there is also no denying that he had *used* India. Any other interpretation is implausible. Austen Chamberlain may have detected how Churchill's mind was working after conversing with him in October 1933.[114] He recorded that Churchill 'anticipates that he and his Indian Die-Hards will continue to hold about 1/3rd of the party' in Parliament and that 'the India Bill will be carried *but that the fight will leave such bitter memories that the Govt. will have to be reconstructed*'.[115] In other words, Churchill perhaps knew that he would lose on India but was seeking to use the emotions aroused by the Empire as a means to cripple the regime and, in the subsequent peace talks, force his way back into office. In such a situation, Churchill told Chamberlain, 'Ramsay [MacDonald], S.B. [Baldwin], Sam Hoare [and] Irwin . . . would have to go'. Churchill wanted to continue the alliance with the Liberals led by John Simon, and 'it would still be a National Government'. As always for Conservatives, then, dominating the centre ground with some form of anti-Labour electoral alliance was the goal; but just as in 1918, 1922, and 1931, the conflict was principally about whom should lead it.

As an adventurer himself, Churchill probably detected something familiar in many of the outstanding international political figures of the 1930s and 1940s. Certainly his famous description of Gandhi during the Irwin negotiations hinted at that. The London-educated Gandhi was, on Churchill's reading, a 'Middle Temple lawyer, now posing as a fakir . . . striding half naked up the steps of the Viceregal Palace, whilst he is still organising and conducting a defiant campaign of civil disobedience, to parley on equal terms with the representative of the King-Emperor'.[116] Presumably Churchill understood it because he would have acted in precisely the same way if he had been wearing Gandhi's sandals and wire-frame spectacles. But there is a wider point. In the eyes of *many* British leaders, Gandhi's brazen approach—his obvious pretence at being a typical Indian, and his willingness to raise the stakes whilst still coming to the negotiating table—was not all that different from that of the dictators later in the decade. Indeed, many of those who had to deal with Mussolini and Hitler in the second half of the 1930s were the same individuals who grappled with Gandhi and the other Indian nationalists in the first. Baldwin, Irwin, Hoare, Simon, and Chamberlain applied the same conceptual framework to the dictators after 1935 that they had to India before 1935. This was to establish the demands of nationalists, whether Indian or German, and then satisfy them within a framework that would deliver stability. Churchill, meanwhile, also applied the same toolkit to Hitler that he had to Gandhi. It is difficult to believe he would be pleased that, in 2015, a statue of the Indian nationalist was placed within yards of his own in Westminster.

Policy decisions in the 1930s cannot be understood apart from the *politics* that provided the backdrop against which they were made. To be sure, this was a complex situation and there were very real national and imperial problems that demanded a response. But those responses were informed by an intricate set of motivations and pressures. Churchill's campaign on India is a powerful example of that. Almost any conceivable policy problem can present alert politicians with a platform on which to take a stand or advertise their wares; politicians are typically willing to exploit even catastrophe as a lever to benefit themselves. Churchill did this over India between 1929 and 1935, only to find that it backfired badly. By 1935, his descent into Conservative disrepute was complete.

3

THE POLITICS OF FOREIGN POLICY

Defining the National Interest

In the second half of the 1930s, the British world-system was confronted by a series of profound geopolitical challenges. The complexity, and connectivity, of these problems can be readily appreciated by examining a world map. The British Isles is located off the coast of north-west Europe. But the Empire was global. Imperial interests in the Western Hemisphere extended from Canada to the Caribbean. Britain controlled parts of northern, southern, eastern, and western Africa. It was the pre-eminent power in the Middle East. In Asia, meanwhile, British India extended for thousands of miles, from the borders of modern-day Iran to China. And in the vastness of the Pacific, British authority ranged across Australia, New Zealand, Malaya, Singapore, parts of Indonesia, and dozens of islands of varying size and importance. Those parts of the map that were shaded red covered an astonishing one-quarter of the world's surface. The land frontiers of the Empire ran to some 20,000 miles. Yet, incredibly, this was merely the tip of the iceberg. British commercial penetration of the rest of the world was even more expansive, and lucrative. Britain remained the globe's leading creditor nation. Its capital for investment and goods for sale lubricated the global economic machinery; the City of London was the world's financial hub. The pound remained the dominant medium of international exchange. Moreover, the laws and practices that governed global trade were unmistakably those set by Britain. Communication across this network was facilitated by undersea cables, telegraph wires, mail services, a merchant marine, railway lines, fast passenger ships, newspapers, and telephones. Businessmen, labourers, administrators, teachers, journalists, and travellers flowed back and forth along its highways. The descendants of British settlers populated large parts of the world, and the cultural pull of the diaspora remained strong. And the whole structure of British power was bound together by a web of sea-lanes controlled by the world's most iconic military force, the Royal Navy. These were sustained in turn by a series of naval bases and coaling stations scattered across the oceans. This world-system was a monument to centuries of diligent statecraft. It constituted power and influence on a planetary scale.

The security of this imperial archipelago depended on an ability to exercise naval control in the waters surrounding the British Isles. Britain also needed to be able to ensure safe passage to the Middle East and Asia through the Mediterranean and Suez Canal, which in time of crisis would mean an ability to defeat any other naval power in that theatre. And it needed to not only control the Indian Ocean but wield sufficient influence in the Pacific to deter any challenge there too. Now examine a map of the British Empire at its territorial zenith during the interwar era. The large sections coloured red convey the extent of the resources and allies that Britain could bring to bear; more than enough to eventually defeat any conceivable adversary. British strength remained vast, even after the horrendous costs of the war of 1914–18. But, crucially, it was also geographically dispersed. This meant that, in shaping international strategy, policymakers had no alternative but to think in terms of the whole globe.

There were a number of states with the potential to manufacture trouble. Germany, Italy, Poland, Japan, and the Soviet Union were all governed by unpleasant regimes. France was powerful but paranoid about its security. Czechoslovakia was a democracy but, given its location and ethnically diverse population, a flashpoint in the geopolitical vacuum that was the heart of Europe. China was huge yet unstable, a tempting target for an avaricious predator. The United States possessed greater potential power than any other country yet sat serenely behind two huge oceans. These states were all important because of their geographical position, and the interactions between them could easily generate conflict. Yet Germany, Japan, and Italy presented the most acute challenges. These were 'revisionist' powers, so-called because of their dissatisfaction with the international status quo. All three were governed by extreme nationalist regimes committed to expanding their international standing, inimical to liberalism, and comfortable with *Machtpolitik* (the politics of force). Their leaders—Hitler's Nazi party in Germany, Mussolini's Fascists in Italy, and the militaristic imperial regime in Japan—employed promises of national greatness to cement their public authority.

Throughout the 1930s their behaviour generated international crises. These crises exposed the toothless nature of the League of Nations, which had been established at the Versailles conference held at the end of the Great War. The League existed to oversee the international system, mediate disputes, and deter aggression from its headquarters in Geneva through a utopian system of 'collective security'. The aspiration underpinning the League was that conciliation might replace competition in the international realm, with the member states acting in unison to bring

THE POLITICS OF FOREIGN POLICY

overwhelming pressure—moral, political, economic, and if necessary military—to bear against 'aggressor' nations. But from the very beginning, the liberal ideal of collective security looked unlikely to work, simply because states have always had very different interests and agendas.

The problem facing policymakers in Whitehall was that while Britain could wage war against one of these revisionist powers—or even a combination of two of them—to fight all three simultaneously would be prohibitively costly. A conflict with Germany, even if fought alongside allies, would necessitate stationing the bulk of Britain's military strength around the homeland and north-west Europe. This would leave Asia dangerously vulnerable to Japanese aggression, for a conflict in which Britain needed to divide its naval power between multiple theatres would be far more winnable for Tokyo. And Italy, sitting astride the Mediterranean, possessed the air and sea capability to threaten Britain's artery from Europe to Asia. The alternative route around the Cape of Good Hope took much longer.[1]

Confident that the Empire would ally with other states in any general war, it was not that policymakers expected to lose such a conflict; quite the opposite. They surmised that, as a rich and powerful nation, Britain would almost certainly be on the winning side. In that they were proven correct. Their anxiety was, rather, what another major war—coming so soon after the shattering struggle of 1914–18—would *cost*. Britain's position in the world would inevitably sustain yet another hammer blow; her financial strength remained precarious after the crises of the previous two decades. The human toll would likely be horrendous. Industrial-scale warfare between the great powers had demonstrated its lethality during the First World War and a second struggle would likely prove still more violent, for the development of airpower meant that civilian areas far behind the front line were now recognized as a theatre of future conflict. Enemy production facilities would be attacked by massed squadrons of bombers and it was widely believed that civilian morale would collapse under an onslaught from the skies. The projected casualty figures from a sustained bombing campaign were chilling. As Harold Macmillan wrote in 1966, 'we thought of air warfare in 1938 rather as people think of nuclear warfare today'.[2] But there was more. Another exhausting war could inflame public demands of government and initiate a radical transformation of democracy at home, just as the previous conflict had done. Here too, the leaders of the National Government were proven percipient.

There was a further major complication. Just as policymakers were prisoners of cartography, they were also prisoners of language. Public opinion was strongly committed to the League of Nations, and collective security was elevated into an article of faith in liberal Britain. Even a decade after being established as public totems at Versailles, the League and collective security still set the tone for debate about international affairs. Yet this was little more than rhetorical liberal posturing; and dangerous posturing at that. The League had been exposed as utterly ineffectual when the organization and its member states could not marshal a collective response to Japan's invasion of Manchuria in China in September 1931. The idea of collective security sounded appealing, but concerted action was simply fantastic. Nevertheless, nostrums about uniting against 'aggressors', the dangers of narrow alliances, the dishonour of states attending to their own interests, and even the abolition of war itself had all been inserted into the prevailing political vocabulary. These concepts, fanciful as they were, carried such appeal because of a pervasive societal belief that the struggle of 1914–18 had been senseless, even pointless. The devastating loss of life and widespread suffering were seared into the British psyche. This mournful feeling of futility was reinforced by such cultural touchstones as John Maynard Keynes's 1919 polemic *The Economic Consequences of the Peace*, Erich Maria Remarque's *All Quiet on the Western Front*, Robert Graves's *Goodbye to All That*, and the poetry of Wilfred Owen. Patriotism had inspired men to fight, and as such it was often held responsible for the wanton violence of the war. It was widely believed that 'arms races' caused wars, as did fixation with 'the balance of power' or 'alliances'. These phenomena had apparently led to the flower of British youth being massacred in foreign fields. In 1933, undergraduates at Oxford University notoriously passed a motion that 'This House will in no circumstances fight for its King and Country'.[3] That made worldwide news and spread to other universities. In October 1933, a by-election at East Fulham saw the Conservatives lose the seat to a Labour candidate preaching a pacifist message.[4] The issue was a factor in the campaigns at other by-elections, too. Meanwhile most of the newspapers loudly propagated a message of 'peace' and the cause of the League.

British government and public alike thus lacked the moral conviction necessary to defend what had been won, at immense cost, in the Great War. This was compounded by a widespread popular belief, which took root in the early 1920s, that the Treaty of Versailles had been unjustly draconian towards the defeated states, particularly Germany. This image of a victimized Germany was fantasy, a product of pervasive German propaganda and misplaced Allied guilt. While the Germans were certainly embittered by the peace settlement, it was not remotely as crippling as successive governments in Berlin wanted both international and domestic audiences to believe it was in hopes of evading the economic punishments and military restrictions that had been imposed upon them in 1919. Versailles was far from a Carthaginian peace—and that, arguably, was its real failing, not that it was too 'harsh'. Though Germany had been bested in the war, its will to fight had not been comprehensively broken on the battlefield at the time an armistice was agreed; and while the subsequent peace settlement infuriated Germany, it did not permanently weaken the country.

This was, then, a difficult environment in which to formulate policy. In 1932, the National Government had finally abandoned the so-called 'ten-year rule' for defence.[5] Established in 1919 and renewed every year thereafter, the rule instructed the armed forces to assume that they would not be engaged in a major conflict for at least a decade. The ten-year rule had been used to justify major cuts to defence spending during the 1920s. It was cancelled in March 1932 amidst alarm over Japan's aggression in Manchuria, but by then the damage to the nation's military capabilities was already done—and it ran deep. The resources devoted to the army, navy, and air force had all been dangerously pared back. Just £107.9 million was committed to defence in the financial year 1933/4, a paltry 2.8 per cent of gross domestic product (GDP). This was consistent with levels of military spending since the mid-1920s. Japan withdrew from the League at the beginning of 1933, additional evidence that not everyone saw merit in liberal institutions. Germany was another potential problem. The Weimar Republic had been engaged in cloak-and-dagger rearmament from almost the moment the ink was dry on the Treaty of Versailles. But when Hitler's Nazi party came to power in January 1933 the pace of this activity, illegal under the peace settlement, was quickened and its scope widened dramatically; the army and the air force were hugely expanded. Intelligence about the secret rearmament reached London during 1933, and in October Hitler followed Japan by withdrawing Germany from the League. He also walked out of the World Disarmament Conference, an ambitious international bid to limit armaments which had been running in Geneva since February 1932.

Within weeks of Hitler's actions, the Cabinet tasked several senior civil servants and military officers with overseeing a new body, the Defence Requirements Committee (DRC), to assess the state of Britain's military and map out a gradual programme of rearmament.[6] The core problem with defence planning is that, by definition, it deals in uncertainty; those engaged in it cannot know the future. It is an exercise in informed guesswork about the capabilities the state will require to preserve its security, the identity of its adversaries, the choices made by those adversaries, and the performance of its armed forces in the kinetic situation of combat waged under the pervasive 'fog' of war as conceptualized by Clausewitz. The DRC was chaired by perhaps the most significant civil servant of the century, the Cabinet Secretary Sir Maurice Hankey, a man with an encyclopaedic knowledge of government and an abiding interest in strategy. The committee agreed that Germany was likely the 'ultimate potential enemy', but Hankey and the military top brass were equally worried about Japan and the demands of imperial defence.[7] Hankey told MacDonald that Tokyo 'respects nothing but force'.[8] The DRC thus advised speedy completion of the major naval base long under construction at Singapore (work had begun in 1921, but ground to a halt amid the defence cuts) in what would be a signal of Britain's resolve to dominate Far Eastern waters. Acting on the DRC's recommendations to press ahead with rearmament, the Cabinet increased defence spending to £136.9 million, or 3.2 per cent of GDP, in the financial year 1935/6. But it was slow going, and the programme was not expected to remedy the problems until the end of the decade. It remained challenging to make defence a public priority, and spending on armaments found few vocal advocates.

When discussing foreign policy, British politicians therefore felt a need to employ the pious rhetoric of the League in order to gain a hearing. To speak to the public in traditional terms—the balance of power, the national interest, the possession of a first-rate military, the sanction of force—was to utilize the same wicked concepts that had supposedly precipitated the First World War. There is little evidence that 'arms races', as distinct from the underlying political conflicts that lead states to seek arms in the first place, cause wars.[9] And humans have been just as happy to kill each other with bare hands as with battleships.[10] As the strategist Colin S. Gray wrote, 'Weapons neither make war nor keep the peace'.[11] Yet a failure to employ soaring rhetoric exposed politicians to being charged by liberal opinion with a truly heinous crime: disregard for the brotherhood of man, as embodied in the Covenant of the League. The 1928 Kellogg–Briand Pact that had formally outlawed war, signed by most nations, was merely the most idealistic example of this proselytizing trend. Politicians were thus very careful to articulate their views on international affairs in the vernacular of peace, collective security, and arbitration. This was frequently a cloak to obscure more traditional and hard-headed calculations about the balance of power, but it was an important rhetorical device nevertheless. These men had little choice but to speak publicly in this way; at every turn, the legacy of woolly thinking and idealistic language threatened to ensnare policymakers. With the liberal aversion to armaments having produced a hollowed-out military, there was scant room for diplomatic manoeuvre. And this became a feature of the struggle at Westminster, too. Liberal rhetorics about international affairs were cynically exploited by those outside government as an instrument to connect themselves with public opinion.

The National Government has been routinely criticized for pursuing naive and weak policies towards the dictator states in the second half of the 1930s. That popular perception still conditions how we recall this period. There is no doubt that the strategy pursued by the National Government under Baldwin and, from

May 1937, Chamberlain was deeply flawed. Whether a major war on the continent could have been averted seems doubtful; Europe lacked equilibrium and its politics were dominated by geopolitical vacuums, fear, and loathing. Yet whether it might have been possible to keep Britain out of such a war, at least at the beginning, and preserve British power seems less improbable. In the event, Britain was not only involved from the outset but formally initiated the conflict by declaring war on Germany in order to resist Hitler's ambitions in central and eastern Europe—a region that had not previously been considered a vital interest for London. The pursuit of a national strategy in a world of self-interested, ambitious, and dissatisfied states proved simply incompatible with the liberal language that public opinion and domestic political calculation both necessitated.

Abyssinia and the Peace Ballot

In such a combustible climate, there was ample scope for foreign policy to become the focal point of British high politics. This first became apparent shortly after India receded into the background, in the events surrounding the general election of November 1935. That election initiated a new and protracted struggle at Westminster. The conflict crossed party lines, drawing in virtually everyone in public life. In advertising the value of international crisis for purposes of domestic intrigue, it altered the rhythms of politics. From 1935 onwards, world events—and particularly the *rhetorical* use that could be made of them—became a key resource to be exploited in the competition for ascendancy in Parliament, Whitehall, and the country. As global interstate relations became increasingly strained, conflict between parties and individuals shifted from the familiar issues of economic management and social affairs to encompass foreign policy. Henceforth British foreign policy *was* British politics. Politicians cynically exploited the atmosphere of international crisis for their advantage at Westminster.

This situation developed as a result of Mussolini's threats towards, and eventual invasion of, the African state of Abyssinia—present-day Ethiopia. The line connecting this episode and subsequent events at Westminster was straight and unambiguous. In 1934, *Il Duce* had determined to expand Italy's colonial territories in the Horn of Africa, which already included part of Somaliland (modern-day Somalia) and Eritrea. His goal was to advance his ambitions of Italian national greatness, and occupying bits of Africa had long been a favourite pastime of Western states anyway. Mussolini said that he wanted a 'place in the sun' for Italy. He needed to secure diplomatic triumphs if the Italian public were to be convinced of his capacity to make Italy a country to be reckoned with. As Churchill later assessed matters,

Mussolini's 'rule, his safety, depended upon prestige'.[12] For more than a year Mussolini postured, made demands, and provoked military skirmishes with the Abyssinians before finally launching an outright invasion in October 1935. An Italian force of almost a quarter of a million men sailed through the Suez Canal and landed on the African coast.

The problems this raised were acute. For London, the Abyssinian expedition badly complicated the bigger strategic picture of British foreign policy. The National Government ardently hoped that Mussolini would work with London and Paris in balancing German ambitions in Europe. Italian participation in a diplomatic alignment to contain Hitler would be hugely beneficial. It also made sense from Rome's perspective. If Hitler became aggressive, Italy—located just over the Alps—could well find itself a target. There was no reason to believe that keeping Italy out of the German camp was implausible, and plenty of reasons to suspect that the rival ultra-nationalist regimes might be adversaries. Italian national interests would be ill-suited by a German-dominated continent. And it had already appeared likely that Mussolini would work with Britain and France in acting as a bulwark: in 1934, when it seemed Hitler intended to annex Austria as part of an unsuccessful coup sponsored by the Nazis, Mussolini ordered Italian forces to the Austrian border and threatened Germany with war. During the attempted coup, the murder of the Mussolini-imitating Austrian Chancellor Dollfuss by Hitler-backed local Nazis underlined the scope for conflict. In April 1935, weeks after an emboldened Hitler went public with Germany's rearmament programme and announced that the Reich now possessed an air force of 2,500 aircraft and an army of 300,000 men, and would be instituting compulsory conscription, a conference between Britain, France, and Italy led to the 'Stresa Front', in which the three powers committed to the status quo in Western Europe. A working alignment with Italy would thus represent a crucial diplomatic chip in the game of international poker. Another consideration underpinning the National Government's desire to remain on cordial terms with Rome was the Mediterranean Sea. A hostile Italy, sitting athwart Britain's lines of communication to the Empire, would pose a threat to that crucial waterway upon which imperial power rested.

In short, there existed a strong imperative to avoid pushing Mussolini into the German camp. Fascist Italy was akin to a carrion bird: likely to prey on weakness, but not a major threat in itself. And Abyssinia was simply not an important country in the minds of British policymakers. Britain could certainly stop Italy in Abyssinia, for as Chamberlain observed, 'by putting his army on the other side of the Suez Canal, Mussolini has tied a noose round his own neck and left the end hanging for anyone with a navy to pull'.[13] But turning Rome into an enemy over an issue that was of no obvious national interest was something policymakers were loath to do. The most sensible course of action would have been to permit Italy to annex an imperial possession in Africa and ignore the matter. This would have consolidated Anglo-French cooperation with Italy in Europe, rendering Germany's flanks more vulnerable. It would also neutralize Italy as a naval rival in the Mediterranean. The dictates of the national interest seemed obvious. Yet there was a problem that simply precluded this: British public opinion, animated as it was by the language of the League of Nations and international 'justice'. The mood of the electorate rendered the wisest policy impracticable.

Politicians quickly grasped the political dangers posed by Abyssinia because the popularity of the linked causes of peace and the League had only recently been driven home to them. In June 1935, the results of the 'Peace Ballot'—a nationwide questionnaire organized by a pressure group, the League of Nations Union (LNU)— had been announced. Led by middle-class moralizers, the Union carried out what was effectively a huge informal referendum. An astonishing 11.6 million people (more than half of the 21 million who participated in the general election later that year, and 38 per cent of the total adult population) took part. The poll—in which respondents were asked a series of questions about foreign affairs—showed large-scale popular support for the League.[14] Several questions returned results of more than 10 million people being in favour of League solutions such as 'disarmament' and 'collective security', versus only a few hundred thousand for the alternatives. Whether the Peace Ballot indicated that the public were willing to fight to uphold the principle of collective security, or, alternatively, revealed the deeply pacific mood of the electorate, remains contested. The questions were also phrased in a leading manner, with the pro-League answer always presented as simple common sense. Moreover—and, one imagines, deliberately—there was no question about whether Britain should undertake rearmament in order to replenish its military capabilities in the face of a deteriorating global situation.

The Peace Ballot was, therefore, a sophisticated propaganda exercise in liberal woolliness and progressive hot air. It was the brain-child of Lord Robert Cecil, a maverick Conservative fully convinced of the mission of the League. He served as president of the LNU from 1923, and turned it into a remarkable association with 40,000 members. It appealed to both the constitutionally credulous and everyday folk who wanted to avoid another major war. Cecil aspired to the transformation of the entire international system, and had faith in the existence of a 'world conscience'. He had been a powerful advocate of the World Disarmament Conference held at Geneva between 1932 and 1934 with the goal of turning disarmament into an ideology by eliminating the possession of offensive weapons. This was millenarian stuff, destined to remain in the realm of fantasy. Hankey thought Cecil 'a crank'.[15] He certainly suffered from a hero-martyr complex, but it turned him into the most prominent peace campaigner in the world; he won the Nobel Peace Prize in 1937.[16] Cecil was dismayed by the collapse of the Disarmament Conference, and with the international environment moving against him, tried to shape the foreign policy of the National Government by harnessing, and weaponizing, public opinion. He was an experienced politician and believed that, with 11 million signatures behind the 'National Declaration' as he called the Ballot, Baldwin could be coerced into a renewed bid to save the world (or, more accurately, the liberal conscience). Whatever its ambiguities and propagandistic purpose, the Ballot constituted a powerful expression of public faith in the League Covenant. Politicians had to take account of that fact. Despite Churchill's later insistence that Baldwin could have, in effect, ignored the evidence presented of the pacific mood of the public and pressed ahead with a more confrontational foreign policy, this was plainly nonsense.[17] Churchill might claim that the Ballot 'intimidated' Baldwin and ministers 'misunderstood' its results—but its results were emphatic.

The need for politicians to speak in terms of collective security and League platitudes was, therefore, only strengthened by the Peace Ballot. This was not an environment in which office-seekers could channel Achilles and bellow, 'Fool, prate not to me about covenants'.[18] Even as Europe lurched towards war over the coming years, competing leaders all expressed and justified their policies in terms of upholding the principles of the League while charging their opponents with failing to do so. As the historian Norton Medlicott observed, 'Every British politician and official in 1935 claimed belief in the League of Nations'.[19] There is no doubt that large segments of public opinion would have been responsive to a traditional rhetoric about the world that emphasized patriotism and an unapologetic pursuit of 'the national interest'; one poll run in the conservative *Morning Post* newspaper in March 1935 attracted some 45,000 votes and found a majority of 82 per cent in favour of 'increasing our defences'.[20] The problem was that there existed a constituency of opinion which it was crucial for the Conservative and Labour parties to capture if they were to win general elections: *liberal* opinion. The Liberal party was dying, and its remaining voters (5.3 million of them as late as 1929) were increasingly amenable to voting for other parties. Liberal opinion therefore represented 'the floating vote'. This meant that foreign policy, and the way in which politicians spoke about the world, had to be tailored to what liberal opinion wanted to hear. The second half of the 1930s constituted a long and painful demonstration of the consequences of this.

Succumbing to Temptation

As Mussolini's ambitions became clear, Sir Samuel Hoare—recently appointed British Foreign Secretary as a reward for passing the Government of India Act without collapsing the ministry in the process—grasped that Italian threats towards Abyssinia might prove a liberal *cause célèbre* at home. He worried that the issue could have a galvanizing effect similar to Gladstone's famous exploitation of Turkish atrocities against their Bulgarian subjects in order to capture popular opinion in 1876.[21] And Hoare was right; getting out the pitchforks proved impossible to resist. With the intensity of Italian demands on Abyssinia increasing, there were excited calls in the press and among liberal opinion for 'collective security' to be enforced, for the League Covenant to be upheld, and for Rome to be brought to heel. There was much public discussion of economic sanctions. Abyssinia was a curious country to be the beneficiary of liberal outrage: embraced as an innocent victim by the Geneva lobby, it was in fact a highly autocratic state that still engaged in the slave trade.

Cognizant of the public atmosphere exemplified by the Peace Ballot, Baldwin, Neville Chamberlain, Hoare, and other senior figures of the National Government immediately discerned the political risks. Austen Chamberlain warned that 'if we edge out of collective action . . . a great wave of opinion would sweep the government out of power'.[22] But the *opportunities* were equally clear as well—and temptation proved too great to resist. Despite its large majority in Parliament and the ineffectiveness of Labour as an opposition, the National Government was concerned about the stubbornly high level of unemployment, persistently around 2 million. Moreover, a string of Labour victories at by-elections in 1933 and 1934 had alarmed the leadership. Adverse local election results also elicited anxiety. The Cabinet was worried that liberal opinion might back Labour in response to the unemployment problem. Chamberlain, in particular, appreciated the issue was a liability. In August 1935, he wrote that government policy on employment was one around which 'we can never win an election'.[23]

As such, he felt that an 'issue' needed to be located which would conveniently place unemployment 'in the background'. It would be even better if that issue could also be used to create 'a fear in the public mind'.[24] In terms of domestic policy, the radical socialist programme advocated by the rising star of the Labour party, Sir Stafford Cripps, was one such fear. Now, with Mussolini's behaviour, international affairs represented another. The opportunity to distract public opinion from dole queues and frame the general election around a fresh issue was a welcome one for the Conservative leaders. Pledging to stand up for the League over Abyssinia would deprive the government's opponents of the language of moral indignation. Moreover, a promise to undertake military rearmament in order to enhance the League's credibility might appeal to heavy industries, such as shipbuilding, in areas that remained economically depressed. Rearmament could offer security and employment. Two birds could be killed with one cunningly tossed stone. Chamberlain wrote that 'the Labour party obviously intends to fasten upon our backs the accusation of being "warmongers"...I have therefore suggested that we should take the bold course of actually appealing to the country on a defence programme, thus turning the Labour party's dishonest weapon into a boomerang'.[25] The Chancellor was thinking first and foremost of political advantage. Earlier in the year, James Ramsay MacDonald had described him as already 'virtually PM'.[26] Chamberlain delivered public speeches in Scotland on defence intended as 'the preliminary to the election campaign'.[27] The press interpreted them as such, which, as Neville told his sister, 'was precisely what I was after!'[28]

Baldwin too believed that the government should fight the election on a foreign policy platform. In fact he was profoundly worried by the unpreparedness of Britain's military. In September his friend, the former deputy Cabinet Secretary Thomas Jones, paid a visit and found the Prime Minister 'marching nervously up and down', ruminating that

> for the last 16 years we've underspent a hundred million on the Navy and Air. If only we had our 1914 naval preponderance neither Japan nor Italy would have shown their ugly faces...We've got the wrong sort of Navy now. Anyone who knew anything at the naval review the other day could see they were all old junk...We are stripped bare. Only 96,000 sailors instead of 150,000 and no stores ready...Of course we shall get them but it will take time.[29]

What was required was an electoral tactic that would permit Baldwin to justify increased defence spending to a public immensely wary of military strength. The old master therefore decided to try a subtly different approach to the one favoured by Chamberlain. Earlier in the year he had taken care to welcome the results of the Peace Ballot, opportunistically appropriating it as an endorsement of the government's pacific policy.[30] It showed, he said, that 'we have a large volume of public opinion behind us in our efforts'. By the summer the Prime Minister appreciated that, despite Labour's lack of credibility, a failure to be seen acting in support of the League over Abyssinia could prompt former Liberal voters—who had backed the Conservatives to devastating electoral effect in 1931—to cast their ballots for Labour in protest.[31] Thus, basing the election campaign around the sanctity of the League would appeal to those electors and encourage them to support the

Conservative party. It would steal Liberal and Labour clothes. 'No political issue' was likely to 'influence them more' than 'the future of the League of Nations', Baldwin was told.[32]

In September, Hoare—with Cabinet approval—was dispatched to deliver a major speech at the General Assembly of the League in Geneva. This was a landmark in his career, and in British policy. As he strode into the chamber of the Assembly on 11 September 1935, Hoare doubtless felt at the very heart of global events. The Assembly chamber was long, high, and narrow, with the national delegates of each member state assembled in three rows facing the platform; they sat soberly behind desks of dark panelled wood. There were also two balcony levels, packed with observers, running around the edge of the room. The setting was a suitably imposing one. The eyes of the world were on the Foreign Secretary as the League faced the sternest test of its short history. Everyone was waiting to see what Britain would do. Hoare's response was unambiguous. He pledged to the assembled delegates that Britain would help to uphold the League despite the difficulties of the present situation. He reaffirmed the government's 'support of the League . . . and collective security'; rebutted those who 'scoff' at 'ideals'; and declared that the League was 'the most effective way of ensuring peace'. As if that was not unequivocal enough, Hoare told his audience that 'His Majesty's Government . . . will be second to none in their intentions to fulfill . . . the obligations which the Covenant lays upon them'. He pledged 'unswerving fidelity to the League and all that it stands for'. The Foreign Secretary finished his speech by telling the Assembly that Britain would offer 'steady and collective resistance to all acts of unprovoked aggression'.[33] Though delivered abroad, the speech had a domestic audience: the intention was to create an impression in the minds of the electorate that the National Government would spearhead the defence of the League Covenant. Hoare himself foresaw 'the making of a first-class crisis' in Britain if the Cabinet struck the wrong note.[34] His speech in fact 'struck oil' at home among pro-League opinion—although, tellingly, the view within the Foreign Office was that 'we have beaten the drum too vigorously in response to the demands of the ignorant public'.[35]

For the election campaign, Baldwin thus decided to build on this success by making the importance of the League Covenant the centrepiece of his message. Conservative propaganda stressed that diplomacy conducted through the League represented the best hope of avoiding war over Abyssinia. The message, in effect, was that the combination of sanctions and diplomacy would force an Italian climbdown and a peaceful resolution. The Prime Minister was encouraging voters to identify his Cabinet as being committed to collective security. Of course, Baldwin understood that the principle of collective security remained incoherent and a case of wishful thinking—enforcing League principles in the face of Italian ambition could only be done through the threat of war, which would spell the end for peace—but, politics being politics, the circle did not have to be squared. As so often before, Baldwin knew what the public wanted to hear and ensured the Conservative campaign said it over and over.

The party's election manifesto drove the point home. The first three sections were entitled 'The League of Nations', 'Peace and Defence', and 'Limitation of Armaments'.[36] There was a pledge that the League 'will remain . . . the keystone of British foreign policy . . . there will be no wavering in the policy we have hitherto pursued'. Meanwhile rearmament would be undertaken, but the explanation for this was closely integrated with the need to uphold the Covenant. A huge campaign of Conservative radio broadcasts, short films shown in cinemas, and pamphlets reiterated these arguments. One poster depicted John Bull, the iconic cartoon personification of Great Britain, with a dove of peace; another poster, intended to chill those who saw it, showed children playing under the shadow of bombers flying overhead; a third, entitled 'Our Word Is Our Bond', depicted a clenched fist slamming down upon a parchment bearing the inscription 'Covenant of the League of Nations'—an unequivocal message that the National Government would support the League.[37]

Presenting the issue in this way was an astute decision on Baldwin's part. It enabled the Conservatives to confront Labour's accusations of being 'warmongers' and stand on a platform of support for the League. It deprived the Labour leadership of an opportunity to preach from the moral high ground. And it offered a rationale for rearmament. Held on 14 November, the general election saw the National Government secure another landslide victory, emerging with 432 Conservative MPs to Labour's 154. They held a massive overall Commons majority of 255. Strikingly, despite four years of economic difficulty the total Conservative vote had barely fallen, from 11.9 million in 1931 to 11.8 million in 1935. It was a major success and demonstrated once again Baldwin's uncanny ability to interpret, and guide, public opinion.

'We Have Had a Political Earthquake'

Readers with a sense of mischief may have guessed that this triumph was to prove remarkably short-lived.[38] In succumbing to the temptation to advertise support for the League partly in order to reap domestic political benefits, the government raised expectations over Abyssinia that its diplomacy simply could not satisfy. Within a mere four weeks of the election, the Cabinet was embroiled in a major scandal stemming from the popular perception that it had 'betrayed' the League.

A belief took hold that Baldwin and his colleagues had brazenly lied in order to retain office.

The crisis stemmed from a proposal to end the war in Abyssinia, devised in early December by Hoare and his French counterpart, Pierre Laval. Giving priority to the relationship between France and Italy in Europe, Laval was desperate to find a workable solution. The Hoare–Laval Pact, as it became known, envisaged partitioning Abyssinia in order to satisfy Italy's aspirations while preserving a symbolic Abyssinian sovereignty. The conquered fertile plains would be recognized as an Italian colony, while the Abyssinian Emperor Haile Sellasie would retain independence in the south.[39] Hoare and the chief civil servant at the Foreign Office, Sir Robert Vansittart, hashed out the terms with Laval after being instructed by the Cabinet to 'press on with peace negotiations as rapidly as possible with a view to bringing the conflict to an end'.[40] Hoare, assisted by Vansittart, brokered the specific details of the Pact on his own initiative without the approval of Cabinet colleagues, but his fellow ministers seemed to approve of the plan when it was communicated to them.[41] They quickly changed their minds after its details were leaked in the French press on 10 December.[42] These proposals generated a public and political explosion.

On balance, the Hoare–Laval Pact constituted a plausible solution to Italian demands. Rome could achieve its imperial objectives while at least part of Abyssinia remained independent. Mussolini was prepared to accept it, and the Abyssinians had little choice in the matter. It was even consistent with the Covenant of the League, for Article 15, paragraph 3 of that document mandated the settling of disputes through conciliation. Indeed, the League Assembly had set up a committee of thirteen member states to seek conciliation, with Britain and France tasked with engineering it.[43] In late November, Hankey—in a rather Machiavellian frame of mind—told Hoare that, with the election over, the government 'no longer had to angle for votes from the left wing' and so 'could do what they liked'. Hoare was at first resistant, saying that 'public opinion would not stand it', but Hankey retorted that 'we knew the facts'.[44] Since October, Mussolini himself had been signalling that he would be willing to back down from his sweeping demands for annexation of the whole of Abyssinia and settle for a more modest outcome, including a territorial swap with Italy's neighbouring colony of Eritrea that would provide landlocked Abyssinia with a commercially valuable outlet to the sea. Agreement thus seemed possible.

The British negotiators were extremely satisfied with the terms brokered. Most importantly, the Pact offered the prospect of extricating Britain from a diplomatic impasse in which her vital interests were not at stake, yet, due to public outrage, Italy was being pushed into the role of an adversary. The economic sanctions imposed by the League at the outset had already antagonized the Italians; but, if sanctions were to truly work, an oil embargo enforced by London and Paris would almost certainly be necessary. At the time of his conversation with Hankey on 25 November, Hoare took the view that oil sanctions must be implemented, not least because it was 'politically impossible' not to do so.[45] Within a fortnight he had changed his mind, and ruled out an embargo. There seemed a real possibility that Mussolini would react to an oil embargo by attacking British and French ships in the Mediterranean. With France most concerned about cultivating Italian support against Germany, Laval initially even refused to promise French support should British ships suffer a 'mad dog' attack, a stance which infuriated the Cabinet; Vansittart raged that it was 'disloyalty and treachery in its dirtiest and blackest form'.[46] The situation thus threatened to spiral rapidly out of control. There was no conceivable British interest that would justify bringing the Royal Navy to bear against Mussolini over a minor colonial disagreement that did not even affect the Empire. The framework crafted by Hoare and Laval offered the basis for an acceptable settlement to an unfortunate episode.

The problem with the Pact was not *strategic*. It was *political*. It represented an intolerable reversal from the policy upon which the National Government had won a general election just weeks earlier. It appeared blatantly opportunistic. Even Ivan Maisky—as Soviet ambassador to London, an official representative of a regime that had long ago perfected the art of saying one thing and doing the precise opposite— was left astonished: 'A plan that marks the most brazen, most impudent betrayal of the League! And when? Three weeks after the election!'[47]

When the details were announced, the Pact generated shock across the political spectrum. The opportunity to get one over on the government proved impossible to resist. The Labour party adopted a stance of moral indignation and insisted that it had been correct about the perfidy of the National Government all along. This afforded Labour a degree of credibility, and appearance of prescience, that the substance of its policies did not merit. Attlee moved a motion of censure on the government in Parliament, and attacked Baldwin's integrity: 'If the Prime Minister won an election on one policy and immediately after the election was prepared to carry out another, it has an extremely ugly look'.[48] And it was not just the Opposition; the press was in absolute uproar, with even the generally supportive *Times* assailing the Cabinet.[49] The editor, Baldwin's friend Geoffrey Dawson, took a strongly anti-Italian line and thought the agreement dishonourable. In a stinging editorial he described the proposed settlement as 'A Corridor for Camels'.[50] The government was inundated as a torrent of violent attacks poured forth. Newspaper after newspaper denounced the policy. Critical messages from prominent figures in public life, including scientists, businessmen, historians, and economists, appeared in the letters page of national and regional newspapers. The weeklies, such as *The Spectator* and *The Economist*, were every bit as hostile. There was also a deluge of letters from ordinary members of the public to Conservative ministers and backbenchers. In the midst of a meeting with Baldwin at Downing Street, Vansittart witnessed a harried secretary enter the room to bring in the latest bundle of angry telegrams.[51] All this represented an expression of popular outrage far greater than anything the recipients had experienced before.[52] Cecil and the League of Nations Union were positively apoplectic.

Many Conservative MPs quickly recognized that the party had just sailed at full-speed into an iceberg, and the Pact could not be accepted as a basis for British policy. Backbenchers were furious that it 'made a nonsense of the general election campaign', and 'plac[ed] us in an impossible situation *vis-à-vis* our constituents'.[53] 'Their election speeches were still warm on their lips', as Macmillan later recalled.[54] Cuthbert Headlam—admittedly one of the most pessimistic backbenchers of the century—confided to his diary: 'It really frightens me that we should have such a crew running the show'.[55] 'How on earth the government can have so misunderstood public opinion', he moaned, 'it is difficult to imagine'.[56]

The Foreign Secretary was not having a good week. Hoare had fallen face-first while indulging his passion for ice-skating during a brief holiday in Switzerland, suffering a badly broken nose in the process. Hurrying home and sporting a plaster across his nose, the battered Hoare touched down at Croydon airport on 16 December. Once in London he was hit by the ferocity of political and media outrage. The Hoare–Laval Pact represented one of the most intense scandals faced by a British government in the democratic age. Vansittart later acknowledged that there was 'a dualism which might look like duplicity' to the government's behaviour.[57] Chamberlain complained that 'our whole prestige in foreign affairs at home and abroad has tumbled to pieces like a house of cards. If we had to fight the election over again we should probably be beaten & certainly would not have more than a bare majority'.[58] (Neville did, though, 'take some comfort' from the thought that 'if I had been Premier', the 'discredit would have fallen on me instead of S.B.')[59] It is difficult to have much sympathy, for back in August the Chancellor had explained the Cabinet's policy to Lord Lloyd: they would not spearhead League action against Italy, but simply wanted to ensure that Britain did not get the blame for the failure to stop Mussolini, a stance which left Lloyd ruminating on 'the manifest dishonesty of the whole policy'.[60] Austen Chamberlain wrote that Hoare had 'blundered badly', for 'I have never known the political sky cloud over so suddenly nor have I seen blacker clouds on the horizon'. Principally concerned about the effects on the government's political stature, he melodramatically concluded that it was 'a tragedy'.[61] Meanwhile Churchill's chief crony, Brendan Bracken, contacted his master who was holidaying in Majorca to say that 'we have had a political earthquake'.[62] He was not wrong.

The combination of public shock, criticism from Labour and the press, and the lack of support within the Conservative party compelled the government to disavow the Pact. This would clearly necessitate tossing the unfortunate Sam Hoare overboard. But Viscount Halifax—the former Irwin, Viceroy of India and now Lord Privy Seal in the Cabinet—believed that the National Government's 'whole moral position' was 'at stake'.[63] At an extraordinary Cabinet meeting on the morning of 18 December, Hoare was effectively put 'on trial' and abandoned by his colleagues.[64] Chamberlain regretfully concluded that the Foreign Secretary had 'committed an error of judgement'. Baldwin told his ministers that 'it was a worse situation in the House of Commons that he had ever known'. Reassurances that Hoare's colleagues were 'of course . . . with him' were palpably false; the Cabinet wanted to ditch the Foreign Secretary in order to save the government. Prodded by a dozen pitchforks wielded by men desperate to hold on to their offices, Hoare was told that he must take the blame and resign: with a resignation, 'the whole thing would be dead'. Halifax suggested that Baldwin—'one of our national anchors'—might be forced to step down if the Foreign Secretary did not go.[65] Reluctantly, an embittered Hoare agreed to do so, and surrendered his office on 19 December—a mere nine days after the proposals were revealed. The National Government promptly distanced itself from the mooted Pact.

Hoare had been made the scapegoat. This seemed rather unfair, because not only had the Cabinet authorized him on 2 December to broker a solution, but his colleagues explicitly told him not to bring the issue back before them unless discussions with Laval 'did not offer any reasonable prospect of settlement'.[66] Hoare was thus provided with clear instructions to resolve the Abyssinian issue, and a free hand to do so. It had been a disaster for a man who a mere six months earlier stood at the pinnacle of his career, having defeated Churchill and navigated the tortuous passage of the Government of India Act. In yet another piece of shrewd Baldwinian calculation, Hoare was succeeded at the Foreign Office by the young and handsome Anthony Eden—whose principal qualification for the post of Foreign Secretary was that he took care to dress fashionably and, as a relentless advocate of the Covenant, appealed to liberal sentiments. He was previously Minister for League of Nations Affairs, a role which afforded plenty of opportunity to spout hot air and thus made him an ideal Foreign Secretary for a government keen to restore its credentials as a patron of the League. Eden was regarded by those in the know as erratic, unstable, and worryingly idealistic, but he looked and sounded the part. Such was the primacy of keeping up appearances.

Grandstanding over Abyssinia in the approach to the 1935 general election thus created acute problems in its aftermath. It altered the whole dynamic of British politics. Strategically the British were short on options, but Conservative election tactics narrowed these considerably. Dropping strong hints about collective security blew up in the government's face because no collective security policy was actually feasible. The problems with the concept were legion. It supposed that member states of the League would combine their resources to overawe any 'aggressor' nation even where their own interests were not threatened. Touching as it was, this overestimated the prevalence of altruism in the international sphere. In its aspirations for the League of Nations, liberal opinion was seeking to make a conscious break with thousands of years of history and its lessons. The dominant mode of thinking about international relations was that it took place in an anarchical, and dangerous, system in which sovereign states needed to be constantly attentive to the protection of their own distinctive interests. There was no higher authority to appeal to, so if they failed to protect themselves, nobody else would. This dilemma was best expressed by the ancient Athenian historian Thucydides, whose conclusions about why states went to war—his famous trinity of 'fear, honour, and interest'—remained the foundation of serious strategic thought. In the interwar era that interpretation of the international system was increasingly viewed not as an indispensable explanatory tool, still less as a guide for actual practice by leaders, but as something to stand condemned. It represented a blueprint for self-interest and conflict, a state of affairs that the League was intended to banish. In the real world, however, the notion that states might subordinate their own concrete needs to the purported interests of a nebulous 'world community' was a pious fantasy. It was positively unstrategic when Britain was confronted with the reality of converting Mussolini into a potential ally of Hitler rather than a bulwark against him.

As Chamberlain privately put it, the British had no objection to Italian colonial aspirations; it was the method and timing that proved inconvenient.[67] Baldwin's view was that he was 'not going to get this country into a war with anybody for the League of Nations or anybody else or for anything else'.[68] The Covenant was an easy thing for which to express rhetorical support; the international status quo suited British interests. The problem came when the expansive principles of the Covenant were challenged and Britain found itself under pressure to defend them. Not only were British interests *unaffected* by Italy gaining colonial territory in Africa; but having to lead the protests to the invasion ran *directly counter to* the larger strategic objectives of British policy. This was the situation that liberal rhetoric created. Moral rectitude was all well and good, but a sentiment was not a policy. 'The League', 'collective security', 'disarmament', 'justice', and 'peace' were powerful slogans, but in the end they were just that: slogans. Collective security was a liberal ideal, but most states in the League were not Western liberal democracies and unlikely to pursue policies along those lines. Moreover, while liberal opinion wanted something to be done to bring Italy to heel, that same liberal opinion recoiled in horror from the employment of force or coercion that would be necessary to do so.

The contradictions at the heart of the liberal view of the world were glaring.[69] If the Covenant of the League was to be upheld, war—and lots of it, in all corners of the world—was likely to be unavoidable. And this was not something public opinion could tolerate. Commitments to the League of Nations landed Britain in difficulties that the rhetoric of the very same organization made it politically impossible to resolve. The mood exemplified by the Peace Ballot was, in the judgement of the MP Harold Nicolson, 'self-contradictory nonsense', an expression of what people wanted the world to look like.[70] Even if collective security was genuinely attempted, the distribution of global power—and the absence of America from the League—meant that in practice the military, economic, and social burden of enforcement would fall on Britain and France.

A further issue with the League was that, by guaranteeing every existing international border, it attempted to preserve the current state of the world in aspic. This only ensured that every future international dispute—even the most routine ones—would have the makings of a first-class world crisis. The nostrums of the League offered vanishingly little flexibility or space for conventional inter-state behaviour. This rigidity doomed it. The message sent out by a blanket guarantee of territorial integrity was 'there will be no change'. This was never realistic. By making adjustment almost impossible—because all parties had to consent, which hardly seemed likely—the Covenant ensured that stability would remain elusive. Whether for reasons of war, conquest, fracture, or ethnic discord, borders shifted; the world evolved. Even the idea of preserving the status quo was thus exceedingly dangerous. Territorial disputes involving minor states, or arguments over the location of a line on a map thousands of miles away, occasionally threatened discord between the great powers anyway; this was routine. But by guaranteeing *every* border, the League also guaranteed that *every* single dispute in the future, between states anywhere in the world, would have the potential to erupt into a major international crisis—with all the implications for great power relations that flowed from that. Every issue could carry serious ramifications for global peace. Routine disputes—in places such as Abyssinia—would demand a response, and thus precipitate diplomatic confrontations, regardless of any actual national interests at stake. The League effectively institutionalized chaos.

Chamberlain complained, unkindly if not inaccurately, that the League of Nations Union was made up of 'fanatics':[71] 'I can find no polite words to express my opinion of the L[eague] of N[ations] Union . . . The kind of person who is really enthusiastic about the League is almost invariably a crank'.[72] Meanwhile, in a sentence dripping with contempt for the curse of middle-class naivety, Churchill later wrote of Baldwin's mistake in seeking to 'comfort the professional peace-loving elements in the nation'.[73] There is certainly little doubt that in diagnosing one pathology, the advocates of the League were inadvertently creating another. But the fact of the matter was that the National Government had made their bed with the League in the election. Now they had to lie in it. The public rhetoric about international affairs which had been inculcated into the electorate by all the major parties since 1919 meant that politicians could not easily sanction a violation of the piety of the League. They certainly could not do so after running a nationwide election campaign on a League platform just weeks before. As Headlam wondered incredulously, 'Surely they might have foreseen all of this before they began playing with sanctions?'[74]

'The Very Midsummer of Madness'

Italy's war in Abyssinia continued into early 1936, and the capital fell in May.[75] The conflict was a long slog and reminded everyone of the limitations of the Italian military, but eventually the whole country was in Mussolini's hands. The war remained a *cause célèbre* in Britain, although some Britons who knew more about Abyssinia were less sad: the novelist Evelyn Waugh went to see events first-hand and wrote back cruelly that 'I have got to hate the Ethiopians more each day goodness they are lousy & I hope the [Italians] gas them to buggery'.[76] Gas them the Italians certainly did, shipping 300 tons of poison gas to the conflict zone and employing it liberally. Abyssinia was merged with Rome's other colonies to form Italian East Africa. In the flush of victory, Mussolini theatrically likened his success to the birth of a new Roman Empire.

Throughout 1935 the National Government felt itself assailed from all sides. In this climate, Baldwin recognized that the Peace Ballot and the Abyssinian question offered valuable opportunities if their symbology could be harnessed for the Conservative party. The result was an electoral triumph and a strategic catastrophe.

Attempting to extricate Britain from what was fast becoming a farce in which vital national interests were being sacrificed on the altar of virtue, in the spring of 1936 Chamberlain argued strongly in Cabinet for the sanctions on Italy to be lifted.[77] He was angry that Baldwin, still frightened by the response to the Hoare–Laval Pact, was reticent to move on the issue. Chamberlain's self-confidence was soaring at this point (the Commons was 'completely under [my] command') and he was looking forward to Baldwin's retirement.[78] MacDonald remarked that the Chancellor 'holds the PM in his pocket'.[79] Eventually, the Chancellor's patience snapped; he concluded that 'if those who should give a lead won't . . . someone else must'.[80] In a public speech in June 1936 calculated to force the Cabinet's hand—Chamberlain himself acknowledged that it was a 'blazing indiscretion'—he declared that to maintain sanctions when they had failed was 'the very midsummer of madness'.[81] Days later, with the war over, sanctions were finally lifted. Flexing his muscles in this way was a signal of Chamberlain's growing power.

It was an overdue conclusion to an ignominious episode. All along, the National Government recognized that belligerence did not serve the wider British interest. Baldwin had repeatedly insisted in public that Britain would take 'no isolated action'. But the Cabinet was equally worried about being seen to abandon the Covenant, wanting to make it 'impossible to criticise us on the ground that we were deserting the League'.[82] This illustrated that the overriding concern at work was not strategy, but politics. The language of the League of Nations had been internalized by the governing classes, becoming a necessary component of their intellectual furniture. From the beginning the government sought to avoid imposing effective sanctions on Mussolini, knowing what that would mean for Anglo-Italian relations, but insisted that 'It must be the League and not the British government that declares that sanctions are impracticable'.[83]

Feeling it necessary to be *seen* to do something, Britain ended up taking half-measures that failed on all counts. The economic sanctions that were imposed did not pack the punch necessary to stop Mussolini. That the sanctions were intended only as a gesture for public consumption can be discerned not simply in the extreme reticence of the Cabinet to impose them in the first place, but Hoare's care to avoid steps—such as an oil embargo—that might prove a particular 'provocation' to Italy.[84] Yet Mussolini did not see matters this way. To his mind, by imposing sanctions at all, Britain made itself an enemy of *Il Duce*. The entire episode was a disaster. London had placed itself in Mussolini's path and, for political reasons, made a symbolic show of resisting him—only to be brusquely shouldered aside. This outcome was the worst of all worlds.

No conclusion seems plausible other than that the National Government had badly miscalculated. Its leaders enthusiastically embraced the Abyssinian issue as one on which to win an election. Meanwhile they sought to avoid the public odium of coming out against League sanctions, whilst secretly trying to ensure that robust measures were not imposed. It was duplicitous, and, with the Hoare–Laval Pact, they had been caught red-handed. Henceforth British politics and British foreign policy would be indistinguishable.

4

DEFENDING THE REALM

The Struggle Against Martyrdom

Initially expected to illuminate the pleasing vistas of a new world order, the concepts of the League of Nations had in fact only plunged policymakers into pitch darkness without so much as a lamp to guide them. Abyssinia had a major impact on the wider political nation as well. Whereas for the National Government the affair was toxic, for others it offered advantages. And few benefited more from the opportunity to talk about something fresh than the Labour party.

Labour had spent four years unsuccessfully seeking to restore its credibility after the disaster of presiding over the 1931 financial crisis. Emerging from the 1931 general election with just fifty-two MPs, for those senior figures who banked on politics as a career there loomed the alarming possibility that Labour was finished as a party of government. Labour lapsed into internal bloodletting and scheming that lasted for most of the decade. Radical socialist ideas were advocated by prominent figures and adopted by the rank-and-file at annual conference.[1] Virtually the whole Labour movement developed admiration for the methods of authoritarian economic 'planning' adopted by Fascist Italy and Communist Russia. There was much talk of the 'socialization' (which meant nationalization or, at the very least, state control) of all key industries and infrastructure. Yet, beneath this, the struggle for power and personal ascendancy was at least as important as the milk of pure doctrine. Political recovery was slow in the years up to 1935, for the small Parliamentary Labour Party (PLP) was 'a poor little affair', and 'isolated' from the National Executive Committee (NEC) which governed the party as a whole and quickly became the real seat of power.[2] The NEC and Labour headquarters at Transport House—located just off the Victoria Embankment at Westminster—spent four frustrating years trying to assert control over the PLP and activists in local constituency parties.

The international crisis of 1935 was thus invaluable. Factions within the party employed it as a welcome instrument to launch a *coup d'état* against a number of leading figures. Most importantly, it was used to jettison the elderly Labour leader,

George Lansbury. A devout Christian and radical socialist MP born in 1859, Lansbury's qualification for the leadership had been that he was one of the few senior figures to retain a seat in the 1931 rout. Others holding what the more moderate Hugh Dalton described as 'purely accidental position[s]' through surviving in 1931 included Clement Attlee ('a small man') and Sir Stafford Cripps (a 'crank').[3] A martyr by temperament, Lansbury devoted his life to campaigning against established authority and was unsuited to a serious job. The Abyssinian issue provided a convenient pretext to force an ineffectual leader into resignation, for Lansbury's Christianity inspired a staunch aversion to military conflict. In 1933 he had declared that 'I would close every recruiting station, disband the army and dismiss the air force. I would abolish the whole dreadful equipment of war and say to the world "do your worst"'.[4] Demands from senior figures at Transport House for Labour to take a more robust line on international affairs created an unbridgeable divide between them and their pacifist leader. While Lansbury publicly agonized over how to respond to the Italian threats, much of the Labour party and its trade union sponsors indicated that they would support a policy of sanctions, including war if necessary. Walter Citrine, chieftain of the Trade Union Congress, expressed disdain for Lansbury's 'pious declarations' of the need for a 'truce of God'.[5]

The stage was set for a public assassination at Labour's annual conference, held at Brighton, in September 1935. Weeks earlier, Lansbury had given an emotional address in which he made clear he could not countenance a policy that might lead to the use of armed force, and asked for direction as to whether he should stay on.[6] Now, in Brighton, the trade union boss Ernest Bevin—arguably the single most powerful man in the entire British Labour movement—took the platform and, in front of the delegates, delivered a speech in which he effectively bludgeoned Lansbury into retirement. Born in 1881, Bevin was the illegitimate son of a midwife. He left school at the age of eleven and worked on the Bristol docks before playing a central role in creating the Transport and General Workers' Union, an industrial titan and the largest union in the country. Ernie was its General Secretary from its founding in 1921 and, though he did not become an MP until 1940—by which time he was fifty-nine years old—Bevin was a political leviathan. Unforgiving by nature, Bevin was not the sort of individual to make an enemy of. He was a giant of a man, both literally—he weighed more than 200lbs—and figuratively. In addition to being Britain's greatest trade unionist, Ernie went on to become one of its greatest ever ministers. Attlee would later describe him as 'a tank'. Bevin did not suffer fools gladly, mastered the detail of a problem better than those around him, and, despite his lack of formal education, was never overawed by anyone and always supremely self-confident. He was also not shy about speaking his mind.

THE END IS NIGH

From the platform in Brighton, Bevin was brutal, even merciless, towards Lansbury. As he began speaking, the dome atop the conference hall was subjected to a fierce hailstorm, which *The New Statesman* described as 'singularly apposite'.[7] In a blistering address that quickly entered political folklore—Ernie's face was flushed with anger and his hands tightly gripped the rail as he spoke—he charged the aged pacifist with 'hawking your conscience round from body to body asking to be told what to do with it'.[8] Lansbury was, he said, 'placing the Labour movement in an absolutely wrong position'. Bevin accused the leader of fatal weakness, and even of 'betray[ing]' his duties. It was an address that none of those who heard it would ever forget. Bevin had crushed Lansbury beneath the wheels of a juggernaut. To some who felt he had been offensive, Ernie dismissively replied that 'Lansbury has been going about in saint's clothes for years waiting for martyrdom. I set fire to the faggots'.[9] The speech destroyed Lansbury's authority, with the delegates backing sanctions by a huge margin of 2.1 million votes to 102,000.[10] Within days the leader resigned, probably happy to be relieved of responsibility, just weeks prior to the general election. Dalton judged that Bevin had 'hammered' Lansbury 'to death'.[11]

Lansbury was not the only one to be forced out. Sir Stafford Cripps, the son of a former Conservative politician, hailed from a privileged background and enjoyed a successful career as a barrister. Cripps was haughty and ambitious. Entering Parliament in 1930, Cripps rapidly became a minister before being one of those to survive the 1931 crisis. The defenestration of the Labour leadership opened up opportunities that would otherwise simply not have been available to a political novice. Forty-two, rich, and possessed of great energy, Cripps saw an opportunity to dominate. The man who had flirted with abandoning Labour and joining the National Government in 1931 promptly reinvented himself as an extreme socialist and spent the next few years pressing for a confrontation with the established social order in order to destroy it. He sought power within Labour by going over the head of the party establishment and appealing directly to activists in the constituency parties. One of his ideas was that a future Labour government should pass emergency legislation that would set up a virtual dictatorship within a matter of hours. This would include the abolition of the House of Lords, the neutering of the Commons to prevent 'obstruction', longer periods between general elections, an empowered executive, a weakened judiciary, and the immediate state ownership of land, finance, and industry. Cripps was easily the most dynamic member of the shrunken parliamentary party. He was also chairman of the Socialist League, a radical party-within-a-party set up in 1932 that extended from the grassroots to debating societies all the way up to the PLP.[12] Its purpose was never quite clear, even to its leaders,[13] but it was really a vehicle for their own capture of the Labour party.

It secured some notable policy victories, including the endorsement of the annual Labour conference for nationalization of the banks. Dalton recalled that Cripps displayed a 'Messianic Marxism',[14] while Bevin—whose entrenched view of the middle-class intellectual was that they were the 'people who stabbed you in the back'—slammed 'the antics of careerists who seem to think we have created the movement as a sort of ladder for individuals'.[15]

Many colleagues thought Cripps a lunatic drunk on the worship of other lunatics.[16] The notion that a Labour government would curtail parliamentary debate and abolish judicial review was unthinkable. In one speech in 1934, Cripps even discussed 'removing the opposition from Buckingham Palace' to a socialist transformation of the country, an implied threat to the wellbeing of King George V which provoked uproar.[17] Cripps thereafter denied that he was referring to the King, but it seems unlikely he was speaking of the servants. He had a zealous, intolerant character. Dalton wrote that Cripps 'seems to think that only he and his cronies know what Socialism is'. His 'gaffes cover an immense range' and 'Tory H.Q. regard him as their greatest electoral asset'.[18] The Abyssinian crisis was, therefore, a helpful instrument in curtailing his influence. In the autumn of 1935, the NEC's strong backing for sanctions against Italy goaded a self-righteous Cripps into resigning from that body in protest at 'capitalist sanctions' that made war likely.[19] The weakening of Cripps made the rebuilding of Labour's credibility as a moderate force substantially easier.

Having exploited the crisis to launch a coup against those who would be an electoral liability, following the election a new, informal ruling group took shape. The most notable of those who came to the fore was Clement Attlee. Attlee was a slight and laconic man, balding, with a distinctive clipped moustache. From an affluent background, Clem was born in 1893 and attended Haileybury College, a public school near Hertford. His life experiences were eclectic: solicitor, social worker in the poverty-stricken East End of London, lecturer at the London School of Economics, and veteran of the Great War who climbed to the rank of Major. That Attlee became one of the political icons of the century has puzzled historians for generations. The fact of the matter is that he possessed no personal charisma whatsoever; he was shy; and he was terrible at making conversation. Few people could say that they knew him. Attlee was very hard to read, a characteristic which baffled contemporaries and has defeated all but a handful of historians. His major interest was watching cricket.

But what Attlee did possess was a capacity for hard work and administrative skill in running committees. He was also indifferent to what other people thought of him, a crucial asset for a politician. Postmaster-General under MacDonald, Attlee was one of the few Labour MPs to survive the 1931 rout and thereafter earned the admiration of the rump PLP for a willingness to assume responsibility for keeping Labour in business as a parliamentary force. This was the key opportunity of his career: the crisis of 1931 permitted a dry, quiet man to come to the fore in a way that would otherwise never have occurred. Such was the loyalty and admiration of MPs Attlee built up that, in November 1935, in a contest held following the general election, he managed to defeat the far more charismatic Herbert Morrison to become leader of the Labour party. Dalton—who organized Morrison's campaign—thought it a 'wretched' result: 'And a little mouse shall lead them!'[20] Attlee was no mouse. He would go down in history as Labour's best-regarded leader. But it would take several years for him to grow to maturity. Until 1939, he proved unwilling to give a lead, avoiding confrontation with his party, and acquiescing in some of its more self-indulgent behaviour.

Besides Attlee, the new leadership grouped consisted of Hugh Dalton and Herbert Morrison, men who had lost their seats in 1931 but through the machinery of the NEC emerged as powerful figures before returning to Parliament. Morrison was the working-class son of a London police constable. He was a formidable organizer who straddled both national and local politics, being Leader of the London County Council from 1934 to 1940. Blind in one eye and bearing a distinctive quiff of hair that was rarely brushed, Herbert—who was also fond of wearing a bowtie—was instantly recognizable and looked perpetually untidy. He had left school at fourteen but took the autodidactic route and became a voracious reader of texts on politics, economics, and history. Politics was his life—his marriage was unhappy—and he often slept in the office. This dedication enabled Morrison to become one of the commanding figures of twentieth-century politics. The many pockets of his jackets were always stuffed with notes on some aspect of public affairs. He was an intriguer to his fingertips, and burned with the ambition to become Labour leader. Even after being defeated by Attlee, Morrison searched constantly for opportunities to supplant his foe; their rivalry was one of the longest in modern political history and did not terminate until both retired in 1955. Widely regarded as Machiavellian, Herbert was a skilled election strategist and shrewd campaigner—traits inherited by his grandson, the 'dark prince' of New Labour, Peter Mandelson. He understood that if Labour was to win elections it had to appeal beyond its core vote and was relentless in preaching that message. In running London, Morrison oversaw one of the world's great metropoles, a city with a population of more than 4 million people. London was employed by Herbert as a proving ground for demonstrating Labour's capacity to govern, whether in tackling the capital's slum problem, constructing new infrastructure, or testing ideas about how socialist 'planning' might be implemented. Morrison was the Labour movement's most capable machine politician.

Dalton, meanwhile, was the son of a senior clergyman who was tutor to the children of Queen Victoria. An academic, he taught economics at the LSE. Boisterous, possessed of a booming voice, and unashamedly ambitious, Dalton was never the subtlest of politicians. Yet he was one of Labour's most capable intellectuals, an expert not only in economics but later foreign affairs and defence. On the trade union side, the new leadership group included Bevin and Walter Citrine, General Secretary of the Trades Union Congress. Relations between these men were far from harmonious. Dalton and Morrison resented Attlee for jumping the queue by surviving in 1931; Morrison coveted his job; and Bevin utterly loathed Morrison for being a 'politician'—by which he meant untrustworthy. But the group worked together fairly well. And they shrewdly employed Abyssinia to begin reconnecting the Labour movement with public opinion. Exploiting the opportunity presented by the Hoare–Laval scandal, Attlee declared that Baldwin 'has killed the League and collective security' and 'never honestly tried to make an effort'.[21] The episode 'blackened the name of this country in every part of the world'. People had 'trusted' Baldwin's 'word', he said, and been 'dupe[d]'. Moreover, Labour was explicitly committed to military sanctions while the government prevaricated.

When the Spanish Civil War erupted in July 1936, Labour politicians were quick to portray it as another confrontation between good and evil.[22] Spain caught the imagination of the political and intellectual left in a way that few wars have. For the next three years, the struggle between the Republicans and the Nationalists was a rhetorical cause célèbre for the party—a ready source of slogans, symbols, and imagery that played well with a socialist audience at home keen to view their left-wing brethren, the Republicans, as heroes fighting the good fight against fascism. With the Republicans aided by the USSR and the Nationalists backed by Hitler and Mussolini, it was all very romantic from afar. Yet in fact it is far from clear that many of the participants in Spain were on the side of morality. The Republicans were as likely to employ the methods of terror and murder as their opponents.[23] It must also be stressed that despite the Labour party's volubility over Abyssinia or Spain, their strategic policy lacked cogency. Labour ignored the fact that the dictators could probably only be restrained by war, yet, incredibly, continued to oppose British rearmament. But this did not in any way lessen the *rhetorical* value of their seizing upon, and utilizing, these crises. After four years in the wilderness, deprived of credibility by the events of 1931 and flirting with extremist policies, foreign affairs finally equipped the Labour party with a means to reach out to the public.

'The Storm Clouds Gather'

For Churchill, whose career appeared finished after India, renewed international instability resembled divine intervention.[24] The crisis with Mussolini therefore constituted an opportunity that he could not miss. As gung-ho as ever, Winston initially flirted with the idea that Britain should act alone to stop Mussolini.[25] As far as he was concerned, the whole conceptual apparatus of the League was irrelevant to the sublunary minds that governed most states. Naval forces in the Mediterranean should thus be immediately strengthened.[26] Churchill was 'deeply incensed' at Mussolini's defiance, and 'all out for blood and thunder'.[27] However, in August 1935 his attitude moderated and shifted towards that of the Cabinet. He came to believe that Britain should only act in concert with the French and pledged to 'support the government on these lines'. Hoare recorded that Churchill was 'anxious to cooperate with us'.[28] This desire to 'cooperate' may have been rooted in Churchill's belief, or hope, that with the Government of India Act on the statute book as of that month and the insurgency defeated, Baldwin would let bygones be bygones and bring him back into the Cabinet. As one scholar observed, with the vast sums earned by Churchill from writing for the press he was probably the best-paid journalist in the country in the 1930s,[29] but the flame of ambition still burned bright.

If Churchill was behaving himself in hope of preferment, he was to be disappointed. The socialite and Conservative MP Nancy Astor implored Baldwin not to 'put Winston back in the government—it will mean war at home and abroad'.[30] She need not have worried. In no mood to offer his adversary a route back to respectability, following the election Baldwin constructed a Cabinet without him. The Prime Minister ignored a suggestion from one of Churchill's friends that the rogue elephant be given ministerial responsibility for expanding Britain's airpower.[31] Fascinated with war and angling for office, for several months Churchill had been issuing public warnings about Hitler's air programme and the need for Britain to achieve parity with Germany.[32] Winston twice caught out the government by revealing in Parliament secret details of German aircraft production that had been leaked to him by a concerned civil servant, Desmond Morton. Perhaps having learnt his lesson over India, this time Churchill began to immerse himself in close analysis of the problem.[33] The result was his rapidly becoming an expert in the question of relative air strengths and rearmament. Few knew more about the subject. His revelations of German aircraft production alarmed the public and were hugely embarrassing to the Cabinet. Churchill felt 'anxious to lay my hands upon the military machine'.[34] And yet the Prime Minister doggedly refused to include him. Baldwin's allies at The Times ran a pair of pointed editorials welcoming the fact that, with his majority secure, the Prime Minister had no need to make 'concessions' to 'extremists' and could work 'without fear of interruption from purely political intrigues'.[35]

Baldwin's rebuff may have been the moment when Churchill began to suspect the party leadership would never willingly take him back.[36] His behaviour since 1929 had permanently poisoned that well. Churchill described this realization as a 'bitter disappointment'.[37] As such, when the government's credibility collapsed with the Hoare–Laval Pact, Churchill and his small band of loyalists rejoiced. His son Randolph recognized that the crisis 'will have lasting repercussions which I am sure will be very much to your advantage'. The Conservative MP Brendan Bracken, Churchill's most faithful disciple, was gleeful at the prospect of 'see[ing] Baldwin exterminated'.[38] Realizing—as he failed to do over Hoare's impeachment—that the wisest course of action was to allow the government to writhe in embarrassment, Churchill wrote to his son that 'it would be . . . v[er]y injurious to me . . . if you publish articles attacking the motives and character of ministers, especially Baldwin'.[39] For good measure he threw in a little emotional blackmail, warning Randolph that if he did so 'I shall not be able to feel confidence in y[ou]r loyalty and affection for me'. With India receding into the background and foreign affairs having suddenly become central to national politics, Churchill spotted an opportunity to restore his fortunes that would also happily align with his lifelong fascination with conflict between the great powers. As he told Clemmie, 'Evidently B [Baldwin] desires above all things to avoid bringing me in. This I must now recognise. But his own position is much shaken, & the storm clouds gather'.[40]

'You Can Smell the Gunpowder!'

Winston was right; the storm clouds certainly *were* gathering.[41] In early 1936, the attention of policymakers was jolted yet again. On 7 March, Adolf Hitler ordered the German military into the Rhineland. Located along Germany's border with France and Belgium, the Rhineland, though part of Germany, had been demilitarized under the Treaty of Versailles. Berlin was forbidden to station armed forces either on the left bank of the river Rhine or within fifty kilometres of the right bank, stipulations intended to leave Germany's western flank vulnerable to a rapid French invasion. Hitler's decision to send the army into the Rhineland thus constituted a flagrant violation of treaties. He publicly justified it as a response to the Franco-Soviet alliance of 1935 which was obviously aimed at encircling Germany.[42] But he was emboldened by the Abyssinian crisis too. The rupture between the Western allies and Italy—the states with the most to lose from a shift in the balance of power in western Europe—created a window of diplomatic opportunity that the Fuhrer was determined to exploit. The action represented a calculated gamble by the Fuhrer to probe the willingness of France and Britain to resist his revisionist aspirations. It was the latest episode in Hitler's testing of behavioural boundaries. Within weeks of coming to power in January 1933 he had embarked upon a secretive and major expansion of the German military. Later in the same year, he withdrew Germany from the League of Nations and the World Disarmament Conference. And in June 1934 Hitler sponsored a failed coup in Austria. The following year the Fuhrer instituted conscription, resolved to increase the peacetime army to 550,000 men, and commenced a major expansion of his air force, the Luftwaffe. The occupation of the Rhineland in 1936 confirmed this trend.

The British ambassador in Berlin from 1928 to 1933, Sir Horace Rumbold, thought the Nazi leadership were 'notoriously pathological cases': 'I have the impression that the persons directing the policy of the Hitler government are not normal. Many of us . . . have a feeling that we are living in a country where fantastic hooligans and eccentrics have got the upper hand'.[43] Rumbold was right; they were indeed 'pathological cases'. Yet in the Rhineland Hitler had not marched across any international borders; he merely dispatched forces into another part of his own country. This was hardly the stuff of which major wars were made. Moreover, after remilitarizing the Rhineland Germany immediately proposed a twenty-five-year non-aggression pact with her Western neighbours, including the establishment of a new demilitarized zone at the borders.

France and Belgium were keen to threaten force in order to turf the German Army out of the Rhineland, but after the crisis over Italy the National Government in London had little appetite for a fresh showdown. Importantly, despite the popular moral indignation over Abyssinia, when the spectre of a major war in Europe loomed public opinion in Britain suddenly proved to be no more in favour of confrontation than was the Cabinet. Upon learning of Hitler's gambit, the Foreign Secretary, Anthony Eden, hailed a taxi and headed to the Foreign Office to discuss the crisis with his officials. En route, Eden asked the cabbie for his view of the situation. The driver's relaxed response has been immortalized in popular memory: 'I suppose Jerry can do what he likes in his own back garden, can't he?'[44]

As a result, although the incident was viewed as a worrying portent in capital cities across Europe, nothing was done to reverse it. It was one thing to succumb to the temptation to strike poses of moral indignation over colonial squabbles affecting Africans in a country many Britons had never heard of; it was quite another to do so when the outcome might be a conflagration in western Europe. Eden had earlier predicted that Hitler would launch 'adventures' in order to 'distract attention' from economic failures at home, and the Rhineland episode seemed to confirm this.[45] Moreover, the British economy was doing well in 1936, with trade 'expanding marvellously' as Chamberlain put it.[46] The National Government thus sought the space to rebuild its shaken credibility. From a strategic perspective, the failure to humiliate Hitler in the Rhineland must be viewed as a huge missed opportunity. The whole endeavour was an elaborate bluff: conscious of his military weakness at this juncture, Hitler ordered his forces to retreat if they met with resistance from the French. Getting away with the occupation emboldened the Nazis in their infatuation with coercive diplomacy.

But for Churchill, scheming on the backbenches, the remilitarization of the Rhineland prompted a frisson of excitement. To a restless man searching for something big to restore him to a position of importance, Hitler's decision must have seemed like manna from heaven. Here was a challenge that he understood; conflict was his natural habitat. Churchill believed that Britain remained a unique global power, and should act like it. From the industrial smog of Manchester to the exclusive clubs of central London, from the beautiful South African veld to the icy wastes of Canada, from the high mountain passes of India to the sweltering jungles of tropical Africa, from the windswept shores of the Falkland Islands to the deserts of Egypt, and from the ancient civilizations of China and India to the relative upstarts of Australia and New Zealand, this was an empire on a planetary scale. In early 1936, Churchill thus resolved to make British defence policy the key issue in national politics.

Adopting an ominous tone, he warned Parliament that Hitler would violate international agreements again in the future and called for 'real collective security under the League of Nations'.[47] He coupled this support for the League—a cynically populist cry in the context of 1936—with advocacy of a formal Anglo-French alliance to deter Germany. Churchill thus wanted to employ 'the League' as the liberal cover for a traditional system of military pacts.[48] He discussed 'a union of nations, all well-armed and bound to defend each other', targeted specifically at Berlin.[49] 'The whole life and industry of Germany is being organised for war preparation', he said; 'Our efforts compared to theirs are puny'.[50] But for all Churchill's talk of upholding the League, the commitment was largely rhetorical. Like his party leaders, he wanted sanctions on Italy to be lifted and advocated non-interference in the Spanish Civil War lest it spiral into a pan-European conflict.[51] On a wide range of issues, the substantive policy differences between Churchill and the government were minimal; the real difference lay in how much more aggressive Churchill's *language* was. He did not advocate military action to turf Germany out of the Rhineland. He even supported the Cabinet's decision not to dispatch a large

British army to defend the frontiers of France and Belgium in an emergency, taking the view that those two states should be told to 'make their own arrangements'.[52] He also agreed with the Cabinet on the need for cutting-edge air defences. Churchill could publicly charge that the National Government was 'shutting its eyes' to Germany, but in view of its launching the largest rearmament programme in modern British history this was an exaggeration.[53] *Politics* was the principal point of conflict between Churchill and the Conservative leaders, not *policy*. He wanted to land blows on the Cabinet.

Personal ambitions in politics are generally irreconcilable, and it was this—rather than contrasting policy programmes—that gave political action its distinctive texture. The ebb and flow of the profession meant that those, like Churchill, who had lost out in the scramble for power were more inclined to adopt contrarian, adversarial, or eye-catching positions in order to stand out. And stand out Winston certainly did; with Churchill breathing down its neck, the government began to feel pressured to speed up the rearmament programme even more.[54] The tabloid and broadsheet press alike continued to petition for him to be put in charge of defence planning.[55] 'Arms and the Covenant' would be Churchill's new political war cry. Henceforth British rearmament and the German question were the twin outlets for his ambition. And in fastening his fortunes to the behaviour of Herr Hitler, this time he chose very wisely indeed.

'I Feel . . . Fully Entitled . . . to State Facts and Draw Morals'

The Defence White Paper of March 1936 symbolized the National Government's recognition of the need to improve Britain's military capabilities.[56] In it, the Cabinet committed to radical increases in defence spending over the next five years.[57] The RAF would receive a major boost in its annual funding—from £20 million to £45 million immediately, and then to £60 million—while the Royal Navy would initiate a large programme of ship construction. That there was no projected increase in the size of the Army indicated much about the type of war the government intended to fight should it come to it. Where Britain had only been spending approximately £110 million per year on defence since the mid-1920s, this was now rising steeply, leaping to £186.1 million for the financial year 1936/7. Moreover, the Cabinet expected that defence spending would keep growing, reaching £417 million by 1940. Ministers also sought to balance military expenditure with the realities of industry and safeguard the prosperity that undergirded British strength. For instance, locating sufficient factories and skilled labour to implement a programme of major military expansion would be difficult; there would be wider economic consequences. It would harm the export trade upon which national wealth depended, while the shortage of labour threatened to have an inflationary effect as trade unions would press for wage increases. Indeed, the major limitation on rearmament was not the availability of money to finance it but the supply of skilled labour to fulfil the orders for new equipment. War was far from certain, so rearmament needed to be balanced with stability. Even so, within twelve months still greater increases in defence spending were planned, totalling £1.5 billion over five years.[58] It was announced that up to £400 million would be borrowed to finance this.[59] In addition, Chamberlain levied a tax of 5 per cent on all business profits.[60] He feared that socio-economic tensions provoked by high profits, an increased cost of living due to rising prices, wage increases, and the loss of exports would 'ruin' both the rearmament programme and prosperity. His tax measures therefore sought to drive home 'the inevitability of sacrifice' that defence spending entailed.[61]

The Defence White Paper confirmed not only the emergence of foreign affairs as the central issue of British public policy, but also its evolution into the principal basis of Westminster intrigue. 'Rearmament' was a profitable battle cry; in early 1936, it was accompanied by calls for the National Government to be reconstructed in order to 'coordinate' defence. The idea of appointing a new Minister for the Coordination of Defence, tasked with closing the gaps in the nation's capabilities, quickly became a focal point of scheming. It was suggested by those outside the Cabinet as an instrument to criticize the leadership of the government, and it was floated by senior figures such as Chamberlain as a means to head off suggestions that the government was not doing enough.

It will come as little surprise to readers that Churchill held out hope that he would get the job—despite having effectively given up on ever joining the National Government mere weeks before. Churchill's case for the post hinged on his fondness for big strategic problems, his mastery of the details of German military developments, and the fact that even his critics recognized him to be a dynamic presence— perhaps just what the Cabinet needed to revive its flagging public fortunes in the aftermath of Hoare–Laval. Churchill and his supporters pressured Baldwin to make the appointment. Several newspapers repeatedly agitated for Winston to be given the role.[62] Churchill was therefore furious when, in early 1936, his son Randolph decided to stand against Malcolm MacDonald, the son of Ramsay MacDonald, at a by-election in the Scottish Highlands. Predictably enough, Randolph went down to defeat. But this did little to alleviate his father's fury that the leadership would view the incident as 'a definite declaration of war by me', one that would make it 'very difficult' to be offered the job.[63] As so often before, for Churchill familial and public policy issues alike were interpreted through the lens of his own ambition.

Still, Austen Chamberlain felt that Churchill was by far the outstanding candidate: 'in my view there is only one man who by his studies & his special abilities & aptitudes is marked out for it, & that man is Winston Churchill'.[64] Churchill took the view that rearmament should have been commenced earlier, and ought to be accelerated still further.[65] The government would have to reorganize industry in order to produce the weapons that were needed; every effort should be made to exploit technological innovation in air power and air defence. Taking the Rhineland crisis as an omen, he wanted British policy to focus on building alliances against Germany. But Austen judged that Baldwin did not want Churchill in power ahead of his retirement, due to 'the risk that would be involved by having him in the Cabinet when the question of the successor becomes imminent'.[66] In other words, Baldwin did not want to run the (remote) risk that a rehabilitated Churchill might employ India and defence to tug on Conservative heartstrings and snatch the leadership. In March 1936, the Prime Minister thus chose to appoint Sir Thomas Inskip, the former Attorney General, to the post instead. This was an appointment that Churchill's friend, the Oxford scientist Professor Frederick Lindemann, denounced as 'the most cynical thing that has been done since Caligula appointed his horse a Consul'.[67] Most of the press was stunned. Inskip was a minor figure who possessed no obvious expertise in the field.

In the end, Inskip played a crucial role in the RAF shifting its focus from bombers (a purely offensive instrument) to fighters (an aircraft with powerful defensive capabilities)—a decision which reaped immense rewards in the Battle of Britain in 1940, most obviously in the form of the Spitfires. By the outbreak of war Britain possessed a world-leading air defence system. But in March 1936 Inskip was considered too obscure an individual for such an important job. Austen attributed Churchill's exclusion to Baldwin having 'a little mind' that did not rise 'above electioneering', and being 'both jealous and unforgiving'.[68] While criticizing Baldwin for conceptualizing matters in terms of tactical advantage is not without merit, as we have seen, the most consistent feature of the world of high-level decision-making was that this practice was universal. And while Churchill's lifelong enthusiasm for defence matters is obvious, whether he had the clarity of mind necessary to accompany it is less clear. Britain's defence programme might well have been harmed by his erratic temperament. He had a tendency to fixate on some technical detail of a weapon system that would consume all of his energy for weeks on end, before he suddenly discovered a new enthusiasm. Churchill's roving, inquisitive mind would arguably not have been suited to the systematic analysis that rearmament demanded.

Yet, politically, the appointment of Inskip in late March represented the final straw for Churchill. His hopes of reconciliation were dashed once and for all.

Winston now had no choice but to accept that his leaders would never accede to his return to office. Once he had absorbed this fact, the next step came rapidly. On 8 April Churchill warned Lord Cranborne, a minister at the Foreign Office, with some frankness that he would henceforth be publicly targeting the National Government over its international policies. He explained that as the Cabinet's foreign policy was 'designed to give satisfaction to powerful elements of opinion here'—by which he meant liberal opinion—'rather than to seek the realities of the European situation', he could not support it. The policy 'is coming to a most dismal and disastrous end', Churchill charged, and he therefore felt 'fully entitled' to 'state facts and draw morals'.[69] He warned Cranborne that responsibility for what followed 'must rest with the government and ministers concerned'. Coming just weeks after the appointment of Inskip to the job that Churchill coveted, this constituted a declaration of political war.

It is striking—and characteristic of the man—that while Churchill denounced the government for seeking to 'give satisfaction to powerful elements of opinion' in one breath, he was not above cynically cultivating those exact same 'elements of opinion' himself in the next. Just *one day* after his missive to Cranborne, Churchill wrote to Cecil, the President of the League of Nations Union, that 'we are in pretty good agreement on several big things'. He warned that perhaps just a year remained to 'marshall superior forces in defence of the League and its Covenant' before free nations were 'smashed up'. Churchill offered to help provide the 'ways and means' to uphold League principles, by which he meant 'military force'.[70] If the cynicism of this was astonishing even by Churchill's standards, it underlines how determined he now was to attack the Conservative leadership—and how unfussy he was about the rhetorics he adopted and the alliances he made. The language of the League provided a useful cloak for Churchill's true worldview of traditional balance-of-power politics, the realm he intuitively understood. One reactionary Conservative, Lady Houston, despaired that Churchill was engaging with the liberal 'fanatics'; yet it was, in fact, a cunning decision on Winston's part, for it afforded him the opportunity to appeal as broadly as possible across the spectrum.[71] He could connect with backbench Conservative opinion, always staunchly pro-defence, and establish himself as a spokesman on the major issue of the moment. Simultaneously it was a way to place himself on the 'right' side of public opinion—and speak from the moral high ground—at a time when the sanctity of the League was a quasi-religious notion. The Soviet ambassador Ivan Maisky recognized the 'tactical-political' motivation at work, and that for Churchill 'collective security' was merely a 'pseudonym' for traditional alliances.[72] It was a pose, but it invested Churchill with a credibility that, after India, he badly needed.

Sure enough, he quickly opened a barrage, and by the summer of 1936 Churchill was freely attacking the government. He was indefatigable in drawing attention to defence shortcomings. Winston focused on what he described as the inadequacy of the rearmament scheme and called for the declaration of a 'state of emergency' about the preparedness of Britain's defences.[73] This captured public and press attention. Importantly, Churchill began penning newspaper articles describing the latest news on German rearmament in exhaustive detail.[74] These articles caused acute embarrassment for the Cabinet, not least because they were accurate. Churchill's statistics were based on the government's own top-secret intelligence, some of which was being passed to him by sympathetic civil servants—sparking a huge search in Whitehall for the source of the leak. In one article he examined the growth in Germany's importation of resources that might be used for arms production ('imports of iron ore have increased 309 per cent . . . bauxite by 153 per cent . . . manganese by 274 per cent') and went on that 'all this has gone into making the most destructive war weapons and war arrangements that have ever been known'. He posed the question: 'What is it all for? Certainly it is not all for fun. Something quite extraordinary is afoot'.[75] Churchill's seizure of the issue had the Cabinet on the back foot. Chamberlain recognized that he was running a campaign accusing the government 'of not taking defence sufficiently seriously'. Baldwin feared that Churchill might get up in the House of Commons and deliver a 'four hour' speech on the subject. And MacDonald worried about the embarrassment if Churchill were to force the issue in Parliament.[76] One Conservative MP told Churchill that he was reaching 'a peak point in your national importance'.[77]

Meanwhile Churchill began attending regular secret dinners with a small number of disaffected Conservative MPs—including Austen Chamberlain and Sir Henry Page Croft—on the question of defence.[78] When the existence of these gatherings was revealed, one Cabinet minister yelled 'traitors' at Churchill and his colleagues as they entered the Commons.[79] The government loyalist Sir Henry 'Chips' Channon thought Churchill was 'consumed with contempt, jealousy, indeed hatred', while Baldwin 'hates [Churchill] so much' in return.[80] Churchill organized a similar venture with a non-party group, 'The Defence of Freedom and Peace Union', which united Conservatives, Liberals, and even the TUC's Walter Citrine.[81] It held a major rally in the Albert Hall on 3 December 1936 to launch a campaign in defence of 'Arms and the Covenant'. Churchill's speech was the centrepiece of the event.[82] He did not appear to feel hypocritical in wrapping himself in the League Covenant; in fact he relished the fact that the 'left-wing' are 'coming to look to me for the protection of their ideas'.[83] Winston continued to engage with the League of Nations Union, the New Commonwealth society, the Anti-Nazi League, and any other popular pressure group that would spread his gospel. The *New Statesman* predicted the formation of a 'Centre front' to unite the political spectrum with 'Winston Churchill as the effective leader'.[84] A select few even began to see Churchill as a prophet: one Conservative MP, Robert Boothby, told Churchill that 'I believe, passionately, that you are the only man who can save this country, and the world'.[85] Channon despaired that, given the feebleness of Labour, Churchill was becoming the real 'Leader of the Opposition'.[86]

But Churchill was not the only embittered Conservative on manoeuvres. Humiliated at having to take the blame over Abyssinia, Hoare resolved to quickly force his way back into office. His method was old-fashioned: blackmail. Over dinner one evening in February 1936—a mere two months after his resignation—Hoare warned Chamberlain that if he was not 'attached' to the government, he would quickly be 'drawn into conflict' with it.[87] Sam had already been approached by a major publisher to write a tell-all book about the Hoare–Laval Pact.[88] He also hinted that he might favour a 'more Conservative' government than was currently in power. This threat jolted Chamberlain and Baldwin, for 'we could not afford' for 'Sam to serve as a focus of back-bench discontent'.[89] Nor could they run the risk of their erstwhile colleague letting rip in print. Hoare even delivered a Commons speech in which he brazenly solicited a return to the Cabinet by hinting that if given a job he would support the government's defence programme; what might happen if he was *not* brought back into the fold was left unsaid.[90] Baldwin decided to bring Hoare back into the Cabinet, and, after some discussion, in June 1936 sent him to the Admiralty. There, he set about rebuilding his battered reputation.

The Erosion of Government Predominance

The events surrounding Abyssinia, the Rhineland, and rearmament underscored the potency of foreign policy as a high-political resource at home. A dialectical relationship between political ascendancy and international crisis had developed; and it proved impossible to break this. By 1936, international instability meant that 'defence' had become the currency of political opportunity at home. However, there was also more to it than this. The mood of the electorate severely restricted options in British foreign policy. It was wishful thinking to believe that international crises could be resolved with the spirit of brotherly love, but *raison d'état* was anathema to the moralizing rhetoric of Geneva. The cause of the League provided a way for the underemployed, the unoccupied, and the unimportant to rationalize their own worldview thorough agitation and self-righteous pressure groups. Of course, none of the advocates of Geneva had to take responsibility for anything. But they still wielded influence. This was a climate in which even a patriotic, sensible man like Attlee declared that Labour 'have abandoned all idea of nationalist loyalty. We are deliberately putting a world order before loyalty to our own country'.[91] 'You have got to put loyalty to the League above loyalty to your country', he said.[92] One Labour campaign poster declared that 'A Vote For The Tories Is A Vote For War'.

In the House of Commons in late 1936, Baldwin—speaking with what he himself acknowledged was 'appalling frankness'—remarked of the 1935 general election that 'supposing I had gone to the country and . . . said that we must rearm, does anybody think that this pacific democracy would have rallied to the cry? I cannot think of anything that would have made the loss of the election . . . more certain'.[93] This was a 'remarkable' admission of which Churchill made a great deal in his seminal account of the 1930s, *The Gathering Storm*:

> It carried naked truth about his motives into indecency. That a Prime Minister should avow that he had not done his duty in regard to national safety because he was afraid of losing the election was an incident without parallel in our parliamentary history . . . The House was shocked.[94]

The speech constituted the 'proof' of Churchill's case against the man who had kept him out of office. In reality what the Prime Minister had been trying to explain was the difficulty of persuading the electorate of the need for rearmament after a generation of politicians preaching the merits of peaceful co-existence. Endless denunciations of armaments as being inherently wicked rendered defence a tricky political issue. The organizers of the Peace Ballot had hoped that, through the exercise, they would scupper any plans for rearmament. And the Labour party voted against defence spending until as late as 1937. This was the climate in which Baldwin was operating. To his mind, the election triumph offered a mandate for rearmament; the cause of collective security and peace could not be made effective if Britain lacked the military capacities to do so.[95] Churchill's accusation that a 'national awakening was not in accord with Mr. Baldwin's outlook or intentions' was, therefore, false.[96] Baldwin *had* exploited the Abyssinian crisis for electoral effect, but also to secure the political latitude to accelerate defence spending. The problem came when British diplomacy thereafter seemed to betray the League.

The Rhineland crisis that followed on the heels of Abyssinia, and the question of rearmament which dominated British politics in 1936, only underlined the difficulties of forging a coherent policy when the imperatives of strategy, public opinion, party calculation, and dictatorial governments did not smoothly align. Speeches delivered in Britain for domestic audiences were scrutinized in foreign capitals. Actions taken in diplomacy would be dissected and distorted in Parliament or the press. Public innocence about foreign affairs complicated matters. Unsurprisingly, balance proved elusive. The National Government had certainly paid a steep price for its electoral tactics in October 1935. In framing the contest as one about the League, Baldwin was too clever by half. He won the election. But his methods came at the cost of making the Labour party relevant again, the rejuvenation of Churchill, the abdication of public trust, and a weakened diplomatic position. In succumbing to temptation, the Prime Minister ushered in a new era in which the competitive struggle for power and advantage that drove the democratic system, and invested it with its acrimonious flavour, had come to centre on the foreign policy of the Cabinet. For his successor, testing times lay ahead.

5

Mr CHAMBERLAIN'S QUEST

'I Know That I Can Save This Country and I Do Not Believe That Anyone Else Can'

The central figure in the remainder of this unfolding drama proved to be Neville Chamberlain.[1,2] The enduring image of that unfortunate man remains the photograph taken on 30 September 1938, showing Chamberlain addressing a cheering crowd on the airport tarmac at Heston mere moments after returning from the Munich conference with Hitler. Proudly waving a document bearing the Fuhrer's signature, the Prime Minister proclaimed that in avoiding a conflict over Czechoslovakia, he had secured peace in Europe. With his high-risk summit diplomacy having paid off, Chamberlain enjoyed the gratitude of a nation. There were scenes of public jubilation, with thousands lining the streets for Chamberlain's journey through the capital before he appeared alongside the Royal Family on the balcony of Buckingham Palace. It was a remarkable political triumph. Just one year later, however, Britain was at war. It therefore makes sense to begin with this curious figure.

By the time he ascended to the premiership in May 1937 the clouds already gathering in the international skies had become dense black thunderheads. The scenario of Britain being faced with three enemies at once—Germany, Italy, and Japan—was coming to pass.[3] Chamberlain saw that France was unreliable while the United States could not be trusted to do anything, anywhere. The strategy he formulated in response was the pursuit of *détente*. This policy was labelled 'appeasement', and it hinged on completing Britain's rearmament programme while seeking out any possibility of negotiated accommodation with Germany in order to defuse tensions in Europe. It failed spectacularly, resulting in the outbreak of a war that, even if it was won, was certain to spell the end for British power. The consequences were equally fatal for the long Conservative ascendancy constructed by Baldwin.

The reality is that international crisis drew out, and accentuated, all of Chamberlain's most deep-rooted flaws. Appeasement was a deeply personal policy; and its collapse constituted a deeply personal failure. Though a senior minister for many

years, when Neville became Prime Minister the public dimension of the role was a
novel experience for him. He had never before encountered popular acclamation—
in fact, he usually felt disdain for the masses. Now he was acutely conscious of the
'wonderful power' he exercised as a world leader. As he boasted to his sister Ida,
'I have only to raise a finger & the whole face of Europe is changed'.[4] The outcome
was a personal quest—for a *quest* is what it was—in the shape of appeasement.
Analysing the policy has animated historians for decades and there is nothing
approximating a consensus. Fundamentally, however, Chamberlain's goal was to
somehow resolve the geopolitical tensions in central and eastern Europe and avert a
war between Germany and its neighbours. It is crucial to emphasize that this region
of the European continent was not an area traditionally considered a matter of vital
interest for Britain; but Chamberlain established it as one. This was, and remains,
puzzling; not least because many of his *own* instincts were strongly against involvement. The result was an incoherent mess. He devised and pursued an enterprise that
was dependent on the behaviour of a German government that one Conservative
MP described in 1935 as 'a professional treaty-breaker'.[5] The strategic rationale
underpinning the quest was deeply flawed, and it quickly ran into difficulties that
suggested it should be abandoned. Yet the idea of doing so was not seriously
entertained.

So how do we explain this? It may be that as the Soviet ambassador, Maisky,
speculated, the Prime Minister's mind was fixated with the political value of international issues. Maisky was one of the shrewdest observers of the Westminster
political scene and recorded in his diary the suspicion that Chamberlain 'wants to
reach an agreement at all costs with Germany and Italy . . . and then go to the polls
in the role of "appeaser of Europe" so as to consolidate the power of his party for the
next five years'.[6] There is certainly some truth to this. But the picture is also more
complex. Maisky came away from socializing with Chamberlain with the firm
impression that 'the PM considers himself a "man of destiny"! He was born into
this world to perform a "sacred mission"'. This was, Maisky thought, 'a dangerous
state of mind'.[7] Chamberlain was resolved that the problems of Europe would yield
to his will. The more they refused to do so, the harder he tried. The harder he tried,
the more entangled he became. And yet still he persevered. The result was a policy
that quickly became detached from its initial moorings and is best explained in
terms of Chamberlain's search for vindication. Maisky described his foreign policy
as 'zigzagging'.[8] That is probably the best characterization. Chamberlain twisted one
way and then the next. He said one thing to the Cabinet and another to Parliament.
He would resolve to take a stand and then abandon it. In order to understand this,
we need to see what Chamberlain was trying to do. He was searching for a personal

triumph—to pacify Europe against all the odds—and was willing to 'zigzag' in any and all directions. He staked so much capital on the quest that even when it became apparent that it was probably doomed, he had journeyed too far to turn back.

Chamberlain instinctively believed that he could somehow solve any problem. 'Like Chatham', he somewhat grandiosely remarked to his sister, 'I know that I can save this country and I do not believe that anyone else can'.[9] But he was also deeply insecure. He continually fretted that if he did not 'make a success' of whatever he was dealing with at a given moment, the consequences for a career that had the potential to be 'momentous' would be grave: 'I shall slowly drop back'.[10] As the historian Keith Neilson observed, 'Thus, for Chamberlain, all decisions—including those dealing with strategic foreign policy—would be viewed, not necessarily on their merits, but with an eye on his own career'.[11] Appeasement was a quest to prove that Neville Chamberlain was right. It was of a piece with the relentless search for approval that dominated the life of a man who had always been seen as the least of the three Chamberlains, and whose strongest impulse as a result was to prove the world wrong.

'If I Were Working the Thing I Should Feel More Confident of Success'

Even before succeeding Baldwin, Chamberlain took a keen interest in foreign affairs.[12] Anxiety about the deteriorating international situation necessitated committing more resources to defence spending, and as Chancellor Chamberlain sought to ensure that a clear strategy guided this expenditure. He was also adamant that his own voice would be paramount in the process. He had to look strong, and he had to give the impression of being a man who could solve problems. Chamberlain was determined to buck the longstanding wisdom that a priority for British rearmament should be building up the army to protect France and the Low Countries against German attack. This had been the main thrust of the recommendations made by the Defence Requirements Committee (DRC), staffed by civil servants and military top brass. Chamberlain did not concur. French defences were thought to be almost impregnable anyway; a large British expeditionary force would probably take too long to arrive; and he had no inclination to repeat the casualty rates experienced in the conflict of 1914–18. The Chancellor's resistance became apparent in May and June 1934, at a series of landmark meetings of a special Cabinet committee convened to discuss the DRC's work. Chamberlain used it to shape the government's strategic objectives. With his customary clarity of mind and vigour in argument, he reasoned that, instead of land forces, 'we ought to put our major resources into our

Navy and our Air Force'.[13] The RAF should, he stated, have the highest priority. This was a climate in which, across Europe, it was widely believed that, in Baldwin's words, 'the bomber will always get through'.[14] Chamberlain too was a firm believer in the transformative impact of airpower. The best means of deterring war would, he argued, be possession of an air force 'of a size and efficiency calculated to inspire respect in the mind of a possible enemy'.[15] Developing a 'deterrent force so powerful as to render success in an attack too doubtful to be worthwhile' should be Britain's priority.[16]

In the eyes of his colleagues, Chamberlain's arguments got to the heart of the issue. They were accepted by the Cabinet, and imposed on the military.[17] This determined the shape of British rearmament over the coming years. From 1935 onwards, spending on the air force and navy skyrocketed; resources devoted to the army grew more incrementally. The emphasis on the RAF was particularly significant. From £17.6 million in 1934, spending on the air force leapt to £27.5 million in 1935, £50.1 million in 1936, and £82 million in 1937. The Chancellor's intervention had been a crucial one. Baldwin informed Parliament that the National Government would ensure that in its airpower Britain was not 'in a position inferior to any country within striking distance of these shores'.[18] The Prime Minister understood there was the need to 'satisfy' a public and political opinion in a state of 'semi-panic' about 'the air'.[19]

Other aspects of Chamberlain's future instincts about foreign policy were also apparent before he replaced Baldwin. He intuitively understood that British interests were not synonymous with those of France, and sought to erode the notion that the security of the two countries was indivisible; that would only leave Britain in the position of having to pull Parisian chestnuts out of the fire.[20] Chamberlain also displayed a keen appreciation of the restrictive effects of public opinion. As early as 1934 he warned his colleagues that the ascendancy of humanitarian rhetoric was something that 'could not be ignored' by the National Government, lest there be an electoral backlash—the people were 'ignorant' about defence but 'not to be regarded as stupid'.[21]

Whatever resilient myths about the 1930s may suggest, if Chamberlain's subsequent European policy between 1937 and 1939 was guilty of anything, it was not 'cowardice'. Rather, it was that he proved far too willing to play the role of an activist when it came to addressing insoluble continental problems. A conceited man, Chamberlain always believed that he could do things better than anyone else. 'If I were working the thing I should feel more confident of success' was a typical comment, but the correspondence with his sisters is littered with hundreds of comparable statements.[22] Despite a conviction that British involvement in a future war should be largely limited to airpower, in terms of *diplomacy* Chamberlain was an enthusiast. He could not resist the siren call of 'involvement', nor turn his back on the opportunity to strut the international stage. Britain must either 'play our part in pacification' or 'resign ourselves' to spending 'staggering' sums on defence.[23] He argued that Britain should back Hitler's proposal for ten-year non-aggression pacts in western Europe and be willing to act as a guarantor of the peace—something that horrified many Conservatives, who did not like the idea of tying Britain's hands.[24]

As much as the modern mind might—in view of what occurred thereafter—recoil at the notion, until 1936 the reality of geopolitics on the European continent was not German expansionism but French primacy. At that stage France was the most powerful state on the European landmass. Germany had been defeated in 1918 and subjected to robust sanctions (though, as was discussed in Chapter 3, these were never as crippling as skilful German propaganda, aimed at tender liberal hearts in Europe and America, maintained). Berlin's major ally, the Austro-Hungarian Empire, was dissolved, leaving a large power vacuum in central and eastern Europe. Russia temporarily retreated from the stage, devoting its energy to internal turmoil and Bolshevik terror. In this environment France, not Germany, was the weightiest state. Paris was paranoid about the restoration of Germany to its former strength, and long before the rise of the Nazis looked for British support in all her diplomatic dealings. French governments insisted on their predominance and expected London to help ensure this. And they sought alignments with the states of central and eastern Europe in order to encircle Germany with a ring of steel. Hitler's objectives in the East were likely to produce a war come what may; but *any* German regime would have found itself in a comparable position, for French efforts to impinge on Germany hinged not on the character of her government but her geographical location at the heart of Europe.[25] Chamberlain understood the divergence between British and French interests, but ultimately his willingness to involve himself in the details of European affairs that were of no direct interest to Britain, rather than divest Britain of responsibility, created a climate in which the National Government lacked the diplomatic flexibility that it might have enjoyed.

In contrast to the traditional Churchillian critique that Chamberlain's instincts in foreign affairs were insufficiently bold, then, we might argue they were too interventionist. Once he became Prime Minister, for all Chamberlain's complaints about the stupidity of Europeans—and he made similar complaints about most everyone he worked with—he concluded that it was his responsibility to solve their problems. A greater willingness to stand back and allow other states to attend to their *own* troubles would almost certainly have served *British* interests more effectively.

'A One-Man Cabinet'

When Neville finally became Prime Minister in May 1937, he was struck by the realization that he was ascending to a post which had eluded both his father and half-brother.[26] (Austen, the elder statesman of the Conservative party, did not live to see it, having died suddenly in March.) But far from being intimidated by the office, Chamberlain was determined to grasp the opportunity and bend the machinery of Whitehall to his will. He told his sister Ida that he was 'keen to leave my mark behind me as PM'.[27] He certainly did that.

The new Prime Minister enjoyed the time and space to take a tight grip on the reins of government. He was popular in the party, commanded a large parliamentary majority, had overseen an expanding economy, and, though aged sixty-eight, was perceived as a more vigorous figure than Baldwin. Conservative prospects of winning the next general election—due to take place in 1939 or 1940—were high. Chamberlain had long liked to project an aura of mastery and methodical reasoning. Unlike his predecessor, his manner was also firmly partisan. This afforded him a large reservoir of Conservative goodwill. Even Churchill was not above angling for a fresh start, being one of four Conservative MPs to formally propose Chamberlain for the leadership when Baldwin resigned.[28] Predictably, Chamberlain rebuffed the approach, fearing that Churchill would 'dominate' the Cabinet.[29] He did not want *anyone* who would 'rock the boat'—which meant challenge his own authority.[30] Chamberlain's ministers, and for that matter the civil servants, would need to do as they were told.

In this the Prime Minister was ably assisted by those around him. The senior civil servant Sir Horace Wilson acted as Chamberlain's principal confidant and enforcer.[31] After starting out as a teenage clerk Wilson rose to the top of the Civil Service through sheer hard graft. He had been a major asset for Baldwin—who confessed that he himself was not necessarily one of life's hard workers—in keeping a close eye on everything that passed through Downing Street. His clarity of mind was exceptional. Recognizing a kindred spirit, Chamberlain retained Wilson in his post at the Prime Minister's side. He was an indispensable actor in Downing Street, working closely with Chamberlain on a daily basis. Everyone entering Chamberlain's office at Downing Street had to pass through Wilson's adjacent room first. Attlee complained that Wilson 'had a hand in everything, ran everything'.[32] Beaverbrook remarked that 'the country at present is being ruled from the anteroom of Downing Street'.[33] Rab Butler thought Wilson 'the uncrowned ruler of England'.[34] He spent his days interviewing ministers, keeping abreast of their activity and impressing the Prime Minister's preferences upon them. Through this, Chamberlain kept his colleagues on a short leash. Lord Woolton believed that Wilson 'had more detailed knowledge of what was happening in government circles than anyone else'. One Labour critic believed he enjoyed greater influence than 'almost anybody since Cardinal Wolsey'.[35] Wilson was devoted to Chamberlain, and when speaking to others referred to him as 'my master'.[36] A small and select antechamber of power soon formed around the Prime Minister, and for the next three years Wilson was its most important member and gatekeeper.

Another member was the government Chief Whip, David Margesson. Tall and imposing, invariably wearing a black morning coat with black and white checked trousers, Margesson was considered the best-dressed man in the Commons.[37] He could be charming, and was often witty. Yet he was also an intimidating and vindictive presence around Parliament who exercised a ruthless control over back-benchers. The strict disciplinarian always lurked beneath the bonhomie. He was Chamberlain's eyes, ears, and blunt-force instrument in the House of Commons. Margesson 'put the fear of God' into Conservative MPs with his insistence on obedience to the government line.[38] Those who made an enemy of Margesson would regret it. 'He never forgives nor forgets' was a typical observation.[39] Samuel Hoare judged him Chamberlain's 'evil genius'.[40] One Conservative thought that, in terms of sheer ruthlessness, Margesson did not pale in comparison to 'the Nazi party machine'.[41] Iron discipline within government and party alike was non-negotiable.

Perhaps the most intriguing member of the antechamber was Sir Joseph Ball. Ball's is a shadowy presence in interwar politics. He existed in the background. It was, and remains, very easy not to notice him. Powerful men who passed Ball in the streets of Westminster would have had no inkling who he was; there was nothing to distinguish him from all the other pedestrians. Yet Ball would have known who *they* were. His background was in the secret world of the intelligence services. He had been thought of as one of the very best officers in MI5 in the years during and after the First World War, but harboured political ambitions and hoped to enter the more lucrative world of Westminster. In 1927, Ball was recruited by J. C. C. Davidson, the chairman of the Conservative party, to direct its publicity machinery. Davidson became a huge admirer and remarked that Ball was not only 'undoubtedly tough', but 'steeped in the Service tradition, and has had as much experience as anyone I know in the seamy side of life and the handling of crooks'.[42] He put Ball in charge of 'political warfare'—propaganda, in other words—and the wisdom of this was quickly apparent. His success in directing the party's propaganda efforts was 'almost instantaneous'.[43] By 1929, Ball was Director of the newly formed Conservative Research Department. Yet from the beginning, he had another, unoffi-cial, job as well: to employ the skills he had acquired in MI5 and gather politically useful information through means fair or foul. Ball thus found himself in an intelligence 'nirvana' in which he could rather do what he liked and operate without supervision.[44] He even planted spies in the headquarters of the Labour and Liberal parties.[45] From 1929 onwards Ball cultivated a friendship with Chamberlain. He rose as Chamberlain did. The two were in constant contact and holidayed together. Noting that Ball's letters to Neville contained plenty of flattery, one historian has speculated that, as someone trained to read people's weaknesses, Ball knew Chamberlain craved approval and thus gave it to him.[46] A master of political espionage, he undertook black operations for both Baldwin and Chamberlain that they could never admit to knowing about.

With Chamberlain determined to dominate major policy deliberations personally, the sense developed that the Prime Minister's style was a 'dictatorship' and a 'one-man Cabinet'.[47] He chose the National Liberal Sir John Simon to be his successor as Chancellor, safe in the knowledge that Simon would obediently continue his policies at the Treasury. Simon possessed 'a sycophantic quality and almost pathetic desire to please' that prompted 'reptilian metaphors' from those who worked with him.[48] Meanwhile Neville moved the independent-minded Conservative Duff Cooper from the War Office—where he had energetically pressed for a commitment to dispatch a large British army to Europe in the event of war—to the Admiralty. Cooper's predecessor at the Admiralty, Samuel Hoare—a man still consumed by 'restless ambition'—was appointed Home Secretary, where he could play a full part in the 'hurly burly of every day politics'.[49] This was how Chamberlain intended to govern.

'A Faintly Bohemian Flavour'

The Prime Minister knew that if a successful challenge to his influence was to arise, it would likely originate at the Foreign Office.[50] Beneath the splendour of George Gilbert Scott's neoclassical building, Chamberlain suspected that the department was packed full of enemies determined to thwart him. Number 10 Downing Street was but a stone's throw away from the Foreign Office, yet that short distance may as well have been a canyon. The Prime Minister loathed the place as being laden down with both idealists and Germanophobes. Hoare warned him that 'the Foreign Office is so much biased against Germany (and Italy and Japan) that unconsciously and almost continuously they are making impossible any European reconciliation'.[51] Wilson judged the problem as being that there 'were too many dilettantes' in the department.[52] By November 1937 the Prime Minister was complaining that, in imposing his own policies, he had to 'fight' the Foreign Office 'every inch of the way'.[53] This would not do.

In December 1937 Chamberlain decided to shunt aside the most senior civil servant at the Foreign Office, the Permanent Under-Secretary (PUS) Sir Robert Vansittart, due to his inflexible anti-German views.[54] Many within Whitehall had, fairly or unfairly, long held 'Van' responsible for negotiating the details of the Hoare–Laval Pact in December 1935 that almost wrecked the government; Chamberlain himself thought Hoare was 'greatly misled by his staff', and there was a widespread suspicion that Vansittart's personal friendship with Baldwin had protected him in the aftermath.[55] Vansittart's independent temperament, and robust conviction that Nazi Germany could not be negotiated with, provided a powerful incentive for Chamberlain to get rid of him. Eden disliked him as well, considering Vansittart too big for his boots, 'much more a Secretary of State in mentality than a permanent official'.[56] In January 1938 the impertinent 'Van' was therefore neutered by being appointed to an impressive-sounding, but purely ceremonial, role of 'Chief Diplomatic Adviser to the Government'. He was replaced as PUS by Sir Alexander Cadogan, a man whose opinions were much closer to those of the Prime Minister. Moreover, in the spring of 1937, a new British ambassador to Germany had been appointed. The Old Etonian Sir Nevile Henderson turned out to be highly strung and emotionally overwrought, yet he saw himself as the Prime Minister's personal representative in Berlin. He had little compunction about bypassing formal Foreign Office channels and reporting to the Prime Minister directly.

However, there were deeper problems besides dislike of the department when it came to Chamberlain's relations with the Foreign Office. The biggest was the Foreign Secretary himself. From the outset, the young and ambitious Anthony Eden—retained by Chamberlain as Foreign Secretary—posed a particular problem for a man who wanted a servile Cabinet. Eden looked like a film star and possessed an easy charm. He was just forty years old in 1937, with his finger on the pulse of popular culture—the floor of his apartment was strewn with gramophone records featuring 'waltzes, foxtrots and polkas'—in a way that most politicians did not.[57] There was a 'faintly Bohemian flavour' to him.[58] Eden had established himself as the heir to Baldwinian liberal conservatism, tactically employing foreign policy, the League, and the rhetoric of virtue in order to make himself a rising star and win admirers on the left; he assured the public that he stood for 'the Covenant, the whole Covenant and nothing but the Covenant'.[59] Eden was also a staunch patriot who had served in the trenches in the Great War. His status as a star-in-the-making might one day pose a threat to Chamberlain.

There were important psychological similarities between the two men which made for a combustible mixture. Eden and the Prime Minister were both prickly and sensitive to slights, particularly the imagined variety. Both were needful of praise, and struggled to manage without it. But Eden was also so concerned with protecting his reputation that the realities of foreign policy—which, as Foreign Secretary, he could hardly avoid—inevitably came into tension with the public image he cultivated. Many of Eden's speeches were plainly aimed at popular consumption and left Cabinet colleagues furious; he appeared to want to be a Foreign Secretary who could distance himself from his own government's policies when it suited him. He had long been cognizant of the domestic implications of international affairs, telling Baldwin as early as 1933 that 'political reaction at home' to foreign policy needed to be managed to ensure the government was perceived as 'the hero'.[60]

Eden always wanted to play 'the hero', and that was his problem. He was widely considered a prima donna, and was certainly prone to tantrums. His focus was on being liked. He enjoyed attention, whether being cheered by the Labour benches after a speech in the Commons or applauded by members of the general public at rallies.[61] He focused on building up 'as broad a popular backing as possible' by making frequent public speeches and being 'seen in different parts of the country'. This would, one of his allies remarked, 'strengthen his position in the country, in the House, and also abroad'; moreover it would 'strengthen his hand in the Cabinet, where all are not too pleased at his growing strength'.[62] The inner circle in the Foreign Office, particularly Eden's Parliamentary Under-Secretary Lord Cranborne and his Private Secretary, Oliver Harvey, idolized him for his 'flair' and had their chief believing that Cabinet colleagues were just 'jealous of him'.[63] They whispered a daily dose of sweet-nothings in Eden's ear which only puffed up his self-regard. Eden believed that the National Government would be stronger if led by a 'younger man' than Chamberlain; he was presumably thinking of himself.[64] Harvey believed Eden would become Prime Minister 'before very long'.[65]

When Eden believed that 'so far as the home front is concerned'—which meant liberal public opinion—a 'political settlement' with Germany would be popular, he advocated it.[66] To that end he was willing to make 'great concessions to German appetites' in the form of territorial adjustments in Europe so long as Hitler would 'sign a disarmament treaty' and take Germany back into the League which it had quit in 1933.[67] And he personally took the lead in resisting calls from Paris for a firm response to the occupation of the Rhineland.[68] Yet, when such an approach to Germany was no longer popular with his liberal constituency from 1937 onwards, Eden's attitudes reversed and he became firmer. His mind was always fixated on appealing to liberal opinion. This made him a dangerous, and unstable, element in the Cabinet. Hankey judged that Eden 'hates Dictators so much that he seems to me unwilling to make a real effort'. He felt Eden 'is personally vain and doesn't like anyone else to get any credit in foreign affairs', and 'plays to the gallery' of the political left.[69]

The Prime Minister and his Foreign Secretary quarrelled quickly, coming to blows in the autumn of 1937 over whether to try and improve relations with Italy. Despite Eden's evident desire to confront Mussolini, Chamberlain judged an improvement in relations to be essential to weakening 'the Rome-Berlin axis'.[70] In this he enjoyed the support of Halifax, now emerging as one of the weightiest ministers in the government. Serving as Lord President of the Council, the former Viceroy of India enjoyed a roving brief and took a close interest in foreign affairs. Eden, on the other hand, was reluctant to be seen to legitimize Mussolini's conquest of Abyssinia—perhaps inevitably so, given that he had employed the crisis to buff up his own reputation in 1935–6—and as a result the Prime Minister's overture had to be launched by ignoring the Foreign Secretary. The materials for a major explosion were all present.

'The Far East Is on Fire'

That the overture failed—Mussolini having identified Britain not only as an adversary, but a weak one—underlined the difficulties confronting Chamberlain.[71] He was also subjected to a continual barrage of paperwork about the ambitions of Imperial Japan. Chamberlain had long been naive about the Japanese and failed to recognize that, in fact, Britain's most natural strategic adversary of the three revisionist states was arguably Japan. German ambitions under the Nazis lay in central and eastern Europe, which was not an area of overwhelming concern to London. Italy was the least of the great powers, and anyway her interests and those of Britain did not obviously conflict. Japan was different. She was the pre-eminent Asian power. In 1921 Britain had not renewed its formal treaty of alliance with Japan, signed in 1902. This was a serious error on the part of London which weakened protections for imperial interests in the Pacific. The motivation for allowing the treaty to lapse had been to court the goodwill of the United States, but it yielded no appreciable advantages for London's relationship with Washington and only created a rift with Tokyo. Meanwhile, in the second half of the 1920s, democratic government in Japan was weakened and the military empowered. The belief grew that Japan should unify Asia under her rule.[72] Manchuria, a huge region in northeast China, was technically a Chinese province but in practice quasi-independent. Moreover, Manchuria was located just over the border from Japanese-controlled Korea. In September 1931, the Japanese army faked an attack by Chinese dissidents on a Japanese-owned railway line in southern Manchuria; this provided a convenient pretext for an outright invasion of Manchuria. An attack on Shanghai and then the Great Wall region followed. Even India, Australia, and New Zealand might one day become targets of Tokyo.[73]

Yet Chamberlain was sanguine and believed there were no insurmountable difficulties in the relationship.[74] In contrast, MacDonald and Baldwin fretted that Japan might be able to 'mop up the whole of our possessions in the East',[75] and the Chiefs of Staff feared that 'the whole of our territory in the Far East as well as the coast line of India and the Dominions and our vast trade and shipping is open to attack'.[76] Chamberlain even sought to obstruct the strengthening of the naval base at Singapore and 'materially reduce the heavy and increasing shipbuilding programme' that the Admiralty was undertaking to expand the Royal Navy.[77] Naval spending did go up, but Chamberlain pared back the Admiralty's requested increase by 62 per cent.[78] His worldview ignored the realities of imperial defence. There existed in Whitehall a perception that Chamberlain was fixated with doing imperial security on the cheap.

Shortly after he became Prime Minister, the Japanese question became more pressing. In July 1937, Japan's predations against China turned into outright war. The two largest nations in the western Pacific were now in conflict; and the Japanese military was inhumanly sadistic. Ivan Maisky recorded that 'The Far East is on fire'.[79] The name the Japanese bestowed on their new empire—the 'Greater Asia Co-Prosperity Sphere'—could not disguise their brutality in carving it out. In August 1937 the British ambassador to China was badly injured when his car was strafed by Japanese planes near Shanghai. This was an accident but there was a deliberate policy of testing London's resolve, for the Japanese navy regularly stopped and inspected British-flagged merchant ships. Chamberlain now appreciated the dangers that could arise if Tokyo concluded that Britain was a soft touch.[80] However, fixated as he was on European diplomacy, the Prime Minister was forced to confine himself to empty protests; the imposition of biting economic sanctions might provoke Tokyo into war and he was unwilling to station sufficient British forces in the Far East to deter such a conflict.[81] Chamberlain was justifiably frustrated at the absence of US support over Japan,[82] remarking bitterly that 'it is always best and safest to count on *nothing* from the Americans except words',[83] but the failure to act decisively to reinforce British imperial power against a major adversary is striking.

It was even more troubling in an environment where the Anti-Comintern Pact signed by Germany and Japan in November 1936 was joined by Italy a year later. The Comintern was the Communist International, a worldwide organization that united communist parties from many nations and advocated global revolution.

The Pact provided a useful basis for anti-Bolshevik nationalist regimes to ally themselves. The worst-case scenario of an alignment between three states that could threaten British power and interests across the globe—via the North Sea, the Mediterranean, and the Pacific—was taking shape.[84]

Chamberlain's pacific response to the Japanese testing of British resolve highlights the flaws in his strategy. If he aimed to avoid facing all three states and to focus on *British* interests rather than those of a nebulous 'international community', the most logical course of action would arguably have been to stand back from European questions in regions—such as the east of the continent—that were of no obvious interest to Britain, and concentrate instead on deterring the Japanese threat given that the Empire *was* a core national interest. Hitler had no desire for a confrontation with the rich and powerful British Empire, and sought to prepare for a conflict against Germany's natural enemy—a status dictated even more by geography than ideology—the Soviet Union. Indeed, from 1935, the Fuhrer searched for a diplomatic rapprochement with Britain that would leave him a free hand to deal with Stalin. That year Berlin and London signed the Anglo-German Naval Agreement, in which Hitler agreed to limit the size of the Germany navy to a third of that of the Royal Navy.[85] (Considering Germany's shortage of the resources and personnel necessary to build a large fleet, this only reflected Hitler's weakness at sea—even at the outbreak of war, the *Kriegsmarine* was nowhere close to a third of the tonnage of the Royal Navy—but it does underline Berlin's desire to avoid confrontation with Britain.) It should have been possible for Chamberlain to steer a course which rendered war with Germany less likely. A good start would have been clarity about the boundaries of British interests, and then sticking to them with consistency. That the Prime Minister failed to achieve this highlights his inability to develop a clear view of the national interest—a weakness that would lead not only to his own 'zigzagging', but to being pulled in one direction and then another by opponents foreign and domestic.

'Take an Aspirin'

By the autumn of 1937, a put-out Eden realized that 'the PM wanted to deal with foreign affairs himself and keep [Eden] out of the picture'.[86, 87] This predictably offended the Foreign Secretary's sense of *amour-propre*, but Chamberlain worried that Eden's 'vibrations' and enthusiasm for grand moral gestures risked 'throw[ing] Germany and Italy together in self defence when our policy is so obviously to try & divide them'.[88] He even sought to veto his Foreign Secretary speaking at a rally in Wales at which 18,000 people had applied for seats.[89]

Eden's disciples in the Foreign Office, Cranborne and Harvey, took the view that their chief had 'the H[ouse] of C[ommons] behind him as well as the country'.[90] They told Eden that he was 'the most important person in the Cabinet', and 'if he went the government would fall'.[91] In November they advised him that Chamberlain would have no option but to give way if he pushed, for he was 'the only Foreign Secretary in sight' and the National Government was 'living on your popularity and reputation'.[92] Eden's coterie thus advised him to leverage his influence and take control of foreign policy by confronting Chamberlain directly: if he quit, the ministry would collapse, meaning that *you are not only entitled to but you are able to impose your terms*.[93] This was an exaggerated assessment of Eden's authority. But it doubtless inflated the Foreign Secretary's sense of his own indispensability.

On 8 December 1937, he tried to impose terms by going to see Chamberlain and demanding that the pace of rearmament be quickened still further.[94] Citing concerns about precipitating an economic crisis, the Prime Minister refused to give way. Chamberlain held that accelerating the intensity of rearmament would necessitate imposing wartime controls on the economy—something that was inconceivable in peacetime. One cannot help suspecting that the issue was selected by Eden to create a point of conflict; Chamberlain's talk of wartime controls may have had a similar motive. The Foreign Secretary tried again several days later. This time Chamberlain's disdain seeped through to the surface: he contemptuously told Eden to 'take an aspirin'.[95]

This was a remark that still moved Eden to fury thirty years later. Chamberlain had long worried about the Foreign Secretary's mental state; it could be seen in his expressing concern in September that Eden should not 'tire himself out' with work.[96] A cynic might think that Chamberlain had already resolved that in the— hardly unthinkable—event of a conflict with his Foreign Secretary, he would play the instability card and write Eden off as 'ill'. But, to be fair, Eden's inner circle shared much the same concerns, with Harvey recording in his diary that 'A.E. MUST have a holiday'.[97]

Incandescent about the 'aspirin' comment, the Foreign Secretary set out his objections at length on paper—doubtless in order to create a basis for threatening resignation.[98] In Halifax's mind, Eden possessed a 'dual personality'. First, there was 'Anthony Eden . . . the generous idealist'. But he could not co-exist with the second 'personality', the 'Foreign Secretary' who had to make choices that were not 'idealistic'. The result was that the first Eden would persuade the second that it was 'all too beastly for words' and abdicate responsibility in order to salve his own conscience.[99] Another Conservative peer, sceptical that Eden was sufficiently robust for the business of diplomacy, had once asked Baldwin 'can your Foreign Secretary frown? Can he rap the table?'[100] Chamberlain believed Eden's fixation with virtue to be sheer self-indulgence, particularly when 'the appeasement of Europe is a complicated and lengthy business'.[101] The Conservative MP Leo Amery had warned the Prime Minister of the need for Britain to stop paying 'lip service' to the empty ideals of the League, but this was something with which Chamberlain instinctively agreed.[102] In early January 1938, when discussing whether to formally recognize Mussolini's conquest of Abyssinia in order to improve relations with Italy, Eden did not want Britain to be seen to enter into any bargain over recognition but to simply do so and then see what Italy offered in response.[103] Chamberlain was astonished. The Prime Minister felt that Eden was worrying too much about a 'clean conscience', and that to simply grant recognition without a clear *quid pro quo* from Rome was 'giving away our best card for nothing'.[104]

The two men had another serious falling out days later, when Chamberlain rebuffed President Roosevelt's vague calls for a global conference to settle international issues without even bothering to consult his Foreign Secretary.[105] Eden was outraged and resolved to pursue Anglo-American collaboration.[106] In contrast, Chamberlain believed such collaboration would not be forthcoming and that a conference would only expose Britain to fresh diplomatic liabilities when America retreated behind its two vast oceans. The Neutrality Acts and a hostile, isolationist Congress rendered genuine assistance from Washington improbable. Yet the real issue was that Chamberlain intended to be the sole architect of British foreign policy, a fact which offended Eden in that it threatened to consign him to irrelevance. Meanwhile the Prime Minister was exhausted by Eden's volatility and aversion to facing up to the sordid nature of diplomacy. As the row over Roosevelt's idea developed, it became apparent that Eden was considering resignation. Harvey advised him to 'take a very strong line', because the Cabinet 'couldn't let you go on this'.[107]

For once, Eden's devotees read the runes correctly; it would be disastrous for Chamberlain to lose a Foreign Secretary because of his own refusal to take seriously a chance at the diplomatic holy grail of Anglo-American cooperation. The Eden camp reinforced their position by threatening to leak the news to the press.[108] Eden himself warned that he had 'a loyalty to his supporters in the country which is of greater importance than that to his colleagues'.[109] Horace Wilson went over to the Foreign Office and threatened that there would be an 'onslaught' from Downing Street if Eden did go.[110] Wilson was in 'a towering rage'—one Eden supporter said it was 'the first time I had seen him with the mask off'—and promised to use 'the full power of the government machine' to expose Eden's 'shameful obstruction...of the PM's attempts to save the peace of the world'.[111] But on

20 January Chamberlain reluctantly gave way and signalled Britain's willingness to support Roosevelt's idea.[112] It was a 'great triumph' for Eden, one that Harvey judged showed Chamberlain was 'afraid of him'.[113] Predictably, the plan for a conference came to naught—Roosevelt put the initiative on hold indefinitely—but the episode left the Prime Minister resolved that Eden would not be permitted to outmanoeuvre him again.

The break between the two men came quickly, in February 1938. That month, through threats of invasion, Hitler pressed the Austrian government to accept the Nazification of the country. The *Anschluss*—unification between Germany and Austria, by means of the forcible incorporation of the latter into the Reich—seemed imminent. Italy was panicked by these developments on its frontiers, and Chamberlain perceived an opportunity to detach Mussolini from Hitler. Time was of the essence. The Prime Minister thus decided upon an approach to Rome in hopes of repairing the damage done since 1935. In this he was strongly opposed by Eden, who was always far more hostile to Mussolini ('the Anti-Christ')[114] than Hitler. Perhaps, as a weaker power than Germany, Italy was a more tempting target for a gesture that boosted one's career prospects. Indeed, Eden's stance of inaction in the face of the impending *Anschluss* rather suggests that his obsession with preaching the immorality of the dictators was primarily a pose; as John Charmley caustically observed, it is telling that over the *Anschluss* Eden conspicuously failed to 'mount his white steed'.[115]

The scene was set for a decisive test of strength. On 18 February, the Italian ambassador, Count Grandi, arrived at Downing Street to meet Chamberlain and Eden. There he found the Prime Minister and the Foreign Secretary in obvious conflict and barely bothering to hide it. Reporting back to Rome, Grandi likened them to 'two enemies confronting each other', like 'two cocks in true fighting posture'.[116] He concluded that while policy disputes were one thing, in reality 'they were fighting for the high stakes of their future destiny in the Cabinet and in the Conservative party'. Interestingly, the meeting with Grandi was partly choreographed by the Prime Minister; unbeknownst to Eden, Chamberlain had already passed discreet assurances to the ambassador about his determination to pursue talks with Rome.[117] As we have seen, Joseph Ball ran a clandestine intelligence unit for the Conservative party, and the Prime Minister tapped into this whenever he wanted to quietly bypass official channels. Without Eden's knowledge, Chamberlain had used Ball as an emissary to Grandi prior to the meeting.[118] The Prime Minister was resolved to stave off the Foreign Secretary's bid to seize control of diplomacy. Chamberlain determined that his policy would hold sway and Eden would be brought to heel. If he refused, the Prime Minister would, he told Wilson, 'stand firm even if it means losing my Foreign Secretary'. 'The issue between us must be faced and faced at once'.[119]

In other words, the Prime Minister was exploiting Eden's obsession with Mussolini as political bait to draw him into a row in which he would either 'tame' the Foreign Secretary and make him an 'obedient tool', or force him out of the government.[120] Chamberlain was sick of Eden's suspicions and resented the 'acute internal crisis in the Cabinet' which they produced.[121] For his part Eden, basking in his 'great triumph' over the Roosevelt proposal, was encouraged by his Foreign Office coterie that he could 'afford to be as firm as he likes' for the rest of the government were afraid of him.[122] The Conservatives had also just lost a by-election, which might have strengthened his conviction that Chamberlain was vulnerable.

The result was a tense discussion with Grandi that led nowhere. When Grandi left Downing Street—getting into a taxi outside, it has been alleged that he found Ball waiting in the back seat for another confab[123]—a furious Chamberlain accused Eden of 'wanting to throw [a chance for peace] away'.[124] But this was an overblown accusation. So too was Eden's remark about a 'fundamental difference' between himself and Chamberlain. In reality the policy differences between the men were fairly minor, more a question of emphasis and timing than strategy. The arguments were synthetic, sharpened and dramatized in order to provide a respectable veneer for a struggle over *who* was in control.

Two tense Cabinet meetings on 19 and 20 February provided the final act. Chamberlain was determined that 'Anthony must yield or go' and so took the unusual step of calling the Cabinet together on a Saturday and Sunday.[125] Around the Cabinet table, the pair laid out their positions. The Prime Minister invited his colleagues to make a choice. Following long and tense discussions over two days, ministers supported Chamberlain's strategy; the Foreign Secretary found not a single backer.[126] A list-ditch effort was mounted to persuade Eden to submit— John Simon endeavoured to convince the Foreign Office that Eden's problem was exhaustion, that he was 'physically and mentally ill', and that he should take a long holiday—but this failed and he promptly resigned.[127] In truth, Eden probably hoped to be out of office as a means to avoid sullying his popularity by making unseemly diplomatic choices.

When the Foreign Secretary departed the Cabinet, Ball wrote to Chamberlain reporting that he had taken 'certain steps privately' to demolish Eden's case; sure enough, one of Eden's admirers in the Foreign Office noted bitterly that 'the government took every possible step to secure the London papers...and the BBC'.[128] Dawson put out an editorial in *The Times* which charged that Eden's position was simply 'waiting virtuously for the next war'.[129] He suggested Eden had 'unbalanced and hostile motives'.[130] Hints were scattered throughout the newspapers that the Foreign Secretary was suffering a breakdown and that his emotional state was not right—hints that clearly bore the imprint of Ball. One journalist at the *Daily Telegraph* was left 'in tears at the way his paper had behaved'.[131] The departure of Eden from the government was not even the first item on that evening's BBC news. The *Manchester Guardian* complained that the rest of the press had 'preserved a unity of silence that could hardly be bettered in a totalitarian state'—a comment that Ball cut out and filed away.[132]

During an emergency Commons debate on the resignation that began the following day, Eden made a disappointingly flat statement while Chamberlain, in contrast, delivered one of the finest speeches of his career.[133] The Prime Minister argued that to believe the League of Nations represented the key to peace was, quite simply, to 'delude ourselves';[134] whether this talk of delusion was intended as yet another jibe about Eden's mental state is unclear. Amery predicted that 'naturally Winston will exploit the situation to the full'.[135] Sure enough, Churchill immediately tried to recruit Eden as a potential ally—encouraging him to attack the government publicly—but was unable to make any headway.[136] Eden had lacked the stomach for diplomacy, and now also lacked the stomach to be an insurgent. Maisky remarked that Eden 'is not made of iron, but rather of soft clay'.[137] He was right.

Ten years later, in the winter of 1948, Eden returned home one evening to find an urgent message asking him to telephone Winston Churchill at Chartwell, no matter how late the hour. He wondered what the emergency was. When he rang through, Eden found Churchill excited: researching the first volume of his war memoirs, he had come to possess a diplomatic dispatch that Grandi sent back to Rome in February 1938. Relaying news of Grandi's alleged rendezvous with Chamberlain's emissary, Ball, in a taxi immediately after the meeting at Downing Street, Churchill told Eden 'it shows that [Chamberlain] was determined to do you in'.[138]

'We Are Not Talking the Same Language'

With the termination of his power struggle with Eden, the Prime Minister's authority in the Cabinet was cemented.[139] Viscount Halifax succeeded Eden at the Foreign Office, completing his journey from Viceroy of India to the apex of Westminster. The measured Yorkshire aristocrat was a much better fit for Chamberlain than the temperamental Eden. In Halifax, the Prime Minister found someone whose mind ran on similar lines and with whom he could work in tandem; Chamberlain felt that 'he and I understand one another very well'.[140] It was the beginning of a crucial new phase for the National Government. The Cabinet decided to increase projected defence spending still further, to £1.57 billion over five years. The resources Britain devoted to rearmament were now vast. In 1938, £82 million was spent on the RAF, £101 million on the navy, and £77 million on the army. Furthermore, the long-standing primacy given to air and naval power over a large army remained intact. Later in 1938, there was a formal shift in RAF planning to prioritise the aerial defence of the British Isles over offensive action. This paid dividends in the Battle of Britain. Events had been moving in the direction of air defence for some time, with innovative developments in radar, anti-aircraft guns, and communications to help convey the whereabouts of enemy planes. Though at the time many—including Churchill—spoke in favour of the offensive capacity of the bomber, the shift to a defensive force built around fighter planes rendered it unlikely that Germany would be able to win an aerial campaign against Britain. This would buy time for a British naval blockade to expose the vulnerabilities of the German economy and for allies to defeat Germany on land. It also complemented Britain's deepest strategic asset, the staying power afforded by its great wealth.

Yet Chamberlain's premiership remained confronted by a growing array of problems. Crucially, with the exclusion of Eden the expansive domestic coalition bequeathed by Baldwin was left significantly smaller. Whatever his failings as a minister, Eden was a *symbol* of liberal values in foreign policy. His removal posed a dilemma. Since succeeding Baldwin, Chamberlain had been more autocratic and intolerant than his predecessor. That enthused backbenchers, but the Prime Minister was slowly eroding the foundation of Conservative predominance: the party's broad-based appeal.

Elsewhere, international instability persisted. On 12 March 1938 the Fuhrer ordered German troops across the border with Austria and formally completed the *Anschluss*. The successful incorporation of Austria into the Reich represented a major diplomatic victory for Hitler, his greatest yet. The *Anschluss* was a watershed moment in European history. For the denizens of Westminster, it also brought the question of what to do about Germany into sharper focus.[141] Hitler was a multifarious political operator whose true aims and ambitions remained elusive, even unknowable. And the confusion about Britain's objectives had been growing since Chamberlain became Prime Minister. Indeed, a meeting between Halifax and Hitler at Berchtesgaden in November 1937 illustrated the nature of the problem. Halifax had spent long periods negotiating with extremists who wanted to overturn the existing order in India; now Europe posed comparable problems. When he arrived to meet Hitler at Berchtesgaden, Halifax mistook the nondescript-looking Fuhrer for a footman, almost handing him his hat. Swiftly recovering from what would have been a disaster for diplomatic etiquette, Halifax expressed the hope that Britain and Germany could construct 'a better understanding between our two nations', upon which 'the future... might well depend'.[142] The Fuhrer stated that professions of goodwill among states was one thing, but it was not 'worth much unless it took account of the realities', including 'unpleasant' ones. These generally centred on eastern Europe. He identified the size and ambitions of Poland as being 'such a reality' that Germans could not help but 'recognise'. Halifax acknowledged that Germany was a 'great power' and that 'nobody in their senses' was committed to the 'status quo'; the 'whole point was *how* changes were to be brought about'. Hitler responded that the two possibilities were either 'the free play of forces'—which 'meant war'—or 'settlement by reason'. The Fuhrer then went on a 'tirade' about 'the difficulty of doing business with democratic countries' due to the 'complicating' factor of 'the party system', which threatened to 'wreck' the scope for sensible agreements between states.

Halifax denied that democracy made coherent policy problematic; but, fanatical as Hitler may have been, he was surely right about the difficulties which had afflicted British policymakers since the 1935 election. Hitler felt Britain lived in a 'make-believe land' and 'clung to shibboleths' such as collective security which 'offered no practical prospect of a solution to Europe's difficulties'. Hitler also denied any scope for 'peaceful revision' of territorial borders as laid out in Article 19 of the League Covenant, for 'it is impossible to imagine peaceful revision with the consent of all'. Halifax explained that in ignoring 'treaty obligations' over the size of the German military and the Rhineland, Hitler had created a climate of mistrust. He identified 'Danzig, Austria and Czechoslovakia' as flashpoints (as they all proved to be) and affirmed once again that Britain did not 'stand for the status quo' in any of these cases; what mattered was *how* the issues were managed. If the strategy of the National Government can be criticized for anything, it is surely that the Cabinet proved willing to engage in diplomatic confrontations, and ultimately go to war, over issues where, from the outset, they were *never* committed to the 'status quo'.[143]

Writing to the Cabinet, Halifax acknowledged the difficulty of dealing with Hitler: 'we are not talking the same language'.[144] But what the situation really signified was the inescapable logic of geopolitics in central and eastern Europe. The affairs of that region had been addressed under the Treaties of St Germain and Trianon in 1919–20. It was hardly a surprise that these failed to offer a durable settlement, for the problems of this part of the world would have vexed anyone. The collapse of the Austro-Hungarian Empire created a chaotic array of power vacuums and contested borders that stretched for hundreds of miles. It was heavily influenced by ancient tensions between Magyar, Teuton, and Slav. The region now consisted of a mixture of newly created states and older countries that were expanded or cut up as diplomacy dictated; Austria, Hungary, Czechoslovakia, Poland, Romania, and Yugoslavia all vied for influence. Austria was deprived of 60 per cent of its pre-war territory; Hungary more than 70 per cent. Ethnic groups suddenly found themselves living in a different country due to territorial adjustments. The dream of cultural unity with one's brethren across the new borders was a constant feature of politics in the region.

Meanwhile, in the East the Romanov Empire disintegrated in the Russian Revolution, and the emergent Soviet Union withdrew into bloody civil war. For a time, Moscow showed little interest in its traditional geopolitical backyard. From the West, Germany straddled this cauldron of chaos. With the Austro-Hungarian Empire consigned to history it was inevitable that another state would fill the gap. Poland was the first to make the attempt. That country was swollen by swathes of land transferred from Germany and Austria at Versailles: eastern Prussia was now divided from the rest of Germany by newly Polish territory, 'the Polish Corridor', meaning that Germany was no longer a territorially contiguous state. Meanwhile the German city of Danzig was declared a 'free city', separated from the Reich, and locked into a customs union with the Poles. Polish leaders dreamt of welding the Baltic states of Finland, Lithuania, Latvia, and Estonia together with Hungary, the Ukraine, Romania, Yugoslavia, Czechoslovakia, and Belarus into a federation under Polish leadership. The Poles won a territorial war with the Ukraine in 1919 and then a further conflict against Bolshevik Russia in 1921. To Polish leaders the *Intermarium* was a precursor to *Prometheism*, the conquest and dismemberment of Russia itself.

This was fantasy. Far more plausible was the notion that Germany would, once she recovered from the Great War, become the regional hegemon. Her location made German assertiveness a matter of time. So too did the fact that the transfer of territory, and millions of German citizens, to Poland left the German people longing for redress. The liberal principle of 'national self-determination', touted loudly by the peacemakers at Versailles, did not seem to apply to Germanic peoples. Invoking that principle alone, Berlin could justifiably press for unity between Germany and Austria as well as the return of territories granted to Poland and Czechoslovakia.

That region of Europe was, therefore, a colossal powder keg. It was shaped by a series of treaty arrangements which were unsustainable in that they reflected neither the power nor the aspirations of the key states. And given that the countries destined to be drawn into a local struggle in central and eastern Europe had enthusiastically resorted to threats, murder, sedition, and outright war since 1919, this imbalance was hardly likely to be corrected without military conflict on a significant scale. Reduced to its essence, war is a device for generating a decision where politics fails to do so. It seems implausible that equilibrium in central and eastern Europe could have been attained without such a military decision. Moreover, a war along these lines was almost certain to see Germany pitched against Russia, for the simple reason that neither state could permit the other to dominate its near-abroad.

That was the underlying logic of geopolitics in the region, even before the personality and goals of Hitler are factored into the equation. The folly of staking the future of British power on developments in this corner of the world should be obvious. Chamberlain himself intuitively felt that Britain 'should leave Eastern Europe to others'[145] and that 'we ought not be entangled in a war on account of Czechoslovakia'.[146] Later the Prime Minister indicated privately that for Germany 'to dominate' eastern Europe was acceptable, and not something that offended him.[147] Yet he was determined that union with Austria or the Germans in Czechoslovakia must not come through 'force'.[148] At the same time he doubted that there was 'any way of preventing German expansion into central Europe short of [Britain] using force' to stop it.[149] As if all that was not contradictory enough, Prime Minister went on that 'our policy ought to be to make [Germany gaining more territory] more difficult'.[150] Quite how these positions were to be reconciled, or whether even attempting to do so would precipitate disaster, was—and remains—unclear. Chamberlain was exasperated by Hitler's refusal to give way to him. His behaviour reads as that of a man convinced of his own capacity to address a problem that, deep down, he already viewed as insoluble. Chamberlain not only 'zigzagged' in terms of policy, but emotionally as well.

The lack of clarity in the British stance is striking. The conclusion must be that while the National Government had a series of *policies*—framed by a diverse range of influences, from personal vindication to the actions of foreign governments, financial pressures to sensitivities to the newspapers, Cabinet tensions to interpretations of public opinion—it did not have a *strategy*. Properly conceived, policy should serve strategy; strategy needs to come first, and underpin policy. Strategy also needs to be consistent. Yet this was not what was happening. The crux of the matter was this: either Britain had a vital interest in central and eastern Europe, or it did not. As we will see, Chamberlain's approach was to spend his time *insisting* that London did not, but then *behaving* in a way which strongly implied that it did.

6

A CACOPHONY OF VOICES

The Restoration of the Labour Party

This confusion abroad created political risks at home. One of these threats originated on the other side of the House of Commons, for in 1938 Chamberlain found himself facing a Labour party that was an increasingly formidable proposition. The Labour leaders had steered their party on a moderate path in the years following 1935, reconnecting with public opinion and gradually restoring credibility. Labour was now well positioned to exploit the difficulties of the National Government. Considering the size of the ministry's parliamentary majority, it seemed unlikely that Labour would win the next general election; but the period of de facto one-party politics wrought by Baldwin was coming to a close.

There were both foreign and domestic dimensions to this bid to restore Labour to the mainstream. Hugh Dalton stood at the centre of a bustling political laboratory aimed at furnishing the party with new ideas for domestic statecraft. He commissioned bright young intellectuals to undertake research projects, and looked to synthesize their findings. Dalton hit upon economic 'planning' as the keystone of Labour's approach. This was a seminal concept, highly mouldable and something that could perhaps win public support whilst simultaneously appealing to the instincts of the socialist mind. It stood for the technocratic and efficient guidance of the national economy by omniscient 'experts' in central government. It was founded on the belief that bureaucrats could identify objective, valid, and even scientific solutions to economic or social problems. 'Planning' was a theme Labour soon rallied behind. Dalton's campaign to rejuvenate the party culminated in the 1937 policy statement *Labour's Immediate Programme*. It was a landmark moment, a decisive break with the extremism of the early 1930s and setting out commitments that would shape Labour policy down to the Attlee government. Pamphlet versions of the *Immediate Programme* sold an incredible 700,000 copies.[1]

But it was international affairs that represented the government's most sensitive weak spot. Abyssinia, the Rhineland, and rearmament afforded Labour leaders the opportunity to talk about something that truly mattered. For moderate elements within the PLP and trade unions, the international crisis was therefore fortuitous. It permitted them to move on from interminable rows about whether the party should stand for 'the abolition of capitalism'. The fact that the party did not need to actually take responsibility for anything in foreign affairs, or grapple with diplomatic, military, or economic practicalities, provided a rhetorical freedom. Equally, however, it was an issue that Labour *had* to get right if the party was to convince voters of its viability as an alternative government. Labour propaganda enthusiastically charged the National Government with a variety of sins, from betraying the League to increasing the likelihood of war. The party could call for alliances without regard for their basis in reality. They could demand British armaments in one breath and global disarmament in another. Herbert Morrison could threaten the dictators with war to teach them a lesson but then advocate population transfers in order to defuse questions of ethnic self-determination.[2] Labour's statements did not need to be coherent; they merely needed to resonate.

Yet the process still took time. Almost everyone within the party spoke in, and was restricted by, the language of the League. Following the occupation of the Rhineland there was deep reticence about confrontation with Germany; even the more robust Labour figures such as Dalton were opposed to economic, let alone military, measures in response. Moreover, much of the Labour party interpreted international relations through an ideological prism of capitalist competition for money and markets, in which war was a by-product of economics. An entrenched Labour view was that increased defence spending would enrich arms manufac-turers and make a war for the capitalists more likely.[3] The new leader, Attlee, was at this stage either worryingly naive or keen to shore up his fragile position, for he made a series of speeches in which he talked a great deal but offered little of substance. In April 1936, Attlee delivered a radio broadcast in which he declared that investment in 'the instruments of death' was not the solution.[4] He charged that since Labour was removed from office in 1931, international stability had collapsed.[5] There needed to be a 'new world order' based, he said, on 'the brotherhood of man'.[6] 'National armaments' were not the answer; the choice was to 'co-operate or perish'.[7] The problem with the dictators was, he argued, that they were 'capitalist dictators'.[8] It is uncertain whether Attlee really believed what he was saying, or simply felt that he had to say it because his party wanted to hear it.

The radical mood within the party, partly incited by Cripps, thus remained a problem. In 1936 Cripps attracted the fury of the National Executive Committee (NEC) when publicly declaring that it would not 'be a bad thing for the British working class if Germany defeated us'.[9] As the threat to peace became more stark,

Cripps and his supporters among the rank-and-file began pressing for a 'Unity Campaign' in which their Socialist League (affiliated to the Labour party) would ally with the British Communist Party (a longstanding enemy of Labour) and the Independent Labour party (which had disaffiliated from Labour in 1932) in a 'United Front' against 'fascism, reaction and war'. Cripps rejected the League of Nations as a 'capitalist' and 'imperialist' organization; instead, he advocated a British alliance with the workers' paradise that was the Soviet Union. But the Unity Campaign was principally a vehicle to force Labour in a more radical direction and enhance the power of Cripps himself. It constituted attempted infiltration of an old-fashioned variety. In 1937, Cripps even began to finance a new socialist newspaper, *Tribune*, from his own pocket—to the tune of around £10,000—to propagate his worldview within the Labour movement.[10]

In this environment, much of the Labour party doggedly refused to take a realistic view of defence.[11] Labour MPs continued to oppose military spending; for many, opposition to armaments felt emotionally pleasing. But for hard-headed men like Bevin, Citrine, and Dalton, this was simple exhibitionism. To them there was no alternative to a major rearmament programme. Anything else made Labour seem weak on what was the major challenge of the decade. In the summer of 1936, Dalton therefore sought to persuade his colleagues not to oppose the government in the annual vote on the Service Estimates, in which the House of Commons granted the money required to finance the armed forces. Labour MPs traditionally voted against the Estimates, but Dalton advocated that they should instead abstain in order to register opposition to the government while not rejecting the principle of military spending.[12] Whichever course Labour chose, the vote would be a potent symbol of its stance. Damagingly, the PLP opposed the idea and voted against the Service Estimates as usual.[13] The public message this conveyed was that the Labour party opposed the maintenance of effective national defence.

Dalton despaired at the 'lame' decision, for it suggested Labour was in favour of 'unilateral disarmament'; the party was 'hopeless', he raged, and 'we shall be out for the rest of our lifetimes'.[14] In response Dalton redoubled his efforts, intriguing away for months behind the scenes. In October the NEC did pass a motion that 'the armed strength' of states 'loyal to the League . . . must be conditioned by the armed strength of the potential aggressors', but it still refused to support rearmament until the National Government devised a foreign policy of which Labour approved.[15] It was an unconvincing attempt to obscure the divisions within the party, as was a resolution from the National Council of Labour—which linked the Labour party with trade union leaders—that 'this country should make its proper contribution to the collective forces which are necessary for the preservation of peace'.[16] Dalton and

Bevin began plotting a confrontation with Cripps, the union boss determined to ask him directly, 'Do you want us to win or not? What are you playing at?'.[17]

In March 1937 an important blow was struck when the NEC rejected calls for the United Front and disaffiliated the Socialist League from the party. The fact that Cripps was using it for his own ends led Dalton to speak of a 'rich man's toy'.[18] Disaffiliated, the League opted to disband itself. Then, crucially, in the summer of 1937, after a year of work Dalton this time managed to narrowly persuade the PLP to abstain on the Service Estimates in Parliament rather than oppose them.[19] This was a bold declaration of Labour's political credibility, one that altered public perceptions. Its ambient effect was important: a few months later, the party conference at Bournemouth endorsed rearmament by a majority of more than 8:1. Dalton unapologetically told the delegates that 'In this most grim situation . . . our country must be powerfully armed'.[20] The socialist intellectual Harold Laski considered Dalton to be Labour's version of 'the Devil',[21] while, in the view of Cripps, Dalton's aim in politics was 'to become the government'.[22] He meant this disparagingly—endeavouring to get into office has always offended some within the Labour party—but Dalton would have embraced the description. He had spearheaded the development of more appealing domestic policies, and, as Shadow Foreign Secretary, Dalton was the author of nearly all significant Labour statements on foreign policy in the late 1930s. Though too combative to be leader himself, Dalton was the most important politician in the Labour party during the period between 1932 and 1938. Nobody had done more to defeat the extremists, bring Labour back to reality, and furnish it with a viable platform on the major policy challenges of the era. By 1938, Labour was ready to take on the National Government and attack the foundations of Conservative hegemony. All the party needed was an opportunity. It did not have to wait for long.

'A Very Troubled World'

The execution of the *Anschluss* represented an ominous development.[23] It under-scored Hitler's ambition to challenge the Versailles order with a directness that even the most sanguine observer had no choice but to absorb. Across Europe, startled governments and anxious publics pondered what the Fuhrer's subsequent move might be. Many suspected that neighbouring Czechoslovakia—the final democracy in eastern Europe—would be next. Czechoslovakia ruled over the Sudetenland and 3.5 million Germans living within it, and promising to redress this had been a regular feature of Hitler's speeches. Sure enough, in the spring of 1938 the Fuhrer began demanding the incorporation of the Sudetenland into the Reich.

There was now a growing conviction across the spectrum that the Cabinet should draw a line in the diplomatic sand. Indeed, just two days after German forces entered Austria, Churchill called for the formation of a 'Grand Alliance' which would consist of 'a number of states assembled around Great Britain and France'.[24] The centrality of foreign affairs to British politics thus became ever more pressing. As we have seen, it had been selected as a theme for conducting personal and party warfare. The issues of foreign policy served as ideal rhetorical cudgels. Malice was at least as important as belief, and there was a striking coincidence between the policy positions professed and the political self-interest of those who held to them. In truth, geopolitical crisis was ideal for this, for speculating about the fates of nations and empires elevated political conflict from its normal humdrum routines and invested it with a sense of the epic.

The Prime Minister himself considered the possibility of 'the Grand Alliance', only to dismiss it: 'it is a very attractive idea; indeed there is almost everything to be said for it until you come to examine its practicability. From that moment its attraction vanishes'. There was 'nothing' that Britain and France could do to save Czechoslovakia from being overrun if Hitler 'wanted to do it'.[25] The Czechs were surrounded on three sides by Germany.[26] But German designs on Czechoslovakia still threatened to trigger a general European conflict, for the French had a treaty of alliance with Prague as part of their network of alliances on the Reich's eastern front. If Germany violated Czech territory and Paris honoured its obligations, France and Germany would be at war. In such a scenario, the Soviet Union would also be obligated by treaty to join the conflict under the Franco-Soviet agreement of 1935. The crisis thus threatened to spiral into a major conflict.

Chamberlain felt not 'the slightest confidence' in the reliability of the French government.[27] He was also acutely aware from British intelligence that the Kremlin was 'stealthily and cunningly pulling all the strings behind the scenes to get us involved in war with Germany'. The great paranoiac Stalin had recently purged the Red Army of approximately 65 per cent of its officers, with grave implications for combat readiness. He wanted someone else take the lead against Germany. Meanwhile the British Ambassador in Prague bluntly advised London that 'Czechoslovakia's present position' over the Sudeten Germans was 'not permanently tenable'.[28] Importantly, public opinion—though less idealistic than at the time of the Peace Ballot in 1935—did not favour plunging into a war over the issue. Another consideration was that, as we have seen, defence planning deliberately concentrated resources on the RAF and Royal Navy, and did not envisage sending the army to fight a continental war in central Europe.

All of this strongly implies that Britain's national interest *did not* lie in issuing a guarantee of Czechoslovakia's territorial integrity. To Chamberlain, calls for a Grand Alliance from critics at Westminster were thus opportunistic 'twaddle . . . calculated to vex the man who has to take responsibility for the consequences'. Given that there was no way to prevent Germany from invading her Czechoslovakian neighbour, no appetite from regional states to permit Red Army forces to march onto their territory, and no desire in London to do Stalin's work for him, the real question was whether Britain was going to use Czechoslovakia 'as a pretext' for war with Berlin. As Chamberlain had no intention of doing so, he wrote that 'I have abandoned any idea of giving guarantees to Czechoslovakia'.[29] The Cabinet concurred. Appropriating Bismarck's famous remark about the Balkans, Halifax and senior colleagues took the view that 'Czechoslovakia is not worth the bones of a single British grenadier'.[30]

The Foreign Secretary recommended advising Prague to seek 'the best terms' they could from Germany over the Sudeten territory.[31] Yet, presciently, Halifax also warned of what was now in danger of coming to pass: that by engaging in diplomatic interventions beyond its own sphere of interest and seeking to control interstate relations in eastern Europe, London might easily provoke the Fuhrer into concluding that Britain was his most dangerous adversary and turn West instead of East.[32]

When the Prime Minister revealed the government's policy to the House of Commons on 24 March 1938, his statement demonstrated a simultaneous determination to evade a conflict that was not in Britain's interests but also his lack of clarity about whether Hitler's *methods* should be a basis for war. And he signalled his sensitivity to political criticism at home. Speaking from the dispatch box, Chamberlain expounded each of Britain's legal obligations under treaties, including to the League Covenant and to defend Belgium and France from unprovoked aggression. Czechoslovakia did not constitute one of those obligations. The message was that Britain was not compelled to go to war simply because France had guaranteed a third-party state. Yet, seeking to both deter Hitler and hold the line at home, Chamberlain was also deliberately ambiguous. While he refused to offer a guarantee of Czechoslovakian independence, he stated that 'if war broke out' it would be 'quite impossible to say where it might end' and 'what governments might become involved'.[33] This was a crucial hint. The relentless public discussion of foreign affairs since 1935, and the enthusiasm with which critics of the government had taken up the theme, created a febrile atmosphere in which standing aside had become politically impossible. Chamberlain knew that.

The speech was well received in Parliament and the press. It thus served its principal purpose: to reinforce Chamberlain's authority at a moment of turbulence by giving the impression that he was in control of events. However, while Chamberlain hoped that ambiguity might deter Germany, his posture also signalled personal indecision. If the Prime Minister really wanted to find an exit from central European affairs, a looming conflict between Germany and the Franco-Soviet-Czech alliance bloc was arguably the ideal opportunity. It was one in which Britain had no direct stake and could justifiably stand back. Yet the Prime Minister failed to seize the opportunity.

This was underlined two months later, in May 1938, when it seemed that Hitler might invade the Sudetenland. Halifax warned Hitler's Foreign Minister, Joachim von Ribbentrop, that Germany should 'not count upon this country to stand aside'.[34] Berlin never intended to invade in May and the scare passed, but Britain's response was important. The government had taken a stand and threatened Germany. Against his own strategic inclinations about the region—but consistent with both his self-assurance that *he* could solve the continent's ills and the political atmosphere at home—Chamberlain effectively erected Britain as a barrier in central Europe. It was a bizarre state of affairs. As Halifax put it, talking tough meant that across the continent the impression took hold that 'we [have] ... committed ourselves morally ... to intervene if there is a European war'. British involvement in regional diplomacy had made 'a much deeper impression' than was intended, and 'we are certainly regarded as now being ... deeply committed'.[35] Hitler was furious, perceiving himself as suffering 'a loss of prestige' due to the British warning which 'he is not willing to suffer again'.[36] Halifax could complain that 'we do not wish to be manoeuvred into the position of arbitrator', but that was exactly what was happening.[37]

Chamberlain was eager to escape the dangerous situation in which he now found himself. Over the summer months he began pressing Prague to improve its treatment of the German minority—warning that if they failed to do so, Britain would not support them. But Hitler had already instructed the leaders of the German minority to avoid any lessening of tensions with the Prague government, in order to preserve a state of hostility that would provide a pretext for intervention. The Fuhrer told the generals it was his 'unalterable will' to 'smash Czechoslovakia' by the end of 1938.[38] Inexorably drawn in, Chamberlain was desperately trying to resolve a political and racial crisis that the local parties had decided should not be resolved. He had deeply invested Britain's credibility in the effort. And he had no way out. Either the National Government was committed to deterring Hitler over a border that it did not actually support, or it was not. The Prime Minister appeared unable to make up his mind.

Conservative Concerns

Nor, it must be said, could anyone else. Nobody at Westminster wanted war. Even Churchill argued that the Czechs 'owe it to the Western powers that every concession compatible with the sovereignty and integrity of their state shall be made, and made promptly'.[39] Yet the intensity of criticism continued to grow. A sense developed that Chamberlain was in danger of 'splitting the country' and alienating public opinion by accepting repeated humiliation in eastern Europe.[40] Importantly, concern about this began to engender anxiety inside the Cabinet. By May 1938, Halifax was apparently worried the National Government was losing 'touch with the floating vote' and that 'the P.M.'s methods were unlikely to retrieve this'.[41] He felt that the ministry was 'too narrow'.[42] An editorial in The Times warned that the government was becoming too divisive.[43]

The Foreign Secretary was concerned by Chamberlain's overt partisan point-scoring in parliamentary debate and 'the harm' that resulted from him 'hitting up' the Labour party at every opportunity; this only ensured that foreign affairs remained a dangerous political football. Halifax, in contrast, favoured a more emollient approach on Baldwinian lines. Harvey sensed that Halifax 'wants to set himself as free as possible to correct the partisanship of the P.M'.[44] The Foreign Secretary was concerned that 'public opinion' was being driven by emotional 'anti-dictator feeling' and feared this might bounce the government into diplomatic commitments which Britain would 'bitterly regret'.[45] He was already hoping for Eden to return to the Cabinet to broaden the government's base.[46] Baldwin, watching from retirement, was suspected of sharing these fears.[47] He was apparently angry that 'all my work in keeping politics national instead of party' was being 'undone'.[48] When Sir Horace Wilson requested that Baldwin give a speech praising Chamberlain, he refused.[49] Chamberlain engendered 'unbelievable . . . personal dislike' among opponents and was deeply 'sarcastic'; his 'cold intellect' saw him 'beat [people] up in argument'.[50] The Prime Minister himself privately acknowledged that he could seem 'pompous'.[51] Three seats were lost to Labour in by-elections during the spring of 1938, and the MP Harold Nicolson predicted that 'the whole show is going to crack up'.[52] Inside the Cabinet, the First Lord of the Admiralty, Duff Cooper, and the President of the Board, Oliver Stanley, both favoured an unequivocal declaration that a German invasion of Czechoslovakia would trigger British intervention.

In this climate, Sir Samuel Hoare began to ponder if the Prime Minister might fall and whether he might be the one to replace him. He was 'very worried' about the government's credibility on the incendiary issue of rearmament, and thought it necessary that the Cabinet take firm action to 'hurry' the military build-up.[53] Now ensconced at the Home Office, he began putting out feelers to supporters about a bid for the premiership. Hoare was, in the words of one historian, a 'trimmer' and a 'multi-purpose politician'.[54] His range of ministerial experience was the strongest in the National Government, and he had done much to restore his reputation following the disaster of the Hoare–Laval Pact. A year at the Admiralty was spent overseeing the expansion and modernization of the Royal Navy, and at the Home Office he implemented major reforms to workplace law. Hoare was below Chamberlain and Halifax in the Conservative party hierarchy, but, crucially, the latter was a peer. Many judged that it would be impossible for an unelected figure, absent from the House of Commons, to become Prime Minister in the democratic age.

Beaverbrook and 'Chips' Channon both favoured Hoare as successor, and discovered that 'even more convinced than we are that Sam Hoare is the PM's logical successor is Sam Hoare himself'. To that end, he sought 'advice' from Lord Beaverbrook on 'how he might become the recognised Heir-Apparent'.[55] It would also be natural if Hoare harboured resentment at Chamberlain's role in forcing his resignation in December 1935. Chamberlain had once been Hoare's closest friend in politics—'Sam and Neville always hunted together',[56] one observer noted, and every morning the two walked around St James's Park, with their wives strolling behind—and it seems likely that Sam felt abandoned by his comrade. Hoare had also been lined up to take the post of Minister for Coordination of Defence in March 1936 before Chamberlain persuaded Baldwin to appoint Inskip instead.[57] He went to the Admiralty shortly thereafter, but it seems unlikely that Sam forgot this. And when Chamberlain became Prime Minister in May 1937, Hoare coveted the Treasury and expected Neville to appoint him Chancellor.[58] That did not transpire either. By the summer of 1938, Hoare felt a declining inclination to prop up a Prime Minister whom he was hoping to replace.

'The Zigzags and Shifts of British Policy!'

On 7 September 1938, a holidaying Chamberlain was indulging his favourite pastime of fishing in a Scottish stream when he was suddenly recalled to Downing Street. The long-expected German invasion of Czechoslovakia now seemed imminent.[59] As foreign policy and domestic political calculation once again collided, this heralded an important mutation in the balance of power inside the Cabinet. Halifax—who described himself as 'groping in the dark like a blind man trying to find his way across a bog'[60]—now advocated that the Cabinet dispatch a clear message to Hitler calling for a negotiated solution and warning that if he became involved in war with France over Czechoslovakia, Britain would be forced to intervene against Germany. This was a crucial decision. Effectively, Halifax favoured clarity whereas Chamberlain did not. It was the first step in his gradual shift away from the Prime Minister. The Foreign Secretary's decision left Chamberlain isolated, and the Prime Minister was compelled to agree to issue an ultimatum to Berlin. Chamberlain clearly believed that his ally was cracking under the pressure: the atmosphere was 'enough to send most people off their heads', he wrote, at least those whose heads 'were not as well screwed on as mine'.[61]

People certainly did seem to be on the verge of going 'off their heads'. When the ambassador to Germany, Sir Nevile Henderson, received the ultimatum, he flatly refused to convey it to Ribbentrop on the grounds that it might tip Hitler over the edge.[62] A highly strung man whose nerves were failing under the enormous strain of conducting diplomacy in Nazi-ruled Berlin, Henderson even wanted the press to write up the Fuhrer as 'the apostle of peace'.[63] In the Foreign Office, Harvey feared Hitler had staked so much social capital on the Sudeten issue that he would choose war over a humiliation that might bring down the Nazi regime.[64] Meanwhile, outside the government Churchill, other Conservative dissidents, and the Labour party all issued dire warnings against 'weakness'.[65] There seemed to be no route forward or back.

In an increasingly bleak atmosphere—and with his Foreign Secretary fast emerging as an independent force—Chamberlain entertained an idea 'so unconventional and daring' that it 'took Halifax's breath away'.[66] He called it 'Plan Z'. This was that he might personally fly to Germany to meet Hitler and try to broker peace. Unscheduled summit diplomacy became common in the second half of the twentieth century, but at the time was fairly unusual. The idea was a closely guarded secret; besides Halifax only Simon, Wilson, and Henderson were told of it.[67] It opened up the possibility that the Prime Minister might be able to regain personal control by going to see Hitler and 'sav[ing] the situation at the 11th hour'.[68] Overestimating his own abilities as much as ever, Chamberlain persuaded himself that such a move might bring 'about a complete change in the international situation'.[69] He was conscious that 'many, including Winston', were lining up to exploit the crisis;[70] indeed, after a Cabinet meeting at Downing Street, the Prime Minister found Churchill waiting outside in the corridor and demanding that Britain dispatch 'an immediate ultimatum' to Berlin.[71] As he told his sister on 11 September, he was not prepared to 'allow the most vital decision that any country could take, the decision as to peace or war, to pass out of our own hands into those of the ruler of a foreign country' and, in Hitler, 'a lunatic at that'.[72] Yet if that was the case, Chamberlain should surely have taken the decision out of Hitler's hands, either by making clear that Britain would fight or signalling that the issue was one for the regional states to resolve themselves. The fatal ambiguity persisted.

The following day, Hitler made a speech at the Nazi party's annual gathering, the Nuremberg Rally, in which he called for self-determination for the Sudeten Germans and pledged support for their cause. In effect, he was demanding that Czechoslovakia agree to be carved in two. This was the final push the Prime Minister needed. Twenty-four hours later, Chamberlain put Plan Z into effect and telegraphed to the Fuhrer that he would fly to Germany to meet him: 'In view of increasingly critical situation I propose to come over at once to see you . . . I propose to come across by air and am ready to start tomorrow'.[73] This message came as a deep shock to Hitler, but faced with a confrontation with the British Empire he accepted. Chamberlain did not tell the Cabinet about Plan Z until Hitler had already given his assent; there was to be no opportunity for quibbling. Hoare thought Chamberlain was 'taking a great political risk', for he was 'likely to fail'.[74]

On 15 September, therefore, Chamberlain boarded a British Airways Lockheed 10-A aircraft at Heston and flew to Munich. His most trusted adviser, Sir Horace Wilson, accompanied him. Upon landing in Germany, the British party found themselves greeted by cheering crowds; the Nazis most likely choreographed this spectacle in order to play on Chamberlain's vanity. From there the Prime Minister was driven to Hitler's residence in the Bavarian Alps, around sixty miles away. High in the mountains at Berchtesgaden, Chamberlain finally came face to face with the man who had so vexed him over the previous sixteen months. The Prime Minister's proposal to break the logjam was to hold plebiscites in the Sudeten territories on the question of either remaining part of Czechoslovakia or joining Germany. Seeing as the people would inevitably vote for independence from Czechoslovakia, this was a device to incorporate them into the Reich without bloodshed. He was additionally willing to offer a guarantee of what remained of the Czech state, if such a guarantee was also signed by Germany, France, and Russia. Chamberlain believed that by travelling to Germany he had staged a 'coup' with 'dramatic force'. The Prime Minister discerned an opportunity to shape the future of Europe.

Yet locked alone with Hitler in a summit meeting that lasted for three hours, with only an interpreter for company, the Prime Minister's weaknesses—disdain for others, conceit about his own abilities, and susceptibility to flattery—all came to the fore. He thought Hitler looked 'entirely undistinguished' when he first met him: 'you . . . would take him for the house painter he once was'.[75] He struck Chamberlain as 'the commonest looking little dog' he had ever seen.[76] In reality, the Fuhrer was an opportunistic gambler who was willing to lie through his teeth. After ranting about the Czechs, Hitler said that he was intent on absorbing the Sudetenland into the Reich and 'prepared to risk a world war' to that end. Yet he also persuaded Chamberlain that he was willing to find a peaceful solution if the British accepted the principle of self-determination for the Sudeten Germans. The Prime Minister responded that his 'personal opinion' was 'I didn't care two hoots whether the Sudetens were in the Reich or out of it'; he was merely concerned with *how* changes were made.[77] Chamberlain proposed going back to London to consult with his colleagues, as well as the French and the Czechs. He promised to return to Germany to meet Hitler again.

Hitler had played on his interlocutor's evident desperation for peace, so much so that Chamberlain came away from Berchtesgaden with the feeling that 'here was a man who could be relied upon when he had given his word'. The Fuhrer buttered him up even more by letting it be known that he was 'very favourably impressed' with Chamberlain, and thought that the Prime Minister was not only 'a man' but one 'with whom I can do business'.[78] Chamberlain heard that 'I am the most popular man in Germany!' Wilson had him believing that he had overseen 'a bold master-stroke in diplomacy'.[79] Such flattery was music to his ears; and the notion that he had scored a major diplomatic success was quickly reinforced by the 'wonderful letters' he received at Downing Street, with gifts 'rain[ing] in' from people thanking him for averting war.[80]

Chamberlain had taken Britain to the precipice of war over a principle that the National Government did not even stand for. It was a baffling position at the time, and remains so decades later. Czechoslovakia was going to be subjected to coercive diplomacy one way or the other; the only concern was whether a plebiscite might provide a device to hide the embarrassment. If this seems to be a strange question on which to rest the whole future of British power, such was the overwhelming self-assurance of Neville Chamberlain and the ascendancy of liberal rhetoric at home. What the Prime Minister wanted to do was to 'go far beyond the present crisis' and effect a permanent improvement in Anglo-German relations.[81] If that was his objective, exactly how meddling in central Europe would contribute to it remained unclear.

This was even more dangerous in an environment in which the French—relieved at being able to pass the diplomatic buck to Britain—were seeking to evade their treaty obligations to Prague. On 18 September the Daladier government in Paris insisted that the plebiscites be abandoned, and Sudeten territory where German-speakers were in the majority simply be ceded to the Reich. This was a blatant abandonment of an ally. The French also proposed that the existing Czechoslovak-ian alliance with France be replaced by an *international* guarantee of the new border. The exact location of this boundary would be determined by an international

117

commission. For his part, Chamberlain was content with this change. Prague was predictably furious, only to be told that if they did not accede to the loss of German-speaking territory they would need to resist Hitler alone. Unwilling to either fight or wash his hands of the region, Chamberlain's hesitant strategizing had not only weakened the Franco-Soviet-Czech alliance that confronted Germany and pinned Britain down in central Europe against its own national interests, it now implicated London in the dishonour of carving up the last remaining democracy in that region. It was an unedifying spectacle. But at home Chamberlain had already 'cut away the ground' upon which his critics stood by informing the Cabinet that the French were unlikely to honour their alliance with Prague.[82] In effect, the Prime Minister was offering his colleagues a choice: his solution, or nothing. When Oliver Stanley complained that he would have preferred 'a different policy', Chamberlain retorted, 'What policy was that?'[83] The question prompted only silence.

Figure 1. Map of the British Empire, 1937.

READY !

" COME THE THREE CORNERS OF THE WORLD IN ARMS,
AND WE SHALL SHOCK THEM : NOUGHT SHALL MAKE US RUE,
IF ENGLAND TO ITSELF DO REST BUT TRUE."—*King John*, Act V., Scene 7.

Figure 2. Britannia standing guard over the realm's frontiers, *Punch*, 18 January 1896.

Figure 3. Stanley Baldwin, January 1923.

Figure 4. Left to right: Mrs Lucy Baldwin, Stanley Baldwin, and Neville Chamberlain, 24 June 1937.

STILL HOPE

Figure 5. Chamberlain as the Dove of Peace, *Punch*, 21 September 1938.

Figure 6. Sir Horace Wilson, *c.*1939.

Figure 7. Neville Chamberlain at Heston aerodrome after returning from the Munich summit with Hitler, 30 September 1938. In his hand is the Anglo-German declaration, signed by Hitler. Viscount Halifax appears at the far left of the image.

Figure 8. Neville Chamberlain, bronze medal by Victor Damanet, 1938. Produced to mark Chamberlain's negotiation of the Munich agreement. The style is deliberately reminiscent of that used to depict emperors and kings on coins.

A FAMILY VISIT

"It was a great work, and I wish you could now add another chapter to your own career."

Figure 9. Winston Churchill and his ancestor, John Churchill, 1st Duke of Marlborough, *Punch*, 2 November 1938.

Figure 10. Clement Attlee addressing a crowd in Hyde Park, *c.*1935.

Figure 11. Ernest Bevin, no date.

Figure 12. Clement Attlee and Arthur Greenwood arriving at 10 Downing Street, 1939.

THE OLD SEA-DOG

" Any telegram for me? "

Figure 13. Winston Churchill as Sir Francis Drake, *Punch*, 12 July 1939.

Figure 14. John Martin, *The Destruction of Pompei and Herculaneum*, 1822. The image of disaster and destruction vividly evokes the themes explored in this book.

7

WHO GOVERNS BRITAIN?

'The Flowers Have Shed Their Petals and the Fires Died Out'

With the framework for a deal in place, a confident Chamberlain flew back to meet Hitler at Bad Godesberg on 22 September.[1] Upon his arrival he was surprised to find the Fuhrer extremely angry. Hitler considered the boundary commission a device to frustrate him from annexing the Sudeten territory, rather than the flimsy fig-leaf it actually was. 'With some heat' he told Chamberlain that in six days he would order the *Wehrmacht* to cross the border and seize the disputed territory. This threatened to toss the Prime Minister from the tightrope he was walking. A shaken Chamberlain expressed his 'disappointment', complaining that he was only a mediator and had 'take[n] his political life into his hands' in pursuit of a deal that would satisfy Berlin. He said that 'public opinion in England' would turn against him. The Fuhrer was unmoved. Chamberlain, Wilson, and the rest of the team spent hours poring over a vast map of the disputed territory produced by Hitler; it was hard work and they were all 'exhausted'.[2]

Sensing that his authority was evaporating, a desperate Chamberlain unilaterally deviated from the position agreed with the Cabinet, France, and the Czechs. He told Hitler that the international guarantee of the rump Czechoslovakia did not mean that the borders could not be revised *again* to Germany's benefit in the future.[3] Chamberlain possessed no mandate or authority to dangle still more of Czechoslovakia before the Fuhrer; yet he did so regardless. Hitler then brazenly introduced a long list of fresh objections to a peaceful settlement, outlining a range of areas in which the Czechs were allegedly untrustworthy. The reality is that Hitler wanted a rapid solution and, recognizing that Chamberlain had come too far to turn back, was willing to gamble on achieving complete satisfaction.

Back in Britain, the situation was equally ominous for the government. A march through Westminster on the evening of 22 September drew thousands of people onto the streets calling for the government to support Czechoslovakia. There were demands from the marchers that 'Chamberlain must go', a personalization of the issue invited by the Prime Minister's own conduct. Public opinion was now plainly a serious problem. The Labour party was in full cry over the crisis: Attlee informed Halifax that if Czechoslovakia was attacked and France honoured its treaty commitments to that country, Britain should declare war alongside the French.[4] Meanwhile Conservative dissidents were also preparing for a showdown in Parliament. Harold Nicolson recognized that this was a world in which foreign policy had been 'popularized', something that yielded acute problems due to the 'emotional fluctuations' in British opinion: 'our external relations have been brought down from the Cabinet room to the arena of party controversy'.[5] Popular opinion 'oscillates from one emotion to another'.[6] Lord Robert Cecil of the League of Nations Union (LNU) was positively demented with fury. The British ambassador to Washington, Lord Lothian, thought that Cecil was 'the real war mind . . . in Europe today'.[7] At the Foreign Office, meanwhile, there was agreement that, for 'internal political reasons', Chamberlain definitely needed to be seen as firm with Hitler.[8] The tide had well and truly turned.

In response, Halifax once again adopted an independent posture. He telegraphed Chamberlain to say that he was 'profoundly disturbed' by the new policy, for Britain was being put in the position of presiding over a dissection of Czechoslovakia.[9] Hoare 'strongly endorsed' this criticism.[10] And many Conservative MPs seemed 'appalled by the force of opinion' in their constituencies.[11] The Foreign Secretary informed Chamberlain that public, party, and Cabinet opinion were all against the deal in which the Prime Minister had effectively trapped the country.[12] He bluntly warned Chamberlain that the 'great mass' of opinion was 'hardening' to the view that 'we have gone to the limit of concession'.[13] This was probably Halifax's *own* opinion as much as anyone else's; he had already tried to discover whether the Soviets would be willing to fight if Germany invaded Czechoslovakia.[14] Halifax suggested recommending to Prague that they should mobilize the Czechoslovakian army.[15] He wanted Chamberlain to inform the Fuhrer that if Germany refused a peaceful solution there must be war.[16] The Prime Minister was clearly losing control of the home front—and, most worryingly, his Foreign Secretary.

Faced with Halifax's revolt, Chamberlain panicked. If he lost control of the Cabinet, he would be finished. Pondering what to do, the Prime Minister decided to dash back to London after just one day in Germany.[17] He arrived in Downing Street around lunchtime on 24 September. There he found the Cabinet intimidated by the climate of public opinion and opposed to forcing the Czechs to accept the decapitation of their country at the barrel of a gun. The Labour leaders were making hay, warning against a 'shameful surrender' and emphasizing Britain's 'moral obligations'. They claimed there was a 'strong feeling of shame and humiliation throughout the nation' and called upon ministers to 'stand fast for peace and freedom'.[18] It was Labour's best opportunity since 1931 to capture public opinion, and ministers were frightened.

Churchill was also quick to rally the troops, inviting dissidents to his flat on 22 September. Nicolson told him 'this is hell. It is the end of the British Empire'.[19] Winston was unsurprisingly eager to exploit Chamberlain's discomfort. Brooding at Chartwell earlier in the year, Churchill instinctively appreciated that his only chance to get back into office was if 'the foreign situation darkens'. In that case, a new government 'may be forced upon us'; 'but events, and great events alone, will rule'.[20] With 'great events' clearly afoot in September, Churchill began chipping away at the Prime Minister. Since 1936 he had hit upon airpower, defence deficiencies, and collective security as valuable political assets, for they combined issues of genuine public fear with a rhetoric that would play well on the government benches. He carefully selected policy dilemmas that would animate opposition to the Cabinet. Major increases in defence spending to compensate for Britain's military weakness made it appear that Churchill had a panicked government on the run. Now, Winston began to convert this into an overt critique of Chamberlain's leadership. During a private thirty-minute meeting with the Prime Minister, Chamberlain assured him that the Fuhrer was 'sincere'. Churchill replied by 'reminding him that there were some sixteen occasions on which Hitler had solemnly made promises which he had broken'.[21] He thought Plan Z 'the stupidest thing that has ever been done'.[22] And Churchill felt that 'everything depends' on 'the willingness of the Czechs to fight at all costs', for such a scenario would inevitably drag in France and Britain. Chamberlain had devised a 'miserable plan', with Churchill anticipating that it would 'loose a tremendous campaign' at home and 'the country will split'.[23]

Predicting that Hitler's ambitions went far beyond a border dispute with Czecho-slovakia, Churchill told the press that:

> It is necessary the nation should realise the magnitude of the disaster into which we are being led. The partition of Czechoslovakia under Anglo-French pressure amounts to a complete surrender...to the Nazi threat of force...The idea that safety can be purchased through throwing a small state to the wolves is a fatal delusion.[24]

This kind of crisis cast Churchill in the best possible light. His propensity for soaring oratory and purple prose seemed eccentric during normal times, but moments in which the fate of nations hung in the balance enabled Churchill to suddenly resemble a giant from the pages of history bestriding the contemporary stage. This was, of course, an impression that the Duke of Marlborough's descendant deliberately cultivated. Winston's use of prophetic tones and tendency to paint even small episodes as an epic crossroad of world history was unique. He advised that 'a solemn warning' should be presented to Berlin making clear that an 'invasion of Czechoslovakia' would 'be taken as an act of war'.[25] As one of the best speakers in Parliament and a Westminster veteran, Churchill's public pronouncements always garnered widespread attention. He declared that 'the government had to choose between war and shame. They have chosen shame and they will get war'.[26] Exploring an alliance with Labour, Churchill raved that 'at the next general election he would speak on every socialist platform in the country against the government'.[27]

Several ministers, including Duff Cooper, Leslie Hore-Belisha, and Oliver Stanley, advocated mobilizing the British military.[28] Feeling his power slipping away, Chamberlain dug his heels in and explained to the Cabinet that Hitler had 'certain standards'. Though 'violently prejudiced' he 'would not deliberately deceive a man whom he respected . . . and [Chamberlain] was sure Herr Hitler now felt some respect for him'. The Prime Minister assured his colleagues that Hitler's ambitions did not extend beyond the Sudetenland; he knew this because the Fuhrer had told him so.[29] Some members of the Cabinet, particularly Cooper and Hore-Belisha, were incredulous. Hoare, probably keen to create political distance between himself and the Prime Minister, argued that the Cabinet would 'find difficulty' in securing popular support for Hitler's proposals.[30] Listening to the Prime Minister from the far end of the Cabinet room, the civil servant Alexander Cadogan recorded in his diary that Hitler 'has evidently hypnotised him'.[31]

But Viscount Halifax had not been hypnotized; far from it. For weeks Foreign Office officials such as Cadogan, Harvey, and Vansittart had been stoking his fears. The same day as the Cabinet meeting, the Czech ambassador forced an embarrassed and chastened Halifax to agree that the British Prime Minister was reduced to being 'an errand boy' for a 'killer and brigand'.[32] That night, the Foreign Secretary struggled to sleep; he woke at 1.00 a.m. and thereafter rest eluded him.[33] Halifax eventually resolved to come out openly against Chamberlain. This was a crucial step. At another Cabinet meeting the next day, Halifax declared that he opposed cajoling the Prague government to accept Hitler's demands.[34] The Foreign Secretary was recorded as declaring, 'Yesterday he felt that the difference between [the original proposals and Hitler's new demands] did not involve a new acceptance of principle. *He was not quite sure, however, that he still held that view*'.[35]

This was a bombshell tossed into Chamberlain's lap. Halifax appreciated that British policy now lacked credibility, and there would be consequences—both internationally and at home—for this perceived weakness. It was a *political* intervention, too, not a strategic conversion. As Halifax told Maisky, the conceptual keystone of his view of international relations was that 'the world is witnessing the struggle of two ideological fronts—fascism and communism. We . . . support neither one nor the other'.[36] Logically, then, this was not something that need involve Britain. And he had wanted the French to extricate themselves from their commitment to Czechoslovakia lest it embroil Britain in war. The strategic logic of the Foreign Secretary's position was that the British should stand well back from a region in which the leading Fascist and Communist powers appeared destined to come to blows. Yet, for reasons of presentation and prestige—the primacy of politics, in other words—Halifax recognized the imperative of being seen to take a firmer line, and impressed this upon the Cabinet.

There may have been another element to Halifax's decision, as well. As his biographer Andrew Roberts observed, at this moment he would have had to be 'superhuman not to have let personal political calculations enter his reasoning'.[37] Chamberlain's support within the government was disintegrating. Having lost Eden in February, he could hardly afford to drive out another Foreign Secretary in September. Halifax was twelve years younger than Chamberlain and commanded tremendous respect within the Conservative party. Meanwhile public opinion was hardening against a diplomatic coercion of the Czechs. By lining up against Chamberlain, Halifax would, at the very least, exert considerable leverage; and he could conceivably become Prime Minister himself should Chamberlain fall.

Halifax told the Cabinet that, because Britain had involved itself in the matter and implored the Czechs to give up the Sudetenland, a 'moral obligation rested upon us'.[38] The decision to resist should be one for Prague alone to make, and if they opted for war 'he imagined that France should join in', and in that case 'we should join them'. Most damagingly, Halifax said that he was 'not quite sure' that his 'mind' and that of the Prime Minister were still working as 'one'. This was a symbolic act of detachment from Chamberlain; a statesman as experienced as the Foreign Secretary knew exactly what he was doing when he uttered these words during a Cabinet meeting. Halifax now went still further and outlined what he described as his 'ultimate aim'—'the destruction of Nazism'.[39] This was not a view he had expressed before, and one that constituted a dramatic political leap by the Foreign Secretary. In the spring of 1940, after pondering Halifax's behaviour for a long time, 'Chips' Channon concluded that he possessed 'eel-like qualities', and a capacity for 'sublime treachery which is never deliberate and, always to him, a necessity dictated by a situation'.[40]

Halifax's act of sabotage was debilitating to Chamberlain, who passed a note to his Foreign Secretary saying that it constituted 'a horrible blow to me'.[41] He implied that he would rather quit the premiership than go to war. The Cabinet revealed itself to be split in half as to whether the Czechoslovakians should be strong-armed into accepting the deal. And three other ministers were contemplating resignation. Meanwhile, on 26 September, Churchill and his fellow plotters on the backbenches— Cecil, Lloyd, Amery, Nicolson, Sinclair, Bracken, Lindemann, Bob Boothby, and Harold Macmillan—agreed that 'if Chamberlain rats again' they would 'form a united block against him'. Even if he did not 'rat', 'we shall press for a coalition government and the immediate application of war measures';[42] presumably there would be posts for themselves in such a new regime. As one member, Amery, put it, the group was a 'queer collection' of the 'usual . . . conspirators'.[43] Lloyd George, still friends with Churchill and still the senior partner in that relationship, was even roped in.[44] Opposition to the Prime Minister was coalescing across the spectrum.

Compelled to retreat before Halifax, a weakened Chamberlain agreed that Britain should leave it up to Prague to decide for themselves what to do.[45] The same day, Czechoslovakia rejected the terms demanded at Bad Godesberg. Halifax also pressured Chamberlain—who was exhausted and felt 'all over the place'—to go on the radio and affirm that if France went to war over Czechoslovakia, Britain would follow.[46] With trepidation the Prime Minister capitulated to this drastic reversal. Without consulting Chamberlain, Halifax also had the Foreign Office release a statement declaring that if Germany invaded Czechoslovakia, 'the immediate result must be that France will come to her assistance, and Great Britain and Russia will certainly stand by France'.[47] He opposed fresh concessions on the grounds they would entail a 'complete capitulation' to Germany, and, exerting himself once again, forced Chamberlain to acquiesce to this in Cabinet.[48]

The outbreak of a general European war now seemed imminent. The Royal Navy was ordered to mobilize, gas masks were distributed among the civilian population, and anti-aircraft guns were deployed in central London. With deep reluctance, the French Army initiated mobilization, while efforts were made to secure Romanian agreement for the Red Army to cross their territory en route to the conflict zone. War with Germany loomed—and over a border that few in Britain considered a vital national interest. It was an extraordinary situation. To a considerable extent, it was a product of high-political conflict, and anxiety, at Westminster.

'People of Whom We Know Nothing'

A Prime Minister who stood at the very apex of his authority six months earlier was now reduced to making a desperate appeal to Hitler.[49] The day after Halifax's bombshell, Chamberlain instructed Horace Wilson to return to Germany. The civil servant was to advise Hitler that the terms outlined at Bad Godesberg would likely provoke war, and ask him to return to the original policy discussed at

Berchtesgaden.[50] The Foreign Secretary would ordinarily have been the obvious one to carry such a message, but given Halifax's manoeuvring Chamberlain likely concluded that he simply could not entrust him with it. In dispatching Wilson instead, the Prime Minister was sending the one person he could still rely on. He told the Fuhrer that Wilson had his 'full confidence': 'you can take anything he says as coming from me'.[51]

Wilson himself was unimpressed by Halifax's abandonment of the man he called 'my master', later bitterly remarking that the Foreign Secretary 'wasn't a man of courage; he didn't readily take responsibility'.[52] He believed that the great Whitehall Germanophobe, Vansittart, was to blame for turning Halifax against Chamberlain. Despite being removed as Permanent Under-Secretary, 'Van' was as energetic as ever and continually bombarded the Foreign Secretary with papers on the German menace. Wilson detested him for his 'usual overbearing vehemence' and being an 'obstructive critic'. Looking back on the crisis three years later, Wilson held that without his own efforts to counter Vansittart, he would have seized control of the Foreign Office and negated Chamberlain's policy. 'When it seemed war would be upon us, I thought it would be hard not to place upon [Vansittart] a good deal of the responsibility'.[53] Wilson's view was that Britain was not 'in a position to enforce' a threat to Germany, and that if a 'transfer of territory is justified and required' it would be absurd not do so simply because of the 'threatening or brutal behaviour of one side . . . [when] the lives and fortunes of millions of people are at stake'.[54]

Received by the Fuhrer late in the afternoon of 27 September, Wilson was immediately subjected to Hitler's ranting. He tried to assure the dictator that Britain had no objection to the transfer of the Sudetenland.[55] As a furious Hitler continually interrupted, Wilson calmly asked the Fuhrer to 'listen' to him: 'the situation in England' was 'extremely serious'; domestic opinion was 'profoundly shocked' at the Fuhrer's demands; and 'the difficulty lay in the manner' in which Hitler was going about things. In response, the Fuhrer 'made gestures and exclamations of disgust', and got up to storm out, but Wilson persisted. He told the Fuhrer it was 'quite clear that the Germans could get what they wanted by peaceful methods'. Hitler explained that he was worried about his own 'position . . . in Germany' should he lose face.[56] Wilson implored the Fuhrer to refrain from military action. Significantly, Hitler was told to ignore any communications from the British side that did not come from Chamberlain personally.

That same day, back in Britain, Chamberlain delivered a national radio broadcast in which he affirmed the position forced upon him by Halifax. Yet, cleverly, he also sought to use the speech to regain the initiative by emphasizing to his listeners the horrific consequences of war. The Prime Minister declared that 'it seems to me incredible that the peoples of Europe . . . should be plunged into a bloody struggle over a question on which agreement has already been largely obtained'. There was a need for Britain to be 'very clear' that 'great issues' were 'really' at stake before entering into such a conflict. He offered to pay a 'third visit' to Germany. And in chilling terms, the Prime Minister went on: 'how horrible, fantastic, incredible it is that we should be digging trenches and trying on gas masks here because of a quarrel in a far-away country between people of whom we know nothing'.[57]

It was a powerful speech, intended to frighten those who heard it. It evoked memories of the Great War; and against a rerun of that nightmarish conflict, the alternative of diplomacy was surely preferable. Meanwhile the space for another round of negotiations was wedged open as the firmer stance engineered by Halifax gave Berlin pause. In another discussion with Wilson, the Fuhrer was warned that Britain would support France if the latter defended Czechoslovakia.[58] Facing war with the British Empire—not a prospect Hitler had earlier entertained—as well as France, Czechoslovakia, and possibly the USSR, the Fuhrer was left seething but hesitant. His coercive diplomacy rested on military and economic foundations that were weaker than they appeared; its success depended on others not calling his bluff. The German armed forces were still poorly motorized and possessed limited stocks of ammunition. Moreover, the Czechoslovakian army was large (thirty divisions to Germany's forty-eight) and, though of inferior quality to the *Wehrmacht*, boasted strong fortifications and would be defending very hilly, rough terrain. The Reich lacked allies and faced a war on two fronts, for the massing of the *Wehrmacht* on the Czech border exposed the western frontier and the industrial heartlands of the Reich to an assault from the fifty-six front-line divisions of the French Army. Germany boasted a paltry eight divisions to hold the west.

As European states roused themselves to resist rather than simply look the other way, Hitler changed tack. He had also grasped that German popular opinion displayed little enthusiasm for war; his own belligerent fury was not shared by the public at large. The Fuhrer thus decided to propose a settlement in which the *Wehrmacht* would occupy those areas of the Sudetenland which Prague had already been willing to cede, while plebiscites would be held in the rest of the disputed territory. Germany would then join a treaty guaranteeing the new Czechoslovakian frontiers.[59]

On the afternoon of 28 September, Chamberlain was in the House of Commons and in the midst of delivering an hour-long speech recounting recent events and seeking to justify his policy in the face of criticism.[60] His future as Prime Minister depended on how MPs reacted. Sensing that the time to strike was at hand, Churchill was probably intending to openly attack the Prime Minister; that would be an irrevocable step, but he was certainly searching for an opportunity to 'fight him in the House'.[61] During Chamberlain's long speech so many slips of paper were passed along the benches to Churchill—presumably notes encouraging him to challenge the Prime Minister directly—that they had to be held together by an elastic band.[62] The moment for crossing the Rubicon seemed to have arrived.

Yet towards the end of Chamberlain's speech, another note appeared. This one was hastily passed along the front bench to the Prime Minister. The folded piece of paper carried word of Hitler's new offer. One observer noted that having read it, Chamberlain's 'whole face, his whole body, seemed to change . . . he appeared ten years younger and triumphant'. The note informed him that the Fuhrer was convening a conference, to be held at Munich the next day; Britain, France, and Italy were all invited. Considering the matter for a moment, the Prime Minister relayed this news to the chamber. The relief was palpable. War seemed to have been averted. MPs on both sides of the House suddenly erupted into a 'roar' of spontaneous and sustained cheering. Harold Nicolson thought it was 'one of the most dramatic moments which I have ever witnessed'.[63] When the Prime Minister took his seat once more, 'the whole House rose as a man to pay tribute'.[64] Such is the speed at which political fortunes can shift. Chamberlain himself told his sister that it was 'a piece of drama that no work of fiction has ever surpassed'.[65] Churchill 'looked very much upset'.[66]

The Prime Minister had somehow slipped the leash which his opponents had forced him to wear. Horace Wilson was certainly due some of the credit, calmly tolerating Hitler's manic outbursts while reiterating that the situation could be resolved peacefully. When Chamberlain spoke of Wilson, 'his eyes lit up'. He called Sir Horace 'the most remarkable man in England. I couldn't live a day without him'.[67] Dashing to Munich to meet Hitler for the third—and final—time on 29 September, Chamberlain entered into a fourteen-hour negotiation that was completed in the middle of the night. His loyal Sherpa, Wilson, was with him once again. Drawing upon their shared ability to anatomize difficult problems, the Prime Minister and the civil servant came away with a deal to avoid war. Under the Munich agreement, the German-speaking areas of the Sudetenland were to be incorporated into the Reich and an international commission would oversee the plebiscites elsewhere. The standoff over Czechoslovakia appeared to have been defused. In addition, Chamberlain and Hitler signed an Anglo-German declaration affirming 'the desire of our two peoples never to go to war again'. This was the symbolic diplomatic victory that the Prime Minister wanted. Against the odds and in the teeth of resistance from colleagues, Chamberlain had succeeded in averting a general war; his mood was one of vindication. The quest he had embarked upon in May 1937 appeared to have culminated in a historic personal triumph.

The Prime Minister returned to England on 30 September, landing at Heston aerodrome. Alighting from his plane and standing on the airport tarmac, he famously brandished the 'piece of paper' bearing Hitler's signature—the Anglo-German declaration—for the press to photograph. It remains one of the most iconic images of the twentieth century.[68] Swept up in a hysterical outpouring of relief that there would be no new Great War, Chamberlain was received as a national hero. His journey back to central London saw thousands lining the streets, 'shouting themselves hoarse', 'banging on the window and thrusting their hands into the car to be shaken'; 'even the descriptions of the papers give no idea of the scenes', the Prime Minister recorded. Chamberlain went to Buckingham Palace and appeared with the Royal Family on the balcony. Later, addressing the delirious crowds from the window at Downing Street, Chamberlain uttered the most memorable words of his career. At Munich, the Prime Minister remarked, he had secured 'peace with honour'. 'I believe', he went on, 'it is peace for our time'.

Tens of thousands of congratulatory letters flowed into Downing Street. Having seized the initiative in dramatic fashion, some began to worry that a triumphant Chamberlain might call a general election in which he would romp to victory.[69] The Prime Minister was certainly pondering an election throughout 1938, for in the spring he had ordered Conservative Central Office to prepare 'propaganda' operations that would commence in the autumn and continue 'until the general election'.[70] His position now appeared to have become unexpectedly impregnable. A panicked Churchill explored building an alliance with Labour, the Liberals, and rebel Conservatives, proposing that a commitment to the League and 'collective security' might form the basis for a common election platform. When Harold Macmillan protested 'That is not our jargon', Churchill roared back: 'It is a jargon we may all have to learn'.[71]

Things Fall Apart

Yet Chamberlain's triumph proved fleeting. The Fuhrer was incandescent that Britain had suddenly threatened war to prevent him from denuding Czechoslovakia of the Sudetenland, and concluded that Britain was not merely a meddler but an enemy. The plebiscites in the disputed areas were never held, nor did Germany guarantee the new Czech borders. In mid-October Hitler issued a twelve-hour ultimatum to the international commission monitoring the settlement of the frontier as to his preferences and then marched German forces into the Sudetenland

and took what he wanted.[72] The process underpinning the Munich agreement unravelled within weeks.

So convinced was Chamberlain of his capacity to avert war, and so determined was he to outmanoeuvre his critics, that he had staked everything—both his own future and a strategy designed to husband British power—on the word of a man whom he already felt to be a 'criminal'. Considering that Britain could do little to save Czechoslovakia, going out on a limb over the issue is only explicable in terms of the intertwined effect of Chamberlain's quest for vindication and the hostile political environment at home. Unable to choose between intervention and turning away, the Prime Minister's approach was the worst of both worlds. Chamberlain should have either called Hitler's bluff or refused to sit at the poker table with him in the first place.

It is true that if war had come in the autumn of 1938 Britain would not have been as prepared as she was a year later, when the RAF and air defence were in a much stronger position. But, by the same token, Germany was also in a markedly weaker position in 1938. Lacking allies and resources, with an economy that was showing signs of failing and a rearmament programme that was incomplete, Hitler's regime could probably not have sustained a prolonged conflict in 1938—much less sweep all before it in the blitzkrieg campaigns of 1939–40. Seeking to bolster support for appeasement, Chamberlain warned his colleagues in September that with the RAF still in the process of expansion and the radar network incomplete, British airpower would be swiftly overwhelmed by the far more numerous *Luftwaffe*. The Cabinet was informed that the RAF boasted 1,606 front-line planes, with 412 in reserve, compared to Germany's 3,200 front-line and reserve of 2,400 planes. The country, particularly the south, would be vulnerable to a German onslaught from the air.[73] But this was a self-serving distortion of the military realities. Without occupying the Channel coast—which hardly seemed feasible given the vulnerable state of the Reich's western frontier in 1938—the Germans would be unable to attack Britain. The size of the *Luftwaffe* had also been overestimated by more than 2,000 planes. Furthermore the construction of British military aircraft was in the process of skyrocketing. 2,827 planes were produced in Britain in 1938, up from 1,830 in 1936. By 1939, Britain's aircraft factories were churning out almost as many planes as those of Germany, 7,940 compared to 8,295, and, in 1940, would comfortably outstrip what the Reich produced, building 15,049 aircraft to 10,247. The Prime Minister's policy also cost the anti-Nazi forces the thirty divisions of the Czech army, as well as the giant Skoda armaments factory—one of the largest in the world.

In 'buying time' for Britain to prepare more fully for war, Chamberlain thus furnished Hitler with the time *he* needed to finish building a world-class military of his own. If forced to go to war in 1938, Germany would have been unable to wage an aerial conflict over the skies of Britain, lacked the raw materials needed to sustain her economy, faced the threat of invasion from the west, and likely confronted an opportunistic enemy in the Soviet Union. The Panzer divisions and powerful *Luftwaffe* that would win lightning victories a year later did not fully exist. In these unfavourable circumstances, the regime may well not have survived.

How secure was Hitler's position at home? In a terror state dominated by a secret police, it would take something dramatic to turn private criticism into active resistance—let alone conspiracy. But many German generals thought Hitler 'cracked' and bound to lead Germany to ruin, and in the summer of 1938 a group of them planned a putsch.[74] They intended to arrest Hitler upon his giving an order to invade Czechoslovakia, seize the government quarter of Berlin, and deploy troops to deal with the SS when they came running to the Fuhrer's rescue. The generals aimed to put Hitler on trial, and have him declared insane. The plotters sent multiple emissaries to London, asking Britain to stand firm if Germany attacked Czechoslovakia. Chamberlain was intrigued, wondering whether 'we ought not to do something to help';[75] so were Halifax and Horace Wilson, who spirited one of the conspirators into Downing Street via the back door.[76] But the coup ultimately came to naught, whether because of Chamberlain's launch of Plan Z or the hesitation of the generals.

Unable to develop a coherent approach in his own mind, much less sell it to his colleagues, Chamberlain singularly failed to take advantage of Britain's considerable strategic advantages over the Third Reich. Moreover, despite the adulation of the crowds, even before the Munich agreement unravelled there was opposition to what Chamberlain had done—predictably so, given that foreign policy was now the principal point of domestic conflict. Many of those who supported the agreement were anxious about where Britain was headed. It is true that when Chamberlain entered the Commons for the first time since his return from Munich the Conservative benches gave the Prime Minister a standing ovation.[77] But one man who was not pleased was Duff Cooper, the First Lord of the Admiralty. He had harboured doubts about Chamberlain's strategy for months. And with the signing of the Munich agreement, he could take no more. Cooper resigned from the government and, in the Commons on 3 October, warned Chamberlain that using 'the language of sweet reasonableness' was pointless when the only thing the Fuhrer understood was 'the language of the mailed fist'.[78] After a brilliant and lengthy speech delivered extempore—Churchill judged it one of the finest parliamentary performances he had ever witnessed—Cooper declared that he, unlike Chamberlain, could 'walk about the world with my head held erect'.

In the Foreign Office, one official, Gladwyn Jebb, characterized Chamberlain's policy as 'riding the tiger'. Proposing a new course of action, Jebb suggested—in words which he admitted were 'reminiscent of Machiavelli'—trying to persuade France to end her alliance with the USSR, a gesture which would have the 'unavowed...intention' of indicating to Hitler that he should divert his efforts towards the Soviet Union.[79] Oliver Harvey thought Munich 'a great humiliation'.[80] Speaking in the House of Lords, Halifax hardly offered a ringing endorsement of Munich when he described the agreement as merely the best 'of a hideous choice of evils'.[81] For its part, Labour was predictably indignant at the 'betrayal' of Czechoslovakia and denounced Chamberlain in Parliament, the press, and across the country. The Labour leaders charged that the Prime Minister had 'sacrificed' 'several million people' in a 'humbug' policy that did not avert war but 'merely postpone[d] it'.[82]

During the Commons debate following the signing of the agreement, Churchill finally felt able to publicly target Chamberlain for presiding over 'a total and unmitigated defeat'. His criticism was deeply personal:

> The responsibility must rest with those who have the undisputed control of our political affairs. They neither prevented Germany from rearming, nor did they rearm ourselves in time. They quarrelled with Italy without saving Ethiopia. They exploited and discredited the vast institution of the League of Nations and they neglected to make alliances and combinations which might have repaired the previous errors...And do not suppose this is the end. This is only the beginning of the reckoning.[83]

It was a scathing oration. And it was one Churchill had been waiting to launch for a long time. It raised issues not only of policy, but of whether those in control even possessed the competence to avoid national humiliation. Once again, the rallying cry of 'honour' and 'prestige' proved the best club with which to beat the government. Other Conservative MPs launched similar attacks.

Churchill had constructed a public persona which seemed to be validated anew every time Hitler misbehaved. It was one that implied a prescience about international affairs. That afforded powerful political advantages. As the warnings he had been delivering since 1936 came to pass, the notion that Churchill was a source of wisdom about what might happen *next* began to gain widespread social currency—a notion furnished by his constant appearances in the press. People even began to refer to him as a 'prophet'.[84]

The idea of Churchill-as-Pericles conformed to Winston's instinctive sense of history and his place within it. These were themes he was thinking deeply about. At the time, he was composing his four-volume *A History of the English-Speaking Peoples*, which charted events from the Roman invasions to the outbreak of the Great War and advanced Churchill's belief that his country had a special purpose. Meanwhile the fourth and final volume of his life of Marlborough was published in 1938. The question of destiny was thus weighing heavily on the mind of the great romantic. It is important to stress that at this point Churchill did not anticipate the premiership—which would have been over-reaching, even by his standards—but instead hoped for a post in the Cabinet. In reality of course, Winston was no prophet. In fastening his fortunes upon the behaviour of Hitler—a fellow opportunist and reckless gambler—he had simply backed a political winner.

The notion that Churchill was a repository of wisdom made it increasingly difficult for his enemies to strike at him. By late 1938, then, Churchill was no longer a voice in the wilderness, but part of the British political mainstream once more. It was a remarkable professional rejuvenation. He was also quite obviously the leading Conservative opponent of appeasement, a mantle once destined to be worn by Eden. Eden's resignation in February 1938 demonstrated that he had been outman-oeuvred by those willing to play on his tantrums. Aged just forty at the time of his resignation, Eden intended to deliver 'big speeches' on questions such as 'Democracy and Young England', advertising his credentials as a symbol of youth as opposed to 'the old men'.[85] He wanted to be thought of as the embodiment of liberal conservatism—in other words, Baldwin's heir. Concerned that Chamberlain was undoing his 'life's work', Baldwin viewed Eden as the man to reconnect the Conservative party to liberal opinion and floating voters.[86] He and Eden saw each other socially and Baldwin helped with his speeches.[87] Eden's team knew the 'immense importance' that Baldwin's 'approval' would carry, and hoped that he would 'play a vital part in securing the succession'.[88] In addition to this support from Baldwin, approximately twenty young Conservative MPs clustered around Eden. Anthony hoped to be Chamberlain's successor, and was continually assured by his friends that he would be. Harvey spoke of the 'switch-over' as if it was a foregone conclusion.[89] Eden himself perhaps thought it 'inevitable'.[90] He probably envisaged being the leader of an 'All-Party Government'.[91]

But, Eden being Eden, he made a hash of it. He did not intend to attack the Cabinet directly, lest it antagonize those who might turn to him when Chamberlain left the scene.[92] Therefore while Eden employed Baldwinian calls for 'national unity' and 'moral regeneration' in his speeches,[93] for the most part he refused to act. His deliberately ambiguous posture was too indistinct. He wanted little to do with Churchill, and had no intention of joining the old man beyond the Conservative pale. The outcome was that, as 1938 progressed, the public statures of Churchill and Eden reversed. Churchill was willing to speak openly against the government on the key policy issue of the day, whereas Eden's criticisms were qualified. Eden expected to be gifted the job of Conservative leader, yet to this end he behaved with such decorum and restraint that he lost all momentum. Eden even made clear that he 'did not intend to lead a revolt'.[94] The result was that, as European crises multiplied, he was 'missing every boat with exquisite elegance'.[95] As his star fell, that of Churchill rose once again. The Eden group of MPs—derisively dubbed 'the glamour boys' by other Conservatives—were not political bruisers. They even decided that while they were a 'group', 'we will not call ourselves a group'—another indication that Eden lacked the guts for a fight.[96]

Eden refused to sign a memorandum to Chamberlain drafted by Churchill and urging a strong line over Czechoslovakia as 'it would be interpreted as a vendetta'.[97] He did criticize the Munich agreement in the House in speaking of 'successive surrenders',[98] and refused to contemplate rejoining the government 'unless it is reconstructed in the most drastic manner',[99] but it was all too late and far too tepid. Eden was a poser, not a statesman. Halifax saw that he was 'not tough enough to be P.M.'[100] Eden was not going to be the Conservative leader of resistance to appeasement. That role could now only fall to Churchill. Winston's position was strong, and becoming stronger with each passing week.

'Like Thunderbolts Upon Us'

Chamberlain profoundly resented the fact that 'all the world seemed to be full of my praises except the House of Commons'.[101, 102] With some political cunning, in early October 1938 the Labour leaders decided to put down a motion of censure on the government in Parliament. This would force a division that would effectively represent a referendum on appeasement itself. It would put Conservative rebels on the spot and hopefully expose the fractures now spreading throughout the National Government. There was much discussion among the Conservative dissidents as to whether they should back Labour's motion, abstain, or reluctantly support the government. To support Labour, or even abstain on the motion, would be seen as a declaration of war against the Cabinet. There were fears that Conservative MPs who did so would be deprived of the party whip, with the leadership seeking to have them de-selected as candidates at the next election.[103] And the Chief Whip, David Margesson, remained an intimidating presence in the Commons. Yet, despite this, many were simply unwilling to back the government. In the vote, Churchill, along with twenty-two Conservative MPs including Amery, Duff Cooper, and even Eden, refused to support the ministry and abstained on Labour's motion of censure. In a move further calculated to 'enrage the government', some, led by Churchill, did not even absent themselves from the House during the vote but defiantly remained seated in the chamber while the division took place.[104] As pieces of political theatre go, it was a powerful one.

This revolt, small in number but not in stature, seemed to 'rattle' Chamberlain,[105] for the Prime Minister took the surprising step of informing the House that there would be no general election. He even admitted that his words about 'peace for our time' may have been ill-chosen.[106] This statement underlined Chamberlain's nerviness. The Prime Minister had taken a beating. He thought that 'Winston was carrying on a regular conspiracy against me', which was attracting the 'weaker brethren' of the Conservative party.[107] Chamberlain's 'blood was up': he wrote to tell Churchill that 'you cannot expect me to allow you to do all the hitting and never hit back'.[108] Indeed, Chamberlain's instincts were to refuse any compromise. Hoare was already petitioning to bring Eden back into the Cabinet (though, naturally, there was no 'basis' for 'a working agreement between Winston and ourselves').[109] Chamberlain refused to even contemplate accommodating Eden because 'I have had enough trouble with my present Cabinet', and wanted 'more support for my policy and not more strengthening of those who don't believe in it'.[110] He also ruled out inviting the Labour party to join a coalition as 'there would be a constant running fight over every move in the international game': 'I am not prepared for . . . a sham unity to take as partners men who would sooner or later wreck the policy'.[111]

With an eye on politics as always, Halifax advised Chamberlain that 'this [was] the psychological moment' to cement 'national unity' under his leadership; such an opportunity might not recur.[112] But Chamberlain would not listen. Whereas Halifax urged a broadening of the Cabinet to include both Conservative rebels and the Labour leaders, the Prime Minister demanded colleagues that supported 'my policy'. He was exhausted and resentful towards his Cabinet for 'assur[ing] me of their complete personal loyalty' but then 'continually harassing me with warnings & doubts'.[113] Though at this point he was even having problems catching trout on his fishing trips, the Prime Minister was determined to yield no additional ground.

Just weeks later, Churchill voted against the government in the Commons for the first time since the India conflict. He supported a Liberal motion calling upon Chamberlain to establish a Ministry of Supply to coordinate Britain's resources.[114] And in response to a barb from Chamberlain that 'If I were asked whether judgement is the first of [Churchill's] many admirable qualities, I should have to ask the House of Commons not to press me too far',[115] Churchill gave a public speech in which he retorted, 'I would gladly submit my judgements about foreign affairs and national defence during the last five years to comparison with [Chamberlain's] own'. He accused the Prime Minister of lacking 'foresight' and, worse, having 'no comprehension of the verities and the realities afoot in the world before they actually fall like thunderbolts upon us'.[116] Long before the Second World War itself began, British politics was in a state of open war.

8

PLANTING THE FLAG

Creaking Cabinet

The Prime Minister now found himself confronted by opposition on three fronts. The Labour party, dissidents on the Conservative backbenches, and members of his own Cabinet were unconvinced of both his policies and his leadership. Chamberlain's vulnerability was compounded by the Nazis' infamous *Kristallnacht* pogroms against Jews on 9 and 10 November 1938. Hundreds were killed, thousands were incarcerated, and thousands of synagogues and businesses were burned. *Kristallnacht* underlined once again the sickening nature of the regime the Prime Minister had staked his career on. The violent persecution was chronicled in British newspapers and shocked public opinion; the photographs provided an unforgettable visual record of Nazi rule.

In this climate many at Conservative Central Office began to fear that the next election—which had to take place in 1939 or 1940—would witness a major reduction in the number of Conservative MPs. By-election defeats continued, with the Conservatives losing two contests in November 1938 alone. As a result, despite Chamberlain feeling that the 'only . . . course of action' likely to improve his situation was to 'get rid of this uneasy and disgruntled House of Commons by a general election', he had no choice but to accept the advice of Conservative staff that 'to have one now or very soon' would be 'suicidal'.[1] He felt that his party was losing its nerve and seemed 'all over the place'.[2] The Prime Minister admitted that he had been glancing around Downing Street and 'wondering how much longer I shall be here'.[3] He felt trapped, complaining that his Cabinet was made up of men likely to be 'a source of trouble'.[4]

A belief was crystallizing amongst politicians and public alike that Nazi Germany was simply not a state one could negotiate with. As such it was increasingly imperative the National Government's approach to international affairs be switched to reflect that mood; domestic political credibility depended on it. Within weeks of the Munich agreement and in the aftermath of *Kristallnacht*, therefore, the Foreign Secretary once again began acting as an independent force. He insisted at Cabinet that the 'immediate objective' of the government should be correcting the public impression that 'we were decadent, spineless and could with impunity be kicked about'.[5] Halifax dramatized this with speculation that Hitler's intention was to destroy the British Empire. He produced a digest of reports from top-secret intelligence sources carefully selected to force the government to move in a new, tougher, direction. Halifax even suggested that Germany might attack India. These reports were cherry-picked for the Foreign Secretary by Vansittart who, through sheer force of will and an enviable series of contacts abroad, had made himself an influential figure at the Foreign Office once more. In terms of remedial measures, Halifax called for longer working hours in aircraft factories and advocated that preparations be made for conscription through the creation of a national register. What he sought was a new strategy to remake public perceptions of the government, one that would have an 'enormous moral and emotional' effect and be seen as 'the organising of an entire nation to meet an emergency'.[6] As soon as the Munich agreement was signed, Halifax privately remarked that he 'foresaw political troubles ahead, both in Parliament and in the country'.[7] Over the next few months, he made concerted efforts to deliver speeches which offered a robust message on foreign affairs. In doing so, he gained greater confidence and boldness. The Foreign Secretary was developing 'his own line', distinct from that of Chamberlain. One of his officials predicted that 'we may have trouble with the P.M. before long!'[8] Despite having been Eden's greatest advocate for years, Harvey now told Halifax that he was the best candidate to replace Chamberlain and should do so as leader of an all-party coalition.[9]

Meanwhile another of the National Government's big beasts, Sir Samuel Hoare, watched the situation with interest. He had even entered into a clandestine relationship with the newspaper magnate Lord Beaverbrook, who offered to secretly pay Hoare the sum of £2,000 per year—a substantial top-up to his ministerial salary of £5,000—in order to remain in politics rather than seek a lucrative job in the private sector.[10] It was an extraordinary episode, and one is compelled to wonder whether the press baron had bought himself a Cabinet minister—a man who Beaverbrook believed might one day be Prime Minister.[11] With good reason was Beaverbrook sometimes called 'been a crook'. Hoare even pressed Chamberlain to give Beaverbrook a ministerial post.[12] Beaverbrook's daughter later described Hoare as 'Father's spy in the Cabinet'.[13] The relationship offered an obvious way of procuring the support of the Beaverbrook press for Hoare's leadership ambitions. In early 1939, Hoare consequently struck independent poses in Cabinet, arguing for Chamberlain to adopt a tougher line in foreign policy. 'Fear' was the only thing that would deter Hitler, Hoare declared, and Britain should make the Fuhrer feel it.[14] He also made lots of reassuring noises aimed at Chamberlain's critics, arguing for discussions with Labour and Liberal leaders.[15] Hoare even expressed sympathy for bringing Churchill into the government.[16] And he advocated the creation of a Ministry of Supply to organize preparations for war as it would 'impress the public', demanded more vigorous rearmament, and pressed the Prime Minister to create a small War Cabinet immediately. Chamberlain was losing control of his government.

The Dark Arts

Yet the Prime Minister was not yet powerless; far from it. The Conservative party machine was swiftly brought to bear, employing underhanded measures against those who questioned the wisdom of government policy. Over subsequent months methods more foul than fair were used to bring rebel MPs to heel. Maisky recorded that 'the power of the party machine has increased immensely and terrorizes many MPs'.[17] The Chief Whip, David Margesson, remained a tyrannical, callous force in the tearooms of the House of Commons. Meanwhile dissident MPs came under pressure from their local constituency associations, with threats of deselection in the air. Eden and the MPs who supported him all experienced 'difficulties' with their local parties.[18] Duff Cooper—MP for the most secure Conservative seat in Britain—was put on notice by his local association that further revolt would not be tolerated. And in November 1938 the anti-appeaser Kitty, Duchess of Atholl, was actually deselected for her seat at Kinross and West Perthshire. When she chose to immediately resign, forcing a by-election and standing as an Independent, the Conservative machine poured a huge number of resources and speakers into the seat. In a poisonous campaign, the party managed to narrowly defeat her. Conservatives who supported the Duchess were threatened with expulsion; Churchill was the only one to express any backing. There were rumblings in Churchill's own constituency at Epping, as well.

There were few lengths to which those around Chamberlain would not go. Horace Wilson, the key figure in the antechamber of power in Downing Street, was at the heart of this effort. Beaverbrook complained that

> Today we are living under despotism by consent . . . The Prime Minister has been able to establish a personal rule under which Parliament is practically ineffective and under which the civil service is silenced by the imposition of Horace Wilson. The power of this man can scarcely be exaggerated . . . even the most minor appointments are contrived in order to fortify his position.[19]

Chamberlain's devoted admirer, 'Chips' Channon, later remembered that at this point Wilson appeared 'all-powerful'.[20] The *Daily Mail* labelled him 'the "mystery man" of Whitehall' and 'one of the Brain Trusters around the Prime Minister', who, through a 'whispered word' in the right ear, could change the direction of policy.[21] The Conservative Rab Butler described him as 'the real P.M.'.[22] Wilson and the ambassador in Berlin, Nevile Henderson, warned Chamberlain that to indulge critics by launching fiery denunciations of Germany would have the 'inevitable result' of prompting the Germans to do 'what they have not hitherto done—prepare plans for war with this country'.[23] Critics within the civil service faced a vigorous clubbing from Wilson if they dissented. The senior official at the Foreign Office, Cadogan, opposed appeasement but later acknowledged that 'Horace Wilson had become an institution . . . If I had tried to fight against him, I should only have been removed'.[24]

Electronic eavesdropping was even employed. This effort was run by Chamberlain's ex-MI5 agent *éminence grise* Sir Joseph Ball. Though the scale of the operation remains unclear, some critics of the government definitely had their telephone conversations intercepted. Eden, his followers, Churchill, and journalists were among those whose communications were monitored at times.[25] Presumably this was done to ascertain what information critics possessed about the defence situation and the alliances they were formulating. Meanwhile Ball ran a longstanding and sophisticated operation to discreetly plant stories in the newspapers, manipulate journalists, and secure favourable press coverage for the National Government. Opponents of appeasement were denigrated through venomous, or mocking, articles initiated by Ball, who also met supportive journalists twice a week to give them secret briefings.[26] Nor was that all. In 1936, working through a proxy organization, Ball had quietly arranged the purchase of a small-circulation weekly journal, *Truth*. This was employed to harangue the adversaries of Chamberlain, not only outside the Conservative party but also within it. Read mainly in Westminster, *Truth* provided a constant diet of venom and bile. Smear tactics and outright abuse were common. *Truth* was essentially a mouthpiece through which Downing Street could seek to influence political opinion using tools that were publicly unbecoming of a Prime Minister. It constituted a device for Chamberlain to sanction the denigration of his enemies. These methods enabled him to run an unattributable operation to manipulate the press throughout his premiership. Considering Ball's close relationship with Chamberlain—they were in constant contact, and enjoyed fly-fishing holidays together—it is inconceivable that the Prime Minister did not know what Ball was up to. Letters to his sisters hint that he was well aware.[27] He may not have orchestrated these intelligence-gathering and black propaganda operations himself, but that was because he had Ball to do it for him. Indeed, when Chamberlain lay dying of stomach cancer in the autumn of 1940, Ball wrote to him reminiscing about their 'great work' in 'countering intrigues' by the Prime Minister's 'enemies' through 'political controversy and propaganda'.[28]

Meanwhile the editor of *The Times*, Geoffrey Dawson, remained supportive of the National Government. His newspaper reflected government preferences to a remarkable extent. After Duff Cooper's brilliant resignation speech, one *Times* journalist wrote a column about it only to find his words rewritten by the editor in order to portray the government in a more favourable light.[29] Meanwhile, despite his anxieties about Wilson, Beaverbrook remained another strong supporter of appeasement and put the *Daily Express* at the service of the government, telling Halifax that 'my newspapers will do anything to help you'.[30] Wilson was routinely employed as a conduit to editors and owners at virtually every newspaper on Fleet Street, as well as the major provincial papers. Intimidation was used too: there were implied threats to censor critical newspapers, with claims about 'national security' or 'the public interest' deployed to discourage publication of articles that might weaken support for the Prime Minister. Notable successes for the policy of shaping press coverage included securing robust backing for Chamberlain's stance over Czechoslovakia, with the *Daily Express* running a headline optimistically declaring, 'There Will Be No European War' and the *Daily Mail* complimenting the Prime Minister for his 'valiant endeavours'.[31] Beaverbrook himself acknowledged that the *Express* 'was invited by the government itself to make these declarations'.[32] Much to Chamberlain's amusement, there was also frequent mockery of Churchill at the behest of Ball.[33]

This was a formidable and powerful operation. Conservative MPs faced coercion, intimidation, and even bugging. The Prime Minister's own fingerprints were, and remain, difficult to detect—but, then, that was the point.

The Expulsion of Cripps

While Chamberlain grappled with the Conservative party, the rebuilding of its rival across the House of Commons proceeded apace. In early 1939 the Labour leadership group finally achieved a decisive victory over the radical socialist elements in the party. Having long beaten the drum of opposition to rearmament, in the aftermath of Munich Cripps opportunistically struck up a new tune. He now began calling for the Labour party to form an alliance with all anti-Chamberlain forces—Communists, Liberals, and even *Conservative* dissidents—in a 'Popular Front'. He demanded rearmament once Chamberlain was removed and a government 'under the control of the common people' established.[34] He reached out to Baldwin, Churchill, and Lloyd George for support. This was 'theatre', an attempt 'to make a 'left-wing' foreign policy the 'centre of power' in a new coalition.[35] But it was also fantasy. The idea of a 'Popular Front' was soundly rejected; Attlee, Dalton, Morrison, Bevin, and Citrine had no interest in alliance with Communists or Liberals. And they were opposed to any alignment with dissident Conservatives unless they were willing to overthrow Chamberlain first. Moreover, a frontal attack from Labour might only rally Conservative backbenchers to Chamberlain's standard. Far better to wait, lecture the government on its failures, and strengthen Labour's hand while the situation developed. What Attlee and his colleagues did do was travel the country, making speeches and attracting the attention of the press with vigorous language rather than the idealistic rhetoric they had talked hitherto. In the months following Munich, Attlee denounced Chamberlain for imperilling 'the very foundations of our western civilisation'.[36]

With the idea of alliance with Conservatives dead, Cripps once again changed tack. Now he spoke of a 'proletarian' Popular Front that linked Labour, Communists, and Liberals but excluded dissident Conservatives (having been cultivated three months earlier, Churchill was now dismissed as a 'reactionary imperialis[t])'.[37] Cripps presented the National Executive Committee (NEC) with a memorandum pressing for the Popular Front and also calling for the party to win the support of 'Youth'—as if young people would offer some magical cure-all. The NEC overwhelmingly rejected the plan by seventeen votes to three. When Cripps angrily responded by circulating a copy of his memorandum throughout the Labour movement regardless, he presented his enemies with a way to deal with him once and for all.

As Dalton put it, the problem with Cripps was that he boasted all 'the political judgement of a flea'.[38] The leaders came down hard, employing the charge of 'disloyalty' to sanction him. On 25 January, the NEC voted overwhelmingly to expel Cripps from the Labour party altogether.[39] Some of his supporters, including the MPs Aneurin Bevan and George Strauss, were purged alongside him. The annual conference later approved the expulsions by a margin of 1.6 million votes.[40] It was a final symbolic victory in the battle for control of Labour—a struggle that had, in Dalton's words, been 'a fight to the finish'.[41] In early 1939, the fight was over at last.

The Destruction of Czechoslovakia

While Labour leaders were purging malcontents, on the green benches across the House of Commons Churchill understood that, for his part, he could now afford patience. Around the world, 'the pigeons are coming home to roost with a vengeance'.[42] He was confident that 'the march of events'—always one of his favourite dramatic phrases—would prove the acid test of whether he or Chamberlain was right.[43] 'By this time next year we shall know whether the Prime Minister's view of Herr Hitler and the German Nazi party is right or wrong', he wrote in the *Daily Telegraph* in November 1938. He did not need to wait a year for his answer—and when it came, it was stark. On 15 March 1939, without prior warning, Hitler ordered his military to invade the remainder of Czechoslovakia and incorporate it into the Greater German Reich. The Munich agreement was instantly destroyed. With it, so was the last shred of Chamberlain's credibility.

The elimination of Czechoslovakia remains a seminal moment in European history. Public opinion immediately hardened still further. A conviction developed that the Nazis could not be dissuaded from aggression and that Britain had a duty to stop them. Germanophobia became the overwhelming public emotion. In Parliament, 'the great majority' of Conservative backbenchers were deeply alarmed at the latest turn of events, and conveyed this to their leaders.[44] 'Chips' Channon judged that the 'whole policy' of appeasement lay 'in ruins'. Channon was Chamberlain's most fervent fan, which might explain his strange reduction of the Czechoslovakian crisis to Hitler's 'callous desertion of the Prime Minister...I can never forgive him'.[45] In something of an understatement, Chamberlain told Parliament that it was 'a terrible shock to confidence'.[46] The Labour party had a field day. The deputy leader Arthur Greenwood stated that the invasion was 'no surprise', while Attlee declared, with scant regard for the facts, that it proved 'Labour's foreign policy has been right'.[47] Morrison exclaimed that 'Chamberlain must go'.[48] But the Labour leaders remained determined that Conservative MPs would have to wield the dagger—not least because they would probably destroy themselves in the process.

The ground on which the Prime Minister had stood since 1937 was thus disintegrating. Observers noted that Chamberlain appeared gaunt and there was speculation about how long he would hold up under the strain. Early in 1939 he had been forced to reverse his stance that a British expeditionary force dispatched to Europe in case of war would be restricted to only five divisions, and accede to a significant expansion of the army.[49] The Secretary of State for War, Leslie Hore-Belisha, had been campaigning for this for months, and the Prime Minister now felt in no position to resist. Meanwhile Halifax sought to bolster the alliance with France by pressing for full-scale joint military planning not only against Germany, but Italy as well.[50] Chamberlain refused to go this far, but in February did agree that any threat to the 'vital interests' of France would 'evoke the immediate cooperation of Great Britain' for the two states enjoyed an 'identity of interests'.[51] This had not been Chamberlain's thinking hitherto; quite the opposite. The shift in tone was evidently intended to appease the Foreign Secretary.[52] Rumours were again circulating that the two no longer saw 'eye to eye'.[53]

Yet the Prime Minister was not ready to concede defeat. Two days after the German invasion, he delivered a speech at Birmingham in which he tried to repeat his old trick of avoiding isolation by moving towards his critics. He acknowledged that the destruction of Czechoslovakia could represent the beginning of 'an attempt to dominate the world by force'. Chamberlain went on that Britain was 'not disinterested in what goes on' in central and eastern Europe, and refuted any suspicion that 'this nation . . . has lost its fibre'. Britain would, if necessary, prosecute war 'to the utmost of its power'.[54] He also attacked the Nazis for their treatment of the Jews.[55] This speech featured such an important change in the language employed by the Prime Minister that one Conservative hyperbolically compared it to something uttered 'by the younger Pitt', Britain's great statesman of the late eighteenth century.[56] But in truth it reflected Chamberlain's profound weakness and recognition of the need to reattach himself to public opinion. Halifax later told Butler that 'it was he who insisted' on the need for Chamberlain to give 'this fighting speech' as 'the prelude to a revolution in foreign policy'.[57]

The Guarantees

What Halifax was aiming at soon became apparent. As authority leached away from the Prime Minister, it passed to his Foreign Secretary. When reports circulated in March of German designs on yet another state, Romania, Halifax began pressing in Cabinet for a British guarantee of that country against attack. This was a crucial step. Romania, like Czechoslovakia, was not an obvious British national interest, yet the Foreign Secretary argued that 'Germany's attempt to obtain world domination' was now 'the real issue'.[58] He also manipulated the Cabinet into accepting his arguments through calculated use of rumours about German troop movements.[59] Halifax's shift away from the Prime Minister was almost complete. Chamberlain was predictably hostile to a unilateral British guarantee of Romania; if he lacked the strength to resist some form of alliance policy, he wanted the USSR, Poland, Turkey, Yugoslavia, Greece, and Romania all sounded out about building a bloc.[60] For all his failings, the Prime Minister was still thinking about co-opting regional states to take responsibility for their part of the continent; Halifax was thinking *politically*. The government had been made to look foolish by Hitler, and this needed to be fixed. This was the climate in which Halifax's outlook was formed. Even supportive newspapers became critical. *The Times* called for Britain to make no more concessions to 'the expansion of political tyranny',[61] and *The Daily Telegraph* argued for a fresh policy which was 'bound to envision new commitments for this country somewhere'.[62] And in a public speech at Birmingham, Attlee made clear that Labour would reject any 'appeals... to rally behind the government in the interests of national unity'.[63] Weeks later he called for 'a government that stands for the whole nation'.[64] Labour was throwing down the gauntlet, declaring they were unafraid to face a general election fought on the basis of 'patriotism'. Eden had already advocated the inclusion of Labour and the Liberals in a new regime.[65] Harold Nicolson recorded that 'The feeling in the lobbies is that Chamberlain will either have to go or completely reverse his policy'.[66]

Halifax therefore understood that if a Conservative victory at the next election was to be obtained, the ingrained perception of British foreign policy must be radically altered. In true Baldwinian style, 'national unity'—or, at least, a variant that would benefit the Conservative party—thus became Halifax's guiding star. His style of conservatism had clear affinities with that of Baldwin. Like the old master, Halifax believed in the value of consensual government. And he knew that a fresh political climate had been created that could spell disaster for the Conservative party. Although Halifax was *instinctually* an appeaser who believed that Versailles was a 'tragedy' for the Germans, had 'liked all the Nazi leaders' on a personal level, and took the view that 'one of the chief difficulties' was the 'unreal position' which France was 'occupying in central and eastern Europe' in its bid to encircle Germany, he realized that political catastrophe awaited.[67] 'The dominating fact', wrote the historian Maurice Cowling, was 'Halifax's belief that the policy would have to be changed if the party was to be saved'.[68]

To this end he sought to recreate the atmosphere of the Baldwin era. The Foreign Secretary had long been in favour of bringing Eden, that symbol of liberal hope, back into government, feeling that Chamberlain was 'unlikely to retrieve the floating vote' alone.[69] In addition, he saw real political and social value in cross-party collaboration. He had 'long antennae' which he used to 'feel every movement' of political opinion.[70] Halifax was also cognizant that Britain's rearmament pro-gramme was nearing fruition. This afforded some leeway to act. The domestic situation necessitated that British foreign policy give an impression of firmness, and Halifax was intent on delivering it. Thus, from late 1938 he began to speak of resisting the dictators in strongly moral terms. Talk of facing down 'evil' played well with crucial liberal and 'floating' constituencies of public opinion. When addressing Conservative backbenchers on foreign policy Halifax was 'brilliant', persuading them with his toughness, 'sincerity', and 'high ideals'. Channon was left wondering, 'Is he saint turned worldling, or worldling become saint?'[71]

The situation in Europe, in which war and peace seemed balanced on a hair-trigger, thus ensured that Halifax retained the advantage. While the Prime Minister was attending a banquet at Buckingham Palace, Hore-Belisha suddenly arrived to whisper into his ear (incorrect) rumours that the Germans had just mobilized twenty divisions on the western borders; Chamberlain could only muse, 'this is like the Brussels Ball', the site of Wellington being informed of Napoleon's movements just prior to Waterloo.[72] On 20 March, Chamberlain therefore once again tacked a considerable distance in a bid to neutralize opposition from Halifax. He suggested pressing for France, Poland, and Russia to join Britain in a formal declaration that, in the event of further German aggression, those states would 'consult' about what should be done, with the 'definite implication' being coordinated military action.[73] A wounded Prime Minister was now proposing a military pact in eastern Europe; and politics, as much as strategy, had driven him to this position. Halifax welcomed the idea, believing that it would have 'immense political influence'.[74] Meeting the Polish Ambassador the following day, Halifax emphasized that Britain would view any Nazi threat to Danzig as a 'grave' issue; Poland was thus erected alongside Romania as another crucial test of German intentions.[75] Halifax was seeking to establish a series of diplomatic and military tripwires in eastern Europe. And he wanted these to be made public.

Chamberlain, in contrast, did not *really* want to extend a guarantee to any of the 'existing frontiers' or the 'status quo', and hoped that 'consultation' between Britain, France, Russia, and Poland would prove sufficient to deter Hitler.[76] It seems that the Prime Minister only entered into this talk of pacts and consultations in order to protect himself at home; privately, he thought the entire initiative impracticable and just wanted someone else to take responsibility for its failure. As he wrote when the Poles refused to sign a commitment to consult with Britain, France, and Russia:

> I could readily understand why. Hitherto [Poland] has skilfully balanced between Germany and Russia so as not to get in trouble with either . . . Was it worth while to go on with Russia in that case? I must confess to the most profound distrust of Russia . . . I distrust her motives which seem to . . . be concerned only with getting everyone else by the ears. Moreover she is . . . hated . . . by many of the smaller states notably Poland, Romania and Finland . . .[77]

Still, given Chamberlain's acute sense of vulnerability, he *was* willing to issue a British guarantee of Poland—though not one that would commit him to going to war over German predations against Danzig.[78] How far this would really constitute a 'guarantee', as opposed to a gesture, is something the reader will have to judge. But on 29 March, 'hair-raising' rumours that Germany was preparing to strike at the

Poles were utilized by the Foreign Secretary to bounce Chamberlain into offering a firmer guarantee.[79] It was widely believed that these rumours were fake as, indeed, they were.[80] But Halifax had a private meeting with the Prime Minister and came away with an agreement that Britain should extend an 'immediate' guarantee.[81] Halifax's imposition of this policy was his greatest success over the Prime Minister. The Cabinet soon endorsed the decision. Butler recorded that 'Halifax is determined to set up a force to counter Germany and . . . is going ahead single-mindedly'.[82] Equally, the Foreign Secretary argued there was a need to bring Churchill and Eden into the ministry. This dispute over 'broadening the base of the government' was thought to be 'his main difference with the P.M.', which rather indicates how far Halifax's policy was being driven by political optics.[83] Chamberlain, in contrast, thought in terms of personal vendettas. As he contemptuously put it, 'our Anthony' is 'in a dilemma from which he would much like me to extract him', and the Prime Minister was not minded to do any such thing unless Eden was willing 'to proclaim his repentance'.[84] And he certainly did not want Churchill let loose in Whitehall.

In Parliament on 31 March, a weakened Chamberlain announced the British guarantee of Poland against 'any action' which 'threatened Polish independence'.[85] The guarantee would commit Britain to war against Germany if Hitler violated it.[86] It was a change in policy compelled by Halifax. The National Government had resisted any military guarantee of Czechoslovakia in the autumn of 1938 because, due to geography, nothing could be done to make it effective. Now a guarantee of Poland—an undertaking which would be even more militarily dubious– was suddenly issued. That there was no obvious way in which Britain could defend Poland underlined the degree to which foreign policy had been reduced to symbolism rather than a hard-headed appraisal of strategic interests and military practicalities.

The guarantee constituted a 'frightful gamble', in the words of Cadogan.[87] Wilson advised against it, and feared Chamberlain had gone 'off the deep end'.[88] But his master possessed more sensitive political antennae and saw no other option. Neville was deeply unhappy, for 'I can never forget that the ultimate decision, the Yes or No which may decide the fate not only of all this generation, but of the British Empire itself, rests with me'.[89] Seeking a possible route of retreat, the Prime Minister was careful to insist that Britain would not guarantee the current *frontiers* of Poland, only the *independence* of the country—and, crucially, 'it is we who will decide whether their independence is threatened or not'.[90] As Geoffrey Dawson of *The Times* dutifully put it, Britain was not committed to 'defend every inch of the present frontiers'.[91] Ball may have been behind this editorial.[92] Channon recognized that Chamberlain's 'heart is not really in' the policy of guarantees.[93] French opinion was scarcely thrilled at the prospect of fighting for Poland, either; the slogan 'Why Die For Danzig?' began to gain traction in France.

Politically, however, the Polish guarantee was welcomed across the spectrum. Even the Labour party supported it. Most importantly, it established important linkages between the government and its critics in the Conservative party. A friend of Halifax, Lord Salisbury, had specifically suggested to the Foreign Secretary that Britain should guarantee Poland.[94] Halifax thus constructed a policy that was acceptable to both the Prime Minister and his critics. Even Wilson acknowledged that it was now 'impossible, *politically*, not to give the guarantee'.[95] Some Labour figures actually tried to claim credit for the development, optimistically declaring that the government was being 'conver[ted]' to their own policy.[96]

Yet international stability remained elusive. In early April, Europe's carrion hunter Mussolini joined Hitler's free-for-all as Italy invaded Albania. Chamberlain's 'faith' in the word of the dictators was close to collapse, for Mussolini had 'behaved liked a sneak and a cad to me'.[97] This was followed in early May by the announcement of a formal alliance between Germany and Italy, the 'Pact of Steel'. An embarrassed Chamberlain was 'depressed', for such episodes 'enable my enemies to mock me publicly and weaken my authority in this country'.[98] Sure enough, Labour launched fresh public attacks with another wave of speeches. Within days of the assault on Albania, Halifax therefore insisted on issuing additional guarantees, this time of the independence of both Greece and Romania. Chamberlain was unhappy about the commitments, but in the face of Cabinet pressure had no choice but to relent.[99] When he relayed news of the guarantees to Parliament he was subjected to stern, even personal, criticism; Attlee, Labour backbenchers, and Churchill all took aim.[100] On 20 April a frail-looking Chamberlain announced the creation of a Ministry of Supply to coordinate the organization of Britain's resources, and shortly afterwards revealed the implementation of six months' conscription for men aged twenty to twenty-one. These were measures he had been determined to avoid but now lacked the power to resist. The Prime Minister was no longer driving the bus.

'A Great Crunch Is Coming'

In contrast, the man whom Conservative leaders had long been determined to keep out of power was quite obviously in the ascendancy.[101] Though still willing to criticize policy when the opportunity presented itself, Churchill now behaved in a noticeably more measured fashion. His public warnings about defence matters were delivered with just as much brio as before, but he was also circumspect about what he said and when. This change was almost certainly made in order to enhance his prospects of being invited into office by a Prime Minister desperate for a political lifeline. When others demanded the introduction of conscription days after the destruction of Czechoslovakia, Winston remained silent. Amery seethed that 'he never said a word. He is still very much . . . a politician'.[102] And he would even pen supportive notes to Chamberlain and Halifax. At moments of tension the Prime Minister found that Churchill was 'telephoning almost every hour of the day' offering unsolicited advice.[103] In April 1939 Winston actually insinuated in the Commons that Wilson was the real source of difficulty, not Chamberlain: there was a hidden 'hand' at work behind the scenes, he said, one which 'intervenes and filters down and withholds intelligence from ministers'.[104] And he let it be known that he had a 'strong desire' to join the government.[105] Chamberlain, exhausted and vulnerable, turned the idea over in his mind, but for the moment did nothing.

Throughout 1939, Churchill cannily sought to build bridges in all directions. His rhetoric about national honour was a fungible language that might mean anything but also resonated widely. He worked to improve relations with Labour and the Eden group. In February he invited Halifax to attend a gathering of cross-party critics of Chamberlain. This was a prospect which the Foreign Secretary admitted 'scared' him;[106] but Halifax was increasingly sceptical about whether Chamberlain could concot the right formula for electoral success. In June, Churchill delivered a speech in which he lauded Halifax, made no mention of their long-running dispute over India, and declared that 'there are no differences between us' apart from 'emphasis . . . and timing'.[107] Just twenty-four hours later Churchill hosted Labour exile Stafford Cripps at his flat, during which he raged against Chamberlain for not taking him into the Cabinet and said that he wanted 'an all-in' coalition regime.[108] Even privately he 'talked about nothing but the prospect of war'; over endless 'whisky and cigars', he regaled dinner guests with his view that 'Chamberlain is not a war Prime Minister' and did not want him in the Cabinet because Winston would be 'so strong' that Chamberlain might be stripped of his power.[109]

The impact of all this on Churchill's fortunes was remarkable. By the summer of 1939, he had comprehensively stolen Eden's 'thunder'.[110] The Prime Minister himself acknowledged that in 'the country', Eden 'was not of the same consequence . . . as Winston'.[111] The press campaigned vigorously for Churchill to join the Cabinet in a senior role, and not only the usual suspects like the *Daily Telegraph*, the *Daily Mail*, and the *Daily Express*; on 3 July nearly every national newspaper ran an article on the subject. Eden's follower 'Bobbety' Cranborne complained of the focus of the press: 'It is Winston, Winston, Winston all the time'. There was, he moaned, 'so little mention of Anthony'.[112]

That Churchill's inclusion in the Cabinet appeared inevitable was symptomatic of both Hitler's behaviour and Chamberlain's vulnerability. But Chamberlain was 'taken aback' by the force of the demands for Churchill to be given a powerful post and deemed it a 'conspiracy'.[113] Channon felt it 'quite threatening'.[114] The Prime Minister still refused to yield, because he would come into 'violent disagreement' with Churchill, because Winston's schemes would 'monopolise the time' of the government, and because he was 'Public Enemy Number 1 in Berlin'.[115] But the correspondence reaching Chartwell over the summer of 1939 indicated that the political nation expected Chamberlain to be compelled to take Churchill into government sooner or later. In this climate, Winston was in better spirits than he had been for years. He described himself as being 'entirely quiescent' as he awaited events: 'a great crunch is coming'.[116]

9

THE DIE IS CAST

The Russian Dimension

That 'crunch' was not long in arriving. Yet in examining the profoundly vulnerable position in which strategic incoherence and political manoeuvre had placed Britain, we need to consider the chessboard of geopolitics from another perspective. This is because the Soviet Union occupied an important place in the minds of British policymakers.

Whispers that the National Government might pursue an alliance with the Soviet Union began to grow louder in early 1939.[1] Such an alignment could represent a means to deter Germany and furnish Britain and France with a powerful ally, possessed of the largest army and air force in the world, and backed by virtually inexhaustible reserves of manpower. The Labour party—including those who had no illusions about Stalin—advocated such a policy. Opinion polling found that 87 per cent of the British public favoured an Anglo-French-Soviet alliance.[2] Within the Cabinet, Hoare shifted from implacable hostility to Moscow to being a strong supporter of a pact.[3] This may have been unconnected to the public popularity of a Soviet alliance; but, equally, for a posturer like Sam Hoare it may also have been motivated by a desire to distance himself from Chamberlain and advertise eye-catching credentials on a big issue.

Left anxious by this public and political pressure, in March 1939 a British Prime Minister attended a reception at the Russian embassy in London for the first time since the Revolution of 1917. It was a calculated gesture of rapprochement. Ministers were routinely invited to the soirees, but never turned up; Maisky was therefore visibly astonished at the sight of Chamberlain crossing the threshold of the communists' embassy. He was accompanied by several members of the Cabinet and their wives.[4] Two months later, Halifax led Cabinet pressure for the National Government to explore a direct agreement with Moscow. The Chiefs of Staff were also now in favour of a 'whole-hog' alliance.[5]

Sipping mulled wine with Maisky at the embassy was one thing; but any notion of formal alliance remained anathema to a Prime Minister who 'hated it' and threatened to 'resign rather than sign'.[6] Maisky realized that Chamberlain wanted 'to use us as a shield against the opposition's attacks', but had no genuine interest in cooperation.[7] Chamberlain told his sister that he distrusted the Soviets' motives, for Moscow '[is] concerned only with getting everyone else by the ears'.[8] The USSR 'is afraid of Germany & Japan and would be delighted to see other people fight them ... Her efforts are therefore devoted to egging on others'.[9] But he knew that 'a failure to associate with Soviet Russia would give rise to suspicion and difficulty with the Left Wing in this country'.[10]

Faced with little choice, the Prime Minister reluctantly sanctioned discussions with Russia because of the 'immense difficulties' a refusal would create.[11] It was yet another blow. 'He is being pushed all the time into a policy he does not like', recorded Amery.[12] Showing a degree of paranoia, Chamberlain complained that the Soviets 'are working hand in hand with our Opposition'.[13] The mood in Parliament remained bitterly hostile, and in turn Chamberlain began to perceive critics as 'traitor[s]'.[14] He knew that Maisky was 'in constant touch' with Churchill, Eden, and Lloyd George, and believed that those three men were plotting to force their way into the Cabinet and substitute Chamberlain for 'a more amenable PM!'[15] The Prime Minister may have seen enemies everywhere, but considering the identities of those men who forced him from office less than a year later, it is difficult to say that he was worrying about nothing. He understood that the next general election would 'be fought mainly around' his record as Prime Minister—and the prospects of that were far from promising.[16] Further weakness in his dealings with Hitler might mean that 'I should be swept out of office without a moment's delay'.[17] Cognizant of the political impossibility of refusal and desperate to find a means of scrambling out of the impasse in which he found himself, the Prime Minister reluctantly permitted the Foreign Office to explore whether an alignment with Moscow might somehow be viable.

The reason for Chamberlain's instinctive hostility was that he understood the principal beneficiary of such a policy would be Josef Stalin. One could argue that the major beneficiary of Britain's botched European strategy in recent years had *already* been the Red Tsar. A binding agreement with Stalin would have conceded him the initiative and, in all likelihood, simply landed Britain and France in a conflict with Germany of the USSR's making and at a time of Stalin's choosing. British foreign policy since 1935 had done the Kremlin enough favours.

Another problem was that talk of alliance with the USSR aroused powerful fears among most Conservatives;[18] Bolshevism was widely seen as being as great a menace as Nazism. To understand this one has to see the interwar world as did those who were there. In interwar Europe, the threat posed by the USSR was a cultural touchstone. The Bolsheviks had been engaging in mass murder, repression, and subversion before the Nazi Party was even a gleam in Hitler's eye. Depicting themselves as the vanguard of 'the people', they had in fact set up the most effective terror state in the world. The Bolsheviks helped overthrow an ancient dynasty, mobilized the support to take over a vast country, and brought about its collapse before re-emerging onto the world stage. They led a totalitarian regime of incredible violence. Their ambitions across Europe, and beyond, were familiar to anyone with access to classified intelligence reports—or even a newspaper. Soviet interference in the Spanish Civil War through the provision of arms, funding, and military 'advisers' for the Republican forces confirmed the suspicion that Stalin hoped to subvert Europe and bring it under his sway—as did encouraging Communist parties around the world to raise volunteers to travel to Spain and fight, a policy which ultimately attracted around 40,000 people in the form of the 'International Brigades'. Soviet intelligence conducted assassinations across Europe of communists who rejected Stalin's authority. The USSR boasted high-level spies in Britain, France, Germany, and Japan with astonishing access to state secrets; the search for traitors funnelling information to the Kremlin occupied much energy. And before Churchill fixed his sights on Hitler in 1936, for almost two decades he had been the staunchest enemy of the USSR in the British polity. His views on the 'foul baboonery' and 'pestilence' of Bolshevism were well known and violent.[19] Indeed, one historian has noted that, taking Churchill's career as a whole, 'the contest with Soviet Bolshevism was what gave his public life the greatest continuity and meaning'.[20]

Discussion of Marxism-Leninism and the reality of life in the Soviet Union were a commonplace in the universities, Westminster, and the serious press. Enough was known in the West to understand that the image of the USSR as a workers' paradise was a fantasy, and that behind the veil of secrecy imposed by the Politburo the remarkable feats of industrial development were built on despotism and murder. Stalin's regime was even more barbarous than that of Hitler. Bolshevism placed such a stress on conspiracy—both as something to be practised and as a conviction that everyone else was engaged in it as well—that it was like a fever. Arbitrary arrest, torture, murder, and the targeting of family members were more likely in the USSR than Germany. There were quotas for arrests and 'liquidations' that had to be met and, preferably, exceeded. The secret police, the NKVD, was a million strong. Something like 100 million people were effectively enslaved under the system of collectivized agriculture. The scale of Soviet success in industrial collectivization was, to Western observers, discomforting at best, and terrifying at worst; meanwhile the purges of the Red Army (under which 40,000 officers were murdered) under-lined the character of the regime. Where the goals of Berlin, Tokyo, and Rome were weighted towards the *particular*—those countries and the territories they aspired to possess—those of the USSR were weighted towards the *universal*. The millenarian objectives of the Soviet Union were potentially all-encompassing. And by the late 1930s, Soviet Russia was re-emerging onto the international scene. It was now a huge industrial power whose military spending outpaced that of all other states besides Nazi Germany. Bolshevism was thus regarded as posing an existential threat to the survival of European civilization itself. Therefore, whilst the tendency of a post-war generation to perceive Germany as the major enemy of the 1930s is understandable, at the time it was far from obvious that the USSR was not as great a threat; and in light of what happened to eastern Europe during half a century of Communist occupation after 1945, it is difficult to view those who warned about the Soviets as alarmist. Western Marxist intellectuals and activists have often argued that the USSR was an aberration. But the application of Marxist-Leninist doctrine led to similar outcomes in China, North Korea, Cambodia, and elsewhere. While leaders grappled with the latest predatory behaviour from Mussolini or Hitler, the spectre of the USSR always loomed in the background.

In 1936, Leo Amery expressed the view that Britain should 'leave the three sources of danger, Germany, Russia and Japan, to neutralise each other'. He feared that alternative approaches—whether those of Churchill or the government— would commit Britain 'to participation in their struggles'.[21] Churchill may have been willing to conveniently set aside two decades of venom towards the Soviet Union in order to focus on Germany, but others were cognizant of a larger picture. Baldwin himself said that 'if there is any fighting in Europe to be done, I should like to see the Bolshies and the Nazis doing it'.[22] 'We all know the German desire, and [Hitler] has come out with it in his book [*Mein Kampf*], to move east, and if he should move east I should not break my heart'.[23] Some were positively enthusiastic about the prospect: 'Chips' Channon wanted to let 'gallant little Germany glut her fill of Reds in the east'.[24] Baldwin and Chamberlain were both determined that Britain would wage war only in her own national interest, but the problem was that their policies had repeatedly done Stalin's work for him. While Hitler and Stalin tearing into—and destroying—one another would be the ideal war if there had to be a conflict, British policymakers had repeatedly interposed themselves in eastern European affairs and rendered it more likely that *they*, rather than the Kremlin, would have to be the ones to confront Hitler. This, arguably, was the real failing of British strategy.

Stalin thus reaped enormous benefits from the conflict and confusion at Westminster that produced the National Government's foreign policy. The British guarantees of Poland and Romania 'have relieved the Soviet Union of anxiety for the greater part of their western frontier', diagnosed one Foreign Office official; 'they can therefore afford to stand out for their own terms' in alliance negotiations.[25] The diaries of Russia's ambassador to London, Maisky, leave the reader in no doubt that Stalin perceived Germany as the USSR's principal adversary. Likewise, those who witnessed Hitler 'all but foaming at the mouth' at the merest mention of communists understood where the Fuhrer's priorities lay.[26] The Spanish Civil War, with Russian proxies fighting against German proxies, was recognized as 'the first serious duel' between the two states.[27] Stalin's view was that if Britain could be prevailed upon to get in the middle, so much the better. Britain was 'a small island', he said, 'but one on which much depends'.[28] It behoved Kremlin diplomacy to try and find someone else to do the job of protecting Soviet interests.

In Europe, the Soviets had expended much energy in trying to guide British policy in directions which served their goals. Maisky was working to persuade the National Government to enter into commitments in central and eastern Europe as early as 1936, long before it was on the agenda in Whitehall.[29] His diary betrays a long-running obsession (understandably so, given that all Soviet diplomats lived in fear of being shot for failure) with cajoling Britain to bear the burden of security in that part of the continent; or, in Maisky's telling phrase, having the responsibility for *bang[ing] one's fist on the table*' when it came to Hitler.[30] The imagery this metaphor evokes is vivid.

Conscious of what an alignment with the USSR would entail, throughout the summer of 1939 the Prime Minister therefore did his best to sabotage the negotiations with the Russians (whom he thought 'peasant[s]').[31] But Chamberlain did not have to try very hard, for the new Soviet Foreign Minister, Vyacheslav Molotov, was intransigent and suspicious. With Britain performing the job of policing his own backyard against the Germans, Stalin was free to drive a hard bargain. On 14 August the talks collapsed when Poland and Romania refused to agree to the Red Army being stationed on their territory. In essence, Stalin was seeking to exploit British anxiety over Germany in order to carve out a de facto eastern European empire without ever firing a shot to conquer it. He envisaged the largest armed forces in the world simply sweeping forward to occupy great chunks of the continent under the pretence of 'protecting' it from Germany. Shamelessly, he wanted Britain and France committed by treaty to defend all states 'bordering on the USSR' from 'the Baltic [to] the Black seas'.[32] Halifax objected that Soviet demands would only 'put us in Russia's power', and, while acknowledging that he was venturing 'a very cynical' perspective, believed that in the event of a crisis 'on the day the Soviet government would act as suited them best at the time without the slightest regard to any prior undertakings'.[33]

Stalin was seeking an agreement in which it would essentially be up to him to determine when and where Britain and France went to war.

Within days of it becoming apparent that Britain would not simply award the Kremlin a sphere of influence which the Western powers would also be committed to defending, Molotov dramatically reversed course and signed a treaty with Hitler instead. The Nazi–Soviet Pact of 23 August 1939 upended the entire international system. It was a diplomatic bolt from the blue. Under the Pact, Germany secured access to the raw materials of the Soviet Union, agreed on a framework to carve up eastern Europe, and was no longer threatened with a two-front war. Berlin and Moscow also secretly agreed to divide Poland between them, while the Baltic states were recognized as an area of Soviet interest. The deal represented a fundamental transformation in the international situation.

Chamberlain was astonished, having believed that no accommodation between these two natural enemies was possible. But, in fact, it was one that his own government had facilitated through several years of British efforts to control geopolitics in eastern Europe. The British guarantee of Poland actually opened up the possibility of the hitherto unthinkable arrangement between Germany and the USSR, because if Hitler was going to face Britain and France, he needed to first secure his rear. Lloyd George had grasped the possibility of this happening when the guarantee to Poland was made on 31 March, and in a private meeting on 1 April urged the Prime Minister to halt an 'irresponsible gamble that may end very badly for our country'.[34] Issued for purposes of politics and symbolism, the Polish guarantee tied Britain to a position that was fundamentally unstrategic. Lloyd George recognized the risks because his mind worked in the same brazen way as the dictators, and he had long anticipated that they would 'wipe the floor' with those who directed British policy.[35] When the old rogue explained his thinking, Chamberlain, apparently stumped, 'did not have an answer'.[36]

If the Prime Minister thought that Lloyd George—whom he 'despised' as much as ever—was an old fool, the events of August suggested otherwise.[37] With the Pact, Stalin secured the European buffer zone he wanted. During the talks with London the Kremlin had sought an explicit British statement that the guarantee of Poland only operated against Germany, a clear indication that Stalin was regarding Polish territory with avaricious eyes. That Hitler conceived of the Nazi–Soviet Pact as a temporary measure until he attacked the USSR did not change the fact that it altered the dynamic of European politics and demonstrated the bankruptcy of the assumptions around which British foreign policy had been based. One is reminded of the comparably shocking 1756 Treaty of Versailles between Bourbon France and Habsburg Austria, two rival great powers that Britain assumed could never ally together. Indeed, the parallels between these 'unnatural' unions do not end there. The strategic vulnerability to which the Bourbon–Habsburg pact gave rise was a product of another era of dangerous and self-defeating British involvement in the geopolitics of central Europe. In many respects, the Nazi–Soviet Pact was the logical culmination of events since 1937. The National Government's interference in the region helped to bring about a marriage of convenience between two natural and deadly enemies and delayed their having to confront one another. This was the vertiginous irony of British foreign policy.

That such a situation was permitted to develop only underlines the almost complete absence of imaginative, counter-intuitive thinking that prevailed at Westminster.[38] Debate and policy were both conducted within simple parameters that were ideal for easy explanation and convenient indignation but insufficiently sophisticated for a situation that demanded ingenuity. British policy enabled Stalin to 'fish in troubled waters', rather than having to worry about his boat capsizing.[39] He should never have been afforded that freedom. As Rab Butler argued, by 'gratuitously planting ourselves in eastern Europe' Britain only served Stalin's interests more than her own.[40] Britain boasted the power, resources, and freedom to exercise much greater discretion in its approach to the international crisis than it did between 1937 and 1939. An island empire, the country did not operate under the same rigid necessities as continental states. But this freedom of choice was consistently squandered. By the summer of 1939, the implications of that were painfully apparent.

Confrontation with Japan

An additional source of discomfort in mid-1939 was the Far East. In recent years, the growing threat posed to the British Empire by Japan had been diverted by Tokyo's war of conquest against China. This was a brutal affair and large swathes of Chinese territory—including Beijing, Shanghai, and Nanking—were added to what would soon boast the rather misleading title of the Greater East Asia Co-Prosperity Sphere, a front for Japanese imperial control of Asia. Yet, from a hard-headed British perspective, China had successfully absorbed Japan's energy in the Pacific region for a number of years. London encouraged this, providing limited financial aid to help prevent the financial collapse of the Chinese state and thus keep Tokyo occupied. (The United States and the Soviet Union followed the same approach.) If Japan was going to be on the rampage in Asia, it was far better that she be tied down fighting someone else. However, far more could perhaps have been done to turn China into a deadly quagmire for the Japanese. The Cabinet held several discussions about expanding the amount of British aid to China, but hesitated lest Japan be provoked into outright hostility. Considering that Tokyo was committed to eliminating British influence in Asia, this seems another mistake.

London's weakness vis-à-vis Japan was painfully demonstrated by the Tientsin crisis of June 1939. Tokyo decided to enforce a military blockade of British possessions in the Chinese city of Tientsin, a port in northern China. This step was undertaken in annoyance at London's decision to guarantee loans for China of £5 million from British banks, as well as the refusal to hand over a number of Chinese accused of terrorism. Around 1,500 British subjects lived in Tientsin, and they suddenly found themselves surrounded by the Japanese military. An electrified fence was constructed, deliveries of food and fuel were prohibited, and Britons were routinely humiliated by being strip-searched at bayonet-point. This outraged opinion at home, particularly when stories of women being strip-searched reached the press. War seemed imminent. Some elements of the Japanese government hoped to exploit difficulties in Europe to provoke an opportunistic conflict against the Empire and expel Britain from the Pacific.

Faced with a serious crisis, the Chamberlain government judged that the only way to compel the Japanese to back down would be to dispatch the full force of the Royal Navy to the Pacific to impose either a diplomatic settlement on Tokyo or, alternatively, a military solution. But with Britain having issued a guarantee of Poland against Germany, the fleet was needed in European waters to enforce a blockade of the Third Reich should war erupt. There could be no prospect of sending the Royal Navy across the world to deal with Japan. Caught between the Devil and the deep blue sea, in mid-August Britain backed down and agreed to turn over the Chinese suspects. It was a humiliation. The blockade was lifted when the Japanese Emperor—worshipped as a living god by his people—made clear to his ministers that he was uneasy about the prospect of a war with Britain while Tokyo was still at war with China and facing rising tensions with the USSR along their borders in northern Asia. Yet the decision to accept embarrassment at the hands of Japan and capitulate at Tientsin amounted to a serious blow to British prestige in the Pacific. Chamberlain's focus on eastern Europe had left Britain unable to defend the Empire. Meanwhile Japan was left convinced that the British position in Asia was ripe for the taking. There would be a price to be paid for that as well.

Purchasing Peace?

In the summer of 1939, an embattled and dispirited Chamberlain made one last-ditch bid to induce the Fuhrer to see sense. Short on options, the Prime Minister was reduced to dangling the carrot of cold, hard cash before Hitler's covetous eyes. In a series of secret meetings undertaken by trusted emissaries, the Prime Minister endeavoured to quietly remind the Nazis of the important economic benefits to be derived from trade between Britain and Germany. This was attempted bribery. He was hoping to appeal not only to Hitler, but also his counsellors—men who might think of the money on offer and whisper peaceable sweet-nothings into the Fuhrer's ear. On 22 July, Chamberlain dispatched Ball and Wilson to meet Helmut Wohltat, a senior official in the German Economics Ministry. Ball floated a scheme of cooperation between British and German companies to develop major new export markets in China, the British Empire, and the USSR; this would be supplemented by a series of loans backed by the British government to the German central bank.[41] It was a plan to pay the Nazis to behave themselves. In return, Wilson wanted a joint Anglo-German declaration that 'forcible aggression will not be employed by either country as an instrument of national policy'.[42] How little the Prime Minister understood his quarry. Wilson told Wohltat that the discussions ought to be kept secret from 'persons who were fundamentally hostile to an understanding', an obvious reference to political opinion at Westminster.[43] Ball communicated to Berlin that the National Government was planning to hold the next general election on 14 November 1939;[44] Chamberlain's desire to broker some kind of settlement, and entrusting his most valued confidantes in Ball and Wilson to pursue it, should be seen through that lens.

The Prime Minister employed another emissary—this time a financier who worked in the City of London—to reach Ribbentrop in Berlin.[45] This man allegedly proposed a British loan to Germany of £1 billion as well as a gift of £100 million. Though the precise details of the offer have never been convincingly established, the suspicion that large sums of money were involved has an air of verisimilitude to it. Considering that British gross national product in 1938 had been £5.1 billion, a loan of £1 billion represented a colossal sum of money.[46] Meanwhile Wilson spoke to Fritz Hesse, an attaché at the German embassy, on behalf of his master and proposed a twenty-five-year defensive pact between Britain and Germany, a commitment to the territorial status quo, and economic cooperation.[47] With no cards left to play, Chamberlain resorted to offering to write a cheque if only Hitler would play by the rules. The problem was that the Fuhrer was uninterested in British bribery. Things had gone too far for that.

Spiralling Towards Disaster

In the aftermath of the Nazi–Soviet Pact, a major war in eastern Europe—launched by Germany against her Polish neighbour—now appeared certain. Indeed, having

THE DIE IS CAST

forged his alliance with the USSR, Hitler quickly utilized the question of Danzig as an excuse to menace Poland. The Fuhrer calculated that Britain would not in fact go to war to resist him there.[48] In late August, left with little choice by the climate at home, a weary Chamberlain informed Parliament that if Germany invaded Poland, Britain would indeed fight to uphold the principles of proper international conduct, upon which 'all possibility of peace and security' depended.[49] The conflagration of an Anglo-German conflict now loomed. Yet whatever he said publicly for political effect, the Prime Minister was *still* doggedly committed to the cause of peace. He refused to permit a general mobilization of the British military lest it provoke Berlin, and when telling the House of Commons that an invasion of Poland would mean war, Chamberlain spoke dispassionately, 'like a coroner summing up a case of murder'.[50] He plainly did not believe in the policy he was being forced to carry out. His own errors, the behaviour of Hitler, and the actions of opponents at Westminster had placed the Prime Minister in a vice. That vice now began to turn.

Undeterred by what he believed to be Chamberlain's empty warning, the Fuhrer decided that the hour had come at last. On the morning of 1 September 1939, Hitler finally unleashed his armed forces. German troops crossed the Polish frontier and commenced the long-planned invasion of their neighbour. The armoured divisions and infantry of the *Wehrmacht* advanced rapidly through the country, while the *Luftwaffe* bombed the capital, Warsaw. Poland was no match for Germany, but this was a lighting operation. It was the first application of the doctrine of *Blitzkrieg* that the German High Command had been working on. Reports from the front made for intimidating reading.

In Britain, the public was far from enthusiastic at the prospect of war but by now largely resigned to its inevitability. The military was finally mobilized and conscription introduced for all men aged eighteen to forty-one, a decision supported by the Labour party. The mood of the country found an eerie reflection in the weather; London was subjected to days of torrential, 'blinding' rain.[51] The Prime Minister appreciated that a general European war was effectively inevitable, but it was an indication of the mistrust he now engendered that his final efforts to avoid a conflict, as well as to coordinate the formal declaration of war with the French, provoked a Cabinet 'mutiny' on 2 September led by Hoare and Simon.[52] Chamberlain issued a warning to Hitler to withdraw immediately, but was willing to discuss the status of Danzig and the Polish border if he did so.[53] It is telling that Halifax now supported him on this. Having forced Chamberlain to adopt a firmer posture throughout 1939, the Foreign Secretary suddenly wilted. Previously categorical in rejecting continued appeasement, he lacked the stomach for a fight when the moment arrived. Halifax had been worried by the commitment to Poland that he had engineered, believing it might encourage Warsaw to be intransigent with Germany over frontier issues. In August, for instance, he stated that 'we must . . . make plain that our guarantee was not a blank cheque'.[54] He was consequently open to pressurizing the Poles to accommodate German demands.[55] This shift in his behaviour reinforces the notion that, in urging a tougher line earlier in 1939, Halifax had perhaps been thinking of domestic perception all along; now that the Polish issue seemed likely to precipitate a major military confrontation, he was quick to backtrack.

Yet after the evasions of the previous two years, the bulk of the Cabinet appreciated that the National Government could not be seen to flinch.[56] Perhaps with an eye on the succession, Hoare led the resistance and argued that Chamberlain was 'running tremendous risks' with 'public opinion'.[57] Even the *impression* of a renewed bout of appeasement would be the end, and the Cabinet came down strongly against additional delay or prevarication. If Chamberlain stuck the boot in to Hoare during his darkest hour in December 1935, the Home Secretary repaid the favour with interest four years later. Astonishingly, however, Chamberlain and Halifax attempted to ignore this expression of Cabinet feeling and continued on their course. The Prime Minister still believed that Hitler was willing to 'work seriously' on 'an agreement with us'.[58]

As it became clear over the course of 1 and 2 September that Chamberlain was seeking to avoid an immediate declaration of war, or even issue a deadline for German withdrawal, the House of Commons was in uproar, the mood around Parliament 'insane'. Some Conservatives believed that 'it was in Winston's power to go to the House of Commons and break [Chamberlain] and take his place'.[59] The stage was set for one of the defining moments in British parliamentary history. Ahead of a statement in the Commons from the Prime Minister on 2 September, many MPs started drinking, steeling themselves with whisky for what was to come.[60] In his speech, Chamberlain explained the gravity of the crisis but was characteristically ambiguous on what would happen next. The address fell far short of a rallying cry. The results were dramatic. When Chamberlain sat down having left open the possibility of further negotiation with Hitler, 'the House gasped'.[61] A rerun of Munich seemed imminent. As the Labour deputy leader Arthur Greenwood—who was standing in for Attlee while he recovered from prostate surgery—rose to reply, a spontaneous 'wave' of cheers suddenly erupted across the Commons. Astonishingly, the Conservative benches cheered him even more vociferously than Labour MPs.[62] Chamberlain flinched. For his part, Greenwood 'almost staggered with surprise' at the roar.[63] Leo Amery—positively 'demented' with fury—famously shouted, 'Speak for England, Arthur!'[64] It was a sight none of those who witnessed it would ever forget.

Greenwood called upon the Prime Minister to issue an immediate declaration of war.[65] He told the House that Chamberlain's speech had 'perturbed' him, and demanded Britain 'must march with the French . . . the die is cast'. Refusing to afford the Prime Minister any additional room for compromise, Greenwood made clear that Labour would fully back such a policy. When he finished his speech, he was again cheered by MPs on the Conservative benches. It was 'an astonishing demonstration . . . here were the PM's most ardent supporters cheering his opponent with all their lungs'.[66]

Labour had left Chamberlain's final effort to avoid a declaration of war in ruins. The Prime Minister feared that the fall of the government was now at hand.[67] Unless war was declared, Chamberlain 'did not believe . . . that the government would be able to maintain itself when it met Parliament the next day'.[68] The face of the Chief Whip, Margesson, was 'purple' with rage at the loss of Commons control; Chamberlain's, by contrast, was 'white as a sheet'.[69] That evening a group of ministers led by Simon bluntly informed him that an ultimatum to Germany must be issued immediately.[70]

Faced with abandonment by his Cabinet and a hostile Parliament, the Prime Minister thus at last relented and sent an ultimatum the following day, Sunday 3 September.[71] Hitler would have two hours to accept it, or war would commence. It was the only way to save his premiership. In July 1939 a journalist at The Times had said that Chamberlain's policy was 'peace at any price except the loss of office'.[72] That remark now appeared to carry a kernel of truth. As Maurice Hankey wrote in 1950, 'Wars usually begin and end in politics'.[73] From 1937 onwards, so many crucial decisions—including the acceleration of rearmament, periodic attempts to appear firm, the decision to guarantee Poland, discussions with the USSR, and the ultimatum of 3 September—had been forced upon the Prime Minister because of high politics.

The final ultimatum was duly presented to Ribbentrop in Berlin by Nevile Henderson at 9.00 a.m. the next morning. No reply was received. Consequently, at 11.15 a.m. on 3 September, with the rainclouds having lifted and the weather turning 'glorious',[74] the moment Chamberlain had laboured to avoid finally arrived. In obvious distress, the Prime Minister went on BBC radio and delivered a sorrowful broadcast. The nation came to a standstill to listen. Chamberlain informed the public that, as no satisfactory assurances had been forthcoming from Berlin, 'this country is at war with Germany'.[75]

Yet it was perhaps the mark of the man that, even now, he could not help but focus on his *personal* disappointment. 'You can imagine what a bitter blow it is to me', he informed his millions of listeners, 'yet I cannot believe there is anything more . . . that I could have done'. Shortly afterwards Chamberlain, looking 'very ill', told Parliament, 'everything I have worked for, everything that I have hoped for, everything that I have believed in during my public life, has crashed into ruins'.[76] The Prime Minister had pursued the policy out of a personal belief that he could somehow spare Europe the agony of war, and continued on this course even when it quickly ceased to serve British interests; now, the failure of the policy was reduced to a personal tragedy for Neville Chamberlain. Exhausted and dispirited, he could not help offering a glimpse of how his mind worked. Neither his speech to Parliament nor his broadcast to the nation was particularly inspiring. Chamberlain looked 'shattered' and 'despairing', his voice 'broken'.[77] When a morose 'Chips' Channon listened to Chamberlain's statement over the wireless, all he could think was that 'our world, or all that remains of it, is committing suicide, whilst Stalin laughs and the Kremlin triumphs'.[78] As the nation's political leaders dispersed that evening, air-raid sirens sounded over Westminster. It was a false alarm, but it was a taste of things to come.

At Downing Street there was one more thing to do, another act which signified the stripping away of Chamberlain's authority. The Prime Minister now had no choice but to bow to the inevitable. Faced with the imperative of shoring up his ministry, on 1 September he had reached out to the Labour party and invited them to join a coalition government—an offer that was immediately rejected. Labour's leaders had no intention of rescuing Chamberlain, and also appreciated that the party would wield little influence if they joined the government at this stage. They preferred to bide their time. After the declaration of war, Chamberlain next approached Conservative critics to participate in a reconstruction of the National Government. There was a job for Eden, though he had squandered so much political capital that it was only a mid-ranking post as Dominions Secretary.

But Churchill—the man who had been right about Hitler all along, and now occupied a unique place in the public sphere—was a fundamentally different matter. The dam constructed to keep him out of power, first built under Baldwin, had finally failed. So great was Churchill's prestige that a mid-ranking role would not do; he would need to be a member of a small inner War Cabinet and possess a prominent voice in strategy. That this would entail other ministers being continually bombarded with lengthy memoranda written in purple prose, transparently composed in order to be quoted in 'the Book' Churchill would inevitably produce after the war, would simply have to be tolerated. With few cards left to play, Chamberlain appointed him First Lord of the Admiralty. When Churchill accepted the post, returning to the office he had first occupied between 1911 and 1915, a short message of just three words was flashed from London to every ship in the Royal Navy. It read 'WINSTON IS BACK'.[79]

The Precariousness of Power

With the declaration of war, the atmosphere at Westminster—and among the public—was largely one of relief. The tension of waiting evaporated; now it was time to get on with the task. There was a striking degree of composure about war, something unthinkable at the time of the Peace Ballot four years earlier. Lloyd George detected a 'grim determination' among 'the masses' to 'carry the war to end'.[80]

Yet how had this situation come about? There was no inescapable logic driving British involvement in the European war that was now underway. This was a dispute about territorial arrangements touching on the frontiers of the Third Reich and the Soviet Union. Britain was not committed to the existing borders. The region was a powder keg. And yet London had been the one to declare war after years of ineffectual diplomacy. Within days the Polish military was crushed, and Warsaw fell to the Germans on 27 September. The Soviet Union joined the invasion to collude in the conquest. The independence of Poland, the cause for which Britain declared war, was swiftly extinguished. In late November, Stalin also attacked Finland in his bid to consolidate Soviet hegemony over the entire region.

Perhaps the most powerful, and culturally influential, criticism of Neville Chamberlain's conduct of British foreign policy after 1937 originates from the standpoint of morality. Indeed, the moral dimension is an enduring aspect of popular views of the 1930s across the Western world, one that still conditions its myths and provides a ready store of 'lessons' about the dangers of appeasement. Chamberlain has frequently been charged with committing a fundamental moral error in failing to confront a uniquely dangerous dictator much earlier; and this criticism is reinforced by hindsight, in our knowledge of the human cost of the Second World War and the German policy of systematic mass murder—most obviously in the Holocaust. Indeed, arguing for a different British policy, one that would have stood back from the regions in which Hitler perpetrated his crimes, can itself seem morally insensitive. Historians who have written along these lines have faced similar accusations. Yet the blunt reality is that while a moral perspective is informative, even inescapable, when assessing the Nazi regime, to mount a critique of British strategy from a moral position runs into immediate difficulties. Coming to grips with that is important in demythologizing this era. The fact is that there was no 'moral' solution on offer. To be sure, Britain could have initiated a war much earlier; but this course of action would, without question, have killed millions—and probably tens of millions. This hardly seems appealing. In addition, a more vigorous policy of deterrence could only have been had either in alliance with, or at the very least by conceding serious diplomatic advantage to, a regime in the USSR that was, if such a thing is possible, even more brutal than Nazi Germany.

The landscape of continental politics, particularly in central and eastern Europe, was not amenable to a morally pleasing approach. There was no clean alternative; simply a range of bad choices. The eventual route to victory in the Second World War was, of course, based around an alliance with the Soviet Union; but it should not be confused with a morally satisfying state of affairs. The only workable approaches on offer were those informed by something quite different: hard calculations of *raison d'état*. We must therefore make a conscious effort to develop criticisms of British policy through the lens of strategy, not morality. That is not to suggest that moral considerations are irrelevant, or worthless in history. Yet it is to point out that they were not an important component in how the practitioners played geopolitical chess during the 1930s. And morality cannot be a central feature of a meaningful strategic critique of British decision-making, because it opens up conundrums which are at least as dubious. We need to avoid undue innocence about the cold relationship between policy and morality.

Mussolini's words had dripped with contempt when, in 1937, he remarked of British policymakers that 'these men are not made of the same stuff as the Francis Drakes and the other magnificent adventurers who created the empire. [They are] the tired sons of a long line of rich men, and they will lose their empire'.[81] The man who had led Britain to victory in 1918, Lloyd George, echoed the suspicion that the strength of the British Empire, acquired over many centuries, was being frittered away. He charged that the Cabinet had 'inherited a rich legacy from their ancestors', which the 'hopeless milksops' were in the process of 'squander[ing]'.[82] It would be another eight months before a 'magnificent adventurer' who was 'made of the same stuff' as the pirates who built the Empire and knew 'how to make the dictators reckon with him' ascended to the premiership.[83] But the game was already up. Within a few years, Lloyd George and Mussolini were proven right.

Perhaps the most important thing the Polish guarantee—given in response to a political crisis at home—had achieved was to grant Stalin room for manoeuvre.[84] Britain and France were committed to bleed in defence of the buffer state, Poland, lying between Germany and the Soviet Union. That Germany's interest was 'Infiltrate East. Bluster West' made sensible strategy all the more important;[85] boiled down to the essentials, its absence between 1937 and 1939 meant that Britain was risking her own power in order to save Stalin from expending his. Thus, by becoming Hitler's adversary in 1938–9, Britain relieved Stalin of an arduous job. And in guaranteeing Poland, Britain permitted the Soviet Union to become the pivot of the entire European balance of power.

The Prime Minister had invested his career, and the future of Britain as a major power, in a personal quest to untie a knot that could not be unravelled. Unable to accept that he had failed, Chamberlain kept 'bargaining...like an old gypsy'.[86] Halifax could emphasize, quite sensibly, that the priority should be to protect Anglo-French 'predominance' in Western Europe as well as in the Mediterranean and the Near East. But if these were the priorities, why the interference in eastern Europe? As the Foreign Secretary himself put it on 1 November 1938, the fact that through its alliance networks France had gotten itself in an 'unreal position' in central and eastern Europe was not a good reason why Britain should clear up the mess;[87] yet Halifax paved the road to war with the subsequent guarantees of Poland, Romania, and Greece. His policy was riddled with as many contradictions as that of Chamberlain. Britain was insisting on a diplomatic veto over a highly unstable region that was not part of its sphere of influence. These commitments—and thus Britain's posture in the final international crisis that precipitated the Second World War—derived from a political struggle at Westminster.

A perceptive man and formidable administrator, Chamberlain was right about many things. He had an acute awareness of what another war would cost Britain, even if she emerged victorious. The Prime Minister also understood that a future conflict was unlikely to be a rerun of the First World War and instead would be marked by mechanization and movement ('I cannot believe that the next war, if it ever comes, will be like the last one and I believe our resources will be more profitably employed in the air and on the sea than in building up great armies').[88] He grasped that in preparing for war, the prosperity required to finance it had to be safeguarded: 'wars are not only won with arms and men. They are won with reserves of resources and credit'.[89] When war came Britain was well equipped to win the conflict, whether it be short or long. But, politically, Chamberlain had failed catastrophically. He was no Baldwin. He had been systematically outflanked. He despised the Labour party and thought their leaders despicable; Attlee was a 'cowardly cur'.[90] He wondered whether Labour's senior figures were agents, unwittingly or otherwise, of the Soviet embassy.[91] Chamberlain felt contempt for Eden and disdain for Churchill, and believed that everyone with a contrary view was an imbecile. He was undoing Baldwin's life's work and destroying the central position occupied by the Conservative party. Baldwin knew how to handle sensitive issues in ways which neutralized public argument. Chamberlain did not even recognize the importance of this.

Abroad, the Prime Minister proved unable or unwilling to follow through on his own instincts to leave central and eastern Europe alone, and could not resist meddling. Chamberlain assumed the premiership aiming to tailor Britain's foreign policy to the requirements of her national interests. Yet the reality was that he did not do so. British foreign policy remained one with expansive burdens, and many of these were of Chamberlain's own creation. If his strategy was not as limitless in its liabilities as that advocated by the likes of Churchill, Labour, and the supporters of the League, it was still very far from 'limited'. Perhaps *that* was Chamberlain's real failing.

10

STATE OF SIEGE

'An Immense and Far-Tentacled Intrigue'

One man who would reap immense benefits from the final months of Chamberlain's regime was not even in Westminster at the moment war erupted.[1] Clement Attlee, leader of His Majesty's Opposition, was in fact 260 miles away at a nursing home on the coast of north Wales. He had been struck down by a problem with his prostate in late May 1939, a condition requiring two surgeries and prolonged recuperation. As he relaxed in a deckchair on the beach, Attlee heard about the Nazi–Soviet Pact over the wireless. Days later, the same wireless set brought him news of the German attack on Poland. He spoke to his deputy, Greenwood, via the telephone and urged him to pressure Chamberlain to declare war: 'We've got to fight'.[2]

On 1 September, the Prime Minister had invited Labour to join a coalition regime. Labour was anticipating this for several months, and senior figures were not keen on the idea. This was not because they were opposed to the notion of coalition; far from it. A cross-party alliance was the only realistic prospect they had of holding office. The problem, rather, was that they had to forge an alliance on the *right* terms. For Labour, coalition politics did not offer happy memories. The Labour party had been torn apart by its participation in the coalition during the First World War; and in 1931, the decision of its leaders to forge the National Government with the Conservatives almost killed the party stone dead. This was seared into its folk memory. The leaders would need to tread carefully. They appreciated that they boasted little political capital that could be translated into leverage. The party was operating from a base of just 167 MPs. Chamberlain loathed them every bit as much as they loathed him, and they knew he would afford Labour little influence over decision-making. As a consequence they were not prepared to serve under him. Dalton believed Chamberlain would give Labour 'the Secretaryship of State for Latrines', and that was about it.[3]

When Hitler invaded Poland, Attlee therefore instructed Greenwood to refuse the offer of coalition. Sensitive that Labour was psychologically fixated with 'betrayal' and 'sell-outs', Clem advised his deputy not to even allow the matter to be the subject of a lengthy discussion by the Executive of the Parliamentary Labour Party (PLP)—lest anyone suspect that a plot was afoot.[4] Any hint of a 'compromise' would only inflame the party's crippling neuroses. Attlee remained confident that Chamberlain was now so fatally discredited he would soon fall. He was adamant that Britain would, in the end, win the war: 'We beat them last time: we'll beat them again. But Chamberlain will have to go'.[5] The PLP Executive followed his recommendation and unanimously rejected the invitation.[6]

The upper echelons of the Labour party were clearly thinking of a *future* coalition, but participation in government would have to be pursued with patience and sensitivity. Moreover, this was not just political expediency; there was deep personal rancour as well. Attlee felt absolutely no inclination to help Chamberlain, a man he 'detested' and thought 'absolutely useless'.[7] Chamberlain returned the feeling. The fact that the Prime Minister had spent the interwar era treating Labour 'like dirt' came back to haunt him. Not only had Chamberlain's policy failed, but his demeanour meant he was positively reviled on the other side of the House of Commons.

When Clem returned to London at the end of September, then, much had changed from the last time he was there in May. Nerves were fraying in Whitehall and Parliament. Electorally, Labour remained pinned to its industrial heartlands and enjoyed little prospect of winning the next general election. For years, the party had been dangerously reticent on the rearmament vital to protect the country— something Conservatives threw in Labour's face at every opportunity. There was also the perpetual risk that someone in the party would do or say something indefensibly stupid. This danger was reinforced when Stafford Cripps—who had, fortunately, been expelled in the spring—expressed his enthusiasm for the Soviet invasion of Poland, believing that the Red Army was a liberating force there to free the Polish people from their class oppressors.

Attlee also had to contend with the fact that a move was now afoot to replace him as leader. In the four years in which he had held the job, Clem made little impression on the general public. He was lacking in charisma, and struggled to set a direction. The bitter factional struggle to renew Labour's ideas, cajole it to toughen up on the dictators, and deal with the internal threat of radical socialists had been waged not by Attlee, but by other men—most obviously Dalton and Morrison and, in the unions, Bevin and Citrine. While Clem was a reassuring and conciliatory presence, since 1935 Labour's leader had not done much in the way of actually *leading*. This was a state of affairs that could not be permitted to persist in conditions of national emergency.

As Attlee travelled to London to chair the meeting of the National Executive Committee (NEC) on 29 September, the vultures were circling. Morrison was one of those preparing to feast. A hugely ambitious man obsessed with becoming leader, Morrison was the most prominent Labour politician in the country and leader of the London County Council. He was dynamic, charismatic, and vigorous—all the things that Attlee was not. He was also a highly capable administrator, and in running the government of London was Labour's biggest success story in the dark years since the 1931 rout. He had been planning to move against Attlee throughout 1939. One newspaper labelled the plot 'an immense and far-tentacled intrigue', while another reported that Morrison's 'closest friends scurry around the lobbies at Westminster ... staking out his claim ... their propaganda is meeting with some success'.[8] They had first attempted to strike within days of Attlee falling ill in May, but the timing was transparent and the move was aborted. By the autumn, Morrison was ready to try again. Attlee's deputy, Arthur Greenwood, was another potential candidate. A tall, lithe, and genial Yorkshireman, Greenwood was popular in the Labour party and had been deputy leader since 1935; and by being the public face of Labour through the final crisis that precipitated the Second World War, he caught the eye of the nation for the first time. Considering that Greenwood was an alcoholic who sometimes turned up to meetings inebriated, and often didn't get out of bed until late afternoon, his sudden ascendancy was rather improbable. *The Times* called him 'the authentic voice of Britain'.[9] In the eyes of some, the former Leeds University economics lecturer suddenly leapfrogged Morrison as the man best placed to dislodge Attlee.[10] Another issue was that the core of the PLP remained the MPs from coalmining areas who had elected Attlee in 1935; many of these were steadfastly loyal to Clem and judged the Cockney Morrison a blatant adventurer. It was thus unclear whether Herbert could win a leadership ballot of MPs before the PLP was flooded with the new members who would hopefully arrive after a general election.[11] Dalton was so desperate to get rid of Attlee that, after witnessing Greenwood's performances in the Commons and at PLP meetings, he switched his support from Morrison to the deputy leader (though, incredibly, he was amenable to replacing Greenwood with Morrison once 'we had loosened the earth' around Attlee!).[12] Attlee's prospects of remaining leader looked bleak.

In early November a backbench MP, Alfred Edwards, wrote to Dalton, Morrison, and Greenwood asking them to permit their names to go forward in a challenge to Attlee.[13] Scenting an opportunity, Morrison was careful in his response. He was at pains to emphasize his loyalty—innocently stating that he was unsure if there existed a 'general or substantial desire' for a leadership election—while simultaneously affirming that '*I should have to reconsider this if a contest were forced from another quarter*'. Herbert stressed that he reserved the right 'to accept nomination at any time'.[14] This was a coded green light to Edwards to force a leadership ballot. At the PLP meeting on 15 November, it became apparent that the names of Dalton, Greenwood, and Morrison had all been put forward.[15] This prompted some pantomime theatre during which there were many bland 'expressions of gentlemanly good will' between the candidates. In other words, all three men would be happy to become leader, but did not want to appear too thrusting in the eyes of the MPs who would make the choice. They thus danced around the issue in hopes that someone else would be the one to demand a ballot.[16]

'Constructive Opposition'

What it swiftly transpired Attlee could do exceedingly well, however, was to take *decisions*. The first eight months of war showed Clem to be a political operator of real cunning and subtlety. He had struggled to set a direction as Leader of the Opposition in peacetime, being unsuited to the game of charisma and appearance; but the Attlee of the Second World War was a fundamentally different creature. He returned from Wales a transformed man, and shone like few others in conditions in which rapid decision-making was essential.[17]

The PLP meeting at which Attlee's fate was to be decided was held, as usual, in a committee room in Parliament. The room was packed, and the atmosphere tense. National emergency and war loomed over the proceedings. The Labour party could not afford a disaster. Clem fully appreciated the game that Morrison and Dalton were playing, and responded to their 'gentlemanly good will' with dexterity. He knocked his opponents off balance by getting to his feet and making a short statement in which he pledged that he would not regard a challenge to his leadership as 'disloyal'.[18] He then sat back down, and quietly waited. It was a masterstroke. This may have seemed like an innocent invitation for his opponents to attack him, but it was much more than that. It was a brilliant defence that threatened to eviscerate any oncoming force. Clem understood that 'disloyal' was the most potent and emotionally charged word in the Labour lexicon, the fear of which fixated both MPs and rank-and-file alike. It raised the spectre of the hated Ramsay MacDonald. By uttering it—even to publicly stress that those who wished to take his job were *not* disloyal—Clem was deliberately playing to the psychology of his party. He knew the power that the word carried and, with his career on the line, planted the seed in the minds of watching MPs. Dalton, Morrison, and Greenwood could ill afford to be viewed as 'disloyal' schemers plotting to enhance their own careers while the country prepared for a fight to the death.

Attlee's words placed enormous pressure on the three men to affirm their loyalty. He sat there amiably, and awaited their response. The result was the rapid deflation of the rebellion. As the assembled MPs looked to the potential challengers, Greenwood told the meeting that he was withdrawing his candidacy. Put in the invidious position of openly placing ambition before party and country if they did not do the same, Dalton and Morrison felt compelled to back down too.[19]

Having faced deposition when he entered the meeting, Attlee left it not only secure, but with a refreshed mandate. He now turned his attention to managing Labour's strategy in the odd atmosphere of what was rapidly becoming known as 'the bore war'. Little of military significance was occurring between the Allies and Germany, and the country waited with bated breath for the 'real' war to get underway. Playing politics in this climate was going to require nerves of steel. At the outbreak of war Chamberlain ordered Whitehall departments to establish liaison arrangements with Labour so as to keep the party apprised of what the different arms of the wartime British state were doing.[20] This was an effort by the Prime Minister to protect himself following the failure to form a coalition. Clem would need to tread carefully lest he step on a political landmine. For one thing, Labour was likely to face toxic Conservative accusations that the party was 'unpatriotic' or 'irresponsible' by refusing to participate in the government or launching criticisms of the war effort. Chamberlain would almost certainly try to depict Labour as exploiting the crisis in order to score points.

Yet it was not enough to simply protect Labour. Attlee also required a means of building up the party's strength for whatever was to come—be it an election, coalition, or long-term uncertainty. He had bold ambitions for the war. Over the final months of 1939 and the first three months of 1940, it became apparent just *how* bold. What Clem really wanted to do was to develop a strategy that would transform the entire British political landscape. He aimed for the Labour party to march onto, and occupy, Baldwin's vaunted centre ground. The catastrophe of foreign policy rendered the longstanding Conservative occupancy of that territory vulnerable; the centre, the place where the 'floating vote' lived, now became a tempting target that Attlee was determined to attack. Over the next few months, his priority was to fuse together four issues—patriotism, the vulnerability of Chamberlain, the emergency of war, and the national desire for strong leadership—into a message that would facilitate Labour's move towards the centre.

Greenwood and others had taken the initial steps in Attlee's absence. The deputy leader publicly described Labour's posture as one of 'patriotic detachment' and 'constructive Opposition'.[21] Greenwood stressed how vital it was that Labour be perceived as behaving 'responsibly' in the national interest.[22] In the House of

Commons, he lambasted Chamberlain for appeasement, while stressing that Labour would stand behind the government in fighting Hitler.[23] It was left somewhat ambiguous as to what exactly standing behind the government meant in practice—beyond assuming an advantageous position from which to plunge the dagger—but this *sounded* right. At a joint meeting of the NEC and the TUC General Council, it was agreed that no Labour MP or trade union official should enter into any arrangement to help the government with the war effort. Tellingly, though, they decided they would not publicize this decision—lest Labour be depicted as behaving unpatriotically.[24]

In an article in *Political Quarterly* that was written anonymously by a senior figure, Labour was advised to bide its time. 'The country will have to pay a heavy price for the sins of the National Government', it thundered.[25] Labour should not 'come to the help of the government too soon', despite the fact that 'false calls of patriotism will no doubt be made' to exhort them to do so. Under no circumstances should Labour participate in a coalition that remained controlled by 'the Men of Munich'. 'It needs tremendous courage in wartime for an Opposition to permit a government to commit suicide; but it is precisely this courage which Labour will need in the coming months'.[26] The party's 'chief objective' should therefore be 'the achievement of a position which can be exploited when hard facts compel the resignation of Mr. Chamberlain'. 'Frontal attack' would be 'politically foolish'. It was, in essence, a strategy that pinned Labour's prospects on military failure. As Dalton put it when referring to the crisis that brought Lloyd George to power, 'the 1916 situation developed as a result of serious reverses in the field'.[27]

When war erupted there was, however, an immediate agreement with the Conservative party to enter into an 'electoral truce' to prevent partisan politics harming national unity. This was all part of the strategy of publicly unimpeachable and 'responsible' behaviour. When a seat in the Commons fell vacant and a by-election was held, the party that previously controlled the seat would not be opposed by a candidate of the other party.[28] This agreement established leverage over the Prime Minister by implicitly reminding him not to provoke Labour into a more vigorous approach. At a local level, meanwhile, Labour looked to keep its constituency parties active in anticipation of a general election; this panicked senior Conservatives, their party having suspended grassroots political activity on 'patriotic' grounds. Douglas Hacking, the chairman of the Conservative party, warned that his party was sleepwalking into a 'disastrous' situation while Labour husbanded its strength.[29] The truce thus constituted a valuable bargaining chip: Labour wrapped itself in the Union Jack while thinking in terms of political advantage. 'Constructive

Opposition' was actually a calculated, and deeply politicized, instrument to enhance Labour's strength.

After seeing off Morrison's bid for the leadership, Attlee quickly put his own stamp on matters. He took on the central role in harrying the Cabinet, both in Parliament and across the country. He travelled Britain to address Labour rallies and delivered speeches on the radio. In the Commons he emphatically rejected any negotiated peace that permitted Hitler to retain his territorial acquisitions. Britain had to pursue the struggle with 'resolution', Attlee declared, for Hitler's word was 'utterly worthless'.[30] He spoke with deliberate vagueness of a 'new' and 'better' world that would emerge from the war.[31] Chamberlain pinpointed 'Attlee's return' as the moment that Labour's 'nagging' and 'fault-finding' became more pointed.[32] Clem reminded the Prime Minister that the electoral truce was not a 'political truce' and emphasized that it could be terminated at any time.[33]

Attlee attacked Chamberlain on literally dozens of occasions for having a War Cabinet composed of members who ran individual departments rather than directing overall strategy, as well as the absence of a domestic supremo tasked with organizing the home front.[34] Clem said, 'I do not understand . . . on what principles the War Cabinet has been founded . . . I gather that it was mainly on the score of personality'.[35] He called for Chamberlain to behave like a 'statesman' and ominously warned that 'if the ministers cannot get on with their jobs then we must get other ministers'.[36] Without irony, Attlee also charged the Conservatives with engaging in 'personal squabbles and petty rivalries' in contrast with his own party: 'We on this side [of the House of Commons] approach this matter from one point of view only, and that is the interests of the country'.[37] In February 1940, the most powerful man in the Labour movement, Bevin, entered the fray and issued an unequivocal warning that if Chamberlain imposed state control of working conditions and wages, 'I will lead the movement to resist this government'.[38] Considering what Bevin had done to old George Lansbury, that was not a threat to be taken lightly.

Adeptly, Attlee leveraged the crisis of war to begin legitimizing Labour's controversial *domestic* agenda in the eyes of the 'floating vote'. As we have seen, the party's major economic concept of the 1930s was 'planning', entailing wide-ranging state intervention in the economy. The problem was that 'planning' sounded sinister to many. How powerful would government need to become in order to do this? Even to those were not immediately alarmed by it, the concept seemed somewhat nebulous. What did it add up to? Was it actually realistic? Now, Clem argued that 'planning' was nothing less than the key to a successful war effort. He thus converted 'planning' from a slogan into one with immediate real-world relevance. 'In this war we need the planning of our resources', Attlee declared in the House of Commons in

February 1940, 'and for that purpose we want ministers who grasp the function of planning'.[39] In a party pamphlet, he wrote that 'the occasion should be seized to lay the foundations of a planned economy'.[40] The message was that Labour's methods of governing were of unique applicability to the prosecution of war, and that the party offered solutions that the Conservatives simply did not possess. This strengthened Attlee's claim to the centre ground, for when presented in terms of the efficient management of Britain's resources for the purposes of war, 'planning' appeared to be simple common sense: who could object to that?

Many Labour backbenchers and activists were unhappy with the approach taken by their leaders and longed to loudly indulge their hatred of the Conservatives.[41] But circumstances required something subtler than an all-out offensive. Attlee and his colleagues knew that to plunge in and denounce the government at every turn would risk appearing unpatriotically opportunistic. It was far wiser to deliberately employ a 'studied moderation of language' when publicly criticizing the Cabinet.[42] The House of Commons thus became a battleground for warfare conducted by stealth. As a result of the political strategy crafted by Attlee, by early 1940 Labour seemed sober and steadfast. While actually engaged in complex machinations, Attlee helped Labour to *appear* as if it stood 'above' politics. It was a remarkable feat of leadership. The policy of 'constructive Opposition' was a huge gamble—a word out of place, an aggressive gesture, or being perceived as too hesitant could have sunk the entire enterprise—but Attlee got it just right. The Labour leaders used the first phase of the war to establish a series of political landmarks. By the spring of 1940, they had captured the language of patriotism.

'The Twilight War'

The eight-month interregnum between the declaration of war on 3 September 1939 and the outbreak of full-scale military hostilities on 10 May 1940 was an odd affair. Many considered it all a little anticlimactic. Within a matter of weeks, 1.5 million people—the majority of them children—were evacuated from British towns and cities in anticipation of the predicted German aerial onslaught. Yet in the event, there was no mass attack of hundreds of bombers bringing death from the skies. When the apocalypse failed to transpire, many of these people began to return home. The country did not seem to be in peril, despite the nightly blackouts. An uneasy calm settled on western Europe. Many different names have been given to this opening phase of the Second World War. The best known is undoubtedly 'the phoney war'. Others called it 'the bore war'. The British press imaginatively adapted the German *Blitzkrieg* into *Sitzkrieg*, 'the sitting war'. In France the period is known as the *drôle de guerre*, 'the funny war'. Yet it was perhaps Winston Churchill, with his rare gift for the English language, who put it most fittingly. He called it 'the twilight war'.

Along the Franco-German frontier there was military stasis as both sides built up their forces. By mid-October 160,000 British troops had been sent to France. This number would soon double. But the British Expeditionary Force was dwarfed by the 104 divisions of the French army; the French would be the ones to do most of the dying, as London had always intended. The Allied forces sat behind the formidable fortifications of the Maginot Line, an intricate barrier of concrete fort-resses, strong points, and emplacements that extended along the French borders with Germany, Switzerland, and Luxembourg (though, fatally, not Belgium). The fortifications snaked for more than 400 miles, and typically had a depth of fifteen miles. The opening phases of the war were thus a stalemate. From the perspective of the Allies, this was probably a mistake. In September 1939 the vast majority of the German army was in the east, conquering Poland. Only twenty-three divisions were stationed on the western frontier. They were vastly outnumbered by the French, and British reinforcements were rapidly arriving. The Nazis were off bal-ance. After the war, members of the High Command in Berlin admitted their belief that if France attacked, the western front would have collapsed within a week. The German heartland lay open to invasion. A lighting Allied assault would certainly be bloody—but it would have posed an existential crisis to the National Socialist state.

It was only at sea that the Second World War felt truly real in its first months. On 4 September, just twenty-four hours after the declaration of war, Britain announced a blockade of Germany to prevent the importation of raw materials and food. The Royal Navy hunted down and either sunk or captured German merchant vessels; many holed up in neutral ports in South America, safe from British attack but useless to the war effort and with their cargos deteriorating in the holds. Around 10 per cent of Germany's normal annual imports were seized by the Royal Navy: 870,000 tons of goods, including 28 million gallons of petrol. Many goods destined for Germany were never even put to sea. On 17 September, meanwhile, the British aircraft carrier H.M.S. *Courageous* was sunk by a U-boat while on patrol off the coast of Ireland. Weeks later, another U-boat slipped inside Britain's naval base at Scapa Flow in the Orkney Islands and torpedoed the battleship H.M.S. *Royal Oak*. These were embarrassing blows to British prestige and a stark warning of the value of submarines. British merchant ships carrying supplies back home were a favourite target. The Royal Navy soon struck back, locating and destroying nine of the elusive U-boats by the end of the year. Merchant ships were organized into convoys and protected with a screen of escorting warships. And in December, three Royal Navy cruisers cornered the German battleship *Graf Spree* just off the coast of Argentina and Uruguay, in the estuary of the River Plate. After sustaining critical damage at the hands of the British forces, the German captain scuttled his vessel. Though still at a lower intensity than would be the case from 1940 onwards, the war on the high seas was very real.

On the home front, the British state began to expand its powers to deal with the challenges of war. Competition for scarce stocks of natural resources and industrial components required government action to organize distribution and determine a hierarchy of priorities. An ever-growing apparatus of regulations was established to control vital resources, fix prices, and purchase commodities on a vast scale. Production of all kinds—from food to munitions—was ramped up as a matter of urgency. A million volunteers flooded into the British armed forces by the end of 1939. And on the financial front, with government spending projected to skyrocket, in September the Chancellor John Simon introduced his first wartime Budget. Defence spending was to be doubled. Taxation was increased to cover the costs of higher spending as far as possible; the rest of the money would be raised from borrowing. Britain's place at the centre of the global system made this task considerably easier than for most of the combatants.

The German High Command knew their prospects of victory in a prolonged struggle with the global power of the British Empire and its French counterpart were bleak. Indeed, from 1938, Hitler's aggressive diplomacy was shaped by awareness that Germany could not outpace the Allies in the long term. He had a window to achieve his objectives; and it was closing rapidly. Moreover, his diplomacy had badly backfired. Hitler's intention all along had been to wage a war against the USSR to annex 'living space' and seize the natural resources of that vast country. Now Germany was forced to temporarily put these ambitions on hold—and sign an agreement with the Bolsheviks—because it found itself faced with another war, against Britain and France. The British enjoyed massive financial strength that Germany simply could not match. Whereas Britain was the hub of the global financial system, Germany was swiftly expelled from it. From September 1939, German imports shrank rapidly under the impact of the Allied blockade—by a staggering 80 per cent.[43] The armament programmes of Britain and France had been operating at a high intensity for several years. Very soon, Germany's lead would be eroded, and thereafter the balance would tip decisively the other way. The military, industrial, and economic potential of the Allies in a prolonged war of attrition dwarfed that of Germany.

Once the conquest of Poland was completed, Hitler therefore put out peace feelers to the Allies. These were swiftly rejected. With Germany having succeeded in its most brazen act of aggression yet, London and Paris deemed that there was nothing further to discuss. From the mid-1930s onwards, the Fuhrer's ambitions were out of sync with the resources at Germany's disposal. A long war would see Germany put under a state of siege, with its industry smashed from the air, and denied raw materials through naval blockade. There was also the possibility that, even if the conflict went well for Germany, the United States might be drawn in— and considering the colossal resources of the Americans, that would be fatal. Time, in short, was not on the side of the Nazis. The Fuhrer appreciated this as well as his generals. Hitler knew that the Allies would endeavour to create the conditions for a war of attrition.

So what to do? One option would be to attempt to deliver a knockout blow to the Western armies by attacking France in a single, mass operation. The Germans calculated that their prospects of sweeping the Allies before them were slight. The problem was that they did not see any more palatable alternative. A long war would be a vice that crushed Germany just as surely as spring follows winter. The Fuhrer thus resolved to pursue a course of action that Chamberlain described as being 'to gamble all on a single throw'.[44] Hitler himself said, 'I am staking my life's work on a gamble'.[45] The High Command was aghast, and once again some contemplated a coup to save Germany. But, as before, they did not have the strength to attempt such an audacious move in the Nazi police state. Importantly, the Fuhrer calculated that he would lose the support of German public opinion if the war turned into a siege. He therefore ordered the High Command to prepare to launch an attack in the West as soon as possible. Hitler aimed to begin this operation on 12 November 1939, but it was repeatedly postponed due to lack of preparedness. It would be May 1940 before the Germans were ready. The prospects of success were not good, but Hitler could not otherwise win the war.

'Hold on Tight'

If it seems curious that Neville Chamberlain clung to the premiership despite presiding over a catastrophic failure of diplomacy, the reality is that there was no obvious successor.[46] Halifax was not in the House of Commons, a serious obstacle to his prospects. Hoare was too adversarial. Eden certainly found being excluded from the inner War Cabinet 'humiliating', but he had blotted his copybook.[47] Churchill was considered untrustworthy at best, and frequently viewed as mad. The Conservative party saw nobody else to rally around. And so Chamberlain carried on.

He was, however, conscious that he might be living on borrowed time. From September, the Prime Minister initiated daily meetings of his nine-member War

Cabinet. Neville was adamant that he would run a tight ship. Besides Chamberlain and Halifax, there was Hoare as Lord Privy Seal; Sir Kingsley Wood (an old friend and colleague of the Prime Minister) as Secretary of State for Air; Simon as Chancellor; Lord Chatfield as Minister for Co-ordination of Defence; Leslie Hore-Belisha as Secretary of State for War; and, perhaps most importantly, Churchill at the Admiralty. There was also a seat for Hankey as Minister Without Portfolio. Hankey provided a valuable link to the past: once Britain's most eminent civil servant, he had served as Secretary to the War Cabinet during the First World War. He was thus a repository of institutional memory in how the British state ran a major conflict. Meanwhile the Chiefs of Staff—General Sir Edmund Ironside, Marshal of the Royal Air Force Sir Cyril Newall, and Admiral Sir Dudley Pound—frequently attended the War Cabinet to discuss strategic operations.

From the beginning, Churchill was a problem. The Prime Minister was antagonized by his relentless strategic activism. In fact Hankey described his *real* 'main job' as being to 'keep an eye on Winston'.[48] Chamberlain knew that Churchill would have been 'a most troublesome thorn in our flesh' if left on the backbenches, but was still determined his old enemy would be watched.[49] In War Cabinet meetings, Winston talked for long periods on all manner of issues relating to the prosecution of the war; and he sent Chamberlain a continual stream of lengthy memoranda. Many of these contained bold, and often fanciful, proposals for British military action. Considering that they saw each other in person every day at the War Cabinet, Neville knew the memoranda were written specifically in order to be quoted in 'the Book' which Churchill would naturally produce when the war was over. After receiving one such missive—that Chamberlain thought transparently intended to advertise Churchill's 'foresight' to posterity—the Prime Minister felt 'I must get something on the record too which would have to be quoted in the Book'.[50] The battle for the post-war record was already being waged. After six weeks of daily letters, Chamberlain sent for Churchill and had 'a very frank talk'. Winston 'swore vehemently' that he had 'no desire or intention of intrigue'.[51] The Prime Minister was not entirely convinced.[52]

Characteristically, the Prime Minister remained determined that he, and nobody else, would direct the British war effort. The membership of the new War Cabinet did not constitute a radical shakeup. With the exception of Churchill and Eden, Neville stuck with the same approach and the same faces. Hoare believed that Chamberlain was influenced by Horace Wilson to exclude as many critics as possible.[53] Even the Prime Minister's offer of coalition to Labour may have been extended in the *hope* that it would be rejected; the last thing he wanted was to be weighed down with people he did not respect. Chamberlain made a similar offer to

Herbert Samuel's Liberal Party. He loathed Samuel as an idiot, and the Prime Minister inspired similar feelings in the Liberal leader. Samuel rejected the invitation, saying that he could not 'accept responsibility for the policy and actions' of the National Government if he did not possess a major voice in strategy.[54] Once again, then, Chamberlain proved to be no Baldwin. The Prime Minister was reminded of the value of the liberal 'floating vote' by both Hoare and Churchill, who told him that building bridges with the Liberals would not only 'eliminate one of the oppositions' but also get 'their very influential press on our side'; Chamberlain, though, did not appear to much care.[55] He was as obdurate as ever.

The Prime Minister had moved only the minimum distance consistent with his own survival. A War Cabinet of nine members was arguably too large and unwieldy for rapid decision-making—five would have been better—but therein lies the nub of the issue. Chamberlain did not truly view his War Cabinet as a decision-making tool. *He* would take the important decisions himself. Politically, the War Cabinet needed to include the obvious big beasts in Halifax, Hoare, and Churchill; but, to the Prime Minister's mind, these men were all of doubtful loyalty and reliability. To ensure his continued ascendancy, Chamberlain thus needed to stack the War Cabinet with ministers who would be loyal to him: Wood, Hankey, Chatfield, and Hore-Belisha. He was simply not inclined to go any further. This was because he was convinced that his war strategy would yield success. Crucially, Halifax agreed with him. The Allies were stronger than Germany, and Hitler could not simply overrun them as he had Poland. The Prime Minister and Foreign Secretary both believed that the stalemate suited British interests, because waging all-out war would be prohibitively bloody and, from the German perspective, doomed to failure. After visiting the Maginot Line, Chamberlain told Ball that 'neither side could or should attempt to break through the fortified [positions]'.[56] Moreover, with the destruction of Poland, the Third Reich and the Soviet Union now shared a common border along which war was likely.

Neville therefore hoped that, far from the war entering a new and more dangerous phase, a peace settlement might soon become feasible: one that would spare Europe the ravages of conflict while satisfying the nervous inhabitants of Westminster. And even if war *did* erupt in the West, Britain and France could hold the line. One could not simply do a deal with Germany and leave it in possession of all its recent gains—that would send the wrong message abroad *and* at home—but the geopolitical and military realities would soon overwhelm Berlin.

One thing *had* definitely changed with the beginning of war, however. Chamberlain had had enough of Hitler. He now felt only a deep personal loathing for the man who had wrecked his plans, and quite possibly his premiership. The Prime Minister was resolved that peace could only be attained via regime change in Berlin. He was not prepared to deal with the Fuhrer anymore. 'Until he disappears and his system collapses', Neville wrote, 'there can be no peace'.[57] Chamberlain hoped that the army would remove him. Hitler was an 'accursed madman': 'I wish he could burn in Hell for as many years as he is costing lives'.[58] The Fuhrer 'must either die' or be imprisoned on 'St Helena', the tiny volcanic island in the South Atlantic, thousands of miles from civilization, to which Napoleon was exiled in 1815.[59] When Hitler offered peace in September, therefore, Chamberlain responded by announcing that Britain was gearing up for a three-year war. He sent a Swiss intermediary to Berlin to demand the liberation of Poland and that Hitler hold a referendum in Germany on his foreign policy. The Fuhrer was apoplectic. Chamberlain had no intention of doing a deal. If the Fuhrer actually wanted peace, it was up to him, not Britain, to prove it.[60]

A stone's throw away from 10 Downing Street, over at the Foreign Office, Halifax was not so sure. He proved markedly less hardline than the Prime Minister. This seems incredible, considering that his behaviour since the autumn of 1938 had forced Chamberlain to adopt a stiffer posture. Yet in the months following the outbreak of war Halifax gave his approval to a series of unofficial and secret conversations—usually held by businessmen who travelled to neutral countries in Europe—with representatives of the Reich on the possibility of a compromise peace. These discussions never bore fruit, but it is clear that the Foreign Secretary was looking for a way out. Halifax was willing to go significantly further than Chamberlain in search of a negotiated end to the conflict. The Foreign Secretary had done much to bounce Chamberlain into a policy which led to war. Yet once war came, Halifax lacked the taste for it.[61] That is a telling commentary on the nature of the Foreign Secretary's conduct over the preceding eighteen months.

Despite the decision to have nothing more to do with Hitler, though, Neville remained clear in his own mind about the type of struggle he was waging. This was a limited war, not all-out conflict. Britain needed to make the Germans realize that 'it isn't worth their while to go on getting thinner and poorer'.[62] Hankey captured it best: it was 'a war of nerves'.[63] As the Prime Minister told his sister:

> My policy continues to be the same. Hold on tight. Keep up the economic pressure, push on with munitions production & military preparations with the utmost energy, take no offensive unless Hitler begins it. I reckon that if we are allowed to carry on with this policy we shall have won the war by the Spring.[64]

As always, Chamberlain persisted in the unshakeable belief that he would be proven right, and that vindication lay just around the next corner. 'I stick to the view that

I have always held that Hitler missed the bus in Sept[ember] 1938. He could have dealt France and ourselves a terrible, perhaps a mortal, blow then. The opportunity will not recur'.[65] He also believed that it would not be 'very long' before peace returned, and when it did he would be 'indispensable' once more in negotiating a lasting settlement.[66] Hopeful that his hour would come and the world would need him, Chamberlain waited.

'Life Is One Long Nightmare'

Yet there is no question that Chamberlain was fundamentally out of his element as a war leader.[67] The Prime Minister knew it himself. Despite being a natural autocrat, Neville lacked dynamism and the capacity to invigorate the public. He gave weekly updates to Parliament but came across as 'depressed', resembling 'the Secretary of a firm of undertakers reading the minutes of the last meeting'.[68] He did not possess 'the gift' of being able to inspire people.[69] Chamberlain wondered whether the German army would dare to move against Hitler before the country received 'a real hard punch in the stomach', yet he hesitated to deliver one.[70] He was ill with a litany of complaints, from gout to catarrh to strange rashes, throughout the final months of 1939. At one point the gout was so severe that he was confined to bed for a week. Neville found it difficult to walk—he had to be carried to a Cabinet meeting in a dining chair, borne aloft like some impoverished potentate—and his hands were bitterly sore as the skin peeled off. Ill health compounded the despondency he felt at his diplomatic failure, and his anger at those who criticized him. 'Life', he wrote to his sister, 'is just one long nightmare'.[71]

When Neville and the War Cabinet agreed to announce Britain was preparing for a war that would last a minimum of three years, one of the Chiefs of Staff, General Ironside, noted that a 'ghastly'-looking Chamberlain 'put his forehead on the table and kept it there for nearly ten minutes'.[72] The Prime Minister remarked, 'I hate and loathe this war. I was never meant to be a War Minister'.[73] His government did not pursue all-out mobilization, hoping to preserve the export trade upon which British wealth depended. He wanted Parliament suspended or at least to meet as infrequently as possible, and was resentful of Margesson's inability to persuade MPs to let the government get on with the job unhindered.[74] He complained that the House of Commons 'gets more and more ill-tempered and unreasonable'.[75] Hoare observed that Parliament 'has nothing to do except to criticise the government ... it means that the fullest possible opportunity is given to nagging'.[76] Chamberlain complained that 'it does not help national unity to have every effort sneered at ... and every complaint exploited to the uttermost'.

Holding a general election in late 1939 was now clearly out of the question; Chamberlain would need to bide his time on that front. Channon watched the Prime Minister perform in the House of Commons and concluded that he 'hates' the chamber; 'certainly he has deep contempt for parliamentary interference and fussiness'.[77] One day, Chamberlain called Attlee, Greenwood, and Sinclair to his room in Parliament and upbraided them for the 'disloyalty' of the Labour and Liberal parties.[78] As so often, his behaviour did nothing to endear him to others.

'Enjoying Every Moment'

Whereas the prospect of all-out war filled the Prime Minister with a bone-chilling, energy-sapping dread, Churchill's mindset was quite different.[79] The new First Lord of the Admiralty was in his element. He had successfully established the defence of British honour and resistance to aggressors as a domestic rallying point that yielded substantial political capital. The effort to return to office had finally borne fruit, and he held a powerful position in the public imagination. From September 1939, Churchill proved an electrifying force in government. His effect on both the Admiralty and the War Cabinet was that of a galvanic current.

Churchill desired one thing above all others: *control*. His search for adventure, his exuberance, and his natural restlessness meant that he interfered in virtually every aspect of Admiralty business—and the work of most of his Cabinet colleagues, as well. Winston's energy drove his officials 'to distraction'.[80] He was as irrepressible as ever. When he entered office, one disparaging adviser at the Admiralty told Amery that 'Winston's first act of state . . . was to order a bottle of whisky', and he doubted that Churchill could stand up to the rigours of ministerial life after 'years of soft living'.[81] Amery, though, had no doubt that Winston's 'power of nervous output and willpower' would prove formidable.

Churchill was suited to executive power. Until April 1940, the war at sea *was* the war; and Churchill was the man who directed it. His energetic leadership of the struggle on the oceans—during which he ensured that even minor naval skirmishes were presented to the public as being only a couple of notches below the Battle of Trafalgar—made for a stark contrast with the sense of stasis elsewhere, both at the front and at home in Whitehall. Active in the War Cabinet and its key subcommittee, the Military Coordination Committee, others struggled to keep up with Winston. His officials were buried in a daily avalanche of memoranda. He did not bother himself overmuch as to whether his schemes were practicable, a tendency that meant his officials often had to spend weeks wrestling with the First Lord until Winston's mind discovered a new enthusiasm. By mid-September he had devised a scheme to invade the Baltic, 'Operation Catherine'. British forces would seize the iron-ore fields in neutral Norway and Sweden in order to deny these raw materials to the German war effort and tighten the Allied stranglehold on the Reich. The idea remained a fixation. He was like a young boy commanding a fleet of model ships in a wargame. Churchill's working hours were also taxing on those around him. He would typically go to bed for a couple of hours after lunch and then keep his civil servants—who did not have the luxury of an afternoon nap—working at the Admiralty until the small hours of the morning. But this was because he was a natural decision-maker. Early in 1940 Churchill ordered that some special stickers be produced for his use. These were red, and bore the words 'ACTION THIS DAY'; famously, Winston would affix them to the most important of his instructions and memoranda. The ACTION THIS DAY stickers were to remain a staple of his wartime leadership for the next five years.

In Parliament, meanwhile, Winston was by far the National Government's most impressive performer. He cheered up MPs with his combination of 'resolution' and 'sheer boyishness'.[82] His quips and energy improved the mood of a depressed House of Commons. Sitting next to him, Chamberlain appeared 'colourless'.[83] Churchill was also a regular feature on the radio and newsreels. On 1 October, he delivered a world broadcast over the BBC; another followed in November. The front page of the Sunday Pictorial featured a photograph of Churchill above the headline, 'THIS IS THE MAN THAT HITLER FEARS'.[84] He presented the war in stark terms and dramatized the stakes: 'either', he said, Britain and France 'will go down, or . . . Hitler, the Nazi regime and the recurring German or Prussian menace to Europe will be broken and destroyed'.[85] Through this Churchill, in the words of one observer, 'brought himself nearer the post of Prime Minister than he has ever been before'.[86] There was a clamour in the newspapers, including the left-wing press, for him to assume the premiership.[87] Winston stood high in public esteem, particularly among men and the young.[88] Close relations between the Admiralty and the media, cultivated by Churchill himself, proved excellent for publicizing the First Lord's gusto. In the view of one admiral, Churchill worked to become 'the popular hero' of the early phase of the war.[89] To this end Winston exaggerated the number of U-boats sunk, insisting that half of the German submarine force had been destroyed when the real number was much lower.[90] Churchill thus utilized the Royal Navy as a powerful personal propaganda tool. One admiral described him as a 'spellbinder' due to his brilliant oratory.[91] Chamberlain correctly discerned that Churchill was 'enjoying every moment' of it.[92]

Meanwhile Winston brought his old crony and 'scientific adviser', Professor Frederick Lindemann, into the Admiralty to lead a new 'Statistical Section'.

191

In practice Lindemann was used less as a facilitator of naval operations than as a Whitehall trawlerman: he cast a net throughout the machinery of state hoping to capture useful intelligence on a wide array of topics. Churchill would then employ this information as ammunition in his War Cabinet performances. The long monologues drove his colleagues up the wall, but there was little they could do; it was not as if they could get rid of him. Winston was not shy about exercising influence. On 10 September 1939, for instance, he sent a minute to Halifax stating that 'I hope you will not mind my drawing your attention from time to time to points which strike me in the Foreign Office telegrams'. It was, he went on, 'so much better' to do so privately 'than that I should raise them in Cabinet'.[93] Halifax was unlikely to have missed the coded warning. Exhausted by Churchill's energy, Neville moaned to his sister that 'it is a heavy price that we have to pay for our Winston'.[94]

On a personal level, Churchill's relations with Chamberlain were cordial enough. On 13 November, he and Clemmie hosted the Prime Minister and his wife Annie for dinner at Admiralty House. The evening passed pleasantly, though it is telling that it was the first 'social conversation' Churchill had experienced with Chamberlain in two decades of acquaintance.[95] But what Churchill was angling for was personal strategic control of Britain's entire war effort and the power to direct operations. He believed that he could do a better job of it than anyone else. He charged that the 'machinery of war-control' was defective and inhibited 'positive action'.[96] In making this argument he was borrowing from the playbook of his old mentor, the Welsh Wizard. In 1916, Lloyd George had made strikingly similar arguments about the machinery of war in seeking to undermine the Prime Minister, Asquith, and accrue the power to take strategic decisions himself. This yielded Lloyd George the premiership.

In the second half of the 1930s, Winston had been engaged in writing a sort of public autobiography as a means to political power. He continued this during the 'twilight war'. The Prime Minister may have been determined to run a tight ship, but the First Lord of the Admiralty was equally determined that *he* would steer the vessel. Upon the declaration of hostilities in September, Amery presciently wrote in his diary that 'I see Winston emerging as PM out of it all by the end of the year'.[97] It would take a little longer than that, but Churchill was in a strong position. The years in the wilderness were emphatically over.

'Nothing Sufficiently Drastic Has Happened to Break the Long-Established Traditions of Party Intrigue'

The more things changed, the more they stayed the same.[98] Despite having little choice but to accommodate Churchill and Eden, and saying all the right things about them in public, privately Chamberlain continued to wage war by proxy against the two men who were now his colleagues. The mendacity of this was extreme. Throughout late 1939 and early 1940, Ball's journal *Truth* never let up in its attacks on Churchill, who was likened to Hitler in his fickleness,[99] and Eden, who was smeared as 'largely instrumental in bringing about' the entire war through his behaviour since 1937.[100] The Prime Minister's director of black operations thus utilized *Truth* to denigrate two of his most important ministers, while keeping Chamberlain's own hands publicly clean. As a 1942 investigation by Vansittart into Ball and *Truth* concluded, 'the policy of *Truth* during this period offers the strongest corroboration of the theory that the inclusion in the Government of Churchill and Eden . . . was to some extent a mere gesture to appease the National Sentiment'.[101] The decision to declare war had been a political necessity. So had the inclusion of Churchill and Eden. Clearly, then, the primacy of intrigue persisted; it had simply been transferred to another plane. The Prime Minister may have been backed into a corner by his critics, but the rules of the game remained the same as always.

Nor did the MPs around Eden rally to the banner of national unity. When war was declared and Eden re-entered the government, his supporters among Conservative MPs—the 'Glamour Boys'—chose to keep up their opposition to Chamberlain. Their meetings were now chaired by Leo Amery, and the group assembled weekly for dinner at the Carlton Hotel restaurant. Eden himself could not attend without appearing disloyal, but he was kept informed; the Prime Minister was not the only one playing a double game. Amery was willing to be far more vigorous as a rebel leader than the hesitant, ineffectual Eden had ever been. Moreover, these men increasingly came to the conclusion that *Churchill* was now the only possible alternative Prime Minister. As Amery put it, Winston 'is the one man with real war drive and love of battle'.[102]

It was indicative of the Prime Minister's growing political ineptitude that his ambition to seize control of the agenda in January 1940 through a 'daring project' of War Cabinet reconstruction descended into embarrassment and failure.[103] Chamberlain tried to shunt the Minister for War, Leslie Hore-Belisha, from his post due to his being despised by the generals. But an angry Hore-Belisha quit the government outright, and launched a damaging attack on the Prime Minister. The press was in uproar. Ball retaliated with a vitriolic assault in *Truth* that veered into anti-Semitism.[104] There were evidently few lengths to which the Prime Minister's antechamber would not go in defence of their chief. Around the same time, the Prime Minister was pondering dropping Hoare and Simon from the War Cabinet. They were not loyal as they had once been. 'Slippery Sam' had been on manoeuvres for more than a year, while Simon was the Cabinet minister who told Chamberlain on 2 September that there was no choice but to issue a final ultimatum to Hitler. Wilson and Margesson were in favour of the scheme, the latter regarding the two as 'egocentric intriguers' who Chamberlain should 'get rid of'.[105] Yet he could not pluck up the courage to face yet another crisis by sacking his old friend Hoare and the 'reptilian' Simon.

By early 1940, therefore, Chamberlain was a man embittered at the world. He felt 'sick' at the 'intrigues' of the Labour party, for they 'only paid lip-service' to the 'otherwise universally accepted doctrine' of national unity.[106] Herbert Morrison, in particular, was 'poisonous'.[107] Labour MPs displayed, he wrote, 'a fine patriotic spirit in wartime!'[108] At least his sarcasm had not been exhausted. Criticism caused Chamberlain to explode, leaving his Private Secretary surprised 'at the violence of [the] fury' emanating from 'such a cold man'.[109] He felt a 'sick resentment' for the newspapers, which 'sell better if they abuse the government'.[110] As the perceptive civil servant Jock Colville recognized, the Prime Minister's chief problem was that 'he likes to be set on a pedestal and adored, with suitable humility, by unquestioning admirers'.[111] This was hardly likely to happen in a war precipitated by the failure of Chamberlain's own foreign policy.

The Prime Minister was not a popular man. His credibility had been shattered, his personality was repellent, and his future looked bleak. Yet neither the enmity of the Labour party nor longstanding adversaries on the Conservative benches would suffice to remove him from power. He retained the backing of the great bulk of National Government MPs, not least because there were no attractive alternatives. What would be required to bring about Chamberlain's fall was a much more drastic shift in mainstream Conservative opinion. As Churchill's most craven crony, Brendan Bracken, put it, the Conservative backbenches were full of 'yes-men', most of whom lived in hope that Chamberlain would give them a job in government.[112] And as Colville noted in a striking, if rather black, diary entry, 'nothing sufficiently drastic has happened to break the long-established traditions of party intrigue'.[113] It would take something dramatic to collapse Chamberlain's support. Unfortunately for the Prime Minister, such a moment lurked just around the corner.

11

DEATH IN THE FJORDS

'One Thing Is Certain: He Has Missed the Bus'

In the final months of 1939 the idea of opening up a new front in the war, in Scandinavia, began to gain traction in Allied capitals.[1] Sweden was a source of valuable iron ore for the German war machine. The ore was transported a short distance from the Swedish ore fields across the Norwegian border to the port of Narvik. From there, it was shipped to the Reich, with German ships hugging the coast in order to remain in Norway's territorial waters. Here, the Royal Navy could not sink them without violating Norwegian sovereignty. Elements within the governments of Britain and France advocated taking military action to sever the flow of the ore. The obvious course was to land Allied forces in Narvik, capture it, and then cross into neighbouring Sweden, where they could seize the ore fields to boot. Without Swedish ore, the Germans would have to fall back on their existing stockpiles—which would run short in perhaps a year. In the War Cabinet, Churchill was the most vocal supporter of this strategy. That Norway and Sweden were formally neutral states did not matter to Winston; there were bigger considerations at stake than the sensibilities of non-combatants.

Chamberlain and Halifax were less sanguine. To sustain a military occupation in the frozen north of Scandinavia would be an arduous logistical operation. To flagrantly violate the neutrality of Norway and Sweden by seizing their territory would have serious diplomatic repercussions; the United States might be outraged. Most importantly, the two men remained hopeful that it would not even be necessary to *really* fight a war. Yet the Prime Minister and the Foreign Secretary lacked the political credibility to simply dictate British, let alone Allied, strategy. Churchill's view was that 'now we had entered the war, we must fight it to a finish'.[2] At a meeting of the Allies' Supreme War Council in February 1940, it was agreed to plan for the opening up of a new front in Scandinavia. The Allies intended to seize Narvik, situated in the fjords of northern Norway, in an amphibious operation. Once ashore, their forces would advance the short distance across the Swedish frontier in order to capture the ore fields.

At the Supreme War Council on 28 March, however, Chamberlain succeeded in having the operation sharply downgraded to simply the mining of Norwegian territorial waters. He was dealing with a new French Prime Minister, Paul Reynaud, who had come to power on 21 March. Reynaud was left 'gasping' as Chamberlain demolished the case for invasion and pressed for more limited action.[3] The new Scandinavian expedition, amended from invasion to merely laying an offshore minefield, would be launched on 5 April. One Downing Street official thought that Chamberlain grasped the 'importance of the psychological factor in the present war', and knew some 'effective action' must be launched as part of 'the necessity of throwing occasional sops to public opinion'.[4]

By early 1940, Neville was at last starting to feel like his old self. He had recovered his self-confidence. The bouts of illness passed, and the war seemed to be going according to plan. He took daily walks around St James's Park. Chamberlain was 'standing the strain wonderfully well', one aide recorded, and in Cabinet remained 'an assiduous reader of all memoranda' who 'masters them in a way no other member of the Cabinet does and by his thorough knowledge of each item on the agenda dominates his colleagues'.[5] In Parliament, Chamberlain's renewed vigour was plain to see: his ability to tear a critical case to pieces returned with a vengeance, much to the discomfort of many Labour backbenchers.

In late March, the Prime Minister resolved upon another tweaking of the War Cabinet. This time Hoare, the Lord Privy Seal, swapped jobs with Kingsley Wood, the Secretary of State for Air. There were also some minor adjustments among lower-ranking ministers. The most important change, though, was in Churchill's position. Rejuvenated, Chamberlain now felt able to come to grips with his Churchill problem. The First Lord was angling to act as a strategic supremo, with oversight of all British military operations. He had been complaining about 'the machinery of war' for months; meanwhile the newspapers were continually pressing for him to be given greater powers. If Chamberlain were to permit Churchill to assume power over decision-making, the effect would be to sanction his own marginalization. This he would never permit. But he judged that some gesture was necessary. The Prime Minister was also confident that he could, in the last resort, handle Winston: after all, he was cleverer than him.

As such, in early April 1940 Chamberlain appointed Churchill the chairman of the Cabinet's Military Coordination Committee. This body consisted of the senior military commander from each of the three Services, and the relevant Secretary of State. It discussed new strategic plans and put them to the War Cabinet, run by Chamberlain, for decision. He thus sought to grant Churchill the *appearance* of authority and initiative while keeping control of the *substance* of decision-making for himself. The press warmly welcomed the development. On 4 April the Prime Minister delivered an optimistic address to the Conservative Central Council in which he boasted that he was 'ten times as confident of victory' as he had been the previous September. He looked 'full of confidence and vim'.[6] Moreover, with Hitler's failure to launch an offensive in the West and the build-up of Allied military strength, 'one thing is certain', Chamberlain declared: Hitler 'has missed the bus'.[7]

Failure in Norway

The problem was that Hitler had not 'missed the bus' at all. Quite the opposite. The British mining of Norway's territorial waters was delayed for three days after the French wobbled on their navy simultaneously mining the Rhine, lest it provoke a German reaction. The Royal Navy finally commenced mining on 8 April. The following day, however, shattering news reached London and Paris: the Germans had begun a pre-emptive seizure of Scandinavia. Denmark was being invaded, while German forces were simultaneously landing in Norway. It had been obvious for some time that the Allies were preparing for offensive operations in Scandinavia, and the Fuhrer was determined to get there first.

Narvik, Trondheim, Oslo, and other major cities were seized within a matter of hours. It was a masterful operation, facilitated by the first-ever airborne drop of paratroopers in combat. Huge numbers of German troops floated down from the skies and secured key targets. Allied decision-making had been glacially slow. Vacillation and excessive caution delayed action. Yet while most of Whitehall panicked, the First Lord of the Admiralty was characteristically buoyant. Here was a chance for sustained combat with the Germans, in an action that the Royal Navy would be central to. He dispatched his forces into the fjords in search of the enemy. British warships promptly engaged the Kriegsmarine in the Bay of Narvik and inflicted a heavy defeat on the Germans, sinking ten destroyers. These ships were carrying thousands of troops for the campaign. Churchill was 'jubilant', advising ministerial colleagues that Britain was 'in a far better position' than had been the case hitherto, because 'we could apply our overwhelming sea-power on the Norwegian coast'.[8] He worked from his bed, examining maps and smoking large cigars while intermittently stroking a black cat named Nelson.[9] He believed that Britain could win a major victory in Norway, capturing the vulnerable 'prizes' that were the German forces, and triumphing in the first major engagement of the war.[10] Confident of naval supremacy in Scandinavian waters, the War Cabinet thus decided to land an army in Norway and turf out the Germans. Chamberlain and Halifax favoured landing south of Narvik, at Trondheim, but Churchill persuaded them to target Narvik too.

Beginning on 14 April British, French, and Norwegian forces totalling around 20,000 men landed and surrounded the Germans in the vicinity of Narvik. The Allies launched additional operations to the south, at Andalsnes and Namos, on 19 April; the forces committed to these missions, numbering 12,000 men, would capture Trondheim in a pincer movement. On 20 April, Chamberlain remained confident that Norway would turn into an 'ultimate disaster' for the Germans.

Yet the whole operation was thrown together in a slapdash fashion. When the intention was to seize a frozen land of mountains and fjords, that was asking for trouble. The result was a bruising defeat. As the landings at Andalsnes and Namos began, they ran into withering resistance from the Luftwaffe. The Germans had seized Norwegian airfields and brought Messerschmitt fighters and Stuka dive-bombers to support their ground troops. The British, by contrast, lacked air support or even adequate numbers of anti-aircraft guns. Only one of Britain's four aircraft carriers was committed to the operation, and the RAF had to hurriedly set up makeshift airfields. The Luftwaffe could put ten times as many planes in the skies as the British. The battlefields proved a bloodbath. The ground forces were frequently cut to pieces, while the Royal Navy, holding position in the fjords, was targeted by the Luftwaffe and sustained a battering.

The Norway campaign offered a stark warning of the importance of securing command of the air in modern warfare. As if that was not bad enough, with the exception of around Narvik itself, the British forces were significantly outnumbered by the Germans. Moreover, most of the British troops earmarked for the operation were from the reservist Territorial Army, the bulk of the regular forces already being in France. Few tanks were sent to support them, and the troops even lacked sufficient winter clothing. Appalling equipment failures, tactical missteps, and amateurish decision-making in London combined to inflict a bloody, and painful, defeat on the Allies. On 27 April—just a week after Chamberlain expressed his confidence in a huge British victory—the decision was taken to evacuate. It was an embarrassing outcome, one that suggested a worrying military gulf between the two sides.

Hitler had not only taken Poland in a bold, lightning assault. He had now repeated the feat in Scandinavia as well. Whether engaging in coercive diplomacy or over-whelming military offensives, time and again since 1936 the Third Reich had achieved its objectives in a rapid fashion. Hitler's credibility rocketed with success. Over and over again he had gambled; and over and over again he had won. Via success on the battlefield, Hitler rendered his position virtually impregnable to internal enemies in the German military.

The impact in London was the diametric opposite. The period between 20 and 27 April was, in Chamberlain's own estimation, 'the worst' of the war.[11] With the failure in Scandinavia, the mood at Westminster shifted and the National Government immediately appeared more vulnerable than ever before. This was telling: while certainly a bad setback, Norway did not in itself constitute a major strategic disaster. Yet, crucially, it was *treated* as one by the government's critics. The botched campaign was thus weaponized and turned against the Prime Minister. As opposition coalesced on all sides, Chamberlain began to realize that the game may, in fact, be up.

'Winston Was Being Maddening'

Churchill did not cover himself in glory, either.[12] He had been pressing for action in Scandinavia for months, and when the campaign came it failed miserably. As the driving force behind the venture, the First Lord bore a considerable degree of the responsibility. Winston's own instructions to naval commanders were vague and contradictory, nor did he ensure that naval and land operations were effectively joined up. His suggestions for action often made little tactical sense. Churchill angrily upbraided the commanders in Norway for lacking offensive spirit, but while this may have been true, they also lacked the equipment to get the job done. Old hands in Westminster were not remotely surprised at the surfacing of all the established Churchill family traits of impetuousness and lack of attention to detail. Kingsley Wood described his chairmanship of the Military Coordination Committee as a 'farce', with Churchill in a 'dreadful state'.[13] The Prime Minister thought Churchill was so ferocious towards his underlings at the Admiralty that everyone there was 'terrified' of him.[14] Winston 'gives me more trouble than all the rest of my colleagues put together', he complained.[15]

Once fighting had commenced in Norway, it was not long before Chamberlain reassumed direction of the Military Coordination Committee—incredibly, at the request of Winston himself. Churchill said that 'they'll take from you what they won't take from me', and surrendered the chair.[16] The Prime Minister looked to impose order on the chaos. He told his sister that Winston's style of leadership engendered 'strained feelings', resulting in a 'sad mess' that it fell to him to clear up.[17] 'This was the committee over which he is supposed to preside but which he had got into an almost mutinous condition'.[18] One observer held that the Prime Minister appeared to be far more exasperated 'by Winston's rampages' than 'the strategical difficulties' in Scandinavia.[19] Meanwhile Horace Wilson received complaints from Simon, Hankey, and Wood that Churchill was even refusing to forward memoranda written by the Service Chiefs—and dealing with their assessment of dangerous operations—to the War Cabinet for consideration.[20] Hankey drew the attention of colleagues to the obvious parallels between Churchill's expedition in Norway and his disastrous campaign in Gallipoli in 1915.[21] In fact, Hankey did not need to point out the Gallipoli analogy—because everyone had thought of it already.

The problem was that Churchill considered himself a military genius along the lines of his ancestor Marlborough, and thus tried to impose himself on the smallest details of operations. The result was a bureaucratic morass, one that required the Prime Minister's brisk chairmanship to resolve. Meetings took place at 10.00 a.m. each morning, and lasted for less than an hour. With Chamberlain back running the show, Churchill veered between being in 'the best of humour' and 'a spoiled & sulky child'.[22] He still made 'nonsensical proposals' that collapsed in the face of 'reasoned argument'.

Yet it should go without saying that the First Lord of the Admiralty's interpretation of the mess was different. Winston's conclusion was simply that he lacked the supreme authority necessary to impose his views on the government and military, and had been 'thwarted' by those who did not understand war. He thus launched a major power-grab in Whitehall. He objected to the fact that 'his opinion [was] to be weighed with other opinions', and threatened to quit the Military Coordinating Committee altogether.[23] Churchill wanted to be appointed 'Minister of Defence' with responsibility for directing the war and control over both strategy and operations. Prior to petitioning Chamberlain to this end, he sought support from the Conservative backbenches, the Labour party, and the Liberals.[24] Winston then drafted a letter to the Prime Minister in which he stated that 'without the necessary powers' he would be unwilling to bear responsibility:

No one is responsible for the creation and direction of military policy except yourself. If you feel able to bear this burden, you may count upon my unswerving loyalty as First Lord of the Admiralty. If you do not feel you can bear it, with all your other duties, you will have to delegate your powers to a deputy who can concert and direct the general movement of our war action, and who will enjoy your support and that of the War Cabinet unless very good reason is shown to the contrary.[25]

Churchill ultimately decided not to send the letter, and went to see the Prime Minister in person to make the pitch—while, naturally, assuring Neville of his 'complete loyalty'.[26] Amidst the failure in Norway, Churchill was brazenly applying to become, in effect, the *real* head of the government—with Chamberlain invited to accept a titular role without responsibility or power. It was Lloyd George in 1916 all over again.

One of Chamberlain's civil service aides picked up rumours that if the Prime Minister refused, Churchill would 'go down to the House and say that he can take no responsibility for what is happening'—in other words, denounce the government and initiate a 'first-class political crisis'.[27] This may have been gossip, but equally it may have had some substance to it; it would certainly have been consistent with the First Lord's penchant for the dramatic. Chamberlain himself resented the fact that Churchill 'is too apt to look the other way while his friends exalt him as the War Genius . . . the good British public does not know the truth'.[28] The Prime Minister played for time by promising to think over the idea. There loomed the distinct possibility that Churchill—'to whom as much blame should attach as any other single individual' over Norway—would 'ride triumphantly forward on the wave of undeserved national popularity'.[29] Yet Neville had absolutely no intention of making him 'sole director of military policy'. While another public gesture of added responsibility might be made to satiate Churchill, Chamberlain was adamant that 'the Cabinet'—in other words, himself—would still take the 'decisions'.[30] Winston's reputation was, he thought, 'inflated' and bore little relation to his actual military knowledge.[31] He eventually decided to concede to Churchill the power to give 'guidance and directions' to the Chiefs of Staff on behalf of the Military Coordination Committee.[32] That would enable Churchill to attempt to impose his views on the military. Even if the War Cabinet could then overrule him where appropriate, it was still an extraordinary promotion for someone intimately involved in the botched Norway campaign.

Yet Chamberlain had little choice but to risk it. Churchill's prestige continued to soar. The mythology Winston had constructed in the 1930s was now so entrenched that public anger at the Norwegian campaign did not fall on his own head. His 'position in the country is, quite unjustifiably, unassailable', remarked one observer; he was 'Public Hero Number One'.[33] In good spirits, Churchill sat 'joking and drinking' with Labour and Liberal MPs in the smoking room of the Commons.[34] 'A Westminster war added to a German war is really too much', complained 'Chips' Channon.[35] The Prime Minister was exasperated by dealing with both military failure in Norway and Winston in the War Cabinet, and in the privacy of correspondence with his sisters flirted with handing the premiership over to someone else.[36] Other days, though, he felt much more confident: 'It's a vile world, but I don't think my enemies will get me down this time'.[37] It is noteworthy that he still had little doubt who his enemies were. Outwardly, Chamberlain betrayed no sign of anxiety. One of his closest aides thought his 'immunity from fatigue' seemed to actually *increase* the worse things got.[38] Channon judged the Prime Minister 'full of fight' and, by granting Churchill additional powers, was 'playing a deep game'. He 'has given Winston more rope'.[39]

It is just possible that Winston would have been trapped by this new arrangement, enjoying the shadow but not the substance of power. But it seems more likely that the irrepressible First Lord would have bulldozed it in short order; Amery, for one, heard that Churchill was 'very unhappy at his false position'.[40] We will never know, because the evacuation from Scandinavia presented the opening that Chamberlain's enemies had long been waiting for.

'We Are Not Satisfied'

The period between 27 April and 10 May 1940 was arguably the most dramatic fortnight in British history.[41] Contemporaries were electrified by it; even grizzled veterans had never seen anything like it before. There has been nothing remotely like it since. With the withdrawal from Norway, Westminster was braced for a serious confrontation between the National Government and its critics. The House of Commons was to hold a two-day debate on the Scandinavian campaign, beginning on 7 May. In the week before, the tension in London ratcheted up to unprecedented levels. Talk of plots, intrigues, and conspiracies filled the corridors of Parliament, the offices of Whitehall, and the dining rooms of the exclusive clubs. It was an atmosphere pregnant with danger—and, for some, opportunity.

The Labour party, under Attlee's guidance, was watching closely. With the war in Scandinavia commencing, on 9 April the Parliamentary Labour Party (PLP) Executive had revisited the notion of joining a coalition led by Chamberlain. Morrison was apparently now in favour of serving under the current Prime Minister. Attlee, by contrast, showed nerves of steel: he still urged caution. The leader managed to carry most of his colleagues in favour of holding out, with the general feeling being that to accept office under Chamberlain would only 'legitimise' him. It was resolved that if the Prime Minister resigned, Labour would immediately reconsider the issue.[42]

Tellingly, there was also discussion of whether, in the event of a subsequent decision to enter a coalition, the leaders should call a special Labour conference and formally ask their party for approval. That would likely take at least a week, though, and nobody could be certain that the party rank-and-file would back alliance with the despised Conservatives. Attlee therefore argued that they should not ask for permission. Instead, they should simply accept office on their own authority and *then* call a conference at which the decision could be endorsed. Clem intended to bide his time for the optimum moment to enter a coalition, but when it came, he would march Labour into government and present his party with a fait accompli. Attlee was a leader transformed, thriving like few others in the pressure-cooker of national emergency.

As the Allied troops were being pulled out at the end of the month, Channon noted his conviction that the Eden group, now led by Amery, would swoop in to attack: 'We are in for a first class political struggle between the Chamberlain men and the "glamour" group'.[43] Yet the Prime Minister's chief problem was not the usual malcontents; it was moderate, mainstream opinion in his own party. The repeated reversals over the preceding two years had incrementally chipped away at the morale of Conservatives, and the lethargy of the 'twilight war' was hardly reassuring. In March, these anxieties had coalesced when the Fourth Marquess of Salisbury—as the scion of the aristocratic Cecil family, the very embodiment of the sober Conservative establishment—formed a new body of Conservative MPs and peers to monitor the war situation.[44] This group, the 'Watching Committee' as Salisbury called it, pressured Chamberlain to carry out a deep reconstruction of the regime at home and adopt a more offensive strategy abroad.[45] These men had a sinking feeling even before the failure in Norway. Salisbury wanted 'decisive' action, and told Halifax that the public 'will not stand for it' if it was not forthcoming.[46] The group supported Churchill's idea that he should be Minister of Defence, appointed as a strategic supremo. They also pressed the National Government to undertake full economic mobilization. Salisbury warned Chamberlain prior to the Norwegian expedition that 'unless we were successful' in Scandinavia, 'the results would be very serious'.[47] 'Another reverse' would be 'fatal to the government', he said; 'the government had already lost two lives and could not afford to lose another'. The recurrent 'loss of credit to this country' could no longer be tolerated.[48]

The Watching Committee represented the respectable and loyalist mass of backbench opinion. They could not be dismissed with a contemptuous snort as some of Churchill or Eden's acolytes might. Another member of the Cecil clan, Salisbury's son Robert Cranborne, complained that Chamberlain's attitude was that of 'Papal infallibility': 'he can't be wrong'.[49] Cranborne was nervous 'for the future of the Conservative party'. A third member of British politics' most illustrious family, Salisbury's brother Lord Cecil, concluded that 'what is really wrong is the supreme direction of the country', specifically 'the Prime Minister'.[50] Yet the Watching Committee was not simply a conspiracy by the denizens of Hatfield House. The disaffection went much deeper, as its membership affirmed: it initially consisted of twenty-eight individuals, but soon expanded. One member took the view that the 'situation demands a change even of the Captain of the Team'.[51] Richard Law—son of the former Conservative leader and Prime Minister Andrew Bonar Law—declared 'there is something wrong with the political direction of the war', expressing his hope that 'the right man' could be found.[52] Another associate remarked that 'Since the Conservative party made the current government, only the Conservative party can destroy it'.[53] This was an ominous sign.

If the situation in the Conservative party was precarious *before* the failure in Norway, it was transformed thereafter. As Allied forces were withdrawn on 29 April, Salisbury led a delegation from the Watching Committee to the Foreign Office to meet with Halifax. In a wide-ranging indictment Salisbury bluntly warned the Foreign Secretary that 'we are not satisfied'.[54] He pressed Halifax on the imperative of radical improvements. In doing so, Salisbury was probably tacitly encouraging the Foreign Secretary to spearhead the resistance and seize the premiership himself. Yet Halifax did not look like a man ready to grab the crown. On the contrary, he seemed 'tired and depressed'.[55] One member of the delegation thought that while Halifax 'understands the situation', he 'does not seem to have any idea about [how] to deal with it'.[56]

Channon observed that 'a cabal against poor Neville' was forming'.[57] On the other side of the Commons, Attlee and Labour vigorously attacked the government for its ineptitude in the frozen north. One Conservative, Cuthbert Headlam, raged that 'the sooner some of these damned Labour people are made to join the Cabinet the better'.[58] The cross-party web of intrigue was embodied by the 'All-Party Parliamentary Action Group', a forum for MPs of all parties to hold meetings and discuss the war which had been formed in September 1939. This was led by a National Liberal MP, Clement Davies, who crossed the floor to sit on the Opposition benches in December 1939. Weekly gatherings at the Reform Club attracted an eclectic bunch: Labour and Liberal MPs, the Eden group, Churchillians, and the Watching Committee. Membership grew to around sixty individuals. Far from missing the bus, Davies told the Commons chamber on 4 May, Hitler 'too often takes a taxi'.[59] And the Sunday newspapers excoriated the National Government over Norway in perhaps the most forceful press attacks in living memory.[60]

At the beginning of May, Churchill's proxy Brendan Bracken joined the Eden group after their weekly dinner for a bout of plotting. He remarked that 'a new government was absolutely essential'. This could be 'either an interim government under Halifax' or, alternatively, 'a new government under Winston'.[61] Did Churchill know what Bracken was up to? It may have been that—as with Chamberlain and Ball—Winston knew when to look the other way. Yet he and Bracken were such irrepressible adventurers for whom life was one endless *Boy's Own* comic strip that this is difficult to believe. Indeed, Jock Colville surmised that while 'Winston himself is being loyal to the PM . . . his satellites (Duff Cooper, Amery, etc.) were doing all in their power to create mischief and ill-feeling'.[62] Cooper—whose fashion sense was so 'dapper' that one journalist thought he looked like a 'pimp' judged that 'there can be no efficient government until Neville goes'.[63]

Colville felt Churchill ought to be 'ashamed of himself' for the plotting.[64] In response, the Conservative Whips under Margesson were 'putting it about' that the Scandinavian setback 'is all the fault of Winston who has made another forlorn failure'.[65] Chamberlain's Parliamentary Private Secretary Lord Dunglass (who himself rose to become Prime Minister from 1963–4) asked Channon whether Churchill ought to be publicly 'deflated', or perhaps sacked from the Admiralty. 'Evidently these thoughts are in Neville's head', 'Chips' surmised.[66] The Prime Minister told his sister that the realities of Norway 'don't square with the picture the gutter press and W.C.'s "friends" try to paint of the supreme First Lord'.[67]

'In the Name of God, Go!'

It was indicative of the degree to which the Prime Minister had lost touch with reality that he confidently expected the Commons showdown to prove a triumph which would see his enemies publicly isolated. In Neville's mind, 'most' of his critics were implacably hostile to him personally; *that* was their real motivation. They were 'traitors' and 'office-seekers' (to be fair, the latter charge was probably true). On 4 May, he actually likened critics such as Morrison to Vidkun Quisling, the Norwegian fascist leader who had recently tried to seize power following the German invasion.[68] This may have been pushing it, but on 6 May Morrison delivered a thunderous assault on Chamberlain in the press with an article entitled 'I Say Get Out' which called for the Prime Minister's immediate resignation.[69] Herbert said it was 'the most bitter indictment' he had ever made. Meanwhile Clement Davies dashed back and forth from one group of critics to the next, urging them to make a stand.

Nevertheless, as Chamberlain settled into his seat in the House of Commons for the first day of the debate on 7 May, he was fairly upbeat. He intended to rout his enemies. Parliamentary confrontations brought out the best in him. At 3.48 p.m., the Prime Minister rose to his feet and opened the proceedings. Yet in the event his statement, which lasted until 4.45, fell utterly flat.[70] Chamberlain came across as lacking in energy. Delivering a bland narrative of the Norwegian expedition, he looked 'tired' and 'fumbled' his words'.[71] More, he was continually heckled with taunts of 'missed the bus' from the Labour benches. Chamberlain appeared a man who had lost control of the House. Revealingly, Neville attempted to convert Churchill's prestige into a shield for the government as a whole: he finished his speech by announcing the news of the First Lord's increased powers over strategy.[72] If this was intended as a dramatic flourish to mollify his critics, it did not work. Amery recorded the speech as a 'flop' that might 'been heard in [Chamberlain's native city] Birmingham'.[73]

Attlee stood up to respond. The difficulty for Labour was the same problem of tactics that had bedevilled them throughout the 'phoney war': how aggressively should they go after Chamberlain? If they were too adversarial, would Conservative MPs instinctively rally to their leader? Clem had long been critical of the 'docile' Conservative backbenchers: 'again and again they will vote against what I believe in their hearts they desire'.[74] Their loyalty to Chamberlain overwhelmed their common sense. Since the previous autumn, therefore, Clem had refused to make the first overt move against Chamberlain.[75] Attlee's stance was that if the Prime Minister was to be brought down, Labour could play a key role—and, naturally, seize a disproportionate share of the fruits of victory—but the main challenge would have to come from Chamberlain's own party. Until they plucked up the courage to strike, Labour would wait. Clem was adamant that Conservatives would need to expose themselves and act as the 'advance guard' for the assault.[76] The longer he held Labour's forces back from either an outright attack or membership of a coalition, the more desperate the Conservatives became. In essence, Attlee had refused to blink first. Now, however, he concluded that the moment for action had finally arrived.[77]

Confident that large numbers of Conservatives would rebel, Clem—the man who had led trench assaults in the First World War—went over the top once more. He told the House of Commons that he was 'disturbed' by what Chamberlain had just said; the Prime Minister had come with a list of 'excuses'. 'We have to face facts. We are not afraid of facing facts'. He savaged the government's conduct of the Norwegian campaign, not least for dispatching unprepared 'boys' instead of 'experienced and older men'. The failures of organization were 'unbelievable', as was the inability to even comprehend 'the vital importance' of adequate air cover. The current War Cabinet was, Attlee said, not 'an efficient instrument'. 'It could only be justified by success, and we have not had that success'. He explicitly stated that Churchill himself was not to blame, but the National Government remained 'blind and deaf', failing to see that the war was not being waged with 'sufficient energy, intensity, drive and resolution'. 'The Prime Minister talked of [Hitler] missing buses', Attlee said. 'What about all the buses which he and his associates have missed?' 'Week after week', Attlee charged, Conservative backbenchers had allowed 'their loyalty to the Chief Whip to overcome their loyalty to the real needs of the country'.[78]

It was a devastating attack. Over the subsequent hours further assaults were made on Chamberlain's position. Several of the most dramatic emanated from the government backbenches. One of those was delivered by the Conservative MP Sir Roger Keyes. Keyes was a decorated Royal Navy officer who had retired from the service in 1935 as Admiral of the Fleet. That evening, in an incredible sight that instantly ensured the rapt attention of all present, Keyes marched into the House in his full dress uniform. Crisp, buttoned-up, and immaculate, Keyes's uniform made for quite a spectacle. It was completely out of the ordinary, yet somehow appropriate for the occasion. When he rose to speak at 7.10 p.m., bedecked with six rows of gleaming medals on his chest, the House of Commons fell silent. Keyes solemnly announced that he was there to represent the 'officers and men'. For twenty startling minutes the Admiral of the Fleet mauled the conduct of the campaign. Speaking from the papers clutched tightly in his hand, Keyes almost quivered with rage. Norway was a 'shocking story of ineptitude', he said. Yet he too specifically exempted Churchill from responsibility for the disaster. Keyes in fact called for the First Lord—a man with 'iron' in his 'soul'—to assume the responsibility for making decisions, because 'the war cannot be won by committees'.[79] When he sat down, there was 'thunderous applause'.[80] Keyes's dress uniform had arguably made the speech, lending added dignity to his words.[81] Maisky thought the fact that Keyes was a poor public speaker, who kept stumbling throughout, was, paradoxically, what produced 'a very moving' address.[82] Harold Nicolson thought Keyes's intervention 'by far the most dramatic speech I have ever heard'.[83]

Thirty minutes later, at 8.00 p.m., Leo Amery stood up. While possessed of a formidable mind, he too was not known as a compelling parliamentary orator. Yet, that evening, Amery secured a place in political history. He wanted to turn the debate into a final 'trial of strength' with Chamberlain.[84] Amery began by reminding the chamber that MPs were faced with 'a grave responsibility'.[85] 'Parliament is on trial in this war', he declared, and 'if we lose . . . Parliament as an institution will be condemned for good and all'. Amery went on that there could be 'no loyalties' except to 'the common cause' of victory. He then narrowed the focus of his attack to the person of Chamberlain himself. Amery charged that there was 'not one sentence in the Prime Minister's speech' which suggested he was capable of 'foresight . . . clear decision and . . . swift action'. As he spoke, more and more members filed into the House to listen, having been fetched from the smoking room by Davies. Amery grew in confidence.

'We cannot go on as we are', he raged; 'There must be a change'. After arguing for a remodelling of the War Cabinet, Amery called for the formation of a new cross-party coalition to bring 'the whole abilities of the nation', including the trade unions, into the heart of the British state. This was, he said, not a moment for 'peacetime statesmen':

> Facility in debate, ability to state a case, caution in advancing an unpopular view, compromise and procrastination are the natural qualities—I might almost say virtues—of a political leader in peace. They are fatal qualities in war. Vision, daring, swiftness, consistency of decision are the very essence of victory.

The country needed 'a man of action', Amery argued, someone 'who can match our enemies in fighting spirit, in daring, in resolution and in thirst for victory'. That was obviously not the Prime Minister. This was vicious enough, but in the climax of his speech Amery launched one of the most famous bombardments in parliamentary history. Quoting Oliver Cromwell's famous injunction from 300 years before, he glared down at Neville Chamberlain and angrily exclaimed:

> This is what Cromwell said to the Long Parliament when he thought it no longer fit to conduct the affairs of the nation: 'You have sat too long here for any good you have been doing. Depart, I say, and let us have done with you. In the name of God, go!'[86]

It was a remarkable ending. Those who heard it would never forget Amery's words. The brilliant usage of Cromwell instantly entered into the annals of parliamentary lore. Amery was anxious beforehand that MPs might see the Cromwell quotation as over-the-top, and had pondered whether to include it at all; but, in the midst of the speech, after a word of encouragement from Davies and feeling the atmosphere in the chamber rise to 'an increasing crescendo of applause . . . I cast prudence to the winds' and went 'full out'.[87] His statement caught the mood of the House perfectly. Amery's contribution was long recalled by Dunglass as 'the dagger' in Chamberlain's 'heart'.[88]

Two of the most powerful speeches in parliamentary history had been heard in the space of little over an hour. They had both been delivered by Conservatives; and they both called for new leadership. With good reason did Chamberlain's devotee 'Chips' Channon open his diary for 7 May with the words, 'A dreadful day'.[89]

'Like a Rat in a Corner'

Attlee and the other Labour leaders now decided to force a division at the end of the debate, effectively acting as a motion of censure on the National Government.[90] This offered the best prospect of breaking the Prime Minister and compelling his resignation; moreover, for Labour to suddenly swoop in and place itself at the centre of events would enhance its negotiating position for a coalition. There was no turning back. As news of the Labour party's decision circulated throughout Westminster on the morning of 8 May, Chamberlain was rattled. At lunchtime he sent his Parliamentary Private Secretary, Dunglass, to speak to Conservative backbenchers and pledge a 'dramatic reconstruction of the government'.[91] Considering that the Prime Minister had explicitly ruled this out in the Commons just the day before, the offer represented an unambiguous sign of panic.

At 4.00 that afternoon, Morrison began the second day of the debate with a highly partisan attack on Chamberlain. The Prime Minister was 'not good enough', Morrison said; he was 'persistently wrong', lacking in 'courage' and 'self-respect', and 'responsible' for the war in which Britain now found itself.[92] The sheer hostility of Morrison's speech 'staggered' Chamberlain.[93] Channon was shocked by its 'vituperation': with Morrison throwing down the gauntlet and declaring that Labour would call a vote, 'we knew then that it was to be war'.[94] 'Showing his teeth like a rat in a corner', the Prime Minister immediately 'jump[ed]' up to respond and made another ill-judged speech in which he reduced the issue before the House of Commons to one of personal loyalty to himself.[95] Characteristically unable to control his disdain for his critics, the Prime Minister took the bait. Chamberlain told the House that 'I accept the challenge'; Morrison had attacked the government, and 'me in particular'. With a look on his face that one critic described as a 'leer',[96] the Prime Minister went on:

I do not seek to evade criticism, but I say this to my friends in the House—*and I do have friends in this House*—no government can prosecute a war efficiently unless it has public and parliamentary support . . . At least we shall see who is with us and who is against us, and I call on my friends to support us in the [division] lobby tonight.[97]

Chamberlain's appeal to his 'friends' went down like a lead balloon. It showed how he thought; it also confirmed his inability to disguise it. The temperature rose. A gleeful Amery, watching from the backbenches, thought it a 'tactless' performance. As both he and Channon noted in their diaries that evening, the ostensible subject of the debate—the Norway campaign—had been 'forgotten' as 'irrelevant'.[98] The *real* focus of the proceedings was the attempted coup against Chamberlain and the National Government. Chamberlain's wife, Annie, sat in the gallery above the Commons and looked down into the 'arena where the lions were out for her husband's blood'.[99] Horace Wilson was also there, and taken aback by the 'hatred written on their faces'; he spoke of years of 'pent-up bitterness and frustration' that was now being let loose.[100]

At 5.37 p.m., Lloyd George stood up to speak. The man who led Britain to victory in the First World War had always detested Chamberlain, yet had prevaricated over whether or not to address the chamber. Clement Davies went to see him in his room at the Commons. Davies had already pressed Amery to stick the boot in to Chamberlain, and now did the same with Lloyd George. 'Has the great Achilles lost his skill?', Davies demanded. As it turned out, Achilles had not. Lloyd George's speech that day represented the final major contribution the Welsh Wizard made to public life prior to his death in 1945. Describing himself as a man 'with some experience of these matters', Lloyd George held the House 'spellbound' as he raged at Chamberlain, while Labour MPs 'shouted themselves hoarse' in the background.[101] Like so many others in the debate, he exempted Churchill from criticism. When Winston made a brief intervention in response to say, 'I take complete responsibility for everything that has been done by the Admiralty, and I take my full share of the burden', the man they called 'the Goat' had a brilliant riposte to his old protégé: 'The right honourable Gentleman must not allow himself to be converted into an air-raid shelter to keep the splinters from hitting his colleagues'.

Deploring Chamberlain's appeal to his 'friends', in a withering put-down the old warhorse declared that Chamberlain could not 'make his personality . . . inseparable from the interests of the country'. Lloyd George went on:

> It is not a question of who are the Prime Minister's friends. It is a far bigger issue. The Prime Minister must remember that he has met this formidable foe of ours in peace and in war. He has always been worsted. He is not in a position to appeal on the ground of friendship. He has appealed for sacrifice. The nation is prepared for every sacrifice so long as it has leadership . . . I say solemnly that the Prime Minister should give an example of sacrifice, because there is nothing which can contribute more to victory in this war than that he should sacrifice the seals of office.[102]

It was brutal. The atmosphere in the chamber was one of 'bedlam'.[103]

Obliged to defend the War Cabinet of which he was a member, Churchill himself wound up the debate that evening with a 'magnificent piece of oratory'. Winston was at pains to be seen as loyal by Conservative backbenchers, and delivered a 'slashing, vigorous speech' against the critics.[104] He even defended Chamberlain's appeal to his 'friends' with a sharp reference to the obeisance of Conservative MPs since 1937: 'I hope he has some friends. He certainly had a good many when things were going well'. Everyone could see the awkward position Winston was in, 'defending his enemies, and a cause in which he did not believe'.[105] When Lloyd George called upon him not to act as an air-raid shelter, one observer thought Winston was 'trying not to laugh' while Cabinet colleagues sat with 'stony faces' on either side of him.[106]

Meanwhile, throughout the day David Margesson had been deploying all of his powers to cajole and coerce Conservative MPs into the division lobby in support of the government. He asked them to back Chamberlain 'just once more'.[107] But the Chief Whip was fighting an uphill battle. That evening, after lobbying from Amery, the Watching Committee unanimously decided to vote against the government.[108] Even larger numbers of Conservatives resolved to abstain.

At 11.00 p.m. on 8 May, the debate finally closed and the division began. The chamber 'buzzed like a disturbed bee hive'.[109] The numbers traipsing into the opposition lobby were high—testament to Davies's efforts to persuade MPs of rival parties to come together to act. Attlee took pleasure in seeing 'Conservative MP after Conservative MP' vote against the government.[110] Channon and others yelled 'Quislings!' and 'rats!' in their direction; they were met with taunts of 'yes-men'.[111] The atmosphere was one of poison. When the results were collated shortly afterwards, the House fell silent in hushed anticipation. Margesson went over to the clerk's table to read out the numbers; the Chief Whip's blood must have run cold when he saw them. '281 to 200', he sombrely announced.[112]

Chamberlain's huge Commons majority of more than 200 had collapsed to a mere eighty-one. Thirty-eight National Government MPs voted outright against the ministry; more than sixty abstained. Chamberlain was 'bowled over' when he heard the numbers. He looked as 'white as chalk'.[113] While on paper a victory, in practice the vote was a huge moral defeat—one that demonstrated the Prime Minister no longer commanded the staunch support even of his own party. The scene was one of pandemonium. Chants of 'Resign, resign!' rang out as Chamberlain stalked from the Commons. Harold Macmillan—like a 'madly grinning schoolboy'—and other MPs on both sides of the chamber launched into a jubilant rendition of 'Rule Britannia'.[114]

12

A NEW ORDER

'A Bad Stomach Ache'

For sheer drama and historical gravity, nothing in living memory can approximate the events of 7 and 8 May 1940.[1] The dialectic between foreign policy and domestic political fortunes retained its potency; 'the whole vigour of the country', Jock Colville recorded, 'is bent towards internal political strife'.[2]

On the morning of 9 May, Chamberlain and his closest advisers circled the wagons. Even now the Prime Minister searched for a way to retain office. Clutching at straws, he hoped that many of the critics could be bought off. He wondered whether, if he dropped Hoare, Simon and several others from the government, discontent might be assuaged.[3] From 8.00 a.m., Chamberlain was therefore on the telephone trying to win the backing of those who had abandoned him the previous evening.[4] He believed that men such as Amery and Cooper were resentful at not being ministers, and remained jealous they 'can only look on' from the outside.[5] Wilson apparently recommended that Chamberlain give Amery—the Conservative who had made the most dramatic speech of the debate—the choice of any Cabinet post he desired as a means of bribing him.[6] Amery derisively described this as 'truly typical of the Horace Wilson methods'. Meanwhile Sir Patrick Spens, the chairman of the 1922 Committee, tried to pep up Chamberlain and talk him out of quitting. He said that resignation would be a 'national disaster'.[7]

While the Prime Minister was searching for ways to stay on, Conservative opinion was increasingly resolved that he must go. Cuthbert Headlam thought Chamberlain was sunk because 'the Socialists won't serve under him'.[8] The House of Commons was 'full of rumour and intrigue, plot and counter-plot', Channon recorded.[9] Even Margesson informed Chamberlain that 'he could no longer command support of a majority in the Conservative party'.[10] At 9.30 that morning, the Watching Committee met to discuss strategy. It agreed that a coalition government with Labour was 'essential', and that Chamberlain, Hoare, and Simon 'must go'.[11] Salisbury immediately went to the Foreign Office to see Halifax and convey this. He said that it was 'impossible' for Chamberlain to form a satisfactory coalition. Importantly, Halifax apparently concurred with this assessment. Salisbury then remarked that the successor must be either Halifax himself or Churchill.[12] Salisbury's preference was probably for Halifax to assume the premiership, rather than the wild man of Chartwell; but, as so often before, the Foreign Secretary lacked the temperament for high-stakes warfare. While accepting that he himself was 'the obvious first choice', Halifax presented his membership of the House of Lords as an insurmountable obstacle: Churchill would be the senior figure in the Commons. A dual arrangement, he argued, was 'impracticable'.[13]

Even before seeing Salisbury, Halifax felt serious reservations about the premiership. Two conversations earlier that morning had cemented this. Rab Butler, Under-Secretary at the Foreign Office, communicated to Halifax details of a discussion the night before with Dalton and Morrison. The two Labour men reiterated that, while their party would not serve under Chamberlain, they favoured Halifax rather than Churchill as Prime Minister: 'Winston must stick to the war'.[14] Attlee too expressed a preference for Halifax.[15] The Labour party thus backed Halifax's candidacy; so would the great mass of Conservative opinion. The premiership was there for the taking. Yet Halifax quailed. The second conversation before he saw Salisbury was with the Prime Minister himself. Chamberlain was now beginning to accept that he would probably have to resign. Neville stated that, if he did so, Halifax, not Winston, would be his preferred successor. Chamberlain offered to serve under Halifax in a new government. He also did not think there would be much resistance in the Commons to Halifax becoming Prime Minister despite being in the Lords. Yet Halifax was apparently unconvinced. 'I put all the arguments I could think of against myself', he recorded, 'laying considerable emphasis on the difficult position of a Prime Minister unable to make contact with the centre of gravity in the House of Commons'.[16]

While one is tempted to view this as false modesty—with Halifax concerned to avoid being seen as *seeking* the job, and hoping instead to have it thrust upon him—such a cynical conclusion would, for once, likely be inappropriate. Halifax in fact felt only a sucking dread when he contemplated the burdens of the premiership. Dealing with a European war, mobilizing the country, and managing the livewire Churchill did not constitute an attractive job. With Churchill effectively running the war from the Commons Halifax feared he would be rendered a 'more or less honorary Prime Minister, living in a kind of twilight just outside the things that really mattered'.[17] Halifax did not believe himself capable of controlling Churchill. He was also a novice in matters of military strategy. The premiership was there to be seized, yet he could not bring himself to reach out and grasp it. As Halifax put it in his diary, 'the conversation and the evident drift of [Chamberlain's mind] left me with a bad stomach ache'.[18]

'Don't Agree, and Don't Say Anything'

While Chamberlain and Halifax were wrestling with what to do on the morning of 9 May, Churchill was in a buoyant mood.[19] He spent time in the Commons smoking room, 'waving a gigantic cigar' and reducing MPs to 'delighted paroxysms of laughter'.[20] He then called Eden to arrange a confab over lunch at the Admiralty. Winston was confident that, as he told Eden down the telephone, 'Neville would not be able to bring in Labour and a national government must be formed'.[21] He suspected that the premiership was about to come his way, and thus felt 'content to let events unfold'.[22] It seems that even Eden—'the film star', as Bracken dubbed him—accepted that he himself could not become Prime Minister.[23]

Still, getting rid of Chamberlain would be facilitated by an important act of betrayal. This originated from an unlikely quarter. Churchill and Eden were joined for lunch by Sir Kingsley Wood, the Lord Privy Seal—and Chamberlain's oldest political ally. While far from a dynamic figure, Wood had risen in tandem with Chamberlain since the early 1920s and was trusted by the Prime Minister in a way that few ministers were. He had been his Parliamentary Private Secretary between 1924 and 1929, and in 1933 Chamberlain pressed Baldwin to bring Wood into the Cabinet. 'At No. 10', he was considered a 'superm[a]n', one civil servant noted.[24] Wood and Chamberlain usually walked around St James's Park together each morning. Yet even Wood now realized that Chamberlain was finished. He therefore suddenly jumped ship and threw his lot in with Churchill. Eden, for one, was 'shocked' at Wood's defection—he had always been 'Chamberlain's man'. But Wood saw the way the wind was blowing. Indeed, one observed wrote that 'he was always an extremely barometrical politician'.[25] When Horace Wilson later realized this, he was seething: Wood had, he charged, 'misled' the Prime Minister about his loyalties.[26] The explanation may be straightforward. Wood had likely heard that he was to be one of the sacrifices offered up by Chamberlain as a means to cling to power. And so he struck first.

Over lunch, the three men discussed what Churchill should do next. Wood advised Churchill to 'make plain his willingness' to become Prime Minister. Eden concurred. Importantly, Wood then proffered some crucial tactical advice that planted a seed in Winston's mind. As Eden recorded the conversation, Kingsley gave 'a warning that Chamberlain would want Halifax to succeed him and would want Churchill to agree. Wood advised: "Don't agree, and don't say anything"'.[27]

One of Chamberlain's closest colleagues thus told Churchill to simply remain silent if asked to serve under Halifax. Wood had seen the Prime Minister that morning, and had probably gathered that he was endeavouring to fix the succession for Halifax. Chamberlain may even have confided in Wood exactly *how* he intended to go about that; Wood's recommendation was certainly very specific. Either way, Wood knew what to expect, and counselled that Churchill stay quiet. It was handy advice that Eden seconded. As events a few hours later would demonstrate, Churchill absorbed it. The historian Maurice Cowling described Wood as 'the indispensable Judas'.[28]

Early in the afternoon, Amery chaired a meeting of Conservative, Labour, and Liberal critics of the government. It was decided to issue a joint statement to the newspapers expressing a willingness to support 'any Prime Minister' who could construct a genuinely 'national' cross-party government.[29] Chamberlain's position was now untenable—and the Prime Minister finally realized it. He called the First Lord of the Admiralty and the Foreign Secretary to a meeting to settle the succession late that afternoon.

At 4.30 p.m., Churchill and Halifax arrived in the Prime Minister's office at 10 Downing Street. Margesson was also in attendance. Sunlight was streaming in through the windows. Margesson remarked that 'unity' was 'essential', and regretfully felt that it could not be attained under Chamberlain. Halifax recorded that with this drift of the conversation, 'my stomach ache continued'.[30] Chamberlain telephoned Attlee and asked him and Greenwood to come to Downing Street. When they arrived shortly afterwards, the Prime Minister posed two questions. The first was whether Labour would now agree to enter a coalition government under his leadership, with a reconstructed Cabinet. The second was whether, if Labour refused to serve under *him*, they would agree to serve under someone else. Attlee was, in his own words, 'very rude' with Chamberlain: 'I have to be quite frank with you, Prime Minister, our party will not serve under you. They don't want you, and in my view the country doesn't want you'.[31] Attlee and Greenwood agreed that they would travel to Bournemouth, where the Labour party's annual conference was due to begin, for a meeting of the National Executive Committee (NEC) the following afternoon. There they would ascertain whether Labour would serve under someone other than Chamberlain, and report back on the decision.[32] 'Until that moment he thought he could hang on', Attlee recalled.[33]

As the Labour leader and his deputy left the four Conservatives alone once more, the crucial moment finally arrived. As Churchill himself recalled in his memoirs, 'I have had many important interviews in my public life, and this was certainly the most important'.[34] Chamberlain said it was now evident that he must resign. The question was whether he should advise the King to send for Churchill or Halifax as his successor. Clearly seeking to steer things towards Halifax, the Prime Minister pointedly asked Churchill if he could see any reason why a member of the House of

Lords should be barred from the premiership.[35] Yet Winston did not answer; he instead just stared out of the window, into Horse Guards Parade behind Whitehall. He had taken Wood's advice. As he himself later put it, 'Usually I talk a great deal, but on this occasion I was silent'.[36] Any signal of agreement that Halifax *could* become Prime Minister would be fatal.

As Churchill continued to stare out of the window, the meeting became awkward. 'As I remained silent, a very long pause ensued. It certainly seemed longer than the two minutes which one observes in the commemorations of Armistice Day'. Churchill was probably exaggerating the duration of the interval, but one imagines that the tension in the room must have been unbearable. In the end, it was Halifax who cracked and broke the silence. The Foreign Secretary reiterated what he had been saying all day: that, as a peer, he was not sure he could provide the proper leadership that Parliament and the country required. As we have seen, he almost certainly did not want the job under these conditions anyway. With that concession, Churchill finally spoke. Winston 'did not demur' from what Halifax had said. He simply stated that he would await the King's commission to form a government.[37]

That was that. Thus was the succession decided. Halifax had, in Churchill's words, 'thrown in his hand'.[38] One can only imagine Chamberlain's face. His efforts to manipulate the proceedings had failed. Halifax wilted—again—and Churchill out-manoeuvred the Prime Minister in one of the most important conversations in modern history. With little choice, Chamberlain agreed to 'put Winston's name to the King' the following day, once he heard from Attlee about the Labour party's willingness to join a coalition.[39] Breaking the habit of a lifetime, Churchill had bitten his tongue. The premiership fell into his lap as a result.

'The Greatest Adventurer of Modern Political History'

The early hours of the following morning, 10 May, brought a startling transformation in the war.[40] Hitler was not content to rest on his success in Scandinavia. At 4.30 a.m., the Wehrmacht and the Luftwaffe began an assault on western Europe. France, Belgium, Holland, and Luxemburg were all attacked in the largest *Blitzkrieg* operation Germany had yet launched. Panzer divisions consisting of dense concentrations of tanks formed a spearhead; ground-attack aircraft offered withering support; and paratroopers dropped from the skies across the Low Countries. The German armies advanced towards France with frightening rapidity, simply circumventing the incomplete Maginot Line. Soon, they were within striking distance of the Channel coast. With the Fuhrer refusing to play ball and send his troops into the fortifications of the Line, as the Allies hoped, officials in both London and

Paris immediately found themselves in the grip of a major crisis. This was combat that made Norway look like a sideshow. And it came at the worst time: the protracted fall of Chamberlain threatened political paralysis in Britain, while across the Channel Reynaud had offered his own resignation, just seven weeks into his premiership. Reynaud immediately retracted this when he learned of the German assault, and got back to work. Yet Hitler had chosen the perfect moment to open up the war in the west.

Reynaud was not the only leader who had a change of heart. When Chamberlain was woken with news of the German attack, he wondered whether the crisis might offer him an excuse to stay on; after all, this was, he reasoned, no time for a change of government. Orders had to be issued and the German advance blocked. For the Prime Minister and his devotees, it looked for a moment as if 'Neville may be saved'.[41] The War Cabinet gathered three times that day. Chamberlain told Beaverbrook that 'we cannot consider changes in the government while we are in the throes of battle'.[42] He telephoned Attlee before the latter went to Bournemouth and indicated that he might now need to remain in post. But those who were resolved upon Chamberlain's resignation were having none of it. When the Prime Minister suggested that the German attack 'changed the whole situation', Attlee brusquely told him, 'Not at all'.[43] The Watching Committee took the same view.[44] And Kingsley Wood openly signalled his defection to the enemy camp by informing Chamberlain that he would still have to resign, and promptly. After the Prime Minister floated the idea of carrying on due to the emergency, Wood replied that 'on the contrary, the new crisis made it all the more necessary to have a National Government'.[45] Chamberlain had precious few 'friends' left.

Late that morning, Attlee, Dalton, Greenwood, and most of Labour's senior leadership caught the 11.34 train from Waterloo Station to Bournemouth. Morrison, as the head of the London County Council, stayed behind in the capital in case of a Luftwaffe attack.[46] The NEC was to meet in the afternoon at the Highcliffe Hotel. If the 'twilight war' had not come to an end, the annual Labour conference would almost certainly have been the scene of violent rows over Attlee's strategy of 'constructive Opposition'. One-quarter of all resolutions submitted to the conference recorded hostility to the policy.[47] For Attlee, then, the transformation in the political situation came just in time. At the NEC that afternoon, Attlee argued forcefully for Labour to refuse to serve under Chamberlain, but also to immediately join a cross-party government led by a different Prime Minister. Clem's colleagues backed his recommendation. The NEC resolved that Labour would 'take a full and equal share as a full partner in a new Government under a new Prime Minister which would command the confidence of the nation'.[48] Attlee's approach had paid off handsomely. Tellingly, the NEC agreed that the conference should be informed of the leadership's *decision* to enter the government, rather than a *recommendation* to do so—hence presenting the action simply for symbolic endorsement, not authorization.[49] Attlee and the rest were adamant that they, and not the activists, would take the important decisions. At 5.00 p.m., Clem left the meeting to telephone 10 Downing Street. He got through to Chamberlain, and conveyed the news of Labour's position.[50] It was thus the Labour NEC, acting on Attlee's recommendation, which finally brought down the National Government. After finishing the call, Clem then hurried to the railway station to catch a train back up to London.

One last desperate bid was made to persuade Halifax to seize the crown. Rab Butler had again worked on Halifax earlier in the day, but still found the Foreign Secretary 'firm'—he 'would not be Prime Minister'.[51] Shortly after Attlee's call to Chamberlain, Dunglass, Channon, and Butler quickly agreed that the latter would speak to the Foreign Secretary yet again and implore him to stop Winston. Yet when Butler went to see him for the final time, he found Halifax had slipped out of the Foreign Office to go to the dentist; apparently the prospect of becoming Prime Minister brought on a toothache as well as a stomach ache.[52] It was now too late. Within an hour of speaking to Attlee, Chamberlain was at Buckingham Palace to see the King. He resigned, and advised George VI to send for Churchill. What was once unthinkable was now unstoppable.

Shortly thereafter, Churchill himself arrived at the Palace. Attempting to lighten the mood, the King said, 'I suppose you don't know why I have sent for you?' Playing along, Winston replied, 'Sir, I simply couldn't imagine why'.[53] At that, King George burst out laughing, and asked Churchill if he would form a new government. Winston said that he would do so. At the age of sixty-five, Churchill had become the Prime Minister of Great Britain. The coup d'état was complete.

That night, Channon, Colville, and Dunglass gathered in Butler's room at the Foreign Office for a drink. It was an emotional get-together. The four men were all deeply morose. They felt 'cheated and out-witted'. Butler was furious: 'the good clean tradition of English politics...had been sold to the greatest adventurer of modern political history'. Chamberlain and Halifax 'surrendered to a half-breed American'.[54] Dunglass—who believed that those around Churchill were 'scum'—was so upset that he 'let himself go'.[55] With nothing left to do, Channon opened a bottle of champagne. 'We four loyal adherents of Mr Chamberlain defiantly raised a toast to "the King over the water"'.[56]

But this was fantasy. There was a new 'King', and he was not 'over the water' either. He was ensconced in Admiralty House, working to build a new administration. Chamberlain had not yet moved out of Downing Street, and so Churchill continued to work from his office at the Admiralty. He toiled for the next nine hours to appoint as many ministers as he could. It was 3.00 a.m. before Winston finally retired to bed. It seems appropriate to allow Churchill himself to describe his feelings as he related them in his post-war paean to himself, *The Gathering Storm*:

> I cannot conceal from the reader of this truthful account that as I went to bed...I was conscious of a profound sense of relief. At last I had the authority to give directions over the whole scene. I felt as if I were walking with destiny, and that all my past life had been but a preparation for this hour and for this trial...Therefore, although impatient for the morning, I slept soundly and had no need for cheering dreams. Facts are better than dreams.[57]

That famous passage offers a remarkable window into the psychology of the Prime Minister. Churchill instinctively described his thoughts in terms of delight at his new status and his victory in the struggle for dominance—and acknowledged he was unable to 'conceal' that fact from 'the reader'. All too often treated as yet another piece of grandiose Churchillian prose, this account of his first hours as Prime Minister illuminates who he was, and always had been.

The Spoils of War

Throughout the 1930s, the notion that Winston Churchill might one day become Prime Minister would have indeed sounded like something from a dream—and, for some, a nightmare. He was yesterday's man, and an unstable one at that. Yet now, remarkably, he was the most powerful politician in the realm. A buccaneering adventurer in the English tradition of Drake and Raleigh had finally ascended to the office of Prime Minister; and politics, not 'destiny', delivered Churchill the job. He immediately appointed himself Minister of Defence as well. This was a new position, with, as Winston put it, 'undefined powers'—but that was the point. He intended to use it to 'assume the general direction of the war'. He would be the 'executive head' of the government.[58] Winston moved to ensure that he, and nobody else, would play the central role in shaping British strategy and the conduct of military operations. The boy who loved toy soldiers now had the might of the British Empire at his command.

Yet Churchill knew that most of the Conservative party still had no love for him. It would be difficult for them to accept him as Prime Minister. He was also a romantic, with his heart in the eighteenth century before political parties existed in their modern form and when, legend had it, governments consisting of men of talent came together to meet national emergencies. Winston therefore decided that, while he would be Prime Minister, he would not seek to become leader of the Conservative party.[59] Chamberlain would retain that position, with a post in the War Cabinet. Churchill would thus be a 'national' figure, symbolically situating himself above party, and leading a government in which the leaders of the Conservative, Labour, and Liberal parties were all represented. There was calculation at work here, too. He needed to bind both Chamberlain and Halifax to him. Their enmity might be fatal if confined to the backbenches. As a result, neither individual was to be sacked. Chamberlain became Lord President of the Council, while Halifax remained at the Foreign Office. Churchill was clever about it. The settling of accounts with these men would come, but it would have to wait.

That said, some other accounts were settled quickly. There was an immediate reckoning with the hated Sir Horace Wilson. On the morning of 11 May, Wilson turned up to 10 Downing Street for work as usual. As he opened the door to his office, adjoining that of the Prime Minister, Wilson found Bracken and Randolph Churchill seated on the sofa and chatting. The 'parachute troops were already in possession', as Macmillan described the scene.[60] The two men simply stared at the civil servant until, without a word, he withdrew—never to return.[61] Within weeks, the authors of the infamous polemic Guilty Men exposed Wilson's work to the world, comparing him to Polonius from Hamlet, the king's chief adviser hiding behind the arras.[62] Churchill apparently told one underling that if Wilson ever dared to visit Downing Street again, 'I'll make him Governor of Greenland!'[63] Joseph Ball's time as one of the most influential men in Westminster was also broken. Chamberlain's feared inner circle was at the end of the road.

Another individual the Prime Minister felt free to remove was Sir Samuel Hoare. The man with whom Winston had clashed over India was immediately sacked from the War Cabinet. Within a fortnight, Hoare was sent as ambassador to Franco's Spain. There is some suggestion that following his sacking Hoare wanted to 'get out' of the country, whether to escape the German bombs shortly expected to fall on London or the public opprobrium soon to be unleashed against the leaders of the former government.[64] After his initial plea to be made Viceroy of India was (unsurprisingly) rejected by Churchill, Hoare himself may have planted the idea of being sent to Madrid. His evident desire to leave Britain at a grim time earned 'Slippery Sam' the enmity of former colleagues; while walking with Halifax and his wife, Alexander Cadogan contented himself with the thought that, with so many German and Italian agents hovering around Madrid, there was at least 'a good chance' of 'S.H. being murdered'. Halifax looked 'pained' at the notion; but the Foreign Secretary's wife 'agreed heartily'.[65] Hoare—'that little blighter'—thus looked to fly out to Madrid 'as soon as he can get a plane'.[66] His job there was to try and keep Spain from joining the war on Hitler's side. Hoare did excellent work in Madrid, succeeding in his brief; though he also quickly requested an increased annual payment of £2,000, which, as the historian Andrew Roberts witheringly points out, was the precise sum he was accustomed to receiving from Beaverbrook for murky purposes.[67]

These cases aside, the Prime Minister was far too savvy to launch a wholesale purge the moment he got his hands on the lever of power. For Conservative rebels, the promotions were not great. With Chamberlain and Halifax still in the War Cabinet, and a need to make room for Labour, there was limited space. Eden was appointed Secretary for War, while Amery was sent to the India Office. Neither man secured one of the top offices of state—though Eden, at least, would do so by the end of the year, despite the fact that his Permanent Under-Secretary at the War Office thought him 'a feeble little pansy'.[68] Margesson was retained as Chief Whip, Churchill putting his talents to good use.

Unsurprisingly, of course, there were several posts for Churchill's friends and cronies. Duff Cooper was made Minister for Information. More importantly, Beaverbrook entered the government in the critical role of Minister for Aircraft Production. Most people thought Beaverbrook a 'crook', but, as an amused Halifax pointed out, 'these days one can't be too particular'.[69] Professor Lindemann retained his all-purpose role at Churchill's side as his chief scientific adviser, while Bracken became the Prime Minister's Parliamentary Private Secretary. The King was apparently unhappy that someone like Bracken might be elevated to the Privy Council; much of Parliament and Whitehall thought it a 'scandal'.[70] Churchill had to insist. Appropriately, there was a reward for Kingsley Wood, too. Wood had advised Churchill how to handle the crucial meeting with Chamberlain and Halifax, and then told Chamberlain in front of the War Cabinet that he would have to go. Winston promoted Wood to be Chancellor of the Exchequer, and tasked him with paying for what would be a stupendously expensive war. Bracken—a man who knew how toadyism worked—complained that Wood 'oiled his way in by flattery'.[71] With the likes of Churchill, Beaverbrook, and Bracken ensconced at the hub of British government, one could forgive Stanley Baldwin if he ruminated that those who had once been inmates were now running the asylum.

Attlee met with Churchill and agreed the Labour party would join the ministry. The Liberals under Churchill's old friend Archibald Sinclair would also enter the coalition. Attlee's stress on patience and patriotism had created the basis for a very favourable division of spoils. While the Conservatives held fifty-two posts in the government compared to Labour's sixteen, this was hardly disproportionate to the balance of MPs in the Commons; and, crucially, Labour had two seats out of five in the new War Cabinet. By contrast, the Liberals had just two ministerial posts in the government and no representative in the War Cabinet. The new War Cabinet would consist of five members: Churchill, Chamberlain, and Halifax from the Conservatives, and Attlee and Greenwood from Labour. Attlee was appointed Lord Privy Seal and rapidly became one of the most influential figures in the machinery of state, extending his influence across numerous key Whitehall committees. The Labour conference in Bournemouth endorsed the decision to enter the Churchill coalition by a majority of more than 25:2.[72] And Attlee made 'the speech of his life' in support of the government.[73] He promised his party that, through membership of the coalition, they would not only serve the country but advance socialism to boot. He was not wrong.

Greenwood was appointed Minister Without Portfolio and Dalton became Minister for Economic Warfare. Morrison went to the Ministry of Supply, not the senior post he had hoped for. Ernest Bevin was a different matter. Churchill was adamant that the trade unions would need to be brought into the heart of the state; and Bevin was the most powerful, and capable, man in the movement. Though he was not even an MP, Churchill brushed this aside. A seat would be found and someone prevailed upon to retire; Bevin would stand at the subsequent by-election. Ernie had never shown any previous interest in being a politician. He despised the manoeuvring and intriguing for small stakes with which most MPs seemed to occupy their time. The exercise of naked power to major ends was the only thing that interested Bevin. Under Churchill, such a role was thrust upon him. Ernie was appointed Minister of Labour and given responsibility for organizing Britain's manpower for the enormous challenges of war production. Bevin, the man Attlee called a 'tank', rolled into Whitehall.

In selecting the personnel of his government, Churchill had laid the foundations of what was, at root, a great team. The ministry encompassed almost all of the available talent in British public life. Career politicians of every stripe and temperament, civil servants, economists, trade unionists, and businessmen were called forth to put their abilities to use. This alliance would endure through five years of dangerous trials and resist all efforts to knock it off course. And it would expand the boundaries of what it was thought possible for the state to accomplish. By the end of the war, the Churchill coalition could lay claim to a central role in Britain's national mythology. The formation of the new regime was, then, not simply another change of government. It was far more than that. Out of the ruins of

Chamberlain's premiership, a new political order had been established. Nothing would ever be the same again.

'Society Is Founded on Hero Worship'

There is an old aphorism that history is written by the victors.[74] Few understood that better than Winston Churchill. A gifted historian with an innate sense of the epic, Churchill correctly discerned that he was living at a crossroads in world history—and he had made sure that, against all the odds and the wishes of his many enemies, he was at the centre of it. He was equally determined that the version of the 1930s that people remembered, the one passed down to future generations, was that which he himself would write. And so he did. Churchill's 1948 book *The Gathering Storm*, one of the great works of twentieth-century literature, built on the hundreds of speeches he had delivered during the 1930s—speeches seemingly vindicated by events—and the example of his war-time leadership to cement a powerful impression in the public mind. Simply put, this held that *Churchill had been right all along*. The inconsistencies and opportunism of his behaviour, and those of others, were glossed over. What had been a complex blend of high-political struggle for advancement and acute strategic dilemma was recast as a morality tale. Given that this version of history remains so deeply entrenched not only in popular culture, but in Britain's very sense of self, it surely represents one of the most remarkable examples of winners' history ever composed.

And there can be little doubt about it. Churchill was *the* great winner of the strife that had torn apart the British polity between 1935 and 1940. By 1931, the dominant political leadership had decreed that Winston was to be kept out of power, and throughout the decade intensive efforts were undertaken, first by Baldwin and then by Chamberlain, to ensure that Churchill would never be able to bulldoze his way back into office again. He was too mercurial, too excitable, and too transparently an adventurer. He had to be isolated and discredited. And yet Churchill quickly discerned, in the 'storm clouds' of international turmoil, the approaching 'great crunch' that would enable him to engineer a dramatic reversal of his fortunes. Treated as some surviving relic of the Pre-Cambrian era in the mid-1930s, within half a decade he was the subject of popular acclamation and Prime Minister with a mandate to wage a war like none before it. Moreover, the rise of Churchill was not yet complete. Through his leadership as wartime Prime Minister, Winston would go on to become the most iconic figure in modern British history. The young man of the 1890s who had been obsessed with the 'Great Men' of history finally, in his late sixties, took his place alongside them.

But, in May 1940, all that lay in the future. The Second World War had begun in earnest. German tanks were racing across western Europe, while the Luftwaffe rained death from the skies. Britain needed to shrug off the shackles of limited war and fully mobilize its vast financial and industrial power for the long struggle to come. In Whitehall, Churchill and his colleagues had no time to waste. They sat behind their new desks and got down to business. There was work to be done.

CONCLUSION

'What a piece of work is a man!'[1]

The End and the Beginning

As the Conservative party tore itself apart in the House of Commons on 7 and 8 May 1940, the long political ascendancy wrought by Stanley Baldwin evaporated like a spring morning's mist. The Baldwinian edifice of British democracy had engendered a stability that few would have expected at the conclusion of the First World War. Baldwin's strategy was founded on a combination of social reform, economic caution, and political inclusivity. In turbulent times, he stressed moderation and patriotism. Baldwin quite consciously appealed to 'national' themes and values, making these the basis of his success. This political ethos proved ideal in meeting the new challenges of mass democracy and the expanded franchise. While Britain faced severe difficulties, and at times was sharply polarized, social conflict on the scale experienced across much of the European continent was conspicuous by its absence. Moreover, Baldwin's ethos secured an era of major electoral victories for the Conservative party. This achievement was never inevitable, and always highly contingent. It renders Baldwin one of the most consequential, and interesting, British political leaders. He was like an old mariner, possessing a remarkable intuition for the political tides and weather.

Yet the democratic settlement established by Baldwin was predicated on a *style* of politics that was destroyed in the coup of May 1940. Public life was upended by the international turmoil of the 1930s, and—still more so—by the acute shortcomings of British strategy in response. The Conservative-dominated National Government was the architect of its own downfall. The credibility of that regime was eroded between 1935 and 1940 and, as this occurred, those people and ideas once consigned to the wilder fringes of politics moved to centre stage. From 1940, Baldwin became a popular bogeyman; Chamberlain even more so. Chamberlain served loyally under Churchill for several months, before being forced into retirement in the autumn due to terminal cancer. He died on 9 November. Churchill replaced

Chamberlain as leader of the Conservative party. Several weeks later, following the sudden death of the British ambassador to Washington, Lord Lothian, Churchill saw an opportunity to rid himself of Halifax too. He was packed off across the Atlantic, to fulfil a crucial diplomatic role as Britain's representative in the United States but never to return to front-line politics. Eden succeeded him as Foreign Secretary.

The Churchill coalition lasted for five years but the credibility of the Conservatives had collapsed, with the party held responsible for the failures of diplomacy and the outbreak of war. The sheer gravity of this failure facilitated a wider, and deeper, indictment of Conservative policies elsewhere: on economics, social reform, and the general state of the nation. The international disaster of the National Government so delegitimized the Conservative party that a stark recalibration of domestic policy seemed appropriate. The entire structure of British democracy was put under siege. With the final discrediting of the National Government in 1940, the foundations of a new democratic settlement were laid.

Over the coming years, the horizons of democracy, the ambitions of the state, and the expectations the public were encouraged to have of their rulers were transformed. The foreign policy failures of the 1930s and the imperatives of war demanded *action*. Perhaps the most striking legacy of the fall of the Baldwinian ethos was the political imperative for the chaos, contingency, and uncertainty of the 1930s to be replaced by a new ethos—one predicated on politicians promising solutions, answers, and decisions. Uncertainty and ambiguity in public life could not be tolerated; henceforth politicians and government had to project an aura of mastery. This new style effectively rewired the entire democratic machine. Decisions and promised fixes were now the common currency of politicians' appeal. They offered, in effect, a magic wand.

Moreover, the rise of Churchill facilitated the triumph of Labour. From Attlee's seizure of power in 1940, the Labour party increasingly resembled the party of the future. The experience of war, and the need to 'plan' the nation's resources for victory, served to validate its doctrines of state control and an empowered government. During the 1940s it looked as if the state could do things dismissed as impossible just a few years earlier; the war seemed to prove it. Active state intervention in the economy on a hitherto-unimagined scale would now be the norm, as would the implementation of 'planning' and 'controls' in order to generate prosperity and guide 'progress'. The 'experts' in Whitehall offered scientific, rationalist, and technocratic solutions to all manner of problems. That, at least, was what Labour maintained. Crucially, Attlee and his colleagues leveraged their new legitimacy to offer a parallel expansion of the welfare state. This was the high tide of statism. And it was hugely popular in a war-weary country. At the

226

July 1945 general election, the Labour party secured a landslide victory over the Conservatives—Churchill's personal popularity having little bearing on the outcome—on a platform of a far-reaching change in the nature of the democratic settlement in Britain. This was a drastic reworking of the Baldwinian architecture established a generation before. It was the type of democracy that many people had been afraid would triumph prior to the extension of the franchise.

The consequences were far-reaching. The legacy endures into the twenty-first century. While the economic statecraft of the 1940s eventually lost its primacy in the 1980s, public spending still remained at the sort of levels established by Labour immediately after the Second World War. And, most fundamentally, the relationship between rulers and ruled remained that developed by Attlee's Labour party. Citizens were encouraged to look to the politicians for the satisfaction of their wants; the new democratic settlement offered, in effect, a simplification of life. Given that this was an abridgement of reality, it arguably never really worked, and growing public cynicism towards politics by the early twenty-first century was the outcome. The magic wand was never real. But a comforting fiction was maintained that it existed.[2] This was a model of politics predicated on a collective suspension of disbelief, and pledges to do things that were mostly undoable. It represents the most important socio-political legacy of May 1940.

High Politics and Foreign Policy

This transformation was one outcome of the dialectical relationship between British strategic policy and the struggle for ascendancy at Westminster in the years between 1935 and 1940. Questions of international crisis and defence were omnipresent themes in high-political conflict. Foreign policy shaped high politics and, in turn, high politics shaped foreign policy. That is, of course, a highly cynical perspective; but then this is a cynical book.

It may be discomforting to think of the road to the Second World War in terms of manoeuvre and counter-manoeuvre in domestic politics, but that is part-and-parcel of how contemporaries perceived things. Strategic issues were understood not only in terms of the problems they presented, but also the personal political capital they might yield. As the strategist Colin S. Gray observed, the interaction between the unknowable shape of the future, the sheer importance of strategic issues, and the imperatives of politics mean it should be no surprise that even in peacetime the strategic arena provides 'a happy hunting ground for political contenders'.[3] Issues of policy 'substance' might carry 'less importance in practice' than 'relative political gain and loss'.[4] Each of the actors involved discerned strong

227

incentives in treating foreign policy as a proving ground. For Chamberlain, it offered the prospect of a famous triumph that would etch his name into the history books and secure the electoral gratitude of a relieved nation. In Halifax's mind, the issue would determine the fate of the government and the Conservative party, and so the Prime Minister had to be supported and, where necessary, challenged. Meanwhile the ascendancy of Baldwinian Conservatism meant that those excluded from office had little choice but to articulate their views and ambitions in the language of oppositional politics. International instability helped critics to secure a theme around which they could rally. Foreign affairs thus became the currency of political power. Churchill's relations with Baldwin were clearly central in determining the positions he adopted—and, indeed, the trajectory of his entire career—after 1929. Meanwhile, Attlee, Morrison, and Dalton recognized valuable opportunities in foreign policy that Labour's limited capital in the domestic sphere would be unlikely to open up. That was simply the nature of political conflict in Britain. As the historian Simon Green eloquently expressed it, the 'clarification of mind' which prompted fixation with how Britain should navigate dangerous international waters 'was often as much the product of political calculation, carefully conceived, as the result of chivalrous sensibility, ultimately aroused'.[5]

The rules of the high-political game meant that virtually all decisions of any consequence had to be contested if politicians were to stand out. What was presented as a titanic clash of principles was actually a highly ritualized form of behaviour; it was the means through which power was accumulated and hierarchies established. This process of contestation determined outlooks and options. Relations were conflictual. There was a striking correlation between the policies that individuals advocated and their personal, and party, advantage that cannot be ignored. Most vividly, for all his rhetorical broadsides and subsequent mythology, Churchill was only ever in opposition to the National Government up to a point. As over India between 1931 and 1935, what he really aimed to do was to *join* the ministry. Churchill may have cast himself as a real-life Apollo—the patron of truth and prophecy, and a guardian—but his behaviour was motivated by a desire to coerce Baldwin and Chamberlain into admitting him into the citadel. And everyone knew it, too. Politicians certainly did argue for policies derived from calculations of British interests, but those policies were developed within a framework of personal conflict and strategies to advance, or maintain, one's influence. Ambition became so interwoven with the issues at hand that the differences between political calculation and national interests were no longer distinguishable; one usually cannot tell where conviction ended and self-interest began.

Churchill's endless invocation of 'the march of events' as his stock explanation for everything was thus as bogus as Attlee's contention that the international crisis revealed the pressing urgency for 'socialism', or Chamberlain's assertion of his own indispensability. This language merely helped politicians to place their actions and decisions in the best possible light. A student of history like Churchill could not but be aware of the power William Pitt the Elder had secured in the 1750s through publicly weaponizing 'patriotism' and British 'honour' before converting his result-ant popularity into office. Churchill similarly utilized foreign-political crises to cut poses and secure advantage within the party system. This was highly reminiscent of Lord Palmerston, the giant of mid-nineteenth-century British politics, too. Crises abroad *confirmed*, and legitimized, existing enmities, ambitions, and intrigues at Westminster; they did not *cause* them. Myth-makers and most historians have presented this in a less sceptical light; but contemporaries discerned the truth, as any reading of correspondence or diaries from the period will attest.

It was only when—in the form of the new Churchill coalition—a group of individuals could reconcile their ambitions and seek to realize them in harness that the political system was finally stabilized. They were, in essence, stockholders in a common venture. Indeed, sustained acrimony between this new elite was rare, and where it did occur (as in the feuds between Bevin and Beaverbrook, or Attlee and Morrison) it was because one of them wanted more authority. From 1940 onwards—just as before—most of the acrimony was between those who ran the system and those excluded from it. The issue, as always, was one of power and influence.

'Meddle and Muddle'

As the Earl of Derby warned in 1864, the great risk in foreign affairs was that Britain—a secure island nation, a wealthy great power, with a liberal parliamentary system—might find itself adopting a policy of 'meddle and muddle'.[6] Politicians could not resist the urge to get involved in international difficulties, and yet were also unsure of what to do about them. This was exactly what happened in the 1930s. There is no question that a variety of approaches were advocated during that decade but, for the inhabitants of Westminster, 'meddle and muddle' was an almost universal tendency. A measured strategy, effectively calibrated to the international situation and British interests, was lacking. The problem was principally conceptual, deriving from a shortage of imagination more than any lack of allies, wealth, or weapons. This proved disastrous. The foreign-political perils confronting the inter-national system during this period were enormous and, for some states, existential.

Hitler seemed to have plans to emulate a Charlemagne or a Khan. Mussolini, albeit preposterously, fancied himself a Caesar. And in Tokyo, a series of militaristic regimes aimed to bring the Asia-Pacific under Japan's imperial sway. Meanwhile France was vacillating and unstable, the United States wrestled with the question of how it should approach the world, and the USSR combined ruthlessness and paranoia with a demonstrated will to subvert. This environment necessitated a cunning British strategy—but none was forthcoming.

There is no tenable conclusion other than that British foreign policy prior to the Second World War was a catastrophic failure. Yet the traditional interpretation of this—deeply embedded as it is in the popular memory, with a cultural half-life that shows no obvious signs of decay—perhaps needs to be revisited. Most criticisms of appeasement have been variations on a Churchillian theme: that British policy failed because, in dealing with the dictators, it was insufficiently bold and interventionist. Britain did not send a signal of strength sufficient to deter Germany, Italy, and Japan. To be clear, this criticism has much to recommend it. But if the priority of policymakers was to uphold *British* power, and advance Britain's own national interests, this traditional criticism perhaps seems problematic. It does not necessarily follow that the sensible alternative would have been deeper, more robust engagement in European affairs—clearer warnings to Hitler and Mussolini, putting the economy on a war footing in 1938, and paying the price of an alliance with the USSR. Meanwhile, the arguments of so-called 'revisionist' scholars—essentially that Chamberlain's approach was a carefully weighed response to international uncertainty and popular scepticism of militarism, one that bought valuable time for British rearmament—can also be looked at afresh. These historians are right that Chamberlain was no coward. Yet the revisionists perhaps do not go far enough. Chamberlain's policy was too active. Like a moth to a flame, he could not resist the siren call to fix the world's problems. In addition, the British government had a capacity to make different choices that many revisionist historians, convinced that there were no other options available, have failed to convey.

As the historian Patrick Finney remarked of the 1930s, 'How policymakers played their hand was as important as the cards in it'.[7] The fact is that policymakers did not play their hands well (nor, for that matter, did the criticisms of their opponents offer much hope of improvement). And political equations were consistently more important than strategic ones. Britain's global power remained unique; it was an empire on a planetary scale. Besides Britain itself it encompassed colonies that were ruled directly by the British, self-governing colonies populated by the descendants of British settlers, protectorates, mandates, treaty ports, areas that were not part of the Empire but commercially dominated by Britain, and a series of military outposts, garrisons, fortresses, and fuelling stations. Britain remained a commercial titan and an industrial giant. It was still the banker and merchant to much of the world. It possessed the largest deep-sea navy on earth, one able to exercise both regional and oceanic supremacy. By the outbreak of war, Britain's air defences were the most sophisticated in the world. Meanwhile the stopping-power of the English Channel inhibited the projection of armies from the continent of Europe onto British soil. The economy had borne the burden of a massive programme of rearmament. Industrial capacity could be—and was—expanded still further as the country was put on a war footing, with astonishing results. Britain also enjoyed important allies. France was another of the great powers, the United States was sympathetic (though not yet engaged), and the British Empire amounted to a permanent military alliance possessing highly integrated armed forces, with stand-ardization of equipment and training, and operating from a global network of bases. In light of how quickly this system unravelled as a result of the Second World War, it is easy to assume that its collapse was in some way inevitable. But that is not obviously the case. While the British world-system had been badly disrupted by the great struggle of 1914–18, it remained very much the central fact of the international landscape. A huge chunk of the earth's surface and seas fell into the orbit of the British world-system and its rules-based international order.

Boasting vast financial, industrial, and human capacity, the British Empire was well placed to eventually win the war. Indeed, as the historian Phillips Payson O'Brien has recently demonstrated, the range of core national strategic assets identified by policymakers in the 1930s—Britain's capacity for perseverance afforded by its wealth, its new airpower, and its great naval strength—proved the keys to eventual victory.[8] The problem, rather, was what it would *cost* to wage such a conflict. The consequences of this, at home and abroad, and in terms of both the present and the future, did not bear thinking about. And yet policymakers did not properly capitalize on Britain's strengths.

Venturing predictions about how things might have turned out if x had not happened or y had been done differently is always a hazardous enterprise, but when attempting to read the chessboard of geopolitics it is a necessary one. Britain was not confronted by predetermined outcomes or inescapable obligations. Instead, it was faced with choices. A more cunning British strategy during the 1930s could have turned the Eurasian landmass into a deadly morass for those states with revisionist aspirations. The key to this would have been a narrower foreign policy, one aimed at breaking out of the tight corner in which Britain found itself and decisively altering the parameters of the strategic game. There was no reason for London to play according to rules devised by others, and every reason to make up new ones in a spirit of *raison d'état*. A narrower foreign policy would have seen Britain take a diplomatic step back from tortuous border and ethnic disputes in eastern Europe in which the country had no strategic interest. It would have identified a small number of core priorities—western Europe, the sea lanes, the Empire—the importance of which was emphasized to all relevant parties and underpinned by a resolve to act with violence if challenged. This would arguably have suited British national interests far better than the more expansive, yet hesitant, policy that was adopted.

To be sure, a narrower foreign policy would have meant abandoning much of the Versailles order; but, as vocally as the liberal conscience protested, it was dead anyway. Crucially, disengaging from central and eastern Europe would almost certainly have compelled the two local great powers of that region, Germany and the USSR, to come to grips with one another much earlier. They were geographical neighbours, and thus natural rivals. Their regimes reviled each other. They were on a collision course for war. If Britain had stood back from playing the role of an ineffectual diplomatic mediator in eastern Europe, this would have upended the entire international dynamic. For one thing, Stalin would not have been able to pass the buck for his own security to London. The effects of this would likely have been transformative. Compelled to take a lead against Hitler, the Kremlin could not have set such an absurd price for cooperation. In this environment, *Britain* would be the state to be courted, *not* the USSR. This could have rewired the whole system. Stalin was in a dangerous geopolitical position, and he knew it. Germany was gearing up for a bid to dominate eastern Europe and, Stalin feared, conquer the Soviet Union itself. Meanwhile in Asia, Japan's fear of the growing power of the USSR was one of the reasons encouraging its bid to conquer China. If Britain had adopted a strategy of what international relations specialists term 'offshore balancing', one that took full advantage of its status as an island nation, this would have compelled the USSR to play a more active role in resisting the challenges to its own security. If in doubt, examine a map of the world. The USSR was threatened by Germany on one flank and Japan on the other. Germany, meanwhile, was menaced by the USSR on one flank and France on the other. Maps certainly reveal the dilemmas of defending Britain's imperial archipelago; but they posed still more acute dilemmas for others. Policymakers and their critics alike failed to surmount this intellectual barrier. Some in the Foreign Office pointed out as early as 1934 that 'the Russian fears of Germany and Japan can be worked to our advantage', but the suggestion had not taken root.[9]

By refusing to play the policeman in an unstable—and unsustainable—region of the world, Britain would perhaps not have been sucked into the maelstrom, certainly not in the way it was. As Hitler and Stalin tore into one another in a protracted rivalry, and probable war, that would exhaust both and which neither would be likely to decisively 'win', Britain would have become stronger while its enemies weakened. Britain could also have done much more to provide aid to China, in order to prop up its war effort and bog down the Japanese. A strategy of offshore balancing would have radically altered the calculations of all other key actors in the international system. It might have turned Eurasia into a quagmire.

As Colin S. Gray put it, the essence of strategy is to seek 'control over an enemy's political behaviour'.[10] British policy not only failed to achieve that, but arguably never created the conditions under which it became a serious possibility. This failure was doubly problematic because, unlike most countries, Britain did not have to adopt the approach that it did. Britain was not imprisoned on the Eurasian landmass by the stark facts of geography. An island state and maritime empire, it was effectively an 'outside' power, not an 'inside' state. This was a luxury of which the 'inside' nations could only dream. Yet during the 1930s Britain failed to exploit the advantages of being an outside power, and behaved like an inside nation instead. This was particularly glaring given that a historical hallmark of British grand strategy had been that of buck-passing: trying to get others to bear the principal burdens of dealing with threats, while Britain remained on the sidelines for as long as possible or, at the very least, needed to shed less of her own blood in confronting them. Adversaries were drawn into a condition of strategic overstretch that proved fatal. That tendency was one of the reasons why Britain had long ago been dubbed 'Perfidious Albion'.

Instead, the British unwisely adopted what Lord Lothian called 'the French view of European politics', concluding that their own security hinged on the efforts of France to encircle Germany in eastern Europe and the importance of trying to exercise a diplomatic veto over events in that corner of the continent.[11] This alignment with the worldview of France had not served Britain well prior to the First World War, and did not do so in the 1930s. There was a fundamental failure to look at the issues through the eyes of a British imperialist; and Britain was, first and foremost, an imperial, global power. The challenges of Germany, Italy, and Japan were all, by contrast, *regional* problems. Britain went to war not to preserve the security of the British Empire, or to advance its interests, but to defend the interests of others. A state demonstrably ruthless about upholding its own distinctive interests would have been more valuable as a partner, and more menacing as an adversary, than one which followed the approach adopted by both the National Government and its critics. Britain failed to take advantage of the benefits of being an offshore empire living in a multipolar system.

'Watch and weaken' was, therefore, a plausible strategic option for Britain in the 1930s. Indeed it was the grand strategy that would likely have served her best. Yet 'watch and weaken' was not an option in the high-political circumstances of British democracy; the urge to 'do something', the language of outrage, the rhetoric of 'the balance of power', and appeals to 'honour' prohibited it. Very few policymakers, or their critics, advocated standing back; the urge to 'meddle' was almost universal. This only underlines the dangerous lack of strategic insight in Westminster and Whitehall. Britain was drawn into the labyrinth of continental paranoia and vendetta; equally, its policy encouraged a culture of dependency, in which European states looked to London to assume responsibility for solving their problems.

As it was, Britain turned itself into a pointless barrier between Nazi Germany and the Soviet Union. All this achieved was to delay their confrontation, antagonize Hitler, encourage Stalin, and tie Britain's hands. By postponing the struggle between the German Fuhrer and the General Secretary of the Communist Party, the National Government and its critics put Britain in the firing line from the outset. This was a fundamental misreading of geopolitics. For centuries, the instability of this crucial geographical locale had perpetually threatened to draw in other states; in 1773, Edmund Burke wrote a celebrated article in the *Annual Register* on the recent partition of Poland by Austria, Prussia, and Russia, in which he argued that Poland was a 'barrier' without which 'the German and Muscovite empires' would soon come to blows. The same geopolitical realities held true in the 1930s, and yet Britain lacked the intellectual fleet-footedness to recognize the opportunity.

And if Britain *was* going to play the active role it did, London should have been robust in sticking to its guns—particularly when it came to Germany and Japan. Hitler should have been met with the threat of force over the Rhineland, the *Anschluss*, and—still more so—Czechoslovakia. In the Pacific, the Japanese should have been confronted with a much more vigorous British strategy. Rearmament could perhaps have been accelerated still further. The domestic ascendancy of the National Government afforded an unusual degree of electoral leeway. And in Stanley Baldwin, they possessed one of the most gifted public persuaders and educators Britain has produced. As the eminent strategist Herman Kahn later wrote with characteristic bluntness, 'Usually the most convincing way to look willing is to be willing'.[12] A firm stand, and resolution to uphold the international status quo, would probably have run greater risks than 'watch and weaken', yet still might have succeeded. But policymakers could not bring themselves to do that, either.

At root, British leaders lacked the insight and intuitive feel for the game of geopolitics—in other words, statesmanship—that the situation required. They settled for a policy of deterrence that failed because it was extended to regions and issues over which adversaries correctly calculated Britain would not, in fact, display the will to act. The revisionist powers weighed British statements and concluded they constituted a policy of bluff, and that the National Government would not take a stand. They were right. This expansive, yet ineffectual, scheme of British deterrence was partly the product of political conflict and competition, partly the product of Neville Chamberlain's own conceit, and partly the product of the higher liberalism. Together, those ingredients made for a potent combination. British leaders and parliamentarians engineered a strategic disaster.

It is by no means easy to discern an easily navigable route out of the crises of the 1930s. Such a suggestion would be grossly unfair. The shaping of foreign and defence policy is always undertaken in the shadow of uncertainty. The future is, quite literally, unknowable. Yet would an alternative strategy to that of Chamberlain or, alternatively, those of his critics have been any more calamitous in terms of both short- and long-term costs? That seems difficult to believe. There was a systemic failure to think imaginatively about British interests and how they might be pro-tected, and advanced, in the world of the 1930s. What was needed was a novel analysis, and even a fresh vocabulary. The prevailing framework within which policy was conceived was not fit for purpose; nor was the language used to discuss British objectives in the world. They provided landmarks which politicians employed to orientate themselves relative to other politicians; what they did *not* do was provide any strategic solutions to the difficulties which Britain faced.

'One Must Wait Until the Evening to See How Splendid the Day Has Been'

In the war that followed, Britain's strength was first exhausted, and then shattered.[13] With France unexpectedly overrun by the Germans in 1940, British strategy had to be hurriedly reconfigured. The endurance and ingenuity of the British public were called upon to rescue their rulers from the catastrophe they had wrought. However, the failure of foreign policy between 1935 and 1939 fostered a situation in which the different parts of the British world-system were placed under such simultaneous strain that, between 1940 and 1942, the system collapsed, never to recover. Britain's staying power afforded by its wealth, naval strength, and Empire enabled it to endure and, in eventual partnership with the Soviet Union and the United State, outlast and defeat the Axis states. But it did so from a position of dependence: on one state that was at least as barbarous as Nazi Germany, and on another that was committed to the dissolution of the British Empire. The country emerged from the war in 1945 almost bankrupt, with the Empire doomed to rapid disintegration and the British world-system a relic of the past. Crippling debts incurred in paying the price of war saddled Britain with heavy burdens for decades. Her leading position in global trade and finance evaporated, as the post-war years quickly, and harshly, demonstrated. Unable to maintain the world-system which had been painstakingly built up over centuries, the Empire was finished. British government and public alike were no longer willing to meet the demands of being an imperial power. India was declared independent in August 1947, crashing out of the Empire in a hard landing which yielded partition and up to 2 million murders during the communal violence that followed. Britain's position as the dominant state in the Middle East was brought to a close soon afterwards. And the maintenance of a first-rate military was equally impossible. In a financially wrecked nation, even the Royal Navy itself was displaced as the world's oceangoing hegemon. Britain was left an international dependant of the United States. It spelled the end for centuries of British, and global, history which had propelled the country to ruling over one-quarter of the earth. What remained was a hollowed-out shell.

At home, the new model of democracy established during the 1940s compounded, and confirmed, this decline. The country turned inwards to wage political warfare over welfare and economic 'modernization'. Under Attlee, a radical economic experiment consumed much of Britain's governmental and moral energy, but failed to restore prosperity or meet the challenges of the time. Yet this new agenda still served the purposes of both politicians and public alike, and was thus sustained permanently thereafter. If the Second World War was a 'victory', for Britain it was a victory of an odd kind. It was like stepping through a door into a new universe. And yet the mythology of the conflict—that which fused Churchillian and Labour perspectives into a story of 'the people's war', 'the little ships' of Dunkirk, 'the finest hour' of the Battle of Britain, endurance under the Blitz, heroism, and the forging of a better tomorrow—obscured this. This mythology deliberately *moralized* the collapse of British power by casting it as a noble cause rather than an utter failure. Thus was the question of what had been *lost* in this endeavour closed down, marginalized, and rarely asked.

Britain's stunning rise to world power in the eighteenth century had been achieved by strategic innovation and dynamism—not least an ability to persuade other powers to do things they did not want to, and shed their own blood in furtherance of British interests. This ability was lacking when Britain needed it once again during the 1930s. The international system was highly unstable, and conflict seemed certain. Yet there was nothing within that system which made Britain's catastrophe inevitable. The explanation lies elsewhere. Britain's life as a great power depended on ingenuity and good judgement, but in the 1930s her executive and

Parliament proved wanting. They lacked the capacity to think the unthinkable; they lacked the sheer ruthlessness that the situation demanded; and they lacked a language to tell the public the truth. Those who had elevated the liberal conscience into a decisive force in public life and foreign policy in interwar Britain had much to answer for. Moreover, the centrality of foreign affairs to high politics created a situation in which strategy was consistently subordinated to conflict in Westminster and Whitehall. The result was a sequence of predictable failures, which eventually culminated in irretrievable disaster. Through this, British power—steadily accumulated over hundreds of years—was finally liquidated by leaders unsuited to wielding it. Britain was trapped between the Scylla of its politicians' pride and the Charybdis of international anarchy. The end was nigh.

NOTES

Preface

1. Herbert Butterfield, *The Peace Tactics of Napoleon, 1806–1808* (Cambridge, 1929), p. 181.
2. 'The continuation of politics by other means': Carl von Clausewitz, *On War* (translated by Michael Howard and Peter Paret) (Princeton, 1984 edn), p. 87.
3. 'Cato', *Guilty Men* (London, 1940).
4. Winston S. Churchill, *The Second World War, Volume I: The Gathering Storm* (London, 1948).
5. For example, A. J. P. Taylor, *The Origins of the Second World War* (London, 1964); Martin Gilbert, *The Roots of Appeasement* (London, 1966); John Charmley, *Chamberlain and the Lost Peace* (London, 1989).
6. For example, R. A. C. Parker, *Chamberlain and Appeasement: British Policy and the Coming of the Second World War* (Basingstoke, 1993); G. C. Peden, *British Rearmament and the Treasury, 1931–1939* (Edinburgh, 1979); Frank McDonough, *Neville Chamberlain, Appeasement and the British Road to War* (Manchester, 1998).
7. Andrew David Stedman, *Alternatives to Appeasement: Neville Chamberlain and Hitler's Germany* (London, 2011).
8. Thomas More, *History of King Richard the Third* (ed. George M. Logan) (Bloomington, 2005), p. 83.
9. Clausewitz, *On War*, p. 87.
10. Hugh Trevor-Roper, *The Wartime Journals* (ed. Richard Davenport-Hines) (London, 2015), p. 52.
11. Edmund Burke, cited in David Armitage, 'The New World and British historical thought: From Richard Hakluyt to William Robertson', in Karen Kupperman (ed.), *America in European Consciousness, 1493–1750* (Chapel Hill, 1995), p. 67.

Chapter 1

1. Studies of the party's success include Stuart Ball, *Portrait of a Party: The Conservative Party in Britain, 1918–1945* (Oxford, 2013) and David Jarvis, 'British Conservatism and class politics in the 1920s', *English Historical Review* (1996), pp. 59–84.
2. Salisbury in *The Quarterly Review* (1861), cited in Paul Smith (ed.), *Lord Salisbury on Politics: A Selection from His Articles in the Quarterly Review, 1860–1883* (Cambridge, 1972), p. 330.
3. Salisbury in *The Saturday Review* (1859), cited in Smith, *Lord Salisbury on Politics*, p. 330.
4. Labour's early history can be explored through David Howell, *MacDonald's Party: Labour Identities and Crisis, 1922–1931* (Oxford, 2002) and David Marquand, *Ramsay MacDonald* (London, 1977).
5. 'To save democracy, to preserve it, and to inspire it': Stanley Baldwin, *On England and Other Addresses* (London, 1926), speech, 27 September 1923, p. 149.
6. *Manchester Guardian*, 18 March 1922.

7. An account of the meeting was published in *The Times*, 20 October 1922.

8. Stuart Ball, 'The legacy of coalition: Fear and loathing in Conservative politics, 1922–1931', *Contemporary British History* (2011), pp. 65–82.

9. Maurice Cowling, *The Impact of Labour: The Beginning of Modern British Politics, 1920–1924* (Cambridge, 1971).

10. The best study is Philip Williamson, *Stanley Baldwin: Conservative Leadership and National Values* (Cambridge, 1999). Its ideas are complemented by S. Nicholas, 'The construction of a national identity: Stanley Baldwin, "Englishness" and the mass-media in inter-war Britain', in M. Francis and I. Zweinigr-Bargielowska (eds), *The Conservatives and British Society, 1880–1990* (Cardiff, 1996) and B. Schwarz, 'The language of constitutionalism: Baldwinite Conservatism', in *Formations of Nation and People* (London, 1984), pp. 1–18.

11. K. O. Morgan, *Consensus and Disunity: The Lloyd George Coalition Government, 1918–1922* (Oxford, 1979), p. 49.

12. *The Times*, 3 November 1923.

13. Stanley Baldwin, *Service of Our Lives* (London, 1937), broadcast, 16 April 1937, pp. 122–3.

14. Robert Boothby, *I Fight to Live* (London, 1947), p. 36.

15. House of Commons Parliamentary Debates (*Hansard*, Fifth Series) (hereafter H.C. Debs.), vol. 276, 29 March 1933, col. 1134.

16. H.C. Debs., vol. 109, 8 August 1918, col. 1600.

17. See Williamson, *Baldwin*, chapter five.

18. Philip Williamson, 'The doctrinal politics of Stanley Baldwin', in Michael Bentley (ed.), *Public and Private Doctrine: Essays in British History Presented to Maurice Cowling* (Cambridge, 1993), pp. 181–208, at 184.

19. Cowling, *The Impact of Labour*, p. 422.

20. W. Steed, *The Real Stanley Baldwin* (London, 1930), p. 147.

21. *The British Gazette*, 5 May 1926.

22. *The British Gazette*, 5 May 1926.

23. H.C. Debs., vol. 195, 3 May 1926, cols 71–2, and 12 May 1926, col. 878.

24. Irwin to Davidson, 25 February 1930, cited in Robert Rhodes James (ed.), *Memoirs of a Conservative: J.C.C. Davidson's Memoirs and Papers, 1910–1937* (London, 1969), p. 306.

25. Stanley Baldwin, *This Torch of Freedom* (London, 1937), speeches to the Brotherhood Movement, 14 July 1930, p. 46 and the Congregational Union, 12 May 1931, p. 87.

26. *The Times*, 23 November 1928.

27. Baldwin speeches in Leeds, 12 March 1925 and Cardiff, 18 October 1924, cited in Williamson, *Baldwin*, p. 178.

28. Baldwin to Monica Baldwin, 22 December 1935, cited in Williamson, *Baldwin*, p. 143.

29. See David Jarvis, 'Mrs Maggs and Betty: The Conservative appeal to women voters in the 1920s', *Twentieth Century British History* (1994), pp. 129–52.

30. On this theme, consult Richard Carr, *Veteran MPs and Conservative Politics in the Aftermath of the Great War: The Memory of All That* (Farnham, 2013).

31. *Conservative Agents' Journal*, April 1928, p. 96.

32. See Ball, *Portrait of a Party*, p. 166.

33. T. J. Hollins, 'The Conservative party and film propaganda between the wars', *English Historical Review* (1981), pp. 359–69. A selection of Conservative propaganda posters can be explored in Stuart Ball, *Dole Queues and Demons: British Election Posters from the Conservative Party Archive* (Oxford, 2011).

34. N. Skelton, *Constructive Conservatism* (Edinburgh, 1924).

35. *The Times*, 23 June 1923.

36. Williamson, *Baldwin*, p. 237.
37. 'Politically we are on velvet': Baldwin to Sir Henry Page Croft, 26 August 1931, cited in John Charmley, *Lord Lloyd and the Decline of the British Empire* (London, 1987), p. 179.
38. Philip Williamson, *National Crisis and National Government: British Politics, the Economy and Empire* (Cambridge, 1992).
39. Baldwin to Sir Henry Page Croft, 26 August 1931, cited in Charmley, *Lord Lloyd*, p. 179.
40. The speech is viewable on YouTube. At the time of writing, the address is https://www.youtube.com/watch?v=0UL5AOgqWLQ.
41. 'Great expectations': H.C. Debs., vol. 288, 17 April 1934, col. 903.
42. Baldwin speech in Welbeck Abbey, 1 June 1925, cited in Williamson, *Baldwin*, p. 179.
43. Baldwin speech at the Hotel Cecil, 11 February 1924, cited in John Ramsden, *The Age of Balfour and Baldwin, 1902–1940* (London, 1978), p. 187.
44. The best study is Robert Self, *Neville Chamberlain: A Biography* (Aldershot, 2006).
45. Baldwin to King George V, 10 July 1926, cited in Self, *Chamberlain*, p. 114.
46. *Clement Attlee: The Granada Historical Records Interview* (London, 1965), p. 19.
47. CAB 24/168, CP 499 (24), 19 November 1924.
48. CAB 24/173, CP 204 (25), 18 April 1925.
49. University of Birmingham, Neville Chamberlain papers, Chamberlain to Hilda Chamberlain, 12 July 1924.
50. H.C. Debs., vol. 277, 25 April 1933, cols 57–61.
51. H.C. Debs., vol. 288, 17 April 1934, col. 903.
52. 'Power without responsibility': *The Times*, 19 March 1931.
53. Stuart Ball (ed.), *Parliament and Politics in the Age of Baldwin and MacDonald: The Diaries of Sir Cuthbert Headlam, 1924–1935* (London, 1992), 20 February 1930, p. 185; T. Jones, *Whitehall Diary, volume II* (London, 1969) (K. Middlemas ed.), 23 October 1928, p. 153.
54. *The Times*, 19 March 1931.
55. Hugo Vickers, *Elizabeth, The Queen Mother* (London, 2006), p. 185.
56. Schwarz, 'The language of constitutionalism', p. 8.
57. N. Nicolson (ed.), *The Harold Nicolson Diaries, 1907–1964* (London, 2004), 10 December 1936, pp. 169–70.
58. Addison, *The Road to 1945*, p. 33.
59. Interview with Herbert Samuel, 19 July 1935, in A. J. P. Taylor (ed.), *W.P. Crozier: Off the Record—Political Interviews, 1933–1943* (London, 1973).
60. Churchill College, Cambridge, Leslie Hore-Belisha papers, HOBE1/2, Hore-Belisha Diary, 7 May 1935.
61. Chamberlain papers, Chamberlain to Ida Chamberlain, 19 June 1927.
62. Robert Rhodes James (ed.), *'Chips': The Diaries of Sir Henry Channon* (London, 1996 edn) (hereafter *Channon Diary*), 30 January 1938, p. 143.
63. *The Times*, 22 May 1950.

Chapter 2

1. J. B. Atkins, *Incidents and Reflections* (London, 1947), p. 122.
2. Cited in R. Blake, *The Unknown Prime Minister: The Life and Times of Andrew Bonar Law, 1858–1923* (London, 1955), p. 189.
3. *The Churchill Archive* online database, Churchill to Clementine Churchill, 28 July 1914.

4. Lucy Baldwin, 'The recollections of a Cabinet breaker's wife on the government crisis, October 1922', in Philip Williamson and Edward Baldwin (eds), *Baldwin Papers: A Conservative Statesman, 1908–1947* (Cambridge, 2004), pp. 70–7, at 71.
5. On this well-known and amusing Churchill phrase which is difficult to source, see https://www.winstonchurchill.org/resources/quotes/re-rat.
6. Rhodes James (ed.), *Memoirs of a Conservative*, p. 238.
7. Stuart Ball (ed.), *Conservative Politics in National and Imperial Crisis: Letters from Britain to the Viceroy of India, 1926–31* (London, 2014) (hereafter *Conservative Politics in National and Imperial Crisis*), Davidson to Irwin, 14 June 1926, p. 51.
8. *Conservative Politics in National and Imperial Crisis*, Dawson to Irwin, 8 June 1926, p. 48; A. J. P. Taylor, *Beaverbrook* (London, 1972), p. 232.
9. *Conservative Politics in National and Imperial Crisis*, Lane-Fox to Irwin, 11 May 1926, p. 30.
10. *Conservative Politics in National and Imperial Crisis*, Davidson to Irwin, 14 June 1926, p. 51.
11. *Conservative Politics in National and Imperial Crisis*, Chamberlain to Irwin, 15 August 1926, p. 78.
12. *The Morning Post*, 29 December 1932.
13. See C. Bridge, *Holding India to the Empire: The British Conservative Party and the 1935 Constitution* (New Delhi, 1986).
14. The best study is Andrew Roberts, *'The Holy Fox': The Life of Lord Halifax* (London, 1991).
15. R. A. Butler, *The Art of the Possible* (London, 1971), p. 77.
16. Robert Self (ed.), *The Neville Chamberlain Diary Letters, Volume 3: The Heir Apparent, 1928–1933* (Aldershot, 2002) (hereafter *Chamberlain Diary, Volume 3*) Chamberlain to Ida Chamberlain, 28 July 1929, p. 152.
17. *Chamberlain Diary, Volume 3*, Chamberlain to Hilda Chamberlain, 26 October 1929, p. 160.
18. John Barnes and David Nicholson (eds), *The Empire at Bay: The Leo Amery Diaries, 1929–1945* (London, 1988) (hereafter *Amery Diary*), 30 July 1929, p. 48.
19. *Chamberlain Diary, Volume 3*, Chamberlain to Hilda Chamberlain, 26 October 1929, p. 160.
20. *Chamberlain Diary, Volume 3*, Chamberlain to Hilda Chamberlain, 26 October 1929, p. 160.
21. *Chamberlain Diary, Volume 3*, Chamberlain to Hilda Chamberlain, 26 October 1929, p. 160.
22. Philip Williamson and Edward Baldwin (eds), *Baldwin Papers: A Conservative Statesman, 1908–1947* (Cambridge, 2004), Lytton to Irwin, 20 November 1929, p. 224.
23. Chamberlain papers, 8/10/6, Walter Bridgeman to Chamberlain, 3 October 1930.
24. This can be charted through Martin Gilbert (ed.), *The Churchill Documents, Volume 12: The Wilderness Years* (London, 1981). See, for instance, Churchill to Baldwin, 26 June 1929, p. 8, Churchill note, 27 July 1929, pp. 25–6.
25. H.C. Debs., v. 230, 24 July 1929, cols 1301–2.
26. *Chamberlain Diary, Volume 3*, Chamberlain to Ida Chamberlain, 28 July 1929, pp. 151–2.
27. Parliamentary Archives, London, David Lloyd George papers, LG/F/7/4/9, Lloyd George to Austen Chamberlain, 14 June 1921.
28. K. Young (ed.), *The Diaries of Sir Robert Bruce Lockhart, vol. 1: 1915–1938* (London, 1973), 21 January 1930 (p. 113).
29. *Daily Mail*, 16 November 1929.
30. *Conservative Politics in National and Imperial Crisis*, Hoare to Irwin, 13 November 1929, p. 289.
31. *Baldwin Papers*, Lytton to Irwin, 20 November 1929, p. 224.
32. *The Times*, 5 July 1930.
33. India Office Library, Sir John Simon India papers, 24/10–12, Simon to Garvin, 1 May 1930.
34. *Indian Statutory Commission—Publications* (London, H.M.S.O., 1930).

35. India Office Library, Lord Reading papers, E238/57/54–111, memorandum, July 1930.
36. India Office Library, 1st Earl of Halifax papers, 18/402a, Irwin to Salisbury, 3 December 1929.
37. Cited in Williamson, *National Crisis*, p. 89.
38. Reading papers, E238/57/54–111, memorandum, July 1930.
39. 'Government of India Dispatch on Constitutional Reform', October 1930: see R. J. Moore, *The Crisis of Indian Unity, 1917–1940* (Oxford, 1974), p. 117.
40. John Arthur Cross, *Sir Samuel Hoare: A Political Biography* (London, 1977); Samuel Hoare, *Nine Troubled Years* (London, 1954).
41. Halifax papers, 19/166e, Lane-Fox to Irwin, 19 November 1930; Hoare memorandum, cited in Moore, *The Crisis of Indian Unity*, pp. 155–6.
42. Halifax papers, 19/161a, Haig to Irwin, 7 November 1930.
43. George Orwell, 'Reflections on Gandhi', *Partisan Review* (January 1949).
44. *Daily Mail*, 21 January 1931.
45. *The Scotsman*, 11 December 1930.
46. *Churchill Documents, Volume 12*, Churchill to Baldwin, 24 September 1930, p. 186.
47. *The Times*, 12 December 1930.
48. H.C. Debs., vol. 247, 26 January 1931, cols 689–703.
49. H.C. Debs., vol. 247, 26 January 1931, cols 744–8.
50. *Churchill Documents, Volume 12*, Churchill to Baldwin, 27 January 1931, pp. 250–1, and Baldwin to Churchill, 28 January 1931, p. 251.
51. *Daily Mail*, 30 January 1931.
52. *Chamberlain Diary, Volume 3*, Chamberlain to Hilda Chamberlain, 31 January 1931, pp. 232–3.
53. John Charmley, *Churchill: The End of Glory: A Political Biography* (London, 1993), p. 258.
54. *Daily Mail*, 25 February 1931.
55. Charmley, *Duff Cooper*, p. 65.
56. *Churchill Documents, Volume 12*, Davidson to Irwin, 6 March 1931, p. 293.
57. *Chamberlain Diary, Volume 3*, Chamberlain to Hilda Chamberlain, 1 March 1931, p. 240.
58. *Churchill Documents, Volume 12*, Thomas Jones diary, 'Conversation with Baldwin', 11 March 1931 (pp. 295–6).
59. *Chamberlain Diary, Volume 3*, Chamberlain to Hilda Chamberlain, 1 March 1931, p. 240.
60. *The Times*, 26 February 1931; *Churchill Documents, Volume 12*, Churchill to Clementine Churchill, 26 February 1931, pp. 280–1.
61. *Churchill Documents, Volume 12*, Thomas Jones papers, 'Jones to a friend', 16 March 1931, p. 302.
62. *Churchill Documents, Volume 12*, Lane-Fox to Irwin, 12 March 1931, p. 297.
63. *Evening Standard*, 9 March 1931.
64. *Churchill Documents, Volume 12*, Goschen to Irwin, 12 March 1931, p. 296.
65. *Churchill Documents, Volume 12*, Thomas Jones papers, 'Jones to a friend', 16 March 1931, p. 302; H.C. Debs., 12 March 1931.
66. *Churchill Documents, Volume 12*, Lane-Fox to Irwin, 12 March 1931, p. 298.
67. *Churchill Documents, Volume 12*, Spender-Clay to Irwin, 5 March 1931, p. 292.
68. *Daily Mail*, 13 March 1931.
69. Churchill's speech to the Constitutional Club, London, 26 March 1931, in Robert Rhodes James (ed.), *Winston S. Churchill: His Complete Speeches, 1897–1963, Volume V* (London, 1974), p. 4984.
70. H.C. Debs., vol. 276, 27 March 1933, cols 713–16.

71. *Sunday Express*, 1 January 1933.
72. *Churchill Documents, Volume 12*, Churchill to Thornton Butterworth, 9 March 1933, pp. 543–4 and Churchill to Salisbury, 12 March 1933, p. 547.
73. HC Debs., vol. 276, 27 March 1933, col. 736.
74. Charmley, *Churchill*, p. 272.
75. *Churchill Documents, Volume 12*, Hoare to Willingdon, 17 March 1933, p. 549.
76. *Churchill Documents, Volume 12*, Hoare to Willingdon, 17 March 1933, p. 549.
77. Hoare to Willingdon, 10 March 1933, cited in Charmley, *Lord Lloyd*, p. 185.
78. *Churchill Documents, Volume 12*, extract from Churchill speech to the Anti-Socialist and Anti-Communist Union, 17 February 1933, in Carson to Churchill, 18 February 1933, p. 529.
79. *Churchill Documents, Volume 12*, Violet Pearman to the Secretary, British Broadcasting Corporation, 1 March 1933, p. 535.
80. *Churchill Documents, Volume 12*, Violet Pearman to the Secretary, British Broadcasting Corporation, 1 March 1933, p. 535, and Churchill to Margesson, 1 March 1933, p. 534.
81. India Office Library, Willingdon papers, E240/3, Hoare to Willingdon, 19 May 1933.
82. India Office papers, Willingdon papers, 240(3)/621–2, Hoare to Willingdon, 3 March 1933.
83. India Office papers, Willingdon papers, 240(3)/621–2, Hoare to Willingdon, 3 March 1933.
84. India Office Library, Willingdon papers, E240/3, Hoare to Willingdon, 31 March 1933.
85. Churchill papers, 2/193/11–12, Churchill to Hoare, 5 April 1933.
86. Graham Stewart, *Burying Caesar: Churchill, Chamberlain and the Battle for the Tory Party* (London, 1999), p. 158.
87. H.C. Debs., vol. 276, 29 March 1933, col. 1099.
88. Dawson to Baldwin, 6 May 1933, cited in Stewart, *Burying Caesar*, p. 161.
89. India Office Library, Willingdon papers, E240(3)3/742, Hoare to Willingdon, 30 June 1943; *The Times*, 29 June 1933.
90. Baldwin speech in Worcester, 29 April 1933, cited in Martin Gilbert, *Winston S. Churchill, Volume V: The Prophet of Truth, 1922–1939* (London, 1990), p. 478.
91. *Churchill Documents, Volume 12*, Churchill, press statement, 30 April 1933, pp. 584–6.
92. Bridge, *Holding India to the Empire*, p. 109.
93. *Churchill Documents, Volume 12*, Douglas Crawford to Churchill, 3 April 1934, p. 741 and Churchill to Captain Fitzroy, 15 April 1934, pp. 755–8.
94. H.C. Debs., vol. 288, 16 April 1934, cols 714–23.
95. *Churchill Documents, Volume 12*, Hoare to Willingdon, 20 April 1934, p. 769.
96. C. Bridge, 'Churchill, Hoare, Derby and the Committee of Privileges, April to June 1934', *Historical Journal* (1979), pp. 215–27.
97. *Churchill Documents, Volume 12*, Hoare to Willingdon, 20 April 1934, p. 769.
98. J. C. C. Davidson to Lord Brabourne, 25 April 1934, cited in Stewart, *Burying Caesar*, p. 178.
99. *Churchill Documents, Volume 12*, Willingdon to Hoare, 21 April 1934, p. 771.
100. *Churchill Documents, Volume 12*, Hoare to Willingdon, 20 April 1934, p. 769.
101. *Churchill Documents, Volume 12*, Cabinet minutes, 16 April 1934, pp. 760–2.
102. H.C. Debs., vol. 290, 13 June 1934, cols 1733–4.
103. H.C. Debs., vol. 290, 13 June 1934, col. 1738.
104. *Churchill Documents, Volume 12*, Churchill to Captain Orr-Ewing, 20 November 1934, p. 928.

105. *Evening Standard*, 24 January 1934.
106. *Churchill Documents, Volume 12*, Churchill to Rothermere, 20 November 1934, pp. 927–8.
107. Charmley, *Churchill*, p. 300.
108. *Churchill Documents, Volume 12*, Churchill 'statement to the Press Association', 19 January 1935, p. 1035.
109. *Churchill Documents, Volume 12*, Churchill, 'broadcast', 30 January 1935, pp. 1053–61.
110. H.C. Debs., vol. 298, 26 February 1935, cols 1043–4.
111. John Darwin, 'Imperialism in decline? Tendencies in British imperial policy between the wars', *Historical Journal* (1980), pp. 657–679.
112. Lord Cecil to Austen Chamberlain, 18 August 1927, cited in Charmley, *Churchill*, p. 236.
113. *Baldwin Papers*, Dawson to Irwin, 8–9 April 1929, p. 216.
114. Robert Self (ed.), *The Austen Chamberlain Diary Letters* (Cambridge, 1995), Austen Chamberlain to Hilda Chamberlain, 28 October 1933, pp. 451–2.
115. Self, *The Austen Chamberlain Diary Letters*, Austen Chamberlain to Hilda Chamberlain, 28 October 1933, pp. 451–2 (emphasis added).
116. *The Times*, 24 February 1931.

Chapter 3

1. CAB 4/21, CID B-1084, 'The Situation in the Far East', 22 February 1932.
2. Harold Macmillan, *Winds of Change, 1914–1939* (London, 1966), p. 575.
3. *Daily Mail*, 14 February 1933.
4. See C. T. Stannage, 'The East Fulham by-election, 25 October 1933', *Historical Journal* (1971), pp. 165–200.
5. CAB 23/70, 19 (32) 23 March 1932; CAB 2/5, CID, 258, 6 April 1933.
6. See K. Neilson, 'The Defence Requirements Sub-Committee, British strategic foreign policy, Neville Chamberlain and the path to appeasement', *English Historical Review* (2003), pp. 651–84.
7. CAB 16/109, DRC 14, 'Report of the Defence Requirements Committee', 28 February 1934.
8. PREM 1.152, Hankey to MacDonald, 5 April 1933.
9. See Colin S. Gray, *Weapons Don't Make War: Policy, Strategy and Military Technology* (Kansas, 1993).
10. Azar Gat, *War in Human Civilization* (Oxford, 2008). On the underlying biological context to the human (particularly male) propensity for conflict, see Stephen Peter Rosen, *War and Human Nature* (Princeton, 2005).
11. Colin S. Gray, *Strategy and Defence Planning: Meeting the Challenge of Uncertainty* (Oxford, 2014), p. 124.
12. Winston S. Churchill, *The Second World War, Volume I, The Gathering Storm* (London, 1948), p. 149.
13. Robert Self (ed.), *The Neville Chamberlain Diary Letters, Volume 4: The Downing Street Years, 1934–1940* (Aldershot, 2005) (hereafter *Chamberlain Diary, Volume 4*), Chamberlain to Ida Chamberlain, 8 December 1935, p. 165.
14. Martin Ceadel, 'The first British referendum: The Peace Ballot, 1934–35', *English Historical Review* (1980), pp. 810–39.
15. Churchill College, Cambridge, Lord Hankey papers, Hankey diary, 11 November 1923.
16. Gaynor Johnson, *Lord Robert Cecil: Politician and Internationalist* (Farnham, 2013).

17. *Churchill Documents, Volume 12*, 'Recollections' (draft for *The Gathering Storm*), 27 June 1935, pp. 1202–3.
18. Homer, *The Iliad*, Book XXII, line 261.
19. Norton Medlicott, 'The Hoare–Laval Pact reconsidered', in David Dilks (ed.), *Retreat from Power: Studies in Britain's Foreign Policy in the Twentieth Century. Volume One: 1906–1939* (Basingstoke, 1981), pp. 118–38 at 129.
20. *Morning Post*, 18 March 1935.
21. FO 800/295, Hoare to Drummond, 27 July 1935.
22. Frank Hardie, *The Abyssinian Crisis* (London, 1974), p. 55.
23. Chamberlain papers, diary, 2 August 1935.
24. Chamberlain papers, diary, 2 August 1935.
25. Chamberlain papers, diary, 2 August 1935.
26. The National Archives, London, James Ramsay MacDonald papers, MacDonald diary, 15 May 1935.
27. *Chamberlain Diary, Volume 4*, Chamberlain to Hilda Chamberlain, 22 September 1935, p. 152; *The Times*, 23 September 1935.
28. *Chamberlain Diary, Volume 4*, Chamberlain to Hilda Chamberlain, 15 October 1935, p. 155.
29. *Baldwin Papers*, Thomas Jones to Lady Grigg, 18 September 1935, pp. 346–7.
30. *The Times*, 25 July 1935.
31. Gower to Baldwin, 1 August 1935, cited in Cowling, *The Impact of Hitler*, p. 93.
32. Gower to Baldwin, 1 August 1935, cited in Cowling, *The Impact of Hitler*, p. 93.
33. *Documents on British Foreign Policy, 1919–1939* online database (hereafter DBFP), Series 2, Volume 14, Appendix IV: 'Sir S. Hoare's speech of September 11, 1935, to the League Assembly'.
34. Chamberlain papers, NC7/11/28/24, Hoare to Chamberlain, 18 August 1935.
35. Cowling, *Impact of Hitler*, p. 89; Ralph Wigram to Eric Phipps, 25 October 1935, cited in Cowling, *Impact of Hitler*, p. 91.
36. The Conservative manifesto for the 1935 election can be examined at http://www.conservativemanifesto.com/1935/1935-conservative-manifesto.shtml.
37. These are reproduced in Ball, *Dole Queues and Demons*, pp. 64–6.
38. 'We have had a political earthquake': *Churchill Documents, Volume 12*, Bracken to Churchill, 11 December 1935 (p. 1348).
39. *The Times*, 11 December 1935.
40. CAB 23/82 (35) 50, 2 December 1935.
41. CAB 23/82, (35) 52, 9 December 1935.
42. *Chamberlain Diary, Volume 4*, 15 December 1935, pp. 166–7; Stuart Ball (ed.), *Parliament and Politics in the Age of Churchill and Attlee: The Headlam Diaries, 1935–1951* (Cambridge, 1999) (hereafter *Headlam Diary*), 11 December 1935, pp. 78–9.
43. Medlicott, 'The Hoare–Laval Pact reconsidered', p. 130.
44. Hankey diary, 25 November 1935, cited in Stephen Roskill, *Hankey: Man of Secrets. Volume III, 1931–1963* (London, 1974), p. 187.
45. Hankey diary, 25 November 1935, cited in Stephen Roskill, *Hankey: Man of Secrets. Volume III, 1931–1963* (London, 1974), pp. 187–9.
46. See *DBFP*, Series II, Volume XV, documents 91, 95, 108, and 115.
47. Gabriel Gorodetsky, *The Maisky Diaries: Red Ambassador to the Court of St James's, 1932–1943* (London, 2015) (hereafter *Maisky Diary*), 24 December 1935, p. 55.
48. H.C. Debs., vol. 307, 19 December 1935, col. 2029.
49. *The Times*, 14 December 1935.

50. *The Times*, 16 December 1935.
51. Ian Colvin, *Vansittart in Office: An Historical Survey of the Origins of the Second World War Based on the Papers of Sir Robert Vansittart, Permanent Under-Secretary of State for Foreign Affairs, 1930–38* (London, 1965), pp. 80–2.
52. Though scepticism about the scale of public outrage is registered in Daniel Waley, *British Public Opinion and the Abyssinian War, 1935–6* (London, 1975).
53. Interviews with H. G. Strauss and Commander R. T. Bower, cited in Waley, *British Public Opinion and the Abyssinian War*, p. 64.
54. Macmillan, *Winds of Change*, pp. 444–7.
55. *Headlam Diary*, 11 December 1935, pp. 78–9.
56. *Headlam Diary*, 17 December 1935, p. 79.
57. Lord Vansittart, *The Mist Procession* (London, 1958), p. 522.
58. *Chamberlain Diary, Volume 4*, 15 December 1935, pp. 166–7.
59. *Chamberlain Diary, Volume 4*, 15 December 1935, pp. 166–7.
60. Lloyd to Blanche Lloyd, 23 August 1935, cited in Charmley, *Lord Lloyd*, p. 199.
61. *Austen Chamberlain Diary*, Chamberlain to Ida Chamberlain, 15 December 1935, pp. 494–5.
62. *Churchill Documents, Volume 12*, Bracken to Churchill, 11 December 1935, p. 1348.
63. Chamberlain papers, diary, 18 December 1935; Halifax to Chamberlain, 26 December 1935; 'Summary of Cabinet Discussion on 18 December 1935 at 10 Downing Street', in *DBFP*, Series II, Volume XV, Appendix III (b).
64. 'Summary of Cabinet Discussion on 18 December 1935 at 10 Downing Street', in *DBFP*, Series II, Volume XV, Appendix III (b).
65. 'Summary of Cabinet Discussion on 18 December 1935 at 10 Downing Street', in *DBFP*, Series II, Volume XV, Appendix III (b).
66. CAB 23/82 (35) 50, 2 December 1935.
67. *Chamberlain Diary, Volume 4*, Chamberlain to Hilda Chamberlain, 14 July 1935, pp. 142–3.
68. Thomas Jones, *A Diary with Letters, 1931–1950* (London, 1954), 30 April 1936, p. 191 and 23 May 1936, p. 206.
69. See Michael Howard, *War and the Liberal Conscience* (London, 1978).
70. Harold Nicolson, 'British public opinion and foreign policy', *The Public Opinion Quarterly*, January 1937, pp. 53–62, at 59.
71. Chamberlain papers, Chamberlain to Hilda Chamberlain, 14 June 1935.
72. *Chamberlain Diary, Volume IV*, Chamberlain to Hilda Chamberlain, 28 July 1934, p. 83.
73. Churchill, *The Gathering Storm*, p. 161.
74. *Headlam Diary*, 11 December 1935, p. 79.
75. 'The very midsummer of madness': *The Times*, 11 June 1936.
76. Quoted in Nicholas Rankin, *Telegram from Guernica* (London, 2003), p. 33.
77. CAB 23/83, 39 (36), 27 May 1936; CAB 23/84, 40 (36), 29 May 1936.
78. *Chamberlain Diary, Volume 4*, Chamberlain to Ida Chamberlain, 25 April 1936, p. 188.
79. MacDonald papers, diary, 26 June 1936.
80. *Chamberlain Diary, Volume 4*, Chamberlain to Hilda Chamberlain, 14 June 1936, pp. 194–5.
81. *Chamberlain Diary, Volume 4*, Chamberlain to Hilda Chamberlain, 14 June 1936, pp. 194–5; *The Times*, 11 June 1936.
82. Chamberlain papers, Chamberlain to Ida Chamberlain, 25 August 1935.
83. Cambridge University Library, Viscount Templewood papers, Hoare to George Clerk, 24 August 1935.
84. Templewood papers, Hoare to Eden, 9 October 1935.

Chapter 4

1. For instance, *1932 Labour Party Annual Conference Report* (London, 1932), pp. 188–94.
2. Ben Pimlott (ed.), *The Political Diary of Hugh Dalton, 1918–40, 1945–60* (London, 1986) (hereafter *Dalton Diary*), 8 October 1932, pp. 168–9.
3. *Dalton Diary*, 8 October 1932, pp. 168–9.
4. Viscount Templewood, *Nine Troubled Years* (London, 1954), pp. 126–7.
5. *Daily Herald*, 6 September 1935.
6. *Manchester Guardian*, 9 September 1935.
7. *New Statesman*, 5 October 1935.
8. *1935 Labour Party Annual Conference Report* (London, 1935), pp. 177–80; Alan Bullock, *The Life and Times of Ernest Bevin, Volume One: Trade Union Leader, 1881–1940* (London, 1960), p. 570.
9. F. Williams, *Ernest Bevin* (London, 1952), p. 196.
10. *1935 Labour Party Annual Conference Report*, p. 193.
11. Hugh Dalton, *The Fateful Years: Memoirs, 1931–1945* (London, 1957) p. 69.
12. See Ben Pimlott, *Labour and the Left in the 1930s* (Cambridge, 1977), chapter five. Also Michael Bor, *The Socialist League in the 1930s* (London, 2005).
13. Pimlott, *Labour and the Left in the 1930s*, p. 48.
14. Dalton, *The Fateful Years*, p. 148.
15. M. Cole, quoted in Bullock, *Bevin, Volume One*, p. 501; Nuffield College, Oxford, G. D. H. Cole papers, Bevin to Cole, 24 September 1932.
16. For example, *Dalton Diary*, 19 January 1934, p. 181.
17. *The Times*, 7 January 1934.
18. *Dalton Diary*, 19 January 1934, p. 181.
19. *1935 Labour Party Annual Conference Report*, p. 158.
20. Cited in *Dalton Diary*, pp. 195–6.
21. H.C. Debs., vol. 313, 18 June 1936, col. 1240.
22. Tom Buchanan, *The Spanish Civil War and the British Labour Movement* (Cambridge, 1991).
23. Julius Ruiz, *The 'Red Terror' and the Spanish Civil War: Revolutionary Violence in Madrid* (Cambridge, 2015).
24. 'The storm clouds gather': Martin Gilbert (ed.), *The Churchill Documents, Volume 13: The Coming of War, 1936–1939* (London, 1982), Churchill to Clementine Churchill, 21 February 1936, p. 54.
25. *Churchill Documents, Volume 12*, 'Sir Samuel Hoare: Record of a conversation between Sir Samuel Hoare, Anthony Eden and Winston S. Churchill', 21 August 1935, pp. 1239–40.
26. Churchill papers, 4/84–5, Churchill to Hoare, 25 August 1935.
27. *Churchill Documents, Volume 12*, 'Sir Samuel Hoare: Record of a conversation between Sir Samuel Hoare, Anthony Eden and Winston S. Churchill', 21 August 1935, pp. 1239–40; Nigel Nicolson (ed.), *Harold Nicolson: Diaries and Letter, 1930–1939* (London, 1966) (hereafter *Nicolson Diary*), 21 August 1935, p. 211.
28. *Churchill Documents, Volume 12*, 'Sir Samuel Hoare: Record of a conversation between Sir Samuel Hoare, Anthony Eden and Winston S. Churchill', 21 August 1935, pp. 1239–40.
29. Charmley, *Churchill*, p. 298.
30. Cambridge University Library, Cambridge, Stanley Baldwin papers, Lady Astor to Baldwin, 17 November 1935.
31. Churchill papers, 2/237, J. L. Garvin to Churchill, 3 September 1935.

32. For example, H.C. Debs., vol. 302, 31 May 1935 cols 1489–96.
33. Churchill papers, 2/244, Desmond Morton to Churchill, 23 August 1935.
34. Churchill, *The Gathering Storm*, p. 160.
35. *The Times*, 18 November and 28 November 1935.
36. *Churchill Documents, Volume 12*, 'Recollections' (draft for *The Gathering Storm*), 14 November 1935, p. 1324.
37. *Churchill Documents, Volume 12*, 'Recollections' (draft for *The Gathering Storm*), 14 November 1935, p. 1324.
38. Churchill papers, 2/238, Randolph Churchill to Churchill, 17 December 1935.
39. *Churchill Documents, Volume 12*, Churchill to Randolph Churchill, 26 December 1935, p. 1364.
40. *Churchill Documents, Volume 13*, Churchill to Clementine Churchill, 21 February 1936, p. 54.
41. 'You can smell the gunpowder!': *Maisky Diary*, 3 May 1936, p. 68.
42. *The Times*, 9 March 1936.
43. *DBFP*, Series II, Vol. V, document 2229, Rumbold to Simon, 30 June 1933.
44. The Earl of Avon (Anthony Eden), *The Eden Memoirs: Facing the Dictators* (London, 1962), p. 346.
45. CAB 27/599, 17 February 1936.
46. *Chamberlain Diary*, Chamberlain to Ida Chamberlain, 2 August 1936, p. 205.
47. H.C. Debs., vol. 310, 26 March 1936, col. 1529 (emphasis added).
48. *Churchill Documents, Volume 13*, Churchill to Lord Londonderry, 6 May 1936 (pp. 142–3).
49. *Churchill Documents, Volume 13*, Churchill to Lord Londonderry, 6 May 1936 (pp. 142–3).
50. *Churchill Documents, Volume 13*, Churchill to Lord Weir, 6 May 1936, p. 141.
51. *Churchill Documents, Volume 13*, Churchill to Lord Linlithgow, 7 May 1936, pp. 143–4, and Churchill to Andre Charles Corbin, 31 July 1936, p. 297.
52. *Churchill Documents, Volume 13*, 'Record of a discussion between Stanley Baldwin and a deputation from both Houses of Parliament', 29 July 1936, pp. 277–94.
53. *Churchill Documents, Volume 13*, Eugen Spier, 'recollections', 19 May 1936, p. 160.
54. *Churchill Documents, Volume 13*, Hankey to Inskip, 22 May 1936, pp. 165–6.
55. *Daily Telegraph*, 3 March 1936.
56. 'I feel . . . fully entitled . . . to state facts and draw morals': *Churchill Documents, Volume 13*, Churchill to Lord Cranborne, 8 April 1936, pp. 92–3.
57. Cmd. 5107, *Statement Relating to Defence* (HMSO, 1936).
58. CAB 23/87, 13 (36) 2, 2 March 1936.
59. H.C. Debs., vol. 320, 17 February 1937, col. 1206–17.
60. H.C. Debs., vol. 324, 1 June 1937, cols 916–17.
61. Chamberlain Diary, Chamberlain to Hilda Chamberlain, 25 April 1937, pp. 246–8.
62. For example, *Daily Telegraph*, 3 March 1936; *Daily Mail*, 26 May 1936.
63. *Churchill Documents, Volume 13*, Churchill to Clementine Churchill, Churchill papers, 8 January 1936, pp. 5–6.
64. *Austen Chamberlain Diary*, Austen Chamberlain to Hilda Chamberlain, 15 February 1936, p. 499.
65. R. A. C. Parker, *Churchill and Appeasement* (London, 2000).
66. Templewood papers, Hoare to Neville Chamberlain, 23 February 1936.
67. Churchill College papers, Lord Lloyd papers, 5/5, Lloyd to David Lloyd, 25 March 1935.
68. *Austen Chamberlain Diary*, Austen Chamberlain to Ida Chamberlain, 23 February 1936, p. 500 and to Hilda Chamberlain, 15 March 1936, p. 502.

69. *Churchill Documents, Volume 13*, Churchill to Lord Cranborne, 8 April 1936, pp. 92–3.
70. *Churchill Documents, Volume 13*, Churchill to Viscount Cecil, 9 April 1936, pp. 93–4.
71. *Saturday Review*, 15 August 1936.
72. Cited in Zara Steiner, *The Triumph of the Dark: European International History, 1933–1939* (Oxford, 2013), p. 431.
73. H.C. Debs., vol. 315, 20 July 1936, cols 99–116.
74. For example, *Evening Standard*, 1 May 1936.
75. *Evening Standard*, 1 May 1936.
76. CAB 23/85, 15 (36) 2, 6 July 1936.
77. *Churchill Documents, Volume 13*, Oliver Locker Lampson to Churchill, 21 July 1936, p. 257.
78. For example, *Austen Chamberlain Diary*, Austen Chamberlain to Ida Chamberlain, 29 May 1936, p. 508.
79. Cited in Stewart, *Burying Caesar*, p. 256.
80. *Channon Diary*, 15 May and 28 May 1936, pp. 60–2.
81. *Churchill Documents, Volume 13*, Eugen Spier, 'recollections', 19 May 1936, p. 160, and A. H. Richards, 'Memorandum', 29 July 1936, pp. 295–6.
82. *The Times*, 4 December 1936.
83. *Churchill Documents, Volume 13*, Churchill to Randolph Churchill, 13 November 1936, p. 401.
84. *New Statesman*, 21 November 1936.
85. *Churchill Documents, Volume 13*, Boothby to Churchill, 11 December 1936, p. 484.
86. *Channon Diary*, 4 May 1937, p. 154.
87. *Chamberlain Diary*, Chamberlain to Ida Chamberlain, 16 February 1936, p. 176.
88. Matthew Coutts, 'The political career of Sir Samuel Hoare during the National Government 1931–40' (unpublished University of Leicester PhD thesis, 2010), p. 166.
89. *Chamberlain Diary*, Chamberlain to Ida Chamberlain, 16 February 1936, p. 176.
90. H.C. Debs., vol. 309, 9 March 1936, cols 1865–73.
91. *1934 Labour Party Annual Conference Report* (London, 1934), pp. 174–5.
92. H.C. Debs., vol. 281, 7 November 1933, col. 148.
93. H.C. Debs., vol. 317, 12 November 1936, cols 1144–5.
94. Churchill, *The Gathering Storm*, pp. 194–5.
95. H.C. Debs., vol. 305, 23 October 1935, cols 151–3.
96. Churchill, *The Gathering Storm*, p. 157.

Chapter 5

1. 'I know that I can save this country and I do not believe that anyone else can': *Chamberlain Diary*, Chamberlain to Ida Chamberlain, 12 March 1939, p. 392.
2. The best study is Robert Self, *Neville Chamberlain: A Biography* (Aldershot, 2006).
3. DBFP, Series 2, Vol. 19, document 401, Cabinet meeting, 22 December 1937.
4. *Chamberlain Diary*, Chamberlain to Ida Chamberlain, 8 August 1937, p. 265.
5. H.C. Debs., vol. 304, 22 July 1935, col. 1523.
6. *Maisky Diary*, draft letter to Litvinov, n.d., c. 20 November 1937, p. 92.
7. *Maisky Diary*, 2 March 1939, p. 161.
8. *Maisky Diary*, 1 December 1937, p. 94.
9. *Chamberlain Diary, Volume 4*, Chamberlain to Ida Chamberlain, 12 March 1939, p. 392.
10. *Chamberlain Diary, Volume 3*, Chamberlain to Hilda Chamberlain, 3 January 1932, p. 300.

11. K. Neilson, 'The Defence Requirements sub-committee, British strategic policy, Neville Chamberlain and the path to appeasement', *English Historical Review* (2003), pp. 651–84 at 655.

12. 'If I were working the thing I should feel more confident of success': *Chamberlain Diary*, Chamberlain to Ida Chamberlain, 27 October 1934, p. 95.

13. CAB 16/110, DC (M) (32) 41, 3 May 1934.

14. H.C. Debs., vol. 270, 10 November 1932, col. 632.

15. CAB 27/511, DC (M) (32) 120, 'Note by the Chancellor of the Exchequer on the Report of the DRC', 20 June 1934.

16. CAB 27/511, DC (M) (32) 120, 'Note by the Chancellor of the Exchequer on the Report of the DRC', 20 June 1934.

17. CAB 23/79, 31 (34), Appendix, 31 July 1934. See also Neilson, 'The Defence Requirements sub-committee'.

18. See H.C. Debs., vol. 295, 28 November 1934, cols 874–82.

19. CAB 27, 507, DC (M) (32), 52, 2 July 1934.

20. CAB 16/111, DC (M) (32) 41, 3 May 1934.

21. CAB 16/111, DC (M) (32) 50, 25 June 1934; MacDonald papers, diary, 25 June 1934.

22. *Chamberlain Diary, Volume 4*, Chamberlain to Ida Chamberlain, 27 October 1934, p. 95.

23. Chamberlain papers, diary, 25 March 1934.

24. Chamberlain papers, diary, 25 March 1934.

25. The classic statement of this way of thinking about international relations is John J. Mearsheimer, *The Tragedy of Great Power Politics* (New York, 2001).

26. 'A one-man cabinet': *Amery Diary*, 13 July 1937, p. 446.

27. *Chamberlain Diary, Volume 4*, Chamberlain to Ida Chamberlain, 16 October 1937, p. 275.

28. *The Times*, 1 June 1937.

29. R. J. Minney (ed.), *The Private Papers of Hore-Belisha* (London, 1960), p. 130.

30. Minney, *The Private Papers of Hore-Belisha*, p. 130.

31. See G. C. Peden, 'Sir Horace Wilson and appeasement', *Historical Journal* (2010), pp. 983–1014.

32. Churchill College, Cambridge, Clement Attlee papers, notes on draft autobiography, 1/16 fo 3.

33. Cited in Martin Gilbert, 'Horace Wilson: Man of Munich?' *History Today* (1982), 32 (10), pp. 3–9, at 9.

34. Trinity College, Cambridge, R. A. Butler papers, F79/93, Butler to Branbourne, 17 February 1939.

35. W. J. Brown, *So Far...* (London, 1943), p. 220.

36. Lord Woolton, *Memoirs* (London, 1959), p. 140.

37. S. Harvie-Watt, *Most of My Life* (London, 1980), p. 31.

38. Harvie-Watt, *Most of My Life*, p. 133.

39. Nigel Nicolson (ed.), *Harold Nicolson: Diaries and Letters, 1930–1939* (London, 1966) (hereafter *Nicolson Diary*), 30 November 1939, p. 231.

40. Templewood papers, XII/3, Hoare notes on April–May 1939, n.d. but 1953.

41. King's College, London, Basil Liddell Hart papers, KH11/HB1939/3, 'Lunch with Hore-Belisha', 27 March 1939.

42. Rhodes James, *Memoirs of a Conservative*, p. 272.

43. Rhodes James, *Memoirs of a Conservative*, p. 338.

44. William C. Mills, 'Sir Joseph Ball, Adrian Dingli, and Neville Chamberlain's "secret channel" to Italy, 1937–1940', *International History Review* (2002), 24 (2), pp. 278–317, at 281.

45. Mills, 'Sir Joseph Ball . . . ', p. 280.
46. Mills, 'Sir Joseph Ball . . . ', p. 281.
47. *Amery Diary*, 13 July 1937, p. 446, and 24 October 1938, p. 533.
48. Paul W. Doerr, *British Foreign Policy, 1919–1939* (Manchester, 1998), p. 124.
49. *Chamberlain Diary*, Chamberlain to Hilda Chamberlain, 30 May 1937, p. 251.
50. 'A faintly Bohemian flavour': *Maisky Diary*, 29 January 1936, p. 63.
51. Chamberlain papers, NC 7/11/30/74, Hoare to Chamberlain, 17 March 1937.
52. Gilbert, 'Horace Wilson: Man of Munich?', p. 5.
53. *Chamberlain Diary*, Chamberlain to Ida Chamberlain, 14 November 1937, p. 283.
54. Lord Vansittart, *Lessons of My Life* (London, 1943), p. 169.
55. *DBFP*, Series 2, Vol. 15, appendix 3, 'Summary of Cabinet Discussion on 18 December 1935 at 10 Downing'.
56. Eden, *Facing the Dictators*, p. 242.
57. *Maisky Diary*, 29 January 1936, p. 63.
58. *Maisky Diary*, 29 January 1936, p. 63.
59. *Western Daily Press*, 13 November 1935.
60. Eden to Baldwin, 24 February 1933, cited in Cowling, *The Impact of Hitler*, p. 63.
61. John Harvey (ed.), *The Diplomatic Diaries of Oliver Harvey, 1937–1940* (London, 1970) (hereafter *Harvey Diary*), 24 February 1937, p. 15, and 10 March 1937, p. 23.
62. *Harvey Diary*, 10 March 1937, p. 23.
63. *Harvey Diary*, 15 October 1937, p. 50, 3 and 7 November 1937, pp. 56–7, and 17 January 1938, p. 72.
64. *Harvey Diary*, 23 March 1937, p. 32.
65. *Harvey Diary*, 12 April 1937, p. 38.
66. CAB 24/259, CP 13 (36), 11 February 1936.
67. *Nicolson Diary*, 13 February 1936, p. 243.
68. CAB 25 (36), 1 April 1936; H.C. Debs., vol. 310, 26 March 1936, cols 1435–49.
69. Hankey papers, HKNY 3/42, Hankey to Robin Hankey, 21 November 1937.
70. CAB 23/89, 34 (37) 6, 8 September 1937.
71. 'The Far East is on fire': *Maisky Diary*, 1 August 1937, p. 85.
72. See M. G. Sheftall, 'An ideological genealogy of Imperial era Japanese militarism', in Frank McDonough (ed.), *The Origins of the Second World War: An International Perspective* (London, 2011), pp. 50–65.
73. CAB 16/609, DRC (1), 14 November 1933.
74. CAB 27/507, DC (M) (32), 41, 3 May 1934.
75. MacDonald papers, diary, 25 June 1934.
76. CAB 23/77, 57 (33) 2, 26 October 1933.
77. CAB 27/511, DC (M) (32) 120, 'Note by the Chancellor of the Exchequer on the Report of the DRC', 20 June 1934.
78. CAB 24/250, CP 205 (34), 'Defence Requirements Report', 31 July 1934.
79. *Maisky Diary*, 1 August 1937, p. 85.
80. CAB 23/89, 34 (37) 1–2, 8 September 1937.
81. CAB 23/89, 37 (3) 3, 13 October 1937.
82. CAB 23/90, 43 (37) 5, 24 November 1937.
83. *Chamberlain Diary*, Chamberlain to Hilda Chamberlain, 17 December 1937, p. 294.
84. *Chamberlain Diary*, Chamberlain to Hilda Chamberlain, 21 November 1937, p. 284.
85. See Joseph A. Maiolo, *The Royal Navy and Nazi Germany, 1933–39: A Study in Appeasement and the Origins of the Second World War* (Basingstoke, 1998).

86. 'Take an aspirin': Avon, *Facing the Dictators*, p. 512.
87. *Harvey Diary*, 22 September 1937, p. 47.
88. *Chamberlain Diary*, Chamberlain to Hilda Chamberlain, 6 November 1937, p. 281, and 12 December 1937, p. 292.
89. *Harvey Diary*, 22 September 1937, p. 47.
90. *Harvey Diary*, 15 October 1937, p. 50.
91. *Harvey Diary*, 17 January 1938, p. 72.
92. *Harvey Diary*, 7 November 1937, p. 57.
93. *Harvey Diary*, 7 November 1937, p. 57.
94. Avon, *Facing the Dictators*, p. 493.
95. Avon, *Facing the Dictators*, p. 512.
96. *Harvey Diary*, 22 September 1937, p. 47.
97. *Harvey Diary*, 5 December 1937, p. 63 (emphasis added).
98. Avon, *Facing the Dictators*, pp. 512–13.
99. FO 800/328, Hal 38/38, Hoare to Sir Roger Lumley, 21 March 1938.
100. J. Vincent (ed.), *The Crawford Papers: The Journals of David Lindsay, Twenty-Seventh Earl of Crawford and Tenth Earl of Balcarres 1871–1940, During the Years 1892 to 1940* (Manchester, 1984), diary, 22 March 1937, p. 578.
101. *Maisky Diary*, 'conversation with Chamberlain', 29 July 1937, p. 83.
102. Cambridge University Library, Leo Amery papers, AMEL 2/1/27, Amery to Chamberlain, 11 November 1937.
103. *DBFP*, Series 2, Vol. 19, document 410, 'Letter from Mr Eden to Mr Chamberlain', 1 January 1938.
104. *DBFP*, Series 2, Vol. 19, document 410, 'Letter from Mr Eden to Mr Chamberlain', 1 January 1938.
105. PREM 1/259, Chamberlain to Sir Ronald Lindsay, 13 January 1938; Chamberlain papers, diary, 19 February 1938.
106. Avon, *Facing the Dictators*, p. 552; PREM 1/259/55, Eden to Chamberlain, 17 January 1938.
107. *Harvey Diary*, note to Eden, pp. 69–70.
108. Avon, *Facing the Dictators*, p. 563.
109. *Harvey Diary*, 17 January 1938, p. 72.
110. *Harvey Diary*, 20 January 1938, pp. 75–6.
111. J. P. L. Thomas to Cranborne, 3 June 1943, cited in Simon Ball, *The Guardsmen: Harold Macmillan, Three Friends, and the World They Made* (London, 2005), pp. 165–6.
112. Chamberlain papers, diary, 19 February 1938.
113. *Harvey Diary*, 20 January 1938, pp. 75–6.
114. *Harvey Diary*, 19–23 December 1937, p. 65.
115. John Charmley, *Chamberlain and the Lost Peace* (London, 1989), p. 46.
116. M. Muggeridge (ed.), *Ciano's Diplomatic Papers* (London, 1948), pp. 182–3.
117. *Ciano's Diplomatic Papers*, pp. 182–3.
118. Chamberlain papers, diary, 19 February 1938. See also Mills, 'Sir Joseph Ball...'.
119. Chamberlain papers, diary, 19 February 1938.
120. *Maisky Diary*, 8 March 1938, p. 103.
121. Chamberlain papers, diary, 19 February 1938.
122. *Harvey Diary*, 20 January 1938, p. 76, 9 February and 17–18 February 1938, pp. 87–94.
123. Avon, *Facing the Dictators*, p. 583.
124. Chamberlain papers, diary, 19 February 1938; Avon, *Facing the Dictators*, p. 583.

125. *Chamberlain Diary*, Chamberlain to Hilda Chamberlain, 27 February 1938, p. 303.
126. CAB 23/92, 6 (38) 1, 19 February 1938; York University, Borthwick Institute, Hickleton papers, A4.410.11, Halifax, 'Record of events connected with Anthony Eden's resignation, 19–20 February 1938'.
127. Avon, *Facing the Dictators*, p. 585.
128. Chamberlain papers, 7/11/31/10, Ball to Chamberlain, 21 February 1938; British Library, Oliver Harvey papers, diary, 23 February 1938.
129. *The Times*, 21 February 1938.
130. *The Times*, 28 February 1938.
131. Harvey papers, diary, 23 February 1938.
132. *Manchester Guardian*, 24 February 1938; John Ramsden, *The Making of Conservative Party Policy* (London, 1980), p. 87.
133. H.C. Debs., vol. 332, 21 February 1938, cols 45–50 and 52–64.
134. H.C. Debs., vol. 332, 22 February 1938, cols 226–9.
135. *Amery Diary*, 20 February 1938, p. 456.
136. *Churchill Documents, Volume 13*, Churchill to Eden, 21 February 1938, p. 914.
137. *Maisky Diary*, draft letter to Litvinov, n.d. *c.* 20 November 1937, p. 92.
138. Avon, *Facing the Dictators*, p. 585.
139. 'We are not talking the same language': *DBFP*, Series 2, Vol. 19, document 336, 'Account by Lord Halifax of his visit to Germany, 17–21 November 1937'.
140. *Chamberlain Diary*, Chamberlain to Ida Chamberlain, 14 November 1937, p. 283.
141. See B. J. C. McKercher, 'Anschluss: The Chamberlain government and the first test of appeasement, February–March 1938', *The International History Review* (2016), pp. 274–94.
142. *DBFP*, Series 2, Vol. 19, document 336, 'Account by Lord Halifax of his visit to Germany, 17–21 November 1937'.
143. *DBFP*, Series 2, Vol. 19, document 336, 'Account by Lord Halifax of his visit to Germany, 17–21 November 1937'.
144. *DBFP*, Series 2, Vol. 19, document 336, 'Account by Lord Halifax of his visit to Germany, 17–21 November 1937'.
145. Chamberlain papers, diary, 27 April 1936.
146. *DBFP*, Series 2, Vol. 19, document 316, 'Record of conversations between British and French ministers held at No. 10 Downing Street on 29 and 30 November 1937'.
147. *Chamberlain Diary*, Chamberlain to Ida Chamberlain, 26 November 1937, pp. 286–7.
148. *Chamberlain Diary*, Chamberlain to Ida Chamberlain, 26 November 1937, pp. 286–7.
149. *DBFP*, Series 2, Vol. 19, document 316, 'Record of conversations between British and French ministers held at No. 10 Downing Street on 29 and 30 November 1937'.
150. *DBFP*, Series 2, Vol. 19, document 316, 'Record of conversations between British and French ministers held at No. 10 Downing Street on 29 and 30 November 1937'.

Chapter 6

1. Dalton, *The Fateful Years*, p. 128.
2. *The Times*, 19 September 1938.
3. *Daily Herald*, 19 February 1936.
4. *Manchester Guardian*, 23 April 1936.
5. *Manchester Guardian*, 8 March 1936.
6. *The Times*, 14 March 1936 and *Daily Herald*, 30 March 1936.
7. *Daily Herald*, 9 March and 16 March 1936.

8. *Daily Herald*, 23 June 1936.
9. *Manchester Guardian*, 16 November 1936.
10. Michael Foot, *Aneurin Bevan: A Biography, Volume I* (London, 1962), p. 245.
11. *Daily Herald*, 3 October 1936.
12. People's History Museum, Labour party archive, Manchester, PLP Executive Committee minutes, 27 July 1936.
13. PLP minutes, 27 July 1936.
14. *Dalton Diary*, 27 July 1936, p. 200.
15. NEC minutes, 6 October 1936.
16. NCL minutes, 15 May 1936.
17. *Dalton Diary*, 11 November 1936, p. 202.
18. *Manchester Guardian*, 12 April 1937.
19. *Manchester Guardian*, 23 July 1937.
20. *1937 Labour Party Annual Conference Report*, p. 138.
21. Beatrice Webb diary, 20 May 1934, cited in Pimlott, *Dalton*, p. 221.
22. Beatrice Webb diary, 16 April 1937, cited in Pimlott, *Dalton*, p. 234.
23. 'A very troubled world': *Chamberlain Diary*, Chamberlain to Ida Chamberlain, 19 September 1937, p. 271.
24. Winston Churchill, *Arms and the Covenant* (1938).
25. *Chamberlain Diary*, Chamberlain to Ida Chamberlain, 20 March 1938, p. 307.
26. DBFP, Series 3, Volume 1, document 140, Newton to Halifax, 12 April 1938.
27. *Chamberlain Diary*, Chamberlain to Ida Chamberlain, 20 March 1938, p. 307.
28. DBFP, Series 3, Volume 1, document 86, 'Mr Newton to Viscount Halifax', 15 March 1938.
29. *Chamberlain Diary*, Chamberlain to Ida Chamberlain, 20 March 1938, pp. 306–8.
30. David Dilks, *The Diaries of Sir Alexander Cadogan O.M., 1938–1945* (London, 1971) (hereafter *Cadogan Diary*), 18 March 1938, p. 63.
31. CAB 27/263, FP (36) 26, 18 March 1938.
32. CAB 27/263, FP (36) 26, 18 March 1938.
33. H.C. Debs., vol. 333, 24 March 1938, cols 1385–1413.
34. DBFP, Series 3, Volume 1, document 264, Viscount Halifax to Sir Neville Henderson, 22 May 1938.
35. DBFP, Series 3, Volume 1, document 264, Viscount Halifax to Sir N. Henderson, 22 May 1938 and document 349, 'Notes by Mr. Strang on his conversations with members of His Majesty's legation at Prague', 26–7 May 1938.
36. Alfred Jodl diary, n.d., cited in John Wheeler-Bennett, *The Nemesis of Power: The German Army in Politics, 1918–1945* (London, 1954), p. 398.
37. DBFP, Series 3, Volume 1, document 347, Viscount Halifax to Sir E. Phipps, 30 May 1938.
38. Cited in Wheeler-Bennett, *The Nemesis of Power*, p. 398.
39. *Daily Telegraph*, 26 July 1938.
40. *Cadogan Diary*, 7 May 1938, p. 75.
41. *Harvey Diary*, 22 April 1938, p. 128.
42. *Harvey Diary*, 19 May 1938, p. 140.
43. *The Times*, 14 June 1938.
44. *The Times*, 14 June 1938.
45. *Harvey Diary*, 19 March 1938, p. 121.
46. *Harvey Diary*, 22 April 1938, p. 128.
47. *Cadogan Diary*, 7 May 1938, p. 75.

48. *Harvey Diary*, 12 March 1938, p. 115.
49. *Harvey Diary*, 7 June 1938, p. 150.
50. Cited in Charmley, *Chamberlain and the Lost Peace*, p. 82.
51. *Chamberlain Diary*, Chamberlain to Hilda Chamberlain, 21 November 1937, p. 283.
52. Nigel Nicolson (ed.), *Harold Nicolson: Diaries and Letters, 1930–39* (London, 1966) (hereafter *Nicolson Diary*), 17 May 1938, p. 341.
53. *Channon Diary*, 13 May 1938, p. 155; *Amery Diary*, 12 March 1938, p. 496.
54. Cowling, *The Impact of Hitler*, p. 342.
55. *Channon Diary*, 1 and 2 June 1938, p. 158.
56. Butler to Brabourne, 14 January 1936, cited in Coutts, 'The political career of Sir Samuel Hoare'.
57. *Chamberlain Diary*, Chamberlain to Ida Chamberlain, 14 March 1936, pp. 179–80.
58. Coutts, 'The political career of Sir Samuel Hoare', p. 192.
59. 'The zigzags and shifts of British policy!': *Maisky Diary*, 6 August 1938, p. 116.
60. FO 800/314, H/XV/81, Halifax to Henderson, 6 September 1938.
61. *Chamberlain Diary*, Chamberlain to Ida Chamberlain, 11 September 1938, pp. 344–5.
62. DBFP, Series 3, Volume 2, documents 770, Henderson to Halifax, 4 September 1938.
63. DBFP, Series 3, Volume 2, document 793, Henderson to Cadogan, 6 September 1938.
64. *Harvey Diary*, 10 September 1938, p. 174.
65. *Daily Herald*, 7 and 8 September 1938.
66. *Chamberlain Diary*, Chamberlain to Ida Chamberlain, 3 September 1938, p. 342.
67. PREM 1/266 A, Sir Horace Wilson memorandum, 30 August 1938.
68. PREM 1/266 A, Sir Horace Wilson memorandum, 30 August 1938.
69. *Chamberlain Diary*, Chamberlain to Ida Chamberlain, 11 September 1938, p. 344.
70. *Chamberlain Diary*, Chamberlain to Ida Chamberlain, 11 September 1938, p. 344.
71. Templewood, *Nine Troubled Years*, pp. 301–2.
72. *Chamberlain Diary*, Chamberlain to Ida Chamberlain, 11 September 1938, p. 344.
73. DBFP, Series 3, Volume 2, document 862, Halifax to Henderson, 13 September 1938.
74. Templewood, *Nine Troubled Years*, p. 300.
75. Templewood, *Nine Troubled Years*, p. 300.
76. John Julius Norwich (ed.), *The Duff Cooper Diaries, 1915–1951* (London, 2005) (hereafter *Cooper Diary*), 24 September 1938, p. 260.
77. *Chamberlain Diary*, Chamberlain to Ida Chamberlain, 19 September 1938, pp. 345–9.
78. *Chamberlain Diary*, Chamberlain to Ida Chamberlain, 19 September 1938, pp. 345–9.
79. Chamberlain papers, NC 8/26/2, 'The Prime Minister's visit to Germany: Notes by Sir Horace Wilson'.
80. *Chamberlain Diary*, Chamberlain to Ida Chamberlain, 19 September 1938, pp. 345–9.
81. *Chamberlain Diary*, Chamberlain to Ida Chamberlain, 11 September 1938, pp. 344–5.
82. Charmley, *Chamberlain and the Lost Peace*, p. 111.
83. CAB 23/95, 40 (38), 19 September 1938.

Chapter 7

1. 'The flowers have shed their petals and the fires died out': *Maisky Diary*, 31 August 1938, p. 121.
2. *Harvey Diary*, 22 September 1938, p. 192.
3. DBFP, Series 3, Volume 2, document 1033, 'Note of a conversation between Mr Chamberlain and Herr Hitler at Godesberg on 22 September, 1938'.

4. CAB 27/279/CP201 (38), Halifax, Czechoslovakia, 16 September 1938.
5. Nicolson, 'British public opinion and foreign policy', pp. 55–6, 62.
6. Nicolson, 'British public opinion and foreign policy', pp. 55–6, 62.
7. Lothian to Astor, 30 September 1938, cited in J. R. M. Butler, *Lord Lothian* (London, 1960), p. 226.
8. *Harvey Diary*, 23 September 1938, p. 194.
9. DBFP, Series 3, Volume 2, document 1044, 'Viscount Halifax to British delegation (Godesberg)', 23 September 1938.
10. *Harvey Diary*, 23 September 1938, p. 194.
11. *Nicolson Diary*, 22 September 1938, p. 197.
12. DBFP, Series 3, Volume 2, document 1058, 'Viscount Halifax to British delegation (Godesberg)', 23 September 1938.
13. DBFP, Series 3, Volume 2, document 1058, 'Viscount Halifax to British delegation (Godesberg)', 23 September 1938.
14. DBFP, Series 3, Volume 2, document 1058, 'Viscount Halifax to British delegation (Godesberg)', 23 September 1938.
15. DBFP, Series 3, Volume 2, document 1027, 'Viscount Halifax to Mr Newton (Prague)', 22 September 1938 and 1030, 'Viscount Halifax to Sir E. Phipps (Paris)', 22 September 1938.
16. DBFP, Series 3, Volume 2, document 1058, 'Viscount Halifax to British delegation (Godesberg)', 23 September 1938.
17. DBFP, Series 3, Volume 2, document 1058, 'Viscount Halifax to British delegation (Godesberg)', 23 September 1938.
18. NCL minutes, 22 September 1938; *Dalton Diary*, 21 September 1938, pp. 244–6; *Manchester Guardian*, 22 September 1938; *The Times*, 26 September 1938.
19. *Nicolson Diary*, 22 September 1938, p. 196.
20. *Churchill Documents, Volume 13*, Churchill to Richard Acland, 26 May 1938, p. 1043.
21. *Amery Diary*, 26 September 1938, p. 517.
22. *Harvey Diary*, 15 September 1938, p. 180.
23. *Churchill Documents, Volume 13*, Sheila Grant Duff to Hubert Ripka, 18 September 1938, p. 1165.
24. *Churchill Documents, Volume 13*, press statement, 21 September 1938, pp. 1171–2.
25. *Churchill Documents, Volume 13*, press statement, 26 September 1938, p. 1177.
26. *Dalton Diary*, 23 September 1939, pp. 242–3.
27. *Churchill Documents, Volume 13*, Duff Cooper diary, 29 September 1938, p. 1189.
28. *Cooper Diary*, 24 September 1938, p. 264.
29. CAB 23/95, 42 (38), 24 September 1938.
30. CAB 27/646/91–2, 'The Czechoslovakian crisis 1938, notes of informal meeting of ministers', 24 September 1938.
31. *Cadogan Diary*, 24 September 1938, pp. 103–5.
32. *Maisky Diary*, 24 September 1938, p. 137.
33. *Cadogan Diary*, 25 September 1938, p. 105.
34. *Cadogan Diary*, 25 September 1938, p. 105.
35. CAB 23/95, 43 (38), 25 September 1938 (emphasis added).
36. *Maisky Diary*, 11 October 1938, p. 146.
37. Roberts, *Halifax*, p. 116.
38. CAB 23/95, 43 (38), 25 September 1938.
39. CAB 23/95, 43 (38), 25 September 1938.
40. *Channon Diary*, 3 June 1940, pp. 255–6.

41. Halifax papers, York, A4 410, 3 7, Chamberlain to Halifax, 25 September 1938.
42. *Nicolson Diary*, 26 September 1938, pp. 366–8.
43. *Amery Diary*, 26 September 1938, pp. 516–17.
44. *Nicolson Diary*, 29 September 1938, pp. 371–2.
45. CAB 23/95, 43 (38), 25 September 1938.
46. *Cadogan Diary*, 27 September 1938, p. 107.
47. *DBFP*, Series 3, Volume 2, document 1111, Viscount Halifax to Sir N. Henderson (Berlin), 26 September 1938; Halifax papers, York, A4 410 19 3, Halifax to Churchill, 3 March 1947.
48. CAB 23/95, 46 (38), 27 September 1938.
49. 'People of whom we know nothing': *The Times*, 28 September 1938.
50. CAB 23/95, 45 (38) 27 September 1938.
51. *DBFP*, Series 3, Volume 2, document 1097, Chamberlain to Hitler, 26 September 1938.
52. Martin Gilbert, 'Horace Wilson: Man of Munich?', p. 6.
53. CAB127/158, memorandum by Sir Horace Wilson, 'Munich 1938', October 1941.
54. T273/403, minute by Sir Horace Wilson, 9 September 1938; T273/403, memorandum by Wilson, n.d., but October 1938.
55. *DBFP*, Series 3, Volume 2, document 1118, 'Notes of a conversation between Sir Horace Wilson and Herr Hitler', 26 September 1938.
56. *DBFP*, Series 3, Volume 2, document 1118, 'Notes of a conversation between Sir Horace Wilson and Herr Hitler', 26 September 1938.
57. *The Times*, 28 September 1938.
58. *DBFP*, Series 3, Volume 2, document 1129, 'Notes of a conversation between Sir Horace Wilson and Herr Hitler', 27 September 1938.
59. *DBFP*, Series 3, Volume 2, document 1144, Sir N. Henderson (Berlin) to Viscount Halifax, 27 September 1938.
60. H.C. Debs., vol. 339, 28 September 1938, cols 5–26.
61. *Nicolson Diary*, 28 September 1938, pp. 368–71.
62. *Nicolson Diary*, 28 September 1938, pp. 368–71.
63. *Nicolson Diary*, 28 September 1938, pp. 368–71.
64. *Amery Diary*, 28 September 1938, p. 521.
65. *Chamberlain Diary*, Chamberlain to Hilda Chamberlain, 2 October 1938, pp. 349–51.
66. *Amery Diary*, 28 September 1938, p. 521.
67. Butler papers, F79/93, Butler to Branbourne, 17 February 1939.
68. The original footage is viewable online at https://www.youtube.com/watch?v=SetNFqcayeA.
69. *Amery Diary*, 3 October 1938, p. 524.
70. Chamberlain papers, NC 8/21/7, Ball to Chamberlain, 1 June 1938.
71. Harold Macmillan, *Winds of Change* (London, 1966), p. 569.
72. Butler papers, RAB G.11/130, 18 October 1938.
73. CAB 23/95, 42 (38), 24 September 1938.
74. See John W. Wheeler-Bennett, *The Nemesis of Power: The German Army in Politics, 1918–1945* (London, 1953).
75. *DBFP*, Series 3, Volume 2, Appendix IV, Chamberlain to Halifax, 19 August 1938.
76. Wheeler-Bennett, *The Nemesis of Power*, p. 418.
77. *Manchester Guardian*, 4 October 1938.
78. H.C. Debs., vol. 339, 3 October 1938, cols 29–40.
79. Gladwyn Jebb memorandum, cited in Donald Lammers, 'From Whitehall after Munich: The Foreign Office and the future course of British policy', *Historical Journal* (1973), 16 (4), pp. 831–56 at 845.

80. *Harvey Diary*, 30 September 1938, p. 203.
81. *House of Lords Hansard*, vol. 110, 3 October 1938, col. 1308.
82. *Manchester Guardian*, 10 October 1938; *The Times*, 10 October 1938; *Daily Herald*, 11 October 1938; *Amery Diary*, 21 October 1938, pp. 532–3.
83. H.C. Debs., vol. 339, 5 October 1938, cols 359–73.
84. *Churchill Documents, Volume 13*, Lord Davies to Churchill, 10 April 1939, p. 1439.
85. *Nicolson Diary*, 11 April 1938, p. 334.
86. *Harvey Diary*, 15 March 1938, p. 117, 13 April 1938, pp. 126–8, and 31 May 1938, pp. 145–6; *Cadogan Diary*, 7 May 1938, p. 75.
87. *Harvey Diary*, 25–6 April 1938, p. 132.
88. *Harvey Diary*, 22 April 1938, p. 131; 1 June 1938, p. 147.
89. *Harvey Diary*, 22 April 1938, p. 131.
90. *Harvey Diary*, 1 June 1938, p. 147.
91. *Harvey Diary*, 26 May 1938, p. 145.
92. *Nicolson Diary*, 18 July 1938, p. 406.
93. *The Times*, 7 May 1938; *Birmingham Post*, 13 June 1938.
94. *Nicolson Diary*, 19 September 1938, p. 195.
95. *Nicolson Diary*, 18 July 1938, p. 406.
96. *Nicolson Diary*, 9 November 1938, pp. 377–8.
97. *Nicolson Diary*, 29 September 1938, p. 201.
98. H.C. Debs., vol. 339, 3 October 1938, cols 77–89.
99. *Churchill Documents, Volume 13*, Churchill to Clementine Churchill, 29 December 1938, p. 1328.
100. *Harvey Diary*, 14 January 1939, p. 244.
101. Like thunderbolts upon us': *Churchill Documents, Volume 13*, speech at Chingford, 9 December 1938, p. 1302.
102. *Chamberlain Diary*, Chamberlain to Ida Chamberlain, 9 October 1938, p. 353.
103. *Nicolson Diary*, 3 October 1938, p. 374; Dalton, *The Fateful Years*, p. 199.
104. *Nicolson Diary*, 6 October 1938, pp. 202–3.
105. *Nicolson Diary*, 6 October 1938, pp. 202–3.
106. *Nicolson Diary*, 6 October 1938, pp. 202–3.
107. *Chamberlain Diary*, Chamberlain to Ida Chamberlain, 9 October 1938, pp. 351–4.
108. *Churchill Documents, Volume 13*, Chamberlain to Churchill, 6 October 1938, p. 1205.
109. *Churchill Documents, Volume 13*, Hoare to Chamberlain, 5 October 1938, p. 1202.
110. *Chamberlain Diary*, Chamberlain to Hilda Chamberlain, 15 October 1938, p. 356.
111. *Chamberlain Diary*, Chamberlain to Hilda Chamberlain, 15 October 1938, p. 356.
112. FO 800/328, Hal/38/38, Halifax to Chamberlain, 11 October 1938.
113. *Chamberlain Diary*, Chamberlain to Ida Chamberlain, 17 December 1938, pp. 369–70.
114. H.C. Debs., vol. 341, 17 November 1938, cols 1128–45.
115. H.C. Debs., vol. 341, 17 November 1938, col. 1196.
116. *Churchill Documents, Volume 13*, speech at Chingford, 9 December 1938, p. 1302.

Chapter 8

1. *Chamberlain Diary*, Chamberlain to Hilda Chamberlain, 11 December 1938, p. 368.
2. *Chamberlain Diary*, Chamberlain to Hilda Chamberlain, 11 December 1938, p. 367.
3. *Chamberlain Diary*, Chamberlain to Hilda Chamberlain, 11 December 1938, p. 368.
4. *Chamberlain Diary*, Chamberlain to Hilda Chamberlain, 11 December 1938, p. 368.

5. CAB 27/627, FP (38) 32, 14 November 1938.
6. CAB 27/627, FP (38) 32, 14 November 1938.
7. *Channon Diary*, 30 September 1938, p. 173.
8. *Harvey Diary*, 17 February 1939, p. 255.
9. Harvey to Halifax, 26 March 1939, printed in *Harvey Diary*, p. 269.
10. Templewood papers, Box x(3), Beaverbrook to Hoare, 22 November 1938.
11. *Channon Diary*, 2 June 1938, p. 158.
12. House of Lords Record Office, Lord Beaverbrook papers, C/99, Hoare to Beaverbrook, 15 February 1943.
13. J. Atkin-Kidd, *The Beaverbrook Girl* (London, 1987), p. 163.
14. CAB 27/625, 19 May 1939.
15. Hoare to Chamberlain, 17 March 1939, cited in Cowling, *The Impact of Hitler*, p. 341.
16. Hoare to W. W. Astor, 13 May 1939, cited in Cowling, *The Impact of Hitler*, p. 342.
17. *Maisky Diary*, 25 November 1938, p. 149.
18. *Harvey Diary*, 10 October 1938, p. 212.
19. Gilbert, 'Sir Horace Wilson: Man of Munich?', p. 9.
20. *Channon Diary*, 14 November 1940, p. 276.
21. *Daily Mail*, 16 September 1938 and 26 July 1939.
22. *Harvey Diary*, 29 January 1939, p. 249.
23. PREM 1/330, memorandum by Sir Horace Wilson, 'Points made by Sir Nevile Henderson', 28 October 1938.
24. Cited in *Cadogan Diary*, p. 53.
25. Hinted at in *Chamberlain Diary*, Chamberlain to Ida Chamberlain, 9 October 1938, pp. 351–2. See Richard Cockett, *Twilight of Truth: Chamberlain, Appeasement and the Manipulation of the Press* (New York, 1989).
26. Halifax papers, A2.278.58.4, Peake to Halifax, 9 August 1957.
27. *Chamberlain Diary*, Chamberlain to Ida Chamberlain, 23 July 1939, p. 432.
28. Chamberlain papers, 7/11/33/19, Ball to Chamberlain, n.d. but autumn 1940.
29. Lynn Olson, *Troublesome Young Men: The Churchill Conspiracy of 1940* (London, 2007), p. 149.
30. Beaverbrook papers, C/152, Beaverbrook to Halifax, 14 November 1938.
31. *Daily Express*, 1 September 1938, and *Daily Mail*, 1 September 1938. See also *The Times*, 3 and 14 June 1938.
32. Beaverbrook papers, G.37, folder VIA, Beaverbrook memorandum, n.d.; C/299, Hoare to Beaverbrook, n.d., September 1938.
33. *Chamberlain Diary*, Chamberlain to Ida Chamberlain, 23 July 1939, p. 432.
34. Dalton papers, diary, 6 October 1938; *Manchester Guardian*, 9 October 1938.
35. Cowling, *The Impact of Hitler*, p. 217.
36. *Manchester Guardian*, 14 November 1938.
37. NEC papers, Cripps memorandum, January 1939.
38. *Dalton Diary*, 19 and 23 January 1939, pp. 252–6.
39. NEC minutes, 25 January 1939.
40. *1939 Labour Party Annual Conference Report*, p. 235.
41. Dalton, *Fateful Years*, pp. 212–13.
42. *Churchill Documents, Volume 13*, Lord Davies to Churchill, 10 April 1939, p. 1439.
43. *Daily Telegraph*, 17 November 1938.
44. *Amery Diary*, 16 and 21 March 1939, pp. 548–9.
45. *Channon Diary*, 15 March 1939, p. 186.
46. H.C. Debs., vol. 345, 15 March 1940, cols 435–40.

47. *The Times*, 8 April 1939; *Manchester Guardian*, 18 April 1939.
48. *Forward*, 15 April 1939.
49. Churchill College, Cambridge, Sir Thomas Inskip papers, Inskip diary, 11 January 1939.
50. CAB 27/264, 36 (39), 26 January 1939.
51. CAB 23/97, 3 (39), 1 February 1939.
52. *DBFP*, Series 3, Volume 4, appendix I, document iv, Halifax to Henderson, 20 February 1939.
53. *Harvey Diary*, 10 March 1939, p. 261.
54. *Daily Telegraph*, 17 March 1939.
55. *DBFP*, Series 3, Volume 4, document 416, Halifax to Lindsay, 18 March 1939.
56. Butler, *The Art of the Possible*, p. 77.
57. Butler, *The Art of the Possible*, p. 77.
58. CAB 23/98, 12 (39), 18 March 1939; FO 371/23062/C4086/3356/18, Halifax in conversation with the Polish ambassador, 24 March 1939.
59. Butler, *The Art of the Possible*, p. 77.
60. CAB 23/98, 12 (39), 18 March 1939.
61. *The Times*, 20 March 1939.
62. *The Daily Telegraph*, 20 March 1939.
63. *Birmingham Post*, 25 March 1939.
64. *Birmingham Post*, 16 May 1939.
65. *The Times*, 1 October 1938.
66. *Nicolson Diary*, 17 March 1939, p. 393.
67. CAB 27/626, FP 39 (36), 26 November 1937; *Channon Diary*, 5 December 1937, p. 141; Halifax to Phipps, 1 November 1938, cited in Keith Neilson, *Britain, Soviet Russia and the Versailles Order, 1919–1939* (Cambridge, 2006), p. 258.
68. Cowling, *Impact of Hitler*, p. 291.
69. *Harvey Diary*, 22 April 1938, pp. 128–32.
70. Butler, *The Art of the Possible*, p. 78.
71. *Channon Diary*, 16 February 1939, p. 184.
72. *Chamberlain Diary*, Chamberlain to Ida Chamberlain, 26 March 1939, p. 395.
73. CAB 23/98, 13 (39), 20 March 1939.
74. CAB 23/98, 13 (39), 20 March 1939.
75. *DBFP*, Series 3, Volume 4, document 471, Halifax to Kennard, 21 March 1939.
76. CAB 23/98, 13 (39), 20 March 1939.
77. *Chamberlain Diary*, Chamberlain to Ida Chamberlain, 26 March 1939, p. 396.
78. CAB 27/624, Foreign Policy Committee minutes, 27 March 1939; PREM 1/321, Chamberlain memorandum, 26 March 1931.
79. *Cadogan Diary*, 29 March 1939, pp. 164–5.
80. CAB 27/624, Foreign Policy Committee minutes, 30 March 1939.
81. CAB 27/624, Foreign Policy Committee minutes, 30 March 1939.
82. Butler, *The Art of the Possible*, pp. 77–8.
83. Butler, *The Art of the Possible*, pp. 77–8.
84. *Chamberlain Diary*, Chamberlain to Hilda Chamberlain, 12 February 1939, p. 380.
85. H.C. Debs., vol. 345, 31 March 1939, col. 2415.
86. See G. Bruce Strang, 'Once more unto the breach: Britain's guarantee to Poland, March 1939', *Journal of Contemporary History* (1996), pp. 721–52.
87. *Cadogan Diary*, 30 March 1939, p. 165.
88. PREM 1/331A, Wilson to Henderson, 12 May 1939; Martin Gilbert, 'Horace Wilson: Man of Munich?', p. 9.

89. *Chamberlain Diary*, Chamberlain to Hilda Chamberlain, n.d. but 1–2 April 1939, p. 399.
90. *Chamberlain Diary*, Chamberlain to Hilda Chamberlain, n.d. but 1–2 April 1939, p. 399.
91. *The Times*, 1 April 1939.
92. R. A. C. Parker, *Chamberlain and Appeasement: British Policy and the Coming of the Second World War* (Basingstoke, 1993), p. 217.
93. *Channon Diary*, 3 April 1939, p. 191.
94. FO 800/315 H/XV/140, Salisbury to Halifax, 23 March 1939.
95. Martin Gilbert, 'Horace Wilson: Man of Munich?', p. 9 (emphasis added).
96. H. C. Debs., vol. 112, 13 April 1939, col. 616.
97. *Chamberlain Diary*, Chamberlain to Ida Chamberlain, 9 April 1939, p. 403, and to Hilda Chamberlain, 15 April 1939, p. 405.
98. *Chamberlain Diary*, Chamberlain to Hilda Chamberlain, 15 April 1939, p. 405.
99. CAB 23/98, 20 (39) 2, 13 April 1939.
100. H.C. Debs., vol. 346, 13 April 1939, cols 5–21, 29–38.
101. 'A great crunch is coming': *Churchill Documents, Volume 13*, Churchill to Rothermere, 19 July 1939, pp. 1569–70.
102. *Amery Diary*, 21 March 1939, p. 549.
103. *Churchill Documents, Volume 13*, Churchill to Chamberlain, 9 April 1939, pp. 1438–9; *Chamberlain Diary*, Chamberlain to Ida Chamberlain, 9 April 1939, p. 403.
104. H.C. Debs., vol. 346, 13 April 1939, col. 34.
105. *Chamberlain Diary*, Chamberlain to Ida Chamberlain, 9 April 1939, p. 407.
106. *Churchill Documents, Volume 13*, Halifax to Churchill, 6 February 1939, p. 1366.
107. *Churchill Documents, Volume 13*, speech notes, 21 June 1939, pp. 1528–9.
108. *Churchill Documents, Volume 13*, Cripps diary, 22 June 1939, p. 1531.
109. *Churchill Documents, Volume 13*, Julian Amery recollections of 18 July 1939, p. 1569; R. Macleod and Denis Kelly (eds), *The Ironside Diaries, 1937–1940* (London, 1962), 25 July 1939, pp. 1575–6.
110. *Channon Diary*, 4 July 1939, p. 204.
111. *Churchill Documents, Volume 13*, Lord Camrose: notes of a conversation with Chamberlain, 3 July 1939, p. 1545.
112. Emrys-Evans papers, Cranborne to Emrys-Evans, 27 June 1939.
113. *Chamberlain Diary*, Chamberlain to Ida Chamberlain, 8 July 1939, p. 426.
114. *Channon Diary*, 3 July 1939, p. 204.
115. *Churchill Documents, Volume 13*, Lord Camrose: notes of a conversation with Chamberlain, 3 July 1939, p. 1545.
116. *Churchill Documents, Volume 13*, Churchill to Rothermere, 19 July 1939, pp. 1569–70.

Chapter 9

1. On the issue of Anglo-Soviet relations, see Keith Neilson, *Britain, Soviet Russia and the Collapse of the Versailles.*
2. G. H. Gallup, *The Gallup International Public Opinion Polls: Great Britain, 1937–75, Volume 1* (New York, 1976), p. 17.
3. CAB 27/624 (38), 27 March 1939; CAB 27/625 (47), 16 May 1939.
4. *Maisky Diary*, 2 March 1939, pp. 158–61.
5. *Cadogan Diary*, 16 May 1939, pp. 179–80.
6. *Cadogan Diary*, 19 May 1939, p. 181, and 20 May 1939, p. 182.
7. *Maisky Diary*, 31 March 1939, p. 169.

8. *Chamberlain Diary*, Chamberlain to Ida Chamberlain, 26 March 1939, p. 396.

9. *Chamberlain Diary*, Chamberlain to Hilda Chamberlain, 29 April 1939, p. 412.

10. CAB 27/624, FP (36) 38, 27 March 1939.

11. CAB 23/99, 30 (38) 1, 24 May 1939; *Chamberlain Diary*, Chamberlain to Hilda Chamberlain, 28 May 1939, p. 418.

12. *Amery Diary*, 19 May 1939, p. 553.

13. *Chamberlain Diary*, Chamberlain to Hilda Chamberlain, 14 May 1939, p. 416.

14. *Chamberlain Diary*, Chamberlain to Ida Chamberlain, 5 August 1939, p. 438.

15. *Chamberlain Diary*, Chamberlain to Ida Chamberlain, 10 June 1939, pp. 420–1.

16. *Chamberlain Diary*, Chamberlain to Ida Chamberlain, 5 August 1939, p. 438.

17. *DBFP*, Series 3, Volume 4, Appendix III, document (i), record of a conversation between Prime Minister and M. Wenner-Gren, 6 June 1939.

18. For example, Churchill papers, 2/253/36, 'Imperial Policy Group statement', April 1936.

19. See David Carlton, 'Churchill and the two "evil empires"', *Transactions of the Royal Historical Society* (2001), pp. 331–51.

20. Carlton, 'Churchill and the two "evil empires"', p. 351.

21. *Amery Diary*, 13 February 1936, p. 407.

22. *Churchill Documents, Volume 13*, 'Record of a discussion between Stanley Baldwin and a deputation from both Houses of Parliament', 29 July 1936, pp. 277–94.

23. *Churchill Documents, Volume 13*, 'Record of a discussion between Stanley Baldwin and a deputation from both Houses of Parliament', 29 July 1936, pp. 277–94.

24. *Nicolson Diary*, 20 September 1936, p. 273.

25. FO 371/23069/C9010/3356/18, Strang to Sargent, 21 June 1939.

26. *Maisky Diary*, 'Conversation with Lloyd George', 1 July 1937, pp. 80–1.

27. *Maisky Diary*, 1 December 1936, p. 73.

28. Cited in Steiner, *The Triumph of the Dark*, p. 430.

29. Printed in *Maisky Diary*, pp. 65–6.

30. For instance, *Maisky Diary*, 7 February 1938, p. 100, 1 March 1938, p. 102, and 26 August 1938, p. 119.

31. *Chamberlain Diary*, Chamberlain to Ida Chamberlain, 10 June 1939, p. 420.

32. *Maisky Diary*, 18 April 1939, p. 176.

33. CAB 27/625, FP (36) 56, 4 July 1939.

34. *Maisky Diary*, 1 April 1939, p. 170.

35. *Maisky Diary*, 'Conversation with Lloyd George', 1 July 1937, p. 81.

36. *Maisky Diary*, 1 April 1939, p. 170.

37. *Chamberlain Diary*, Chamberlain to Hilda Chamberlain, n.d., 1–2 April 1939, p. 401.

38. On the fundamental importance of imaginative insight in the formulation and execution of strategy, see Colin S. Gray, *The Strategy Bridge: Theory for Practice* (Oxford, 2010).

39. K. Neilson, *Britain, Soviet Russia and the Collapse of the Versailles Order*, p. 5.

40. Butler papers, RAB G.10/28, 'Character sketch', summer 1939.

41. *Documents on German Foreign Policy, Series D, Volume VI: The Last Months of Peace, March–August 1939* (Washington, 1954), Wohltat minute for Goering of conversation with Sir Joseph Ball and Sir Horace Wilson, 24 July 1939, pp. 977–83.

42. *Documents on German Foreign Policy, Series D, Volume VI: The Last Months of Peace, March–August 1939* (Washington, 1954), Wohltat minute for Goering of conversation with Sir Joseph Ball and Sir Horace Wilson, 24 July 1939, pp. 977–83.

43. *Documents on German Foreign Policy, Series D, Volume VI: The Last Months of Peace, March–August 1939* (Washington, 1954), Wohltat minute for Goering of conversation with Sir Joseph Ball and Sir Horace Wilson, 24 July 1939, pp. 977–83.
44. *Documents on German Foreign Policy, Series D, Volume VI: The Last Months of Peace, March–August 1939* (Washington, 1954), Wohltat minute for Goering of conversation with Sir Joseph Ball and Sir Horace Wilson, 24 July 1939, pp. 977–83.
45. PREM 1/335, note of an interview with E. W. Tennant by Sir Horace Wilson, 24 July 1939; PREM 1/335, report of a meeting with Herr von Ribbentrop by E. W. Tennant, 31 July 1939.
46. Scott Newton, 'The "Anglo-German connection" and the political economy of appeasement', *Diplomacy and Statecraft* (1991), pp. 178–207, at 197.
47. Fritz Hesse, *Hitler English* (1954), p. 68.
48. Ian Kershaw, *Hitler: 1936–1945: Nemesis* (London, 2001), p. 218.
49. H.C. Debs., vol. 351, 24 August 1939, cols 8–10.
50. *Nicolson Diary*, 24 August 1939, p. 216.
51. *Channon Diary*, 2 September 1939, p. 214.
52. *Chamberlain Diary*, Chamberlain to Ida Chamberlain, 10 September 1939, pp. 443–6.
53. FO 800/317/84, Halifax, 'Record of events', 1 September 1939.
54. FO 371/23025, C11185/4/18, Halifax minute, 10 August 1939.
55. *Harvey Diary*, 27 August 1939, p. 307.
56. FO 800/317/84, Halifax, 'Record of events', 1 September 1939; CAB 48 (39) 1–2, 2 September 1939.
57. CAB 23 (100), 48 (39), 2 September 1939.
58. *Chamberlain Diary*, Chamberlain to Ida Chamberlain, 10 September 1939, pp. 443–6.
59. *Cooper Diary*, 3 September 1939, p. 275.
60. *Channon Diary*, 2 September 1939, pp. 212–13.
61. *Nicolson Diary*, 2 September 1939, p. 220.
62. *Nicolson Diary*, 2 September 1939, pp. 418–20.
63. *Nicolson Diary*, 2 September 1939, pp. 418–20.
64. *Amery Diary*, 2 September 1939, p. 570; Stewart, *Burying Caesar*, p. 382.
65. H.C. Debs., vol. 351, 2 September 1939, col. 282.
66. *Nicolson Diary*, 2 September 1939, p. 220.
67. FO 800/317/84, Halifax, 'Record of events', 2 September 1939.
68. CAB 23/100, 2 September 1939.
69. *Nicolson Diary*, 3 September 1939, p. 221.
70. CAB 23/100, 2 September 1939; R. J. Minney (ed.), *The Private Papers of Hore-Belisha* (London, 1960), diary, 2 September 1939, p. 226.
71. CAB 23/100, 49 (3) 1, 2 September 1939.
72. *Churchill Documents, Volume 13*, Boothby to Churchill, 6 July 1939, p. 1551.
73. Lord Hankey, *Politics, Trials and Errors* (London, 1950), p. vii.
74. *Channon Diary*, 3 September 1939, p. 215.
75. The original broadcast can be found at https://www.youtube.com/watch?v=rtJ_zbz1NyY.
76. *Nicolson Diary*, 3 September 1939, p. 221; H.C. Debs., vol. 351, 3 September 1939, col. 292.
77. *Maisky Diary*, 3 September 1939, p. 223.
78. *Channon Diary*, 3 September 1939, p. 215.
79. *Churchill Documents, Volume 13*, Admiralty to all ships: naval signal, 3 September 1939, p. 6.
80. *Maisky Diary*, 13 September 1939, p. 225.

81. *Ciano diary, 1939–1943*, pp. 9–10.
82. *Maisky Diary*, 'Conversation with Lloyd George', 1 July 1937. pp. 80–1.
83. *Maisky Diary*, 'Conversation with Lloyd George', 1 July 1937. pp. 80–1.
84. Charmley, *Chamberlain and the Lost Peace*, p. 195.
85. RAB G.9/120–2, speech, November 1938.
86. *Maisky Diary*, 18 May 1939, p. 190.
87. *DBFP*, Series 3, Volume 3, document 285, Halifax to Phipps, 1 November 1938.
88. *Chamberlain Diary*, Chamberlain to Hilda Chamberlain, 9 February 1936, pp. 174–5.
89. H.C. Debs., vol. 333, 7 March 1938, col. 1558.
90. *Chamberlain Diary*, Chamberlain to Ida Chamberlain, 26 February 1939, p. 387, and to Hilda Chamberlain, 15 April 1939, pp. 405–6.
91. For example, *Chamberlain Diary*, Chamberlain to Hilda Chamberlain, 14 May 1939, p. 416.

Chapter 10

1. 'An immense and far-tentacled intrigue': *Sunday Express*, 1 January 1939.
2. Attlee interview, cited in Kenneth Harris, *Attlee* (London, 1982), pp. 165–6.
3. *Dalton Diary*, 6 September 1939, p. 297.
4. Attlee interview, cited in Harris, *Attlee*, pp. 165–6.
5. Attlee interview, cited in Harris, *Attlee*, pp. 165–6.
6. *Dalton Diary*, 6 September 1939, p. 297.
7. *Clem Attlee: The Granada Historical Records Interview* (London, 1967), p. 17.
8. *Sunday Express*, 1 January 1939; *Daily Herald*, 9 June 1939.
9. *The Times*, 11 September 1939.
10. *Dalton Diary*, 18 September 1939, pp. 301–2.
11. Bernard Donoughue and G. W. Jones, *Herbert Morrison: Portrait of a Politician* (London, 1973), p. 245.
12. *Dalton Diary*, entries for November 1939, pp. 311–13.
13. Dalton papers, 5/6 (3) (5), Alfred Edwards to Dalton, 11 November 1939.
14. Dalton papers, copy of Morrison letter to Edwards, 11 November 1939 (emphasis added).
15. *Dalton Diary*, entries for November 1939, pp. 311–13.
16. *Dalton Diary*, entries for November 1939, pp. 311–13.
17. Robert Crowcroft, *Attlee's War: World War II and the Making of a Labour Leader* (London, 2011).
18. Dalton, *Fateful Years*, p. 281.
19. *Dalton Diary*, entries for November 1939, pp. 311–13.
20. H.C. Debs., vol. 351, 3 September 1939, cols 293–4.
21. H.C. Debs., vol. 351, 3 September 1939, cols 292–4; see also 1 September 1939, col. 133–5; *The Times*, 4 September 1939.
22. NEC minutes, 2 September 1939.
23. H.C. Debs., vol. 351, 24 August 1939, cols 10–14.
24. National Council of Labour minutes, 25 August 1939.
25. 'Politicus', 'Labour and the War', *Political Quarterly* (1939), 10, pp. 477–88.
26. 'Politicus', 'Labour and the War', *Political Quarterly* (1939), 10, pp. 477–88.
27. Cited in Pimlott, *Hugh Dalton*, p. 272.
28. NEC Election committee minutes, 5 September 1939.
29. Crowson, *Facing Fascism*, p. 169.

30. H.C. Debs., vol. 351, 3 October 1939, cols 1862; vol. 352, 12 October 1939, cols 568–70.
31. C. R. Attlee, *Labour's Peace Aims* (London, 1939).
32. *Chamberlain Diary*, Chamberlain to Ida Chamberlain, 23 September 1939 (pp. 449–52).
33. *The Times*, 11 December 1939; Bodleian Library, Oxford, Clement Attlee papers, box 8, Attlee to James Middleton, January 1940 (n.d.).
34. For instance, H.C. Debs., vol. 352, 18 October 1939, cols 963–5, vol. 351, 26 September 1939, cols 1246–50, and vol. 356, 16 January 1940, cols 49–50.
35. H.C. Debs., vol. 356, 1 February 1940, cols 1414–22.
36. H.C. Debs., vol. 355, 28 November 1939, col. 19, and vol. 358, 19 March 1940, cols 1845–53.
37. H.C. Debs., vol. 356, 16 January 1940, cols 43–4.
38. Bullock, *Bevin, volume one*, p. 644.
39. H.C. Debs., vol. 356, 1 February 1940, col. 1414.
40. *1940 Labour Party Annual Conference Report* (1940), pp. 191–5.
41. For example, *Tribune*, 26 January 1940.
42. H.C. Debs., vol. 351, 21 September 1939, col. 1103.
43. Adam Tooze, *The Wages of Destruction: The Making and Breaking of the Nazi Economy* (London, 2007), p. 332.
44. *Chamberlain Diary*, Chamberlain to Ida Chamberlain, 30 March 1940, p. 514.
45. *Documents on German Foreign Policy, 1919–1939* (London, 1956) Series D, Volume VIII, document 384, memorandum of a conference of the Fuhrer with the principal military commanders, 23 November 1939.
46. 'Hold on tight': *Chamberlain Diary*, Chamberlain to Ida Chamberlain, 8 October 1939, p. 456.
47. Avon, *The Reckoning*, p. 91.
48. Hankey to Lady Hankey, 3 September 1939, cited in Stephen Roskill, *Hankey: Man of Secrets, Volume III* (London, 1974) p. 419.
49. *Chamberlain Diary*, Chamberlain to Hilda Chamberlain, 17 September 1939, p. 448.
50. *Chamberlain Diary*, Chamberlain to Hilda Chamberlain, 17 September 1939, p. 448.
51. *Chamberlain Diary*, Chamberlain to Ida Chamberlain, 8 October 1939, p. 457.
52. *Chamberlain Diary*, Chamberlain to Ida Chamberlain, 8 October 1939, p. 457.
53. Beaverbrook papers, C/308, Hoare to Beaverbrook, 15 February 1943.
54. National Records of Scotland, Edinburgh, Lord Lothian papers, GD40/17/404, Samuel to Lothian, 13 September 1939.
55. Chamberlain papers, NC7/11/32/131, Hoare to Chamberlain, n.d.
56. Bodleian Library, Oxford, Sir Joseph Ball papers, Eng.c.6656/17, Chamberlain to Ball, 26 December 1939.
57. *Chamberlain Diary*, Chamberlain to Hilda Chamberlain, 15 October 1939, pp. 458–9.
58. *Chamberlain Diary*, Chamberlain to Hilda Chamberlain, 15 October 1939, pp. 458–9.
59. *Chamberlain Diary*, Chamberlain to Ida Chamberlain, 5 November 1939, p. 467.
60. CAB 65, WM 45 (39) 7, 12 October 1939.
61. Scott Newton, *Profits of Peace: The Political Economy of Anglo-German Appeasement* (Oxford, 1996), pp. 154–7.
62. *Chamberlain Diary*, Chamberlain to Ida Chamberlain, 5 November 1939, p. 467.
63. Hankey papers, HNKY11/1, 'War Policy', 12 September 1939.
64. *Chamberlain Diary*, Chamberlain to Ida Chamberlain, 8 October 1939, p. 456.
65. *Chamberlain Diary*, Chamberlain to Hilda Chamberlain, 30 December 1939, p. 483.
66. *Chamberlain Diary*, Chamberlain to Ida Chamberlain, 10 September 1939, pp. 443–5.

67. 'Life is one long nightmare': *Chamberlain Diary*, Chamberlain to Ida Chamberlain, 10 September 1939, pp. 443–5.
68. *Nicolson Diary*, 20 September 1939, p. 35, and 26 September 1939, p. 37.
69. *Nicolson Diary*, 20 September 1939, p. 35, and 26 September 1939, p. 37.
70. *Chamberlain Diary*, Chamberlain to Ida Chamberlain, 3 December 1939, p. 475.
71. *Chamberlain Diary*, Chamberlain to Ida Chamberlain, 10 September 1939, p. 443.
72. *Ironside Diary*, 10 September 1939, p. 106.
73. *Chamberlain Diary*, Chamberlain to Hilda Chamberlain, 15 October 1939, p. 458.
74. *Chamberlain Diary*, Chamberlain to Ida Chamberlain, 23 September 1939, p. 449.
75. *Chamberlain Diary*, Chamberlain to Ida Chamberlain, 22 October 1939, p. 462.
76. Hoare to Lothian, 11 November 1939, printed in Templewood, *Nine Troubled Years*, p. 409.
77. *Channon Diary*, 14 December 1939, p. 226.
78. *Colville Diary*, 24 October 1939, p. 44.
79. 'Enjoying every moment': Chamberlain *Diary*, Chamberlain to Ida Chamberlain, 8 October 1939, p. 456.
80. *Channon Diary*, 24 September 1939, p. 220.
81. *Amery Diary*, 5 September 1939, p. 572.
82. *Nicolson Diary*, 26 September 1939, p. 37.
83. *Channon Diary*, 26 September 1939, p. 222.
84. *Sunday Pictorial*, 1 October 1939.
85. *The Times*, 13 November 1939.
86. *Nicolson Diary*, 26 September 1939, p. 37.
87. *Daily Mirror*, 3 October 1939.
88. *News Chronicle*, 1 January 1940.
89. Cited in Paul Addison, *The Road to 1945: British Politics and the Second World War* (London, 1975), p. 79.
90. Addison, *The Road to 1945*, p. 80.
91. Martin Gilbert (ed.), *Churchill Documents: Volume 14, At the Admiralty, September 1939–May 1940* (London, 1993), Admiral Sir William James to a friend, 1 October 1939, p. 187.
92. *Chamberlain Diary*, Chamberlain to Ida Chamberlain, 8 October 1939, p. 456.
93. *Churchill Documents: Volume 14*, Churchill to Halifax, 10 September 1939, pp. 64–5.
94. *Chamberlain Diary*, Chamberlain to Ida Chamberlain, 27 January 1949, p. 492.
95. Churchill, *The Gathering Storm*, pp. 443–4.
96. FO 800/328, Churchill to Halifax, 13 January 1940.
97. *Amery Diary*, 3 September 1939, p. 571.
98. 'Nothing sufficiently drastic has happened to break the long-established traditions of party intrigue': *Colville Diary*, 24 October 1939, p. 44.
99. For example, *Truth*, 29 September 1939.
100. *Truth*, 8 March 1940.
101. Churchill College, Lord Vansittart papers, II/32, 'Report on Truth', cited in R. B. Cockett, 'Ball, Chamberlain and Truth', *Historical Journal* (1990), pp. 131–42, at 139.
102. *Amery Diary*, 14 March 1940, p. 584.
103. *Chamberlain Diary*, Chamberlain to Ida Chamberlain, 20 January 1940, p. 491.
104. Richard Cockett, *Twilight of Truth: Chamberlain, Appeasement and the Manipulation of the Press* (New York, 1989), p. 168.
105. *Colville Diary*, 4 November 1939, p. 47.

106. *Chamberlain Diary*, Chamberlain to Ida Chamberlain, 20 January 1940, p. 491; *Colville Diary*, 17 January 1940, p. 72.
107. *Colville Diary*, 24 January 1940, p. 74.
108. *Chamberlain Diary*, Chamberlain to Ida Chamberlain, 20 January 1940, p. 491.
109. *Colville Diary*, 24 January 1940, p. 74.
110. *Chamberlain Diary*, Chamberlain to Ida Chamberlain, 27 January 1940, p. 493.
111. *Colville Diary*, 2 February 1940, p. 79.
112. Bracken interview, 29 March 1940, in Crozier, *Off the Record*, p. 156.
113. *Colville Diary*, 24 October 1939, p. 44.

Chapter 11

1. 'One thing is certain: he has missed the bus': Chamberlain papers, NC4/5/66, Chamberlain speech to the Conservative Central Council, 4 April 1940.
2. CAB 65/6, WM (40) 67, 13 March 1940.
3. *Ironside Diary*, 28 March 1940, p. 237.
4. *Colville Diary*, 6 April 1940, pp. 96–7.
5. *Colville Diary*, 6 February 1949, p. 82; Jones (ed.), *Diary with Letters*, Thomas Jones to A. Flexner, 12 January 1940, p. 445.
6. *Headlam Diary*, 4 April 1940, p. 185.
7. Chamberlain papers, NC4/5/66, Chamberlain speech to the Conservative Central Council, 4 April 1940; *Manchester Guardian*, 5 April 1940.
8. *Colville Diary*, 9 April 1940, p. 99; CAB 65/6, WM(40)85, 9 April 1940.
9. John Peck, *Dublin from Downing Street* (London, 1978), pp. 65–6.
10. CAB 65/6, WM(40)85, 9 April 1940.
11. *Chamberlain Diary*, Chamberlain to Hilda Chamberlain, 20 April 1940, pp. 519–21.
12. 'Winston was being maddening': *Colville Diary*, 23 April 1940, p. 107.
13. Charles Stuart (ed.), *The Reith Diaries* (London, 1975), 14 April 1940, p. 245.
14. *Chamberlain Diary*, Chamberlain to Ida Chamberlain, 13 April 1940, p. 517.
15. *Chamberlain Diary*, Chamberlain to Ida Chamberlain, 13 April 1940, p. 517.
16. *Chamberlain Diary*, Chamberlain to Hilda Chamberlain, 20 April 1940, pp. 519–21.
17. *Chamberlain Diary*, Chamberlain to Hilda Chamberlain, 20 April 1940, pp. 519–21; PREM 1/404, Sir Edward Brudes memoranda, 25 April 1940.
18. *Chamberlain Diary*, Chamberlain to Ida Chamberlain, 27 April 1940, pp. 521–4.
19. *Colville Diary*, 23 April 1940, p. 107.
20. PREM 1/404, memorandum by Horace Wilson, 25 April 1940.
21. *Colville Diary*, 17 April 1940, p. 104.
22. *Colville Diary*, 17 April 1940, p. 104.
23. PREM 1/404, Wilson and Bridges memoranda, 25 April 1940; *Ironside Diary*, 26 April 1940, pp. 283–6.
24. Churchill, *The Gathering Storm*, p. 505.
25. Churchill to Chamberlain, unsent letter, 24 April 1940, printed in Churchill, *The Gathering Storm*, p. 576.
26. *Chamberlain Diary*, Chamberlain to Ida Chamberlain, 27 April 1940, pp. 521–4.
27. *Colville Diary*, 25 April 1940, p. 108.
28. *Chamberlain Diary*, Chamberlain to Hilda Chamberlain, 4 May 1940, p. 527.
29. *Colville Diary*, 27 April 1940, p. 112.
30. *Chamberlain Diary*, Chamberlain to Ida Chamberlain, 27 April 1940, pp. 521–4.

31. *Reith Diary*, 3 May 1940, p. 249.
32. H.C. Debs., vol. 360, 7 May 1940, cols 1084–5.
33. *Colville Diary*, 26 April 1940, p. 111, and 27 April 1940, p. 112.
34. *Channon Diary*, 1 May 1940, p. 244.
35. *Channon Diary*, 1 May 1940, p. 244.
36. *Chamberlain Diary*, Chamberlain to Ida Chamberlain, 27 April 1940, pp. 521–4.
37. *Chamberlain Diary*, Chamberlain to Hilda Chamberlain, 4 May 1940, p. 528.
38. *Colville Diary*, 24 April 1940, p. 108.
39. *Channon Diary*, 1 May 1940, p. 244.
40. *Amery Diary*, 30 April 1940, p. 590.
41. 'We are not satisfied': cited in Larry L. Witherell, 'Lord Salisbury's "Watching Committee" and the fall of Neville Chamberlain', *English Historical Review* (2001), pp. 1134–66, at 1153.
42. *Dalton Diary*, 9 April 1940, p. 326; Dalton, *Fateful Years*, p. 297.
43. *Channon Diary*, 26 April 1940, p. 243.
44. Witherell, 'Lord Salisbury's "Watching Committee"'.
45. Salisbury, 'Interview with Neville Chamberlain', 10 April 1940, cited in Witherell, 'Lord Salisbury's "Watching Committee"', pp. 1150–1.
46. Salisbury to Hankey, 18 September 1939 and Salisbury to Halifax, 22 September 1939, cited in Witherell, 'Lord Salisbury's "Watching Committee"', p. 1152.
47. Salisbury, 'Interview with Neville Chamberlain', 10 April 1940, cited in Witherell, 'Lord Salisbury's "Watching Committee"', pp. 1150–1.
48. Salisbury, 'Interview with Neville Chamberlain', 10 April 1940, cited in Witherell, 'Lord Salisbury's "Watching Committee"', pp. 1150–1.
49. Cranborne to Salisbury, 15 April 1940, cited in Witherell, 'Lord Salisbury's "Watching Committee"', p. 1152.
50. Cecil to Salisbury, 17 April 1940, cited in Witherell, 'Lord Salisbury's "Watching Committee"', p. 1151.
51. Davies to Salisbury, 15 April 1940, cited in Witherell, 'Lord Salisbury's "Watching Committee"', p. 1152.
52. *The Times*, 4 May 1940.
53. Edward L. Spears memorandum, spring 1940, cited in Witherell, 'Lord Salisbury's "Watching Committee"', p. 1154.
54. Cited in Witherell, 'Lord Salisbury's "Watching Committee"', p. 1153.
55. *Nicolson Diary*, 29 April 1940, p. 73.
56. Emrys-Evans to Cranborne, 5 May 1940, cited in Ball, *The Guardsmen*, p. 210.
57. *Channon Diary*, 30 April 1940, p. 243.
58. *Headlam Diary*, 5 May 1940, p. 195.
59. *The Times*, 4 May 1940. On this group, see D. M. Roberts, 'Clement Davies and the fall of Neville Chamberlain, 1939–40', *Welsh History Review* (1976), pp. 188–215.
60. See, for example, *Manchester Guardian*, 5 May 1940.
61. Cited in Dutton, 'Power brokers or just "glamour boys"?', p. 420.
62. *Colville Diary*, 3 May 1940, p. 116.
63. N. J. Crowson (ed.), *Fleet Street, Press Barons and Politics: The Journals of Collin Brooks, 1932–1940* (Cambridge, 1998), 18 April 1940, p. 266; *Amery Diary*, 3 April 1940, p. 585.
64. *Colville Diary*, 1 May 1940, p. 115.
65. *Nicolson Diary*, 30 April 1940, p. 74.
66. *Channon Diary*, 25 April 1940, p. 242.
67. *Chamberlain Diary*, Chamberlain to Hilda Chamberlain, 4 May 1940, p. 527.

68. *Chamberlain Diary*, Chamberlain to Hilda Chamberlain, 4 May 1940, p. 526.
69. *Daily Herald*, 6 May 1940.
70. H.C. Debs., vol. 360, 7 May 1940, cols 1073–86.
71. *Channon Diary*, 7 May 1940, p. 244.
72. H.C. Debs., vol. 360, 7 May 1940, col. 1085.
73. *Amery Diary*, 7 May 1940, pp. 592–3.
74. H.C. Debs., vol. 356, 1 February 1940, col. 1422.
75. Attlee interview in Francis Williams, *A Prime Minister Remembers* (London, 1961), pp. 20–1, 28.
76. Attlee interview in Williams, *A Prime Minister Remembers*, pp. 20–1, 28; Attlee, *As It Happened*, iii.
77. *Dalton Diary*, 1 May 1940, p. 332.
78. H.C. Debs., vol. 360, 7 May 1940, cols 1086–95.
79. H.C. Debs., vol. 360, 7 May 1940, cols 1125–30.
80. *Nicolson Diary*, 7 May 1940, pp. 76–7.
81. *Channon Diary*, 7 May 1940, p. 245.
82. *Maisky Diary*, 8 May 1940, p. 274.
83. *Nicolson Diary*, 7 May 1940, pp. 76–7.
84. Leo S. Amery, *My Political Life, Volume 3: The Unforgiving Years, 1929–1940* (London, 195), p. 358.
85. H.C. Debs., vol. 360, 7 May 1940, cols 1140–51.
86. H.C. Debs., vol. 360, 7 May 1940, cols 1140–51.
87. *Amery Diary*, 7 May 1940, p. 592.
88. Lord Home, *The Way the Wind Blows* (London, 1976), p. 74.
89. *Channon Diary*, 7 May 1940, pp. 244–5.
90. Williams, *A Prime Minister Remembers*, p. 30; Herbert Morrison, *An Autobiography* (London, 1960), pp. 172–3; Nuffield College, Oxford, Herbert Morrison papers, 'Draft autobiography'; *Dalton Diary*, 8 May 1940, p. 340.
91. Emrys-Evans diary, 8 May 1940, cited in Dutton, 'Power brokers or just "glamour boys"?', p. 421.
92. H.C. Debs., vol. 360, 8 May 1940, cols 1251–65.
93. Donoughue and Jones, *Herbert Morrison*, p. 271.
94. *Channon Diary*, 8 May 1940, pp. 245–6.
95. *Dalton Diary*, 8 May 1940, p. 341; H.C. Debs., vol. 360, 8 May 1940, col. 1266.
96. *Nicolson Diary*, 8 May 1940, p. 78.
97. H.C. Debs., vol. 360, 8 May 1940, col. 1266 (emphasis added).
98. *Amery Diary*, 8 May 1940, pp. 610–11; *Channon Diary*, 8 May 1940, pp. 245–7.
99. *Channon Diary*, 8 May 1940, pp. 245–7.
100. *Colville Diary*, 8 May 1940, p. 119.
101. *Colville Diary*, 8 May 1940, p. 119.
102. H.C. Debs., vol. 360, 8 May 1940, cols 1277–83.
103. *Channon Diary*, 8 May 1940, pp. 245–7.
104. H.C. Debs., vol. 360, 8 May 1940, cols 1348–61; *Channon Diary*, 8 May 1940, pp. 245–7.
105. *Channon Diary*, 8 May 1940, pp. 245–7.
106. Cited in Andrew Roberts, *Eminent Churchillians* (London, 1994), p. 139.
107. *Amery Diary*, 8 May 1940, pp. 610–11.
108. Witherell, 'Lord Salisbury's "Watching Committee"', p. 1160.
109. *Maisky Diary*, 8 May 1940, p. 275.

110. Williams, *A Prime Minister Remembers*, p. 32.
111. *Channon Diary*, 8 May 1940, pp. 245–7.
112. *Channon Diary*, 8 May 1940, pp. 245–7.
113. *Maisky Diary*, 8 May 1940, p. 275.
114. *Channon Diary*, 8 May 1940 (pp. 245–7); Charles Waterhouse diary, 11 May 1940, cited in Roberts, *Eminent Churchillians*, p. 147.

Chapter 12

1. 'A bad stomach ache': Halifax diary, 9 May 1940, cited in Robert Blake, 'How Churchill became Prime Minister', in Blake and William Roger Louis (eds), *Churchill* (Oxford, 1993), pp. 257–73, at 265.
2. *Colville Diary*, 8 May 1940 (p. 119).
3. *Chamberlain Diary*, Chamberlain to Ida Chamberlain, 11 May 1940, pp. 528–30; *Channon Diary*, 9 May 1940, pp. 247–50.
4. *Dalton Diary*, 9 May 1940 (pp. 343–4).
5. *Chamberlain Diary*, Chamberlain to Ida Chamberlain, 11 May 1940, pp. 528–30.
6. *Amery Diary*, 9 May 1949, pp. 611–13.
7. Chamberlain papers, NC7/11/33/162, Spens to Chamberlain, 9 May 1940.
8. *Headlam Diary*, 9 May 1940, p. 196.
9. *Channon Diary*, 9 May 1940, pp. 247–50.
10. Home, *The Way the Wind Blows*, p. 75.
11. *Nicolson Diary*, 9 May 1940, pp. 80–1.
12. Salisbury, 'Memorandum on interview with Lord Halifax', 9 May 1940, cited in Witherell, 'Lord Salisbury's "Watching Committee"', p. 1162.
13. Salisbury, 'Memorandum on interview with Lord Halifax', 9 May 1940, cited in Witherell, 'Lord Salisbury's "Watching Committee"', p. 1162.
14. Cited in Roberts, *The Holy Fox*, p. 199.
15. *Dalton Diary*, 9 May 1940, pp. 343–4.
16. Halifax diary, 9 May 1940, cited in Blake, 'How Churchill became Prime Minister', p. 265.
17. Halifax diary, 9 May 1940, cited in Roberts, *The Holy Fox*, p. 205.
18. Halifax diary, 9 May 1940, cited in Blake, 'How Churchill became Prime Minister', p. 265.
19. 'Don't agree, and don't say anything': Avon, *The Reckoning*, pp. 96–7.
20. *The Spectator*, 16 May 1940.
21. Avon, *The Reckoning*, pp. 96–7.
22. Churchill, *The Gathering Storm*, p. 596.
23. *Colville Diary*, 2 October 1940, p. 255.
24. *Colville Diary*, 11 May 1940, p. 124.
25. Colin Coote, *Editorial* (London, 1965), pp. 203–4.
26. Interview with Sir Horace Wilson, 4 April 1967, cited in Addison, *The Road to 1945*, p. 102.
27. Avon, *The Reckoning*, pp. 96–7 (emphasis added).
28. Cowling, *The Impact of Hitler*, p. 385.
29. *Amery Diary*, 9 May 1940, p. 612; *The Times*, 10 May 1940.
30. Halifax diary, 9 May 1940, cited in Blake, 'How Churchill became Prime Minister', p. 266.
31. *Attlee: Granada records interview*, p. 21.
32. Attlee papers, 1/16, autobiographical notes.
33. Attlee interview, cited in Harris, *Attlee*, p. 174.

34. Churchill, *The Gathering Storm*, p. 597.
35. *Colville Diary*, subsequent reflection, p. 123.
36. Churchill, *The Gathering Storm*, p. 597.
37. Churchill, *The Gathering Storm*, p. 597. See also the contemporary account in *Cadogan Diary*, 9 May 1940, p. 280.
38. Lord Moran, *Winston Churchill: The Struggle for Survival, 1940–1965* (London, 1966), p. 323.
39. *Chamberlain Diary*, Chamberlain to Ida Chamberlain, 11 May 1940, p. 529.
40. 'The greatest adventurer of modern political history': *Colville Diary*, 10 May 1940, p. 122.
41. *Channon Diary*, 10 May 1940, pp. 248–50.
42. Beaverbrook papers, C/80, Chamberlain to Beaverbrook, 10 May 1940.
43. *Amery Diary*, 10 May 1940, p. 613.
44. *Amery Diary*, 10 May 1940, p. 613.
45. Churchill, *The Gathering Storm*, p. 597.
46. *Dalton Diary*, 10 May 1940, pp. 344–5.
47. NEC papers, 'Resolutions for annual Conference 1940'; Attlee Papers, James Middleton to Attlee, 15 March 1940, box 7.
48. NEC minutes, 10 May 1940.
49. NEC minutes, 10 May 1940 (my emphasis).
50. *Dalton Diary*, 10 May 1940, pp. 344–5.
51. *Channon Diary*, 10 May 1940, pp. 248–50.
52. *Channon Diary*, 10 May 1940, pp. 248–50.
53. Churchill, *The Gathering Storm*, p. 599.
54. *Colville Diary*, 10 May 1940, p. 122.
55. Cited in Roberts, *Eminent Churchillians*, p. 164.
56. *Channon Diary*, 10 May 1940, pp. 248–50.
57. Churchill, *The Gathering Storm*, p. 601.
58. Churchill, *Their Finest Hour*, pp. 15–16.
59. *Amery Diary*, 10 May 1940, p. 613.
60. *Dalton Diary*, 16 May 1940, p. 9.
61. Dalton, *Fateful Years*, p. 321; *Maisky Diary*, 26 May 1940, pp. 280–1.
62. 'Cato', *Guilty Men* (London, 1940), chapter fourteen.
63. Cited in Gilbert, 'Horace Wilson: Man of Munich?', p. 9.
64. *Cadogan Diary*, 19 May 1940, p. 286.
65. *Cadogan Diary*, 20 May 1940, p. 287.
66. *Cadogan Diary*, 21 May 1940, p. 287.
67. Roberts, *Eminent Churchillians*, p. 149.
68. Cited in Sheila Lawlor, *Churchill and the Politics of War, 1940–1941* (Cambridge, 1994), p. 37.
69. Halifax papers, diary, 15 May 1940; *Headlam Diary*, 1 August 1940, p. 215.
70. Halifax papers, diary, 5 June 1940; *Headlam Diary*, 18 June 1940, p. 208; *Colville Diary*, 1 June 1940, p. 145.
71. *Colville Diary*, 2 October 1940, p. 255.
72. *1940 Labour Party Annual Conference Report*, pp. 128–33.
73. *Daily Herald*, 14 May 1940.
74. 'Society is founded on hero worship': Thomas Carlyle, *On Heroes, Hero-Worship, and the Heroic in History* (London, 1841), p. 13.

Conclusion

1. William Shakespeare, *Hamlet*. Act Two, Scene Two, 303–12.
2. Robert Crowcroft, 'The role of the politician in the democratic regime', in David Brown, Robert Crowcroft, and Gordon Pentland (eds), *The Oxford Handbook of Modern British Political History, 1800–2000* (Oxford, 2018).
3. Gray, *Strategy and Defence Planning*, p. 142.
4. Gray, *Strategy and Defence Planning*, p. 141.
5. S. J. D. Green, 'Appeasers and anti-appeasers: All Souls and the international crisis of the 1930s', in S. J. D. Green and Peregrine Horden (eds), *All Souls and the Wider World: Statesmen, Scholars, and Adventurers, c. 1850–1950* (Oxford, 2011), pp. 223–62, at 248–9.
6. H.C. Debs., Third Series, vol. 173, 4 February 1864, cols 22–41.
7. Patrick Finney, *Remembering the Road to World War Two: International History, National Identity, Collective Memory* (London, 2010), p. 213.
8. Phillips Payson O'Brien, *How the War Was Won* (Cambridge, 2015).
9. FO371/18305/N6328/16/38, minute by J. L. Dodds, 13 November 1934.
10. Gray, *The Strategy Bridge*, p. 7.
11. Cited in Martin Gilbert and Richard Gott, *The Appeasers* (London, 1967), p. 8.
12. Herman Kahn, *On Thermonuclear War* (New Brunswick, 1960), p. 287.
13. 'One must wait until the evening to see how splendid the day has been': Attributed to Sophocles or, alternatively, Richard Milhous Nixon.

PICTURE ACKNOWLEDGEMENTS

INDEX

Note: References to figures are indicated by an italic 'f' following the page number.